Mortal Pages, Literary Lives

Mortal Pages, Literary Lives

Studies in Nineteenth-Century Autobiography

Edited by

VINCENT NEWEY and PHILIP SHAW

© Vincent Newey, Philip Shaw and the contributors, 1996

All rights reserved. No part of this publication may be reproduced, stored in a retrieval system, or transmitted in any form or by any means, electronic, mechanical, photocopying, recording, or otherwise without the prior permission of the publisher.

Published by
SCOLAR PRESS
Gower House
Croft Road
Aldershot
Hants GU11 3HR
England

Ashgate Publishing Company
Old Post Road
Brookfield
Vermont 05036-9704
USA

British Library Cataloguing in Publication Data

Mortal Pages, Literary Lives: Studies in
  Nineteenth-Century Autobiography.
  (Nineteenth Century Series)
  1. Autobiography — 19th century.
  I. Newey, Vincent, 1943–.   II. Shaw, Philip, 1965–.
  820.9'492'09034

ISBN 1-85928-206-7

Library of Congress Cataloging-in-Publication Data

Mortal pages, literary lives : studies in nineteenth-century
  autobiography/edited by Vincent Newey and Philip Shaw.
      p. cm. - (The Nineteenth Century)
    Includes bibliographical references and index.
    ISBN 1-85928-206-7 (cloth)
    1. Authors, English—19th century—Biography—History and
criticism. 2. Authors, American—19th century—Biography—History
and criticism. 3. American prose literature—19th century—History
and criticism. 4. English prose literature—19th century—History
and criticism. 5. Autobiography. I. Newey, Vincent. II. Shaw,
Philip. III. Series: Nineteenth Century (Aldershot, England)
  PR778.A9M67   1996
  820.9'008—dc20   96–5204
                                                                   CIP

ISBN 1 85928 206 7

Typeset in Sabon by Manton Typesetters, 5–7 Eastfield Road, Louth, Lincolnshire.

**Printed and bound in Great Britain by
Hartnolls Limited, Bodmin, Cornwall**

Contents

Notes on Contributors   ix
Acknowledgements   xii

1. Introduction
   Philip Shaw and Vincent Newey   1

2. Romantic Self-Representation: The Example of Mary Wollstonecraft's *Letters in Sweden*
   Peter Swaab   13

3. The Shock of the Old: Wordsworth and the Paths to Rome
   Keith Hanley   31

4. Autobiography as Self-Indulgence: De Quincey and His Reviewers
   Julian North   61

5. The Romance of Sickliness: Leigh Hunt's *Autobiography* and the Example of Keats
   Nicholas Roe   71

6. Why Do We Remember Forwards and Not Backwards?
   Philip Davis   81

7. Autobiography and the Illative Sense
   William Myers   103

8. Displacing the Autobiographical Impulse: A Bakhtinian Reading of Thomas Carlyle's *Reminiscences*
   David Amigoni   120

9. Victorian Women as Writers and Readers of (Auto)biography
   Joanne Shattock   140

10. 'Fathers' Daughters': Three Victorian Anti-Feminist Women Autobiographers
    Valerie Sanders   153

11. Mark Rutherford's Salvation and the Case of Catharine Furze
    Vincent Newey   172

12	Seconding the Self: *Mary Chesnut's Civil War* *Rosemarie Morgan*	204
13	Autobiography as Prophecy: Walt Whitman's 'Specimen Days' *Nicholas Everett*	217
14	Buried in Laughter: The *Memories and Adventures* of Sir Arthur Conan Doyle *Diana Barsham*	235

Index   253

The Nineteenth Century
General Editors' Preface

The aim of this series is to reflect, develop and extend the great burgeoning of interest in the nineteenth century that has been an inevitable feature of recent decades, as that former epoch has come more sharply into focus as a locus for our understanding not only of the past but of the contours of our modernity. Though it is dedicated principally to the publication of original monographs and symposia in literature, history, cultural analysis, and associated fields, there will be a salient role for reprints of significant texts from, or about, the period. Our overarching policy is to address the spectrum of nineteenth-century studies without exception, achieving the widest scope in chronology, approach and range of concern. This, we believe, distinguishes our project from comparable ones, and means, for example, that in the relevant areas of scholarship we both recognize and cut innovatively across such parameters as those suggested by the designations 'Romantic' and 'Victorian'. We welcome new ideas, while valuing tradition. It is hoped that the world which predates yet so forcibly predicts and engages our own will emerge in parts, as a whole, and in the lively currents of debate and change that are so manifest an aspect of its intellectual, artistic and social landscape.

Vincent Newey
Joanne Shattock

University of Leicester

Contributors

David Amigoni has taught at Liverpool Polytechnic, University College of Wales, Aberystwyth, and the University of Sunderland, and is now Lecturer in English at Keele University. He is the author of *Victorian Biography: Intellectuals and the Ordering of Discourse* (1993) and co-editor of *Charles Darwin's 'Origin of Species': New Interdisciplinary Essays* (1995). He is currently researching the relationship between nineteenth-century literary criticism, ethics and science.

Diana Barsham is Head of Literature at the University of Derby, having taught previously at the University of Warwick and the University of Central England. Her book on Victorian parapsychology and the Victorian Women's Movement, *The Trial of Woman*, appeared in 1992. She is writing a critical study of the works of Sir Arthur Conan Doyle.

Philip Davis is Senior Lecturer in the Department of English, University of Liverpool. His publications include *Memory and Writing from Wordsworth to Lawrence* (1983), *In Mind of Johnson* (1989), *The Experience of Reading* (1991) and *Malamud's People* (1995), and an edition of *Ruskin's Selected Writings* (1995). Forthcoming in 1996 is a collection of essays by divers hands, *Real Voices: On Reading*.

Nicholas Everett is Lecturer in American literature in the Department of English at the University of Leicester. He has published articles on John Ashbery and William Faulkner, and reviews poetry collections regularly in the *Times Literary Supplement*. He is preparing a monograph on Walt Whitman.

Keith Hanley is Professor of English Literature and Director of the Wordsworth Centre at Lancaster University. He has published many essays on nineteenth-century literature, edited selections of the works of Landor (1981) and Meredith (1993), co-edited collections of original criticism, including *Revolution and English Romanticism: Politics and Rhetoric* (1990) and *Romantic Revisions* (1992), and has compiled an *Annotated Bibliography of William Wordsworth* (1995). He is co-editor of the interdisciplinary journal *Nineteenth-Century Contexts* and of the annual *News From Nowhere*.

Rosemarie Morgan lectures in English literature at Yale University. She is the author of *Women and Sexuality in the Novels of Thomas Hardy* (1988), *Cancelled Words: Rediscovering Thomas Hardy* (1992) and several articles in the fields of Victorian studies and literary biographies of women writers. Her work on the holograph manuscript of Hardy's *Far From the Madding Crowd* is due for publication in 1996.

William Myers is Professor of English Literature at the University of Leicester. His publications include *Dryden* (1973), *The Teaching of George Eliot* (1984), *Milton and Free Will* (1987), *Evelyn Waugh and the Problem of Evil* (1991) and most recently an edition of four plays by Farquhar. His current research is on the metaphysics of John Henry Newman and John Stuart Mill.

Vincent Newey is Professor of English at the University of Leicester. He is the author of *Cowper's Poetry: A Critical Study and Reassessment* (1982) and *Centring the Self: Subjectivity, Society and Reading from Thomas Gray to Thomas Hardy* (1995), editor of *The Pilgrim's Progress: Critical and Historical Views* (1980), and co-editor of *Byron and the Limits of Fiction* (1988) and *Literature and Nationalism* (1991). His numerous articles encompass, especially, Puritan writers, eighteenth-century literature and the Romantic poets. He is an editor of *The Byron Journal* and past president of the British Association for Romantic Studies. He is at present investigating modern critical responses to Wordsworth.

Julian North received her doctorate, on the work of Thomas De Quincey, from the University of Oxford. She has held a lectureship at the University of Reading and is currently Lecturer in English at De Montfort University. She has published on De Quincey, Wordsworth and nineteenth-century drug culture. Her book, *De Quincey Reviewed*, will appear in 1996.

Nicholas Roe is Professor of English at the University of St Andrews. His publications include *Wordsworth and Coleridge: The Radical Years* (1988), *The Politics of Nature* (1992) and, as editor, *Keats and History* (1995), a topic on which he is carrying out further research. He is a founding editor of the journal *Romanticism*.

Valerie Sanders is Senior Lecturer in English at the University of Buckingham. She has published *Reason Over Passion: Harriet Martineau and the Victorian Novel* (1986) and *The Private Lives of Victorian Women: Autobiography in Nineteenth-Century England* (1989), and edited *Harriet Martineau: Selected Letters* (1990). Her study of Margaret Oliphant, Eliza Lynn Linton and Charlotte M. Yonge, entitled *Victorian Anti-Feminist Women Novelists: Eve's Renegades*, is forthcoming.

Joanne Shattock is Reader in English at the University of Leicester, and Director of the Victorian Studies Centre. She is the author of *Politics and Reviewers* (1989) and *The Oxford Guide to British Women Writ-*

ers (1993), editor of *Dickens and Other Victorians* (1988) and co-editor of *The Victorian Periodical Press* (1982). She is editing the volume on the nineteenth century in the *Cambridge Bibliography of English Literature* (third edition) and writing a book on literature and journalism in the period.

Philip Shaw is Lecturer in the Department of English at the University of Leicester. His main research interest is in Romantic poetry and British culture during the Napoleonic wars. His recent publications include essays on topography and subjectivity in Wordsworth's *Prelude*, Romanticism and literary theory, and the Romantic treatment of Waterloo. He is working on a book about Romanticism and warfare.

Peter Swaab was Director of Studies in English at Corpus Christi College, Cambridge, and is now Lecturer at University College London. He is editor of *Lives of the Great Romantics: Wordsworth* (1996) and is completing a study of Wordsworth and patriotism. He has also published work in the fields of contemporary poetry and film studies.

Acknowledgements

Thanks are due to Alec McAulay, Caroline Cornish and Anne Nolan, all of Scolar Press, for their invaluable help and support in producing this volume. We are grateful to Angie Kendall, Chief Clerk in the English Department at Leicester University, who brought her usual skill and resourcefulness to bear in several tasks relating to the project.

CHAPTER ONE

Introduction

Philip Shaw and Vincent Newey

Mortal Pages, Literary Lives. The title of this volume is an attempt to convey an idea of what is at stake in *the right to autobiography*. An acute sense of what it would mean to be denied this right is given in a passage from the autobiographical fragments of John Clare:

> the continued sameness of a garden cloyed me and I resumed my old employments with pleasure were I coud look on the wild heath, the wide spreading variety of cultured and fallow fields, green meadows, and crooking brooks, and the dark woods waving to the murmering winds   these were my delights and here I coud mutter to myself as usual unheard and unnoticd by the sneering clown and conscieted coxcomb, and here my old habits and feelings returnd with redoubled ardour for they left me while I was a gardiner[1]

Clare's self writes through its subjection to the constraints of labour, class and education. It is a self *literally* brought into being; an 'I' manifested in the contrast between the verbal compression of the first clause and the expansiveness of the passage that follows. The pleasure of the biographical 'subject', the life that had known the delights of unrestricted growth, is expressed in the verbal life of the prose. For a short space the *autos* (or, autobiographical impulse) seems wholehearted in its commitment to the propagation of times past: 'I resumed my old employments with pleasure were I coud look on the wild heath, the wide spreading variety of cultured and fallow fields, green meadows, and crooking brooks, and the dark woods waving to the murmering winds.' Through a combination of nouns and headwords, modifiers and qualifiers, the language forces the life out of memory and into the experiential present. Here, more specifically, the self is a function of a creative will coming to consciousness through its engagement in the story-making process. In what might be termed an act of spatio-temporal condensation, Clare presents something essential about autobiography: as gardens of constraint melt into landscapes of liberty so the course of one's life – the *bios* – blends imperceptibly into the ichnographical view of the all-seeing I. The panoramic force of narrative enables the writer to encompass both the cultivated and the fallow, the wide and the narrow, the green and the dark.

The emphasis falls next on the lyrical spirit of rejuvenation: everything is 'resumed'; 'and here my old habits and feelings returnd with redoubled ardour.' But the sense of restorative power is framed by a discourse more attuned to the revelatory aspect of autobiography: 'for they left me while I was a gardiner'. As the adverb 'here' signals the existence of a turning-point in Clare's past, the pressure of opposing and contradictory forces – felt by the younger man at a crucial stage in his development – continues to impinge on the present. In the absence of punctuation, it is not only the 'ardour' of the first half of the phrase that is 'redoubled', it is also the poignancy of its conclusion. The sensation of bereavement – 'for they left me' *then* – is with Clare even *now*; it is the threat that drives the author to acts of verbal accountability – acts that bypass the gulf between the feelings the person had at the time and the feelings and consequences that remain.

Will this story survive? Will this have been the story of my life? Clare's autobiography is invested in a relation with the future anterior; in the virtual time of a life that *will have been* lived. And because of its commitment to the future, the autobiographical subject risks an encounter with that which cannot be predicted or brought to account. In this respect perhaps there is no more audacious opening to a story than that of Rousseau's *Confessions*: 'Let the trumpet of the Day of Judgement sound when it will, I will present myself before the Sovereign Judge with this book in my hand. I will say boldly: "This is what I have done, what I have thought, what I was."'[2] Yet not even Rousseau can guarantee the temporal integrity of the I that underwrites this claim. Just as, in Derrida's view, a signature must announce its involvement in repetition (for a signature to be a signature it must be repeatable in other contexts), so autobiography is predicated on the idea that there is no 'private language', no memory that does not depend on the promise of a public recollection. Even as I insist on the unique character of the autobiographical 'voice', and defend its efficacy against the proponents of the death of the subject, the fact remains that in order to be accountable, even recognizable, such moments of pure self-presence can only be thought when the conditions of its possibility are repressed. However deep or ungraspable the essence of the self may be, its very identity as 'graspable-as-ungraspable' is made possible only through the structure of repetition it is supposed to disallow.[3]

With these deconstructive reflections in mind, and with a glance towards the opening of Kierkegaard's *Repetition*, let us return to Clare. In this case the moment of spiritual regeneration is a repetition in the fullest sense: an event in the course of one's life which is 'recollected forwards' so that its very possibility is put into question. On one level Clare experiences repetition as the return of 'old habits and feelings'.

This corresponds to Kierkegaard's first stage of repetition: the stage where freedom is defined as pleasure or desire.[4] The second stage, in which desire is threatened by repetition and the loss of 'a glory from the earth', is countered by a recognition of the aesthetic possibilities of repetition. In Wordsworthian terms, the subject explores the novelty of return: 'A timely utterance gave that thought relief; / And I again am strong.'[5] In the third and final stage, repetition is no longer sought in terms of happiness – as a eudemonic principle – but as a deed of knowing. Clare seeks now not for new experiences but, by going back to his first feelings, to repeat the experience of repetition as a work of art, as autobiography. But the question of repetition can never be taken for granted. For in so far as the final stage, defined by Kierkegaard as the 'religious', also presents repetition as an aesthetic event, it is one that lays much store on the possibility that restoration might not occur; that the future anterior – the feelings that will have been – is breached by its necessary relation with finitude: with death; with the end of 'my' story.

Where Clare seems to differ from Wordsworth therefore, is in his sense that while writing may enshrine the past for future restoration it can only do so in the midst of life's passing. For better or for worse, Clare's prose is committed to showing what it is like to make sense of life while that life is happening. The shift from one temporal marker to another, a process of conjoining 'and' with 'and', or 'here' with 'here', leaves no room for sustained reflection, no space to assert an organizing centre – an *autos* that shapes and controls the story of its life – but it does indicate that which is at stake in Clare's preferred vocation: that the life of a poet is a vicarious one – subject to the ability of the transcendent 'I' to maintain its resistance against the sequential logic of prose. On this basis let us venture a critical distinction: that the poetry of 'I Am' fails where the autobiography succeeds: in encouraging us to realize, however briefly, the notion of a centred self against the passing shows of being. Moreover, it is a distinction that forces us to re-evaluate the privilege accorded to Romantic notions of self-autonomy. Is there not a very strong sense that the transcendent self exists, to the extent that it does exist, only in the act of narration? That its claim to infinity – to property without bounds – is dependent on an a priori relation to finitude; to the act of writing as it reveals the presence of thought in the here and now of making?

Clare's perception of what it would mean to inscribe one's life is then a perilous one. Between work and pleasure – a transition effaced by the use of the word 'employments' – the writer is faced with a real challenge that his work will not survive:

> I now ventured to commit my musings readily to paper but with all secrecy possible, hiding them when written in an old unused cubbard in the chamber which when taken for other purposes drove me to the nessesity of seeking another safety in a hole under it in the wall
>
> here my mother when clearing the chamber found me out and secretly took my papers for her own use as occasion calld for them and as I had no other desire in me but to keep them from being read when laid in this fancied safe repository that desire seemd compleated and I rarely turnd to a reperusal of them
>
> (Clare, p. 429)

But now, as then, the question of literary property is at one with the question of mortal property. Looking back on those early years, Clare's autobiography contains, among so many other things, a lesson in wisdom; a lesson concerning the lines that delimit the right of property to one's own life. However well secreted the autobiography, for it to be autobiography it must enter the domain of the readable. In a further Wordsworthian moment Clare states, the 'hiding places of [one's] power' must be seen, even if only by 'glimpses'. In this case the issue turns on the relation between imitation and appropriation. When Clare's mother discovers her son's first attempts at poetry 'she thought they was nothing more then Copies as attempts at improving my self in writing   she knew nothing of poetry, at least little dreamed her son was employd in that business' (p. 429). The ostensible concern with the oppositions of art and utility, labour and 'business', masks a more fundamental regard: that Clare wishes to fashion himself as a poetic original, not as a 'Copy'. Yet even as originality takes priority in Clare's writing, it is haunted by its dependence on literary precedents: chiefly Wordsworth and Byron, though one also thinks, perhaps more immediately, of Thomson, Cowper and Goldsmith.

In this speculative context one could invoke the revisionary ratios of Harold Bloom and his theories of 'the anxiety of influence' and of creation as oedipal struggle. For the purposes of introducing this volume, however, we would draw the reader's attention to the essay by David Amigoni which defines autobiography, in Bakhtinian terms, as a narratological relation between self and other: 'the self which writes does not exist as a given: the self can only be articulated evaluatively as a process, through its inscription in and relation to an other – or to use Bakhtin's terminology, a hero, or the topic of a particular utterance.' In this reading, Clare's history is not so much the product of an autobiographical impulse as it is the result of a complex act of intertextuality, involving questions of authorship, cultural value and literary style. Clare's claim to originality rests on his ability to create himself as a generic hero, composed 'out of dialogues first with images of the other within the narrative, and second in response to other authorial acts formed in different contexts'. Here one thinks especially of the dialogue between Clare and Burns and the image of the other in 'The Mouse's Nest'.

Where Amigoni is keen to locate the autobiographical self within a differential network of force-relations – textual, cultural, historical – William Myers and Philip Davis argue vigorously for a reappraisal of more traditional concepts of personhood and agency. Whilst not denying that the internal 'essence' of autobiography is far removed from the notion of the classical subject, both would be loath to forego the idea that autobiographical writing, even as it dissembles personal integrity at the level of theory, nevertheless reasserts it on the plain of experience. Whether that experience is addressed in terms of the illative sense, which Myers makes primary, or more generally as the experience of reading, the autobiographical text offers 'momentary glimpses of a missing or elusive centre'. The classic dramatization of that which is at stake in this approach to autobiography can be found in Wordsworth:

> so wide appears
> The vacancy between me and those days,
> Which yet have such self-presence in my mind
> That, sometimes, when I think of them, I seem
> Two consciousnesses, conscious of myself,
> And of some other Being.[6]

Leaving aside, for the moment, the question of whether or not *The Prelude* counts as autobiography in the strict sense, what fascinates this writer is the differential relation between *autos* and *bios* – the gap between now and then, self and life, which both produces and is produced by the signifying structure of language. The self that we read in this poem comes into being only as the result of a linguistic act – an act that must be identified with the shaping presence of an 'I', narrating the events of its *bios* and creating itself as *autos*, through and over time.[7] But whether one is reading from a deconstructive or a 'reconstructive' perspective, to be conscious of oneself as two consciousnesses, 'myself, / And ... some other Being', is to encounter what is most estranging and most intimate about the act of autobiography: the fact that autobiographical writing simultaneously defaces and restores the deeper self that it is struggling to create. In the very act of weighing and summing up what has happened in our lives, language threatens to lay waste the most treasured of beliefs: the belief that we are able to convey, in writing, that which is most personal and proper to ourselves. Whether that property is dissolved in the blankness of verbal succession (the diachronic imperative) or convulsed by the aberrant energy of tropes (the black holes of synchronicity) one is never sure that one's story is entirely one's own. To a critic such as Philip Davis, however, 'it is only in its breakdowns and failures ... that ... autobiography ironically succeeds'. The centre of life-consciousness will be found not in 'the succession of mental attitudes' but in the space between sentences. Here, where the illusory control of the *autos* is no longer evident, 'there is time itself: inner thinking and inner recollecting time'. This is the life that our concentration on the self risks forgetting.

As the essays in this volume indicate, Wordsworth remains central to the developmental narrative of literary history. In some sense his presence confirms the suspicions of new historicist critics such as Marjorie Levinson and Clifford Siskin that high Romanticism is 'the very form of our own literary criticism'.[8] Our intention, therefore, is less about celebrating or demeaning the power of Wordsworthian discourse than about exploring this power – the ways in which it shapes and has been shaped by literary culture, the extent to which it informs critical practice and the forms that have resisted it. To regard Wordsworth in this way is to avoid both the unhappy consciousness of modernism (the decisive break that perpetuates the hold of the past) and the delirious indiscriminations of postmodernism (a levelling discourse that erases its difference from the past). The significance of Wordsworth's role as a 'vital connection' in autobiographical writing is investigated in Keith Hanley's essay, 'The Shock of the Old: Wordsworth and the Paths to Rome'. By way of Hopkins, Baudelaire and George Eliot, Hanley points to the ways in which Wordsworth has been used to 'recharge' the discourses in which his poetry is inscribed. To recall the language of the old is to insulate oneself from the trauma of the new. Starting with Wordsworth's recovery of the pre-established scripts of biblical and epic tradition, nineteenth-century autobiographers are drawn to a model of self-representation that becomes increasingly unavailable as the century proceeds. The 'survival' of Wordsworth in the writings of this period offers an illuminating take on the powerful vulnerability of the autobiographical subject in its relations with temporality – to the language of the past, the present and the future.

A number of essays – those by Davis, Everett, Swaab and Morgan spring to mind – touch on the question of genre. Again, what these authors are concerned with has a direct bearing on an established tradition of criticism. Paul de Man was one of the earliest literary critics to place the question of genre within a specifically theoretical matrix:

> autobiography lends itself poorly to generic definition; each specific instance seems to be an exception to the norm; the works themselves seem to shade off into neighbouring or even incompatible genres and, perhaps most revealing of all, generic discussions, which can have such powerful heuristic value in the case of tragedy or of the novel, remain distressingly sterile when autobiography is at stake.[9]

The problem, for anyone interested in the question of genre, is that autobiographies 'involve less the formal shape of a text than extra-textual and even extra-literary concepts of intention, authorial sincerity and truthfulness'. Thus, what links *The Prelude* with *The Confessions of an English Opium Eater* has little to do with genre *per se* but quite a bit to do with authorial intention, self-declaration and verisimilitude. Despite de Man's mandarin disavowal of the significance of genre, such matters continue to haunt the discussion of autobiography.[10] A thoughtful response to the generical status of the diary, for instance, underpins Rosemarie Morgan's exploratory account of the life of Mary Chesnut. From a stylistic point of view the diary form presents a challenge to traditional concepts of auto-revelation. With its 'interrupted syntax', non-linearity and 'staggered composition', Chesnut's diary blurs the distinction between composition and decomposition. The laying bare of autobiographical devices such as 'artlessness', 'mimesis' and 'sincerity' culminates in a form of ironic self-consciousness where narrator and text intentionally 'objectify' themselves so that interiority may be displayed as pure, unmediated transparency.

From the same period, Walt Whitman's *Specimen Days & Collect* can be read in a similarly ambivalent relation to the 'secular', Rousseauian 'narrative of the author's unfolding mind and fortunes'. Nick Everett's essay, 'Autobiography as Prophecy: Walt Whitman's "Specimen Days"', presents a subject in complex dialogue with the forms and meanings of individual and national self-consciousness. A committed self-revisionist, Whitman wishes to extend the ambit of the autobiographical genre to encompass the realm of collective accountability. Again, Wordsworth too had been interested in the affinities between personal and corporate identity. The difference between Wordsworth and Whitman, however, is that the latter writes within the progressive context of republicanism. In a subtle variation on Foucault's critique of the sovereign self, '"Specimen Days" is not so much about an individual's past as about a nation's future'.

A related set of concerns emerges in Peter Swaab's discussion of Mary Wollstonecraft. Like Whitman and Chesnut, the subject of *Letters in Sweden* bears little relation to the generical subject of Rousseau's *Confessions*. 'Hesitant between travel record, political speculation and confession of the heart', the text of *Letters in Sweden* charts a bibliotopia of 'emotional intensity'; looking back to its prose origins (travel writing, romance, political tract) and forward to its poetic tendency (Wordsworth, Shelley, Byron), Wollstonecraft attempts to synthesize a number of disparate voices. That the attempt should be deemed to have failed is as much a symptom of the history of Romantic critical discourse (to be authentic one must triumph over fragmentation) as it is of an ineluctable truth of language. Reading Wollstonecraft's text might lead us to contest the assumption, promoted by canonical Romanticism, that autobiographies are to be judged on the basis of their ability to sustain an ideal of heroic self-mastery. J. Hillis Miller's De Quincey is a case in point:

> The fleeting accidents of a man's life, and its external shows, may indeed be irrelate and incongruous; but the organizing principles which fuse into harmony, and gather about fixed pre-determined centres, whatever heterogeneous elements life may have accumulated from without, will not permit the grandeur of human unity greatly to be violated.[11]

Thus, to adopt a phrase of Julian North's ('Autobiography as Self-Indulgence: De Quincey and His Reviewers'), 'the fantasy of the autobiographer' is transferred to the fantasy of the critic. Autobiographical criticism, in Hillis Miller's view, is all about discovering those 'fixed pre-determined centres' which gather together in the course of an author's writings to convey the sense of 'an underlying vital unity' (Miller, p. 15). In his own readings of De Quincey, Browning, Brontë, Arnold and Hopkins we encounter a familiar pattern: Hillis Miller provides details of every aspect of a writer's career – from letters to diaries to unfinished fragments to complete published works; the idea being that only an exhaustive work of scholarship can convey a complete picture of a writer's essential unity. In North's essay, De Quincey's fascination with indulgence – indulgence of and towards the self – becomes an extended meditation on the nature of the autobiographical pact between author and reader. Pushing the idea of confession to its limit, the opium-eater makes repeated claims on our own addiction to power and authority. In doing so, he inadvertently exemplifies the way in which the 'quest for personal salvation' involves a deep engagement with a number of psycho-political questions.

In a recent article on William Hazlitt's *Liber Amoris* and Sarah Hazlitt's *Journal of My Trip to Scotland*, Sonia Hofkosh speculates on the ideological premises operative in the definition of autobiography. She notes that Sarah Hazlitt's journal 'has been read as a footnote in the chronicle of William's life, as a marginal gloss to his experience rather than a record or a revelation of her own'. Echoing Kristeva's view of femininity as the iconic boundary of masculine culture, 'at once perpetuating conventional definitions and "threatening to disrupt or transform them"', she calls attention to a conflict within the autobiographical tradition 'that literary history, with its normative aesthetics and values, has refused to acknowledge'. The conflict turns on the issue of 'narrative mastery', the very right to autobiography that William Hazlitt invokes towards the end of *Liber Amoris*. Both stories tell of the effects of a divorce but where the male autobiographer can define his identity outside the sexual economy of marriage, 'the woman may never conclude that she is her own except in contesting the very oppositions within which she is essentially aligned'. Put another way, where William can write himself out of contradiction, recuperating a unified subject position in the claim that 'It is all over and I am my own man', Sarah is constrained by social conventions that delimit the range and extent of her authorial identity. Far from being her own woman, her situation remains 'pretty much the same as it had long been'.[12]

In Hofkosh's view, women's autobiography speaks not only of 'the differences within tradition' but of 'tradition's difference from itself'. The writing of Victorian women offers a particularly illuminating example of the way in which tradition works to neutralize this difference. In Joanne Shattock's essay, 'Victorian Women as Writers and Readers of (Auto)biography', Margaret Oliphant, George Eliot and Eliza Lynn Linton are the focus for an investigation of the links between autobiography, professionalism and concepts of femininity. Oliphant's life offers a particularly instructive account of the 'creative tension' between the demands of art and family. Disappointed with the 'myth of progress' which dominates J.W. Cross's *George Eliot's Life as Related in Her Letters and Journals*, Oliphant chooses instead to concentrate on the fragmented, inner world of 'domestic memories, friendships, and griefs, the stuff of women's lives'. There is a sense here in which the autobiographer's rejection of professionalism becomes a silent revolt against the dictates of masculine culture. As Oliphant writes in her review of the *Life*: 'That it should be George Eliot, with her voice and touch of power, her large freedom of speech, her emancipation from all bondage of the petty and proper, who was the heroine of this little conjugal drama, is in the highest degree bewildering.' In her (auto)biography, reduced to the condition of 'a women writing a man's story', Eliot becomes a 'lifeless silhouette'.

The story of Victorian women's struggle with traditional forms of authorial identity is picked up in Valerie Sanders's essay, '"Fathers' Daughters": Three Victorian Anti-Feminist Women Writers'. Citing De Quincey's opinion of Dorothy Wordsworth, Sanders argues that the history of nineteenth-century women's autobiography is one of 'self-bafflement' and 'self-counteraction'. Upon entering the public sphere, the woman autobiographer (this time with reference to formulations by Sidonie Smith) 'assumes the adventurous posture of man'; and in doing this she represses the mother in her, perpetuating 'the political, social and textual disempowerment of mothers and daughters'. In the case of anti-feminist autobiographers such as Charlotte Yonge, Eliza Linton and Mary Ward, the situation is even more fraught: 'How did they sustain the pressure of an inward desire to tell and an outward injunction to remain silent?' Caught within a male value-system, their stories speak of their frustration with traditional womanly paradigms. Following Hofkosh we might say that the energy of such writing cannot be made to disappear within history; at the very least it is expressive of the way definitions of femininity depend on the suppression of differences that would disturb the male aesthetic norm of unity, visibility and heroic achievement.

A notable exception to this norm is the *Autobiography* of Leigh Hunt. In 'The Romance of Sickliness: Leigh Hunt's *Autobiography* and the Example of Keats', Nicholas Roe argues that Hunt 'elaborates an alternative Romantic identity, a "feminized" self associated (after Burke's *Philosophical Inquiry*) with ill-health, weakness and vulnerability'. The question of whether or not the adoption of such an example offers much of an advance on traditional forms of gendered self-representation is a moot one, yet in the world of mid-Victorian commercial society where masculinity is bound, as in Pip's dream, to the infernal machine of capital, the foregrounding of a 'feminine' self offers one of the few, perhaps the only, species of symbolic resistance.

Further testimony to the collapse of traditional concepts of self-identity is provided in the writings of William Hale White, who called himself Mark Rutherford. According to Vincent Newey in his essay 'Mark Rutherford's Salvation and the Case of Catharine Furze', Hale White's prose throws into relief the late-Victorian, and modern, quest for new ways of understanding personal salvation. Taking up Pater's comment on autobiographical consciousness as a 'continual vanishing away, that strange perpetual weaving and unweaving of ourselves', Newey highlights the difference between George Eliot's reformulation of orthodox models of the self (exemplified in Bunyan and Wordsworth) and Hale White's driven attempts to move beyond them. Both *The Autobiography of Mark Rutherford* and the novel *Catharine Furze* evince a concern with the passing of established theological, ontological, moral and gender positions, yet, rather than simply lamenting their loss, or worse still, proselytizing in the name of communal 'positivism', these texts remain stubborn in their commitment to the idea of transcendence: to its psychological necessity and its intellectual impossibility. Here, as with Hunt, in an age in which social and symbolic forces conspire to construct a 'subject' (disenfranchised and dispersed) where there was once free will (self-determining and whole), femininity is figured as the spirit of the age. In a sense, the preoccupation with gender is indicative of a more widespread crisis in the forms of mimesis. At the same time, however, the symbolic equation of femininity and loss speaks volumes about the political unconscious of the period.

Finally, Diana Barsham's essay on Conan Doyle ('Buried in Laughter: The *Memories and Adventures* of Sir Arthur Conan Doyle') examines yet another aspect of late nineteenth-century autobiographical scepticism. Like Whitman and Hale White, Doyle is suspicious of the confessional impulse in autobiography. His 'fear of intimacy' is based not only on an artistic dislike of Rousseau but also on a more subversive intellectual distrust of Romantic notions of subjectivity. As Barsham notes, '*Memories and Adventures* runs counter to that "shift of attention from *bios* to *autos*" which James Olney sees as largely responsible for opening up "the subject of autobiography for literary discussion"'. Interestingly enough, Doyle's rejection of Rousseau and Romanticism is concomitant with the same current of feeling that impels Hunt and Hale White: the belief that confession unsettles rather than supports the ideal of heroic self-mastery. This deconstructive awareness emerges in a form of episodic consciousness where the avoidance of introspection is a means of protecting the vital unity of the self from its linguistic displacement.

In many respects, Doyle's gay science is the heir *manqué* of Rousseauian sincerity. At once a product of artistic decadence as well as of the official discourses of empire, *Memories and Adventures* also prefigures a great deal of the self-authoring of our own times: from the brusque plain-dealing of the popular confessional to the post-ironic consciousness of the contemporary novel. Given the general scepticism towards concepts of personal identity – a scepticism that in Terry Eagleton's view is pervasive enough to encompass both post-structuralism and global capitalism – it is a miracle that anything like a confessional impulse manages to survive. Yet, authors and readers are persistently drawn to those accounts which offer witness to the ability of an 'I' to assert itself as a presence. Whether we should regard such writing with nostalgic longing or with revolutionary impatience is beyond the scope of this introduction. We will conclude, then, with an unscientific postscript from the autobiography of Roland Barthes: 'I do not say: "I am going to describe myself" but: "I am writing a text, and I call it R.B.".'[13] The spectral reality of R.B. is the best that any autobiographer can achieve: not the life as a recounting of literal or external fact, but the life as a record of internal significance.

Notes

1. *John Clare*, ed. Eric Robinson and David Powell, The Oxford Authors (Oxford: Oxford University Press, 1984), p. 429 (hereafter, Clare).
2. Jean Jacques Rousseau, *Confessions*, Everyman Library (London: Dent, 1943), p. 1.
3. The most enabling account of Derrida's interest in the structure of the signature can be found in Geoffrey Bennington and Jacques Derrida, *Jacques Derrida*, trans. Geoffrey Bennington (Chicago and London: Chicago University Press, 1993), pp. 148–66. The relevance of Derrida's theory to the question of autobiography has been addressed by Robert Smith in *Derrida and Autobiography* (Cambridge: Cambridge University Press, 1995).
4. Søren Kierkegaard, *Fear and Trembling and Repetition*, ed. and trans. Howard V. Hong and Edna H. Hong (Princeton: Princeton University Press, 1983), p. 301.
5. William Wordsworth, 'Ode' ('There was a time'), ll. 23–4; *Wordsworth*, ed. Stephen Gill, The Oxford Authors (Oxford: Oxford University Press, 1984), p. 298 (hereafter, Gill).
6. Wordsworth, *The Prelude* 1805, II. 28–33; Gill, p. 393.
7. The centrality of James Olney's work on autobiography is such that it is hard to envisage a discussion of the genre that avoids it. See, in particular, *Autobiography: Essays Theoretical and Critical*, ed. James Olney (Princeton: Princeton University Press, 1980), p. 21. For an excellent discussion of Olney and other theorists of autobiography, see Jonathan Loesberg, 'Autobiography as Genre, Act of Consciousness, Text', *Prose Studies*, 4 (September 1981), 169–85.
8. Marjorie Levinson, Introduction, *Rethinking Historicism: Critical Readings in Romantic History*, ed. Marjorie Levinson (Oxford: Basil Blackwell, 1989), p. 49.
9. Paul de Man, 'Autobiography as De-Facement', *The Rhetoric of Romanticism* (New York: Columbia University Press, 1984), p. 68.
10. For the background to de Man's essay, see the works mentioned in note 7 (above) but also Elizabeth W. Bruss, *Autobiographical Acts: The Changing Situation of a Literary Genre* (Baltimore: Johns Hopkins University Press, 1976) and Philippe Lejeune, 'The Autobiographical Contract', trans. R. Carter, in *French Literary Theory Today: A Reader*, ed. Tzvetan Todorov (Cambridge: Cambridge University Press, 1982).
11. Thomas De Quincey quoted by J. Hillis Miller in *The Disappearance of God: Five Nineteenth-Century Writers* (Cambridge, Mass.: Harvard University Press, 1963), pp. 15–16 (hereafter, Miller).
12. Sonia Hofkosh, 'Sexual Politics and Literary History: William Hazlitt's Keswick Escapade and Sarah Hazlitt's *Journal*', in *At the Limits of Romanticism: Essays in Cultural, Feminist, and Materialist Criticism*, ed. Mary A. Favret and Nicola J. Watson (Bloomington and Indianapolis: Indiana University Press, 1994), pp. 125–42 (pp. 135–8 *passim*).
13. *Roland Barthes by Roland Barthes*, trans. Richard Howard (New York: Hill and Wang, 1977), p. 56.

CHAPTER TWO

Romantic Self-Representation: The Example of Mary Wollstonecraft's *Letters in Sweden*

Peter Swaab

On 10 October 1795, the day of her second suicide attempt, Mary Wollstonecraft wrote a farewell letter to Gilbert Imlay, her inconstant lover and the father of her child:

> I shall plunge into the Thames where there is least chance of my being snatched from the death I seek ... Should your sensibility ever awake, remorse will find its way to your heart; and, in the midst of business and sensual pleasure, I shall appear before you, the victim of your deviation from rectitude. MARY[1]

Even *in extremis*, she interprets her experience as morally instructive; she makes herself an exemplary figure, as a victim, but also as a monitory presence. Imagined in this way, her posthumous appearance will turn the tables in the power relations between the two of them. It will also serve to inspire remorse and keep Imlay on the straight and narrow amid the lures of 'business and sensual pleasure' (for Wollstonecraft never loses sight of her conviction about the relatedness in Imlay of his sordid commercialism and his infidelity as her lover). In the event she was rescued, so Imlay was spared this visitation; the interest of the letter lies in its suggestion of a rooted habit of didactic self-fashioning. Suicide notes are likely to involve self-dramatizing elements; but Wollstonecraft's combination of pathos and didacticism is distinctive. To the end she pictures herself and her experience in ethical terms which may give benefit.

Throughout her writing career she had created portraits of exemplary figures – from the virtuous Henry in *Mary* (1788), to the rather alarmingly omnicompetent Mrs Mason in *Original Stories* (1788), to the stoical widow in the *Vindication of the Rights of Woman* (1792). The important comparable presence in *Letters in Sweden* (1796) is Queen Matilda of Denmark; in a larger sense, however, the narrating persona of the book is herself its crucial exemplary figure, at once autobiographically circumstantial and didactically selective.

Like many of the women writing in the last two decades of the eighteenth century, Wollstonecraft was mobile between an impressive array of genres. She wrote, for example, an educational anthology, political pamphlets, a historical chronicle and more than one kind of novel. But in Wollstonecraft's hands all these genres have affinities with autobiography; her biographer, Claire Tomalin, points out that 'she never could write without inserting more or less veiled remarks about ... the state of her own life'.[2] Her earliest published books, *Mary*, *Thoughts on the Education of Daughters* and *Original Stories*, have been construed by Mitzi Myers as 'experiments in selfhood' in which she 'transforms personal dilemma into alternative images of female selfhood'.[3] And it is fascinating to learn that among her later works she attempted a comic play based on her own experiences: 'this comedy was in fact offered to two producers in a rough draft and then set aside when they rejected it'.[4] Godwin felt that it was in too 'crude and imperfect a state to warrant preservation'.[5] Wollstonecraft's final novel, *The Wrongs of Woman* (1798), is also markedly autobiographical in that its protagonist's experiences closely reflect her own life. Its narrative strategies, however, suggest that she judged the risky and experimental autobiographical method of the *Letters in Sweden* to have had limited success. In *Maria* she separates the narrator from the protagonist, and so provides a relatively detached and unimpassioned framework to mediate the several life stories which the novel includes.[6] Throughout her career, then, she was concerned to mingle autobiographical elements with various different genres. For the *Letters in Sweden*, the crucial informing genre was that of travel writing.

Wollstonecraft, in her capacity as a book reviewer, had plenty of opportunity to consider the possible scope and nature of travel writing; she had reviewed some 24 travel books for Joseph Johnson in the *Analytical Review*, mostly in 1790 and 1791.[7] Only three of these were written in epistolary form, and only one is by a woman (Mrs Piozzi's *Observations and Reflections, made in the Course of a Journey through France, Italy and Germany*). Many of the books record travels undertaken in connection with commercial or government business. In her reviews Wollstonecraft tends to commend precision, curiosity and a sense of history; she also praises writing able to combine the virtues of sociological investigation and descriptive prose. She is severe on the language of feigned rapture, on incuriosity and 'while-a-way' shallowness.[8] Mrs Piozzi comes in for a Johnsonian putdown: 'Those who can readily gather flowers, will not laboriously turn up the earth for the most valuable materials.'[9] The imagery rather priggishly contrasts an implicitly feminine attention to pleasing surfaces with the right kind of stamina, implicitly masculine by association with farming (or possibly mining).

It is worth looking at one of Wollstonecraft's reviews in more detail to discover her developing notions of the possibilities of travel writing; and to see how far the criticism of travel writing engages her central ethical concerns.

> These amusing letters are full of information, delivered in that connected form, which characterizes a thinking mind, for the ingenious writer appears to have always had in view the natural history and antiquities of the places he describes; and the desultory manner that casually occurs, entertains, without turning the attention from the main subject. We have before observed, that travels would be very useful repositories of knowledge, if the traveller always had a particular pursuit in his head; not merely to serve as a clue to the judgment, plunged into a maze of enquiries; but as a solid foundation for the work, only trusting to chance for the ornamental parts of the structure. The imagination would not then be racked to give the air of adventures to common incidents, or to spin sentiments out of the brain that never agitated the heart: – nor would the trivial occurrences of each day be noted with puerile exactness, and vacant indiscriminate surprise. But when a man only travels to *while-away* the time, when leisure is, literally speaking, idleness, his eyes are turned on every prominent novelty, and the mind, quite afloat, catches at every straw and bubble that crosses it, not having previously determined what it should wish to examine, excepting the vague desire of seeing something new. – An old propensity, as St Paul informs us, that led to vice by encouraging a vain curiosity, though a thoughtless restlessness of mind scarcely deserves the name of that useful impulse, and seldom acts as an incitement to acquire knowledge, or to search into the reason of things. The art of travelling is only a branch of the art of thinking, or still more precisely to express ourselves, the conduct of a being who acts from principle; – but we are stepping out of our province.
> (*Works*, vol. VII, pp. 276–7; review of *Letters Concerning the Northern Coast of the County of Antrim ...* by the Revd William Hamilton)

These are very much the terms of the *Vindication of the Rights of Woman*, insisting that rationality consists not in surrender to exteriors, but in a conscious principle of selection. The appeal to St Paul suggests Wollstonecraft's roots in a tradition of Protestant dissent, a likely source for the anti-sensualism in much of her early writing. In *Letters in Sweden*, Wollstonecraft wants to emulate this uncasual desultoriness of Hamilton's; to combine vivacity of observation with depth of insight; her grievance against sensuality, essentially, is not against the sins of the flesh (on three occasions she uses the word 'voluptuously' approvingly[10]) but against a lack of depth – neglecting the 'most valuable' depths for the visible 'flowers'. Sexual permissiveness, then, is the equivalent of the 'mind, quite afloat, [that] catches at every straw and bubble that crosses it'. These terms also suggest the source of her discontent about homelessness, an unhappiness which pervades both the *Letters in Sweden* and the letters she wrote to Imlay. Restlessness trespasses against the need for roots, for fixity, just as thoughtlessness entails no foundation, no depth. For Wollstonecraft, there are strong correlations between restlessness and superficiality, as also between settled domesticity and the groundworks of reason. The title, which is in full *Letters Written During a Short Residence in Sweden, Norway and Denmark,* offers only 'A Short Residence' when what she wants is a permanent dwelling-place.

Wollstonecraft makes further remarks on the proper conduct of travel in the *Vindication of the Rights of Woman*. Once again she insists that the traveller's mind needs to be purposefully prepared. The gender implication is further developed on this occasion by means of a hostile association of femininity with frivolity of mind and vanity of person:

> A man, when he undertakes a journey, has, in general, the end in view; a woman thinks more of the incidental occurrences, the strange things that may possibly occur on the road; the impression that she may make on her fellow-travellers; and, above all, she is anxiously intent on the care of the finery that she carries with her, which is more than ever a part of herself, when going to figure on a new scene; when, to use an apt French turn of expression, she is going to produce a sensation. – Can dignity of mind exist with such trivial cares?[11]

Inconstancy of attention, then, can only be justified in these writings of the early 1790s by a deliberated unity of purpose. How readily can this be discerned in the *Letters in Sweden*?

The book begins with an 'Advertisement', giving us a mixed generic message from the first: 'The writing travels, or memoirs, has ever been a pleasant employment', she blandly opens, adding sharply that 'vanity or sensibility always renders it interesting'. Travels or memoirs, which is it to be? It's as though she were combining in one book the methods of Johnson's *Journey to the Western Islands of Scotland* and Boswell's *Tour to the Hebrides* (Johnson's *Journey* was probably a particular influence on the *'men's questions'* (p. 68) that Wollstonecraft asked). The advertisement is uneasy about the propriety of her prominence as 'the little hero of each tale'; the unease being registered in the way she gives three different justifications. First, the criterion of accuracy: 'I could not give a just description of what I saw, but by relating the effect different objects had produced on my mind and feelings'; secondly, interesting the affections of the reader: 'A person has a right ... to talk of himself when he can win on our attention by acquiring our affection'; but third, 'my plan was simply to endeavour to give a just view of the present state of the countries I have passed through' (p. 62). This third statement comes across more as a retraction than a restatement, diluting the empathetic and subjective emphases in favour of something more functional.

The distinction between these emphases suggests the question that has occupied commentators on the *Letters in Sweden* from its first reviewers until now: namely, whether its rapid shifts of tone and subject – its 'desultory' character in Wollstonecraft's term – constitute a charming informality, a purposive tension or just a hasty mess. One view of the matter may be represented by Claire Tomalin: 'There was no pretence of a systematic approach; Mary had simply allowed her eye for nature, her curiosity about mankind and her bent towards didacticism to run together in oddly successful harmony.'[12] This is generous in a way, but it attributes the book's success to the author's undesigning permissiveness, and it says little about how the 'oddly successful harmony' is brought about. At the other extreme, Mitzi Myers finds that 'Underlying the seeming duality of personal and social motifs in the *Letters* is a continuous concern with human identity and self-realization, developed in counterpoint to the related themes of society's improvement and nature's values.'[13] I am in sympathy with Myers's idea of the continuity of the book's concern, but she too is unspecific about the 'counterpoint', and her essay does little to clarify the rather unfocussing ideas of 'nature's values' and 'self-realization'. I hope to offer a fuller characterization of Wollstonecraft's attempt to synthesize the various elements in the book; and to describe its possible influences, negative and positive, on subsequent self-representation in the Romantic period.

Letters Written During a Short Residence in Sweden, Norway and Denmark: the full title brings out that this travel book, written as it is in 25 letters, shares some of the features of an epistolary novel.[14] We never discover the identity of the addressee of the letters. Contemporary readers outside the author's circle would not have known anything about the figure of Gilbert Imlay, on whose behalf Wollstonecraft was undertaking an intricate business venture of dubious legality.[15] Indeed, although we now know that the book derives in large part from Wollstonecraft's correspondence with Imlay, he is not in any transparent way its addressee. It is never unambiguous that the letters are written to a faithless lover; nor indeed do we know that the writer has been abandoned, though she often bemoans her loneliness. We know she has a child, but not whose. She always refers to Fanny as 'my child', never 'ours'. Is she a respectable widow or a ruined woman? Her situation is certainly startling, and romantic partly in that it suggests a novel whose plot shadows and precedes the book. But the allusions stop short of a recoverable narrative, and the roles of writer and addressee are generalized beyond biographical circumstance. Comparison with the unpublished letters to Imlay shows elements of shaping. Early on, for example, she was knocked out in what sounds like a highly dramatic fall from some rocks: 'how I escaped with life I can scarcely guess' (*LMW*, p. 299). Imlay gets to hear about this, but perhaps she thought it would come across too designingly as heart-wrenching for other readers. Similarly, the lover's appeals in her personal letters to Imlay are suppressed, except as moralized reproach. She disconcertingly brings her situation to bear as a pervasive influence on the book; but withholds any explanation of its crucial circumstances.

The narrator, then, is not a neutral observer, and her observations take the colour of her fluctuating emotional state. The relative blitheness in the early descriptions of Norway, for instance, is connected to the returning health Wollstonecraft was enjoying; while the sombre and sometimes apocalyptic reflections in the concluding letters from Hamburg accompany her sense of finally abandoned love. Our main impression of the narrator is of her emotional vulnerability; we frequently hear of 'clouds of sorrows' and 'black melancholy' (to take two examples among many), and hints are offered about 'various causes'.[16] Details of landscape start up reflections on her own place within it; in Letter Ten, for example, the way that a group of trees 'stood to brave the elements' prompts her to romanticize her own isolated and buffeted state:

> Sitting then in a little boat on the ocean, amidst strangers, with sorrow and care pressing hard on me, – buffeting me about from clime to clime, – I felt
> > Like the lone shrub at random cast,
> > That sighs and trembles at each blast!
>
> (p. 126)

The quotation, variously appropriate to Wollstonecraft, is adapted from Goldsmith's *The Traveller, or a Prospect of Society* (1764) (it is unidentified both in Holmes's edition and in Butler and Todd's *Collected Works*). Goldsmith's narrator offered Wollstonecraft a close precedent in his obscure melancholy, his vain search for a place to settle, and his political acumen. The relevant lines in *The Traveller* are these:

> Here for a while my proper cares resigned,
> Here let me sit in sorrow for mankind,
> Like yon neglected shrub at random cast,
> That shades the steep and sighs at every blast.[17]

Wollstonecraft's alterations produce a simpler pathos, notably by omitting the altruistic context of Goldsmith's 'sorrow for mankind' (although such altruism figures importantly elsewhere in the *Letters*). The 'neglected' shrub becomes more straightforwardly 'lone' in Wollstonecraft's memory, and she also misses out the suggestion of its protective resilience. Her abbreviation of the lines into octosyllabics moves away from the basic sturdiness of the heroic couplet tradition into a more simply pathetic movement. And the effect of adding the words 'lone' and 'trembles' is to give an undertone of erotic appeal to the lines, the kind of thing to which Godwin famously responded in his sense of 'a book calculated to make a man in love with its author' (p. 249).

Godwin's words are indeed more suggestive than he may have intended. The pathos is 'calculated', and the man whose love it first requires is not Godwin, but Imlay. One aspect of Wollstonecraft's persona can be suggested by the raw fact that she wrote most of the book between two suicide attempts. The book is a suicide note; it tells Imlay and intimates to other readers that her lover has driven her to wish her own destruction.

Wollstonecraft's characteristically speculative attitude to her own experience means that she does not only threaten suicide; she also considers it philosophically. Just as the forlorn lover remains a diligent observer of the travelled scene, so the suicidal woman thinks searchingly about death and immortality. Indeed, some of the most fascinating (and least commented on) writing in the book is born of these discussions.

Wollstonecraft's ideas about the persistence of the self beyond death are psychologically and theologically idiosyncratic, and they are produced by various contexts in her travels. In Letter One, to take an early example, the natural scene 'made me feel that I was still a part of a mighty whole, from which I could not sever myself', not even 'by snapping the thread of an existence which loses its charms' (p. 70). This attunement to nature is ambivalent; it has equally the possibility of reconciling her to life and of consoling her about the non-finality of suicide. In Letter Two the landscape again works a reconciling charm, with pacifying intimations of immortality: 'The waters murmur, and fall with more than mortal music, and spirits of peace walk abroad to calm the agitated breast. Eternity is in these moments' (p. 75). What exactly are these 'spirits'? Here as elsewhere her language intimates pagan presences, sometimes modestly unspecific ('spirits unseen'), but more often characterized in further, half-parodic detail – 'hapless nymphs', 'hospitable sprites of the grots', 'light-footed elves' (pp. 134, 156, 127, 80). Like Coleridge's 'Religious Musings' (1794–96), Wollstonecraft's are ecumenical and speculative; and again like the early Coleridge, she is curious to investigate the psychological origins of diverse religious beliefs. Passing through groves of trees, she is struck with a mystic kind of reverence:

> Not nymphs, but philosophers, seemed to inhabit them – ever musing; I could scarcely conceive that they were without some consciousness of existence – without a calm enjoyment of the pleasure they diffused.
>
> How often do my feelings produce ideas that remind me of the origin of many poetical fictions. In solitude, the imagination bodies forth its conceptions unrestrained, and stops enraptured to adore the beings of its own creation. These are moments of bliss; and the memory recalls them with delight.
>
> (p. 119)

The 'poetical fictions' we are likely to think of are Wordsworth's, because of the anticipation of 'Lines written in Early Spring' ('I must think, do all I can, / That there was pleasure there'),[18] and because the incarnational theory of the creative imagination prefigures Book V of *The Prelude* and the 'Essay Supplementary' to the 1815 edition of his poems. The imagination, sensing life all around, produces fictions (nymphs, sprites, gods); in giving these fictions supernatural status, it is partly worshipping its own reflections, and its own creative powers. Like Wordsworth, Wollstonecraft is curious about the frequently pagan reference of eighteenth-century loco-descriptive poetry;[19] and she resembles Wordsworth again in that her location of the origin of supernatural forms in the mind itself actively confirms her in a strong but not quite orthodox religious sentiment.

To find such congruence of supernatural forms and human imagination is sustaining. Her shocked reaction to the embalmed bodies she sees at Tønsberg comes from her sense that this process mistakes the character of what is truly imperishable in humanity. 'Life, what art thou? Where goes this breath? this *I*, so much alive? In what element will it mix, giving or receiving fresh energy?' (p. 109). Here again her metaphysical speculation takes it for granted that death is not the end; the self will continue in new combinations, a consoling view couched in terms remote from Christian eschatology. 'It appears to me impossible that I should cease to exist, or that this active, restless spirit, equally alive to joy and sorrow, should only be organized dust.'[20]

Wollstonecraft's thoughts keep returning to death, but her faith in a persistent vital principle is never shaken. From the point of view of autobiographical writing this means that suicide would not exactly bring a life-story to an unhappy end because it would not exactly bring it to an end. 'I cannot tell why – but death, under every form, appears to me like something getting free – to expand in I know not what element' (p. 152). The self-destructive impulse, indeed, had for

Wollstonecraft always had a connection with divine discontent. 'Delusions of passion', she argued in *A Vindication of the Rights of Woman*, are 'a strong proof of the immortality of the soul'.[21] Earlier yet, she had written robustly about the edifying aspect of worldly unhappiness in the *Thoughts on the Education of Daughters*:

> I have very often heard it made a subject of ridicule, that when a person is disappointed in this world, they turn to the next. Nothing can be more natural than the transition; and it seems to me the scheme of Providence, that our finding things unsatisfactory here, should force us to think of the better country to which we are going.
>
> (*Works*, vol. IV, p. 37)

This sense of the world as a vale of tears persisted with Wollstonecraft, so that her suicidal reflections in the *Letters in Sweden* evoke her as a rare spirit – a troubling romantic figure, like Goethe's Werther, the object at once of compassion and admiration.

The idea that suicide is a mortal sin does not enter the picture, not even to be denied. The omission is striking, given the strict piety and frequent biblical reference of her early works. But although Wollstonecraft retained from her Protestant dissenting roots an emphasis on the unrelaxing will, her writings come to distance themselves from Christian eschatology. The author of creation is frequently discerned in the *Letters in Sweden*,[22] but not as a figure of judgement. Her expressions of suicidal feeling in this book are presented as valuable discoveries of sublimity and dignity. At the falls near Frederikstat, for instance:

> my thoughts darted from earth to heaven, and I asked myself why I was chained to life and its misery? Still the tumultuous emotions this sublime object excited, were pleasurable; and, viewing it, my soul rose, with renewed dignity, above its cares – grasping at immortality – it seemed as impossible to stop the current of my thoughts, as of the always varying, still the same, torrent before me – I stretched out my hand to eternity, bounding over the dark speck of life to come.
>
> (pp. 152–3)

It is an enigmatic passage. The grandeur of the falls recommends life by helping her transcend her cares and by producing pleasure. But it also makes her feel immortal longings, born of the sense that the process of life can never be extinguished. The end of the passage metaphorically suggests a suicidal plunge into partnership with eternity; one wonders about Wollstonecraft's influence on Shelley.

Such passion in her response to scenery repeatedly threatens to unbalance the narrator. The endings of the letters, in particular, frequently find in the description of nature an impetus to personal introspection. Her capacity to feel is presented as a dangerous susceptibility. It is in one aspect a legacy of 'sensibility'; Wollstonecraft, in common with other women writing at the time, was not so much in reaction against 'sensibility' as determined to recuperate it by discrediting the affectation and falsity from which it needed to be differentiated. Hence the pressure of attention visited in her writings on the word 'sensibility'; it is an effort of redefinition. Wollstonecraft projects her persona in the *Letters in Sweden* as a figure of exemplary sensibility:

> Nature is the nurse of sentiment, – the true source of taste; – yet what misery, as well as rapture, is produced by a quick perception of the beautiful and sublime, when it is exercised in observing animated nature, when every beauteous feeling and emotion excites responsive sympathy, and the harmonized soul sinks into melancholy, or rises to extasy, just as the chords are touched, like the aeolian harp agitated by the changing wind. But how dangerous it is to foster these sentiments in such an imperfect state of existence; and how difficult to eradicate them when an affection for mankind, a passion for an individual, is but the unfolding of that love which embraces all that is great and beautiful.
>
> (p. 99)

In this passage nature is the 'nurse' of sentiment, but to 'foster' responsiveness is a danger. The love plot shadowing the book exactly reflects this situation: the narrator's feeling heart exalts her but makes her suffer. Wollstonecraft is arguing that there is a vital interconnection between political altruism, erotic love, and enthusiasm for nature. They are aspects of a particular kind of personality, of which the narrator of the book stands as the example. To read the book is to be solicited to fellow-feeling in all these areas; Wollstonecraft is representing herself as exemplary partly in order to evoke a correspondingly exemplary reader.

That reader would share Wollstonecraft's capacity to be depressed and distressed by the political imperfections she encounters. 'The heart sickens', she writes, at the sight of 'poverty and dirt' (p. 185); the fire at Copenhagen has 'much to afflict the benevolent heart' (p. 163); and in one prescient passage of Malthusian speculation about the planet's finite resources she succumbs to the neurosis of rigorous utilitarian thinking: 'I really became distressed for these fellow creatures, yet unborn.'[23]

Letters in Sweden considers blighted hopes and ideal prospects as the contexts for political thinking as well as for the drama of love. Wollstonecraft's previous book had been *An Historical and Moral View of the French Revolution* (1794). Many of the discussions in the *Letters in Sweden* take place within the recognized lexicon of post-revolutionary political debate; the nature of the monarchy, for example, the effects of wealth on morality, issues concerning law reform and the punishment of crime. The *Historical and Moral View* was a moderate book, its burden that the Terror was a price worth paying for social progress. Wollstonecraft holds fast to an optimism about beneficial political change in the *Letters in Sweden,* but does so amid realistic provisos. Satirical moments check visionary ones. There are a number of emblematic moments in which excessive hopes meet with more than expected resistance in the real world. None the less, she writes predominantly as a witness to improvements in knowledge and science, especially in Norway. When Wollstonecraft indulges what she ruefully calls 'my favourite subject of contemplation, the future improvement of the world' (p. 187), her favourite word is 'enlarged'.[24] It is a useful word for her because it suggests improvement in both quantity and quality: with 'enlarged views' you know more things, and you know them in a wiser spirit, that of educated understanding. One might suggest that the Johnsonian aspects of her style work towards such an enlargement. When she writes that 'their manners will naturally improve in the same ratio as industry requires ingenuity' (p. 121), the conceptual density of the prose compels the reader to think through an idea of improvement, charting the relations between hard work, intellectual energy and social refinement. The complexity of the style grounds its aspiration in a discriminating moral intelligence. Again:

> The domestic happiness, and good-humoured gaiety, of the amiable family where I and my Frances were so hospitably received, would have been sufficient to insure the tenderest remembrance, without the recollection of the social evenings to stimulate it, when good-breeding gave dignity to sympathy, and wit, zest to reason.
> (p. 116)

The last phrases sketch a diagram of the way in which good qualities can better themselves.

Although the book deals many checks to idealism, Wollstonecraft finds a space to value and endorse it as a source of energy and precondition of amelioration. Her ambivalence between maintained hope and suffered despair defines the characteristic tension of the *Letters in Sweden*. Hearing of the inhabitants of northern Norway, for example, she hesitates between scepticism and enthusiasm:

> The description I received of them carried me back to the fables of the golden age: independence and virtue; affluence without vice; cultivation of mind, without depravity of heart; with 'ever smiling liberty', the nymph of the mountain. – I want faith! My imagination hurries me forward to seek an asylum in such a retreat from all the disappointments I am threatened with; but reason drags me back, whispering that the world is still the world, and man the same compound of weakness and folly, who must occasionally

> excite love and disgust, admiration and contempt. But this description, though it seems to have been sketched by a fairy pencil, was given me by a man of sound understanding, whose fancy seldom appears to run away with him.
>
> (p. 149)

She is drawn to this imagined model community partly as a counterpart to the agrarian ideal which she had hoped to share with Imlay in America: 'I should have been content, and still wish, to retire with you to a farm' (*LMW*, p. 274; letter of 9 January 1795).

The *Letters in Sweden* are haunted by the idea of homelessness, and Wollstonecraft's phrasing frequently conceives of fulfilment in terms of a dwelling-place: 'human happiness, where, oh! where does it reside?' (p. 122), she asks, and conjures the 'ideal forms of excellence! again enclose me in your magic circle' (pp. 128–9). She recalls that it was 'in returning to my home' (p. 189) that she discovered Imlay's infidelity, and feels an especially bitter pang at Tønsberg because though it 'was something like a home – yet I was destined to enter without lighting-up pleasure in any eye' (p. 135). As a quest for a settled home, the *Letters in Sweden* may anticipate such Romantic poems as, for instance, Coleridge's *The Rime of the Ancient Mariner* and Shelley's *Alastor*. The difference is structural: Coleridge has a wedding-guest, part of the community, as well as a mariner cursed to wander; Shelley has a narrating poet who takes warning from his unrequited solipsist double. But Wollstonecraft is at once wanderer and aspirant dweller; she does not separate the suffering protagonist from the chastened commentator. It is one and the same figure, hence some of the fluctuations in her narrative manner. In this passage, then, the balance between wishfulness and scepticism remains finally unstable. For all her saltiness about 'Rousseau's golden age of stupidity' (p. 122), her imagination is allured by this reverie of republican virtue, and the intervention of reason does not wholly negate it. A view of society continues to soothe a personal disappointment. Wollstonecraft's prose leaves it behind, projecting the ideal into a dubious state between 'sound understanding' and 'a fairy pencil'.

Her reformist ambition had been directed in the second *Vindication* towards enlarging the narrow educational prospects of English women; in the *Letters in Sweden* it looks to the prospects of nations abroad. Her faith in such international progress sounds shaken in the more sombre later letters of the book. Letter Twenty-Two, especially, is prompted by 'German despotism' to a tremendously imagined panorama of waste and destruction, in which she expresses a horrified pre-Darwinian presentiment that the species may flourish while individuals fall by the wayside and the presiding intelligence watches indifferently.

Such darker currents of feeling threaten in the later stages of the book to overthrow its exemplary purposes. In its concluding pages she has finally given up on her lover; everywhere she looks she sees the blight of commerce, which she vehemently and repeatedly demonizes in an unusually crude simplification of her socio-political understanding; and she is fed up with travelling. Wollstonecraft may have sensed that the book was being too negatively determined by its emotional intensity; this might account for the way it concludes in recuperating gestures of reformism. The short and wretched final letters are followed by a much more measured 'Appendix', looking to gradual 'alterations in laws and governments' (p. 198). She warns against internationalist aspirations and against revolutionary upheaval: improvements 'must be the growth of each particular soil, and the gradual fruit of the ripening understanding of the nation, matured by time, not forced by an unnatural fermentation' (p. 198). To embody the counsel of patience, she follows the appendix with statistical supplementary notes about Norwegian trade and, in conclusion, its fiscal system.

Her narrative persona is characterized above all by its susceptibility to strong feeling. Hesitant between travel record, political speculation and confession of the heart, *Letters in Sweden* provides many contexts for emotional intensity: landscape, in the ardent and theologically speculative natural descriptions; love, in the increasing desperation of the shadowy love story; and politics, in the negotiations between reformist ardour and pessimistic indignation. This mobility between generic precedents suggests a thoroughgoing sense of the connections between private and public concerns. Wollstonecraft constructs a self which is both exemplary and endangered, both politically progressive and by the same token emotionally vulnerable. She implies that the same outgoings of the heart are the motor for social good and the cause of possibly disabling emotional hurt. Lovers of mankind will be at risk in private life; political and personal disappointment overlap.

She presents herself, then, both as an inspiring and a pathetic figure. In this she resembles Queen Matilda, in whom Wollstonecraft finds a haunting counterpart for herself. Matilda, the wife by an arranged marriage to King Christian of Denmark, lived a life marked by reformist ambition, audacious independence about love and, ultimately, by disappointment. Christian's mental instability required medical restraint. The royal physician, Struensee, became Matilda's lover, and probably the father of her child. Together they initiated a liberal reforming regime, but they were eventually overthrown by their enemies in Christian's family. Struensee was beheaded, and Matilda died in exile, aged 24.[25] Wollstonecraft undertakes to defend Matilda against censure; her way of doing so shows her affinity with this forerunner. She describes, first, Matilda's tough-minded child-rearing; then her good public works, in which she erred only 'in wishing to do immediately what can only be done by time' (p. 166) – the same kind of over-zealousness that the 'Appendix' will warn against; then her freedom in love: 'she certainly was not a woman of gallantry', Wollstonecraft begins approvingly, 'and if she had an attachment for him [Struensee], it did not disgrace her heart or understanding, the king being a notorious debauchee, and an idiot into the bargain' (p. 166). That nice touch of asperity leads to the mingling at the end of the letter of indignation and lament that the king, now 'absolutely an idiot' (p. 167), should live on, 20 years after Matilda's early death. 'What a farce is life! This effigy of majesty is allowed to burn down to the socket, whilst the hapless Matilda was hurried into an untimely grave' (p. 167).

When Wordsworth echoes these lines in 'The Ruined Cottage' (written in 1797), he brings out their pathos but deflects the politicized anger. The Wanderer in the poem is telling its narrator of Margaret's death: 'O Sir! the good die first, / And they whose hearts are dry as summer dust / Burn to the socket.'[26] The Wanderer is thinking of his own emotional desiccation in age; the anger in the tragic contrast is turned inward, with an effect of doubled poignancy.[27] Wordsworth's lines are quoted in their turn as a climactic conclusion to Shelley's 'Preface' to *Alastor*: 'Those who love not their fellow-beings live unfruitful lives, and prepare for their old age a miserable grave. "The good die first, / And those whose hearts are dry as summer's dust, / Burn to the socket!"'[28] It is tempting to speculate that Shelley was thinking back through Wordsworth to Wollstonecraft. Although her quest is love-stricken rather than solipsistic, still her restlessness and the landscape she travels may have contributed to the situation of *Alastor*. That Shelley's poem has affinities with the writings of Wollstonecraft (his late mother-in-law, after all) is vividly apparent from this passage in one of her letters to Imlay: 'Believe me, there is such a thing as a broken heart! There are characters whose very energy preys upon them; and who, ever inclined to cherish by reflection some passion, cannot rest satisfied with the common comforts of life' (*LMW*, p. 304; 7 July 1795). In October 1814, the year before he wrote *Alastor*, 'Shelley read a canto of *Queen Mab* and some of Mary Wollstonecraft's love letters out loud' to Jane Clairmont and his wife Mary.[29]

According to Wollstonecraft's recent editors, Marilyn Butler and Janet Todd, the *Letters in Sweden* had a particularly powerful influence; the book 'moved and haunted the leading men writers of her generation, Coleridge, Wordsworth, Southey, Hazlitt and Godwin, and several of the women too – Seward, Hays and Alderson' (*Works*, vol. I, p. 21). The echoes and analogues from Wordsworth and Shelley suggest this influence. In conclusion, however, I want to argue that her self-representation in the *Letters in Sweden* failed to have the influence she intended. What Wollstonecraft meant as exemplary was taken as cautionary; cautionary in a punitive sense to her political adversaries, and in an elegiac sense to her sympathizers.

Several critics have described the recoil against Wollstonecraft, prompted after her death by the publication in 1798 of Godwin's *Memoirs*.[30] Her principled sexual freedoms shocked even her admirers, and hostile critics pilloried her on this account. 'For years after 1798 there was scarcely an unwanted pregnancy anywhere in England for which Mary Wollstonecraft did not take a share of the blame.'[31] Whereas the *Letters in Sweden* construct sensibility as a progressive principle, Wollstonecraft's critics came to see her sensibility more straightforwardly — as a quality to which she was a martyr. Mary Hays, for example, performs a lament which is also a diagnosis: 'persons of the finest and most exquisite genius have probably the greatest sensibility, consequently the strongest passions, by the fervor of which they are too often betrayed into error'.[32] Hays converts fervent sensibility into a symptom of false vision. Other critics make much the same assumption, in various modes from elegy to lampoon. Contemporary readers of *Letters in Sweden* fail even to grasp, never mind credit, its attempt to unify its generic elements. Amelia Alderson, for instance, wrote to Wollstonecraft admiringly about the book, but in terms which separate the love and the politics: 'as soon as I read your letters from Norway, the cold awe which the philosopher has excited, was lost in the tender sympathy called forth by the woman'.[33] T.J. Mathias comparably finds her a mass of contradictions: 'Fierce passion's slave, she veer'd with every gust / Love, Rights and Wrongs, Philosophy and Lust ...'.[34] And Thomas Brown's poem of 1816, 'The Wanderer in Norway', manages to 'turn the *Letters* into a moralistic narrative poem illustrating the dangers of a woman, even one with "a mind of no common order", indulging in passion'.[35] Intellect and passion, once again, are kept apart.

From the point of view of subsequent autobiographical writing, this widespread failure to understand (or credit) the synthesizing design of the *Letters in Sweden* has important consequences. Wollstonecraft had advocated and attempted a voice which could be at once passionate and authoritative, at once symptomatic and diagnostic. The *Letters in Sweden* represents that ambition, even if it only partially succeeds in fulfilling it; the ruptures and shifts of tone in the book have much to do with its intellectual reach and literary vitality, but they show the strain in its project of synthesis.

The most important subsequent writers in the Romantic period, the poets, characteristically push apart the voices whose inseparability

Wollstonecraft propounds. Hence the prevalence of 'doubled' figures – voices of passion and their more detached counterparts; unbalanced, self-destructive figures and their more prudent shadows. Notable instances include the Wanderer tempering the narrator's gloom early in Wordsworth's *Excursion*, and 'correcting' the Solitary's despondency later in the poem; Byron's separation of narrator and protagonist in *Don Juan*; and, as I have already discussed, the poet-narrator's wary ambivalence about the visionary solipsist of *Alastor*. One of Shelley's finest poems, 'Julian and Maddalo' (1819), separates its competing companionable voices further still. Maddalo, of course, is based on Byron, and Julian on Shelley himself (with added sanguineness); but what of 'the Maniac'? Is the Maniac Mary Wollstonecraft in disguise? The similarities are striking. A deserting paramour has driven him to distraction; he imagines himself 'wide awake, though dead'; and sufferingly fills the role of world-conscience 'as a nerve o'er which do creep / The else unfelt oppressions of this earth'.[36] The Maniac resembles Julian – 'he was ever talking is such sort / As you do' (ll. 236–7) – but in Shelley's poem Julian survives to tell the story while his Maniac double enigmatically dies. Maddalo goes travelling in Armenia, Julian returns to Venice, and the Maniac lives on in his memory and the poem. The structure of the poem keeps the writer's various impulses separately figured. Wollstonecraft's unwillingness in the *Letters in Sweden* so to separate the voices of her self (political scientist, natural historian, abandoned lover) defines the originality of her experiment in autobiography. Perhaps its failure turned out to have no less influence on subsequent autobiographical writings than any success we may imagine.

Notes

1. *Collected Letters of Mary Wollstonecraft*, ed. M. Ralph Wardle (Ithaca and London: Cornell University Press, 1979), p. 317 (hereafter, *LMW*).
2. Claire Tomalin, *The Life and Death of Mary Wollstonecraft* (London: Weidenfeld and Nicolson, 1974), p. 40.
3. Mitzi Myers, 'Pedagogy as Self-Expression in Mary Wollstonecraft: Exorcising the Past, Finding a Voice', in *The Private Self: Theory and Practice of Women's Autobiographical Writings*, ed. Shari Benstock (Chapel Hill and London: University of North Carolina Press, 1988), pp. 192–210 (p. 195).
4. Tomalin, p. 188.
5. Mary Wollstonecraft and William Godwin, '*A Short Residence in Sweden, Norway and Denmark*' and '*Memoirs of the Author of "The Rights of Woman"*', ed. Richard Holmes (Harmondsworth: Penguin Books, 1987), p. 235. All unattributed page references henceforth are to this edition.
6. For a cogent discussion of the narrative strategies of *Maria*, see Nicola J. Watson, *Revolution and the Form of the British Novel 1790–1825: Inter-*

cepted Letters, Interrupted Seductions (Oxford: Clarendon Press, 1994), pp. 51–7: 'Assembling her social anatomy, Wollstonecraft resorts to the third person for social and moral authority beyond individual feeling, containing the subjective within a series of ever-larger box-narratives which isolate Maria's central first-person narrative, insulating the reader's sympathies' (p. 55).

7. I have followed the attributions in *The Works of Mary Wollstonecraft*, ed. Marilyn Butler and Janet Todd, 7 vols (London: Pickering and Chatto, 1989), vol. VII (hereafter, *Works*). Some of the books reviewed have an uncertain generic status.
8. 'Flying and loitering, sprightly and *vapourish* travellers, have given us, in their minute diaries, written at the moment, different views of the objects, which enabled them to *while-a-way* some leisure time which hung heavy on their hands' (*Works*, vol. VII, p. 301; review of Samuel Ireland, *A Picturesque Tour through Holland, Brabant, and Part of France*).
9. *Works*, vol. VII, p. 110.
10. See pp. 81, 94 and especially 83: 'there is always a mixture of sentiment and imagination in voluptuousness'.
11. Mary Wollstonecraft, *A Vindication of the Rights of Woman*, ed. Carol H. Poston, second edition (New York and London: W.W. Norton & Co., 1988), p. 60.
12. Tomalin, p. 190.
13. Mitzi Myers, 'Mary Wollstonecraft's "Letters Written ... in Sweden": Toward Romantic Autobiography', *Studies in Eighteenth-Century Culture*, 8 (1979), 165–85 (p. 166).
14. Imlay's epistolary novel, *The Emigrants* (1793), offered a precedent for combining a love story in letters with discursive reflections on topics of socio-political importance.
15. Per Nyström has researched the circumstances of the journey in *Mary Wollstonecraft's Scandanavian Journey*, Acts of the Royal Society of Arts and Sciences of Gothenburg, Humaniora No. 17, 1980. Richard Holmes's introduction to his Penguin edition summarizes Nyström on pp. 21–6.
16. Pp. 127, 141, 97; see also, pp. 111, 151, 178.
17. *The Traveller*, ll. 101–4; *The Poems of Gray, Collins and Goldsmith*, ed. Roger Lonsdale (London: Longman, 1969), p. 637.
18. 'Lines written in Early Spring', ll. 19–20; William Wordsworth and Samuel Taylor Coleridge, *Lyrical Ballads*, ed. Michael Mason (London: Longman, 1992), p. 145. See also, 'And 'tis my faith that every flower / Enjoys the air it breathes' (ll. 11–12), and 'the least motion which they made, / It seemed a thrill of pleasure' (ll. 15–16).
19. Geoffrey Hartman has been an excellent interpreter of this aspect of Wordsworth. See especially 'Inscriptions and Romantic Nature Poetry', in his *The Unremarkable Wordsworth* (London: Methuen, 1987).
20. P. 112. Compare her reflections on departed greatness at the palace of Rosenborg: 'Could they be no more – to whom my imagination thus gave life? Could the thoughts, of which there remained so many vestiges, have vanished quite away? And these beings, composed of such noble materials of thinking and feeling, have they only melted into the elements to keep in motion the grand mass of life? It cannot be!' (p. 175). An early letter to Joseph Johnson about Samuel Johnson had also expressed Wollstonecraft's faith in some sort of persistence beyond death; she had been reviewing

Johnson's *Sermons* (see *Works*, vol. VII, pp. 36–42), and found them affecting, 'a just tribute of respect to the memory of a man – who, spite of his faults, I have an affection for – I say *have*, for I believe he is somewhere – *where* my soul has been gadding perhaps' (letter of *c.* July 1788; *LMW*, p. 179). 'I believe he is somewhere': the phrasing could hardly specify less.

21. *Vindication*, ed. Poston, p. 74. See also, pp. 53–4, 124.
22. See, for example, pp. 65, 87, 94, 111. Wollstonecraft's imagination was especially stirred (both geologically and theologically) by the rocky coasts: see her fine passage describing 'the huge, dark rocks, that looked like the rude materials of creation forming the barrier of unwrought space' (p. 65).
23. P. 130. Compare, from her letters to Imlay: 'My mind however is at present painfully active, and the sympathy I feel almost rises to agony' (*LMW*, p. 306; 30 July 1795); and 'the lively sympathies which bind me to my fellow creatures, are all of a painful kind' (*LMW*, p. 311; 6 September 1795).
24. See, for instance, pp. 79, 93, 126, 131, 182. 'Expand' is a cognate term to which she also has recourse. Its opposite, 'narrow', recurs even more often – examples can be found on pp. 79, 84, 114, 121, 124, 141, particularly in the context of the blighting emotional effect of commercial ambition.
25. I take these details from Richard Holmes's edition (see note 5 above), pp. 290–1.
26. 'The Ruined Cottage', ll. 96–8; *William Wordsworth*, ed. Stephen Gill, The Oxford Authors (Oxford: Oxford University Press, 1984), p. 33.
27. Wollstonecraft's dismayed reaction to the deserted state of a nobleman's house in Tønsberg may also have influenced the tragic dereliction of 'The Ruined Cottage': 'A stupid kind of sadness, to my eye, always reigns in a huge habitation where only servants live to put cases on the furniture and open the windows' (p. 118), she writes; and continues, 'The mildew respects not the lordly robe; and the worm riots unchecked on the cheek of beauty', phrasing which may have prompted Wordsworth's 'She is dead, / The worm is on her cheek' (ll. 103–4).
28. *Shelley's Poetry and Prose*, ed. Donald H. Reiman and Sharon B. Powers (New York and London: W.W. Norton & Co., 1977), p. 70.
29. Richard Holmes, *Shelley: The Pursuit* (London: Quartet Books, 1976), p. 257.
30. Tomalin, pp. 232–42 and Watson, pp. 61–8 have documented this with especially valuable fullness.
31. William St Clair, *The Godwins and the Shelleys: The Biography of a Family* (London: Faber and Faber, 1989), p. 188.
32. *Memoirs of Mary Wollstonecraft* (1800); cited in Watson, p. 62.
33. May 1796; cited in Tomalin, p. 190.
34. *The Shade of Alexander Pope on the Banks of the Thames* (1798); cited in Watson, pp. 65–6.
35. Gary Kelly, *Revolutionary Feminism: The Mind and Career of Mary Wollstonecraft* (London: Macmillan, 1992), p. 195.
36. 'Julian and Maddalo', ll. 388–92, 449–50; *Shelley's Poetry and Prose*, ed. Reiman and Powers, pp. 122–3.

CHAPTER THREE

The Shock of the Old: Wordsworth and the Paths to Rome

Keith Hanley

There is a passage in Gerard Manley Hopkins's correspondence with Canon Dixon written from University College, Dublin, where he tries to characterize the impact of the Wordsworthian revelation:

> There have been in all history a few, a very few men, whom common repute, even where it does not trust them, has treated as having had something happen to them that does not happen to other men, as having *seen something*, whatever that really was. Plato is the most famous of these ... human nature in these men saw something, got a shock; wavers in opinion, looking back, whether there was anything or no; but it is in a tremble ever since. Now what Wordsworthians mean is, what would seem to be the growing mind of the English speaking world and may perhaps come to be that of the world at large is that in Wordsworth when he wrote that [Immortality] ode human nature got another of those shocks, and the tremble from it is spreading. This opinion I do strongly share; I am, ever since I knew the ode, in that tremble. You know what happened to crazy Blake, himself a most poetically electric subject both active and passive, at his first hearing: when the hearer came to 'The pansy at my feet' he fell into a hysterical excitement. Now common sense forbid we should take on like these unstrung hysterical creatures: still it was a proof of the power of the shock.[1]

Hopkins was probably reacting to Arnold's scepticism about the faith of the Wordsworthian church, aware of the obscurities of Wordsworth's 'obstinate questionings', yet, though revolted by the excess of nonconformist (Blakean) enthusiasm, none the less more willing than Arnold to see in the latter's acknowledgement that Wordsworth indeed 'has something to say'[2] ('had seen something') that that 'something' ('far more deeply interfused'[3]) was not after all soothing in its predictability, but even *shocking* in its claim to ground a spiritual discourse.

Hopkins was responding to the ode's celebration of the kind of experience Wordsworth claims to be both representative ('that dream-like vividness and splendour which invest objects of sight in childhood', to which he believed 'everyone ... could bear testimony') and yet in his case peculiarly insistent ('particular feelings or *experiences* of my own mind'):[4]

> ...those obstinate questionings
> Of sense and outward things,
> Fallings from us, vanishings;
> Blank misgivings of a Creature
> Moving about in worlds not realised,
> High instincts before which our mortal Nature
> Did *tremble* like a guilty Thing surprised.
>
> (ll. 142–8; my italics)

The claim Hopkins was making for the broad cultural effect of Wordsworth's vision could hardly have been stronger: the ode's readers have been electrified, and the charge is being conducted into the language every since throughout the English-speaking world. On behalf of the Wordsworthians, Hopkins is telling the Arnoldians, who so mistrusted them, that far from safely '[laying] us as we lay at birth / On the cool flowery lap of earth'[5] he had jolted his readers into a reawakening from that fall into 'a sleep and a forgetting' ('Ode', l. 58).

For Hopkins, the agitation was specifically, as he had expressed it in 'The Wreck of the Deutschland', for the reconversion of 'rare-dear Britain' to Rome: 'For my part I sh. think St George and St Thomas of Canterbury wore roses in heaven for England's sake on the day that ode, not without their intervention, was penned' (*Correspondence*, p. 148). Hopkins's focus on the inspired and inspiring occasion of poetic composition is crucial: 'when [Wordsworth] wrote that [Immortality] ode human nature got another of those shocks'. The later poet is separating the claim for some kind of imaginative experience prior to the writing from the achievement of the poem itself, and locating it as the moment when the discourse of religious nationalism had first become embedded in Wordsworth's poetry. Later, Wordsworth's poetry had become far more evidently instrumental in promoting the discourse of Anglo-Catholic revivalism, a tendency that had been received in some quarters as (scandalously) shocking in its influence towards Romanism. But what Hopkins is already recognizing in the ode is a crisis of representation through which what is in large measure a private revelation was offering itself also as a paradigm for a resurgence of Christian imperialism.

Wordsworth's own most evolved model for the national culture, which Hopkins may also have had in mind, is that imaged in the spider's web in *The Convention of Cintra*:

> The outermost and all-embracing circle of benevolence has inward concentric circles which, like those of a spider's web, are bound together by links, and rest upon each other; making one frame, and capable of one tremor; circles narrower and narrower, closer and closer, as they lie more near to the centre of the self from which they proceeded, and which sustains the whole.[6]

The 'one tremor' afterwards became the Wanderer's principle of British colonization in *The Excursion*, conducting outwards a vision that depended ultimately on the resonance between the 'particular feelings or *experiences* of [Wordsworth's] own mind' and the terms of a re-created Christian civilization powered by the British industrial-military machine:

> Change wide, and deep, and silently performed,
> This Land shall witness; and as days roll on,
> Earth's universal frame shall feel the effect;
> Even until the smallest habitable rock,
> Beaten by lonely billows, hear the songs
> Of humanised society; and bloom
> With civil arts, that shall breathe forth their fragrance,
> A grateful tribute to all-ruling Heaven...
> –Vast the circumference of hope – and ye
> Are at its centre, British Lawgivers.
> (*Excursion*, IX. 384–91, 398–9)

More obviously than Wordsworth, however, Hopkins laid great stress on the legislative power of poets and the efficacy of literature itself in spreading the empire. Writing from Dublin some months earlier to thank Coventry Patmore for a new edition of his works, his 'trembling' has become more disconcerting, more biblical, when he proclaims: 'Your poems are a good deed done for the Catholic Church and another for England, for the British Empire, which now trembles in the balance held in the hand of unwisdom.' He answers his own question: 'How far can the civilisation England offers be attractive and valuable and be offered and insisted on as an attraction and a thing of value to India for instance' by offering 'a continual supply' of literature, 'and in quality excellent'?[7]

Hopkins's plan prefigures George Orwell's at the end of the Second World War, broadcasting British poetry over 'the aether-waves' at the BBC to 'a small and hostile audience' of Indian university students, who were 'unapproachable by anything that could be described as British propaganda'.[8] Rather than propaganda by another name, and despite all the potential abuses, Orwell felt that the transmission of poetic language had an immediacy that could contribute to the 'aesthetic improvement' of the 'spiritual and economic' ugliness of his times and become 'a necessary part of the general redemption of society'.[9] Some indication of the actual effectiveness of such a cultural programme is reflected in the Wordsworth Centenary Number of *The Government College Miscellany, Mangalore*, the Republic of Indian Union, 1951,[10] which could hardly provide a more convincing example of Wordsworth's poetry being received in the way invited by Hopkins and Orwell as the universalizing stimulus of British cultural values. Dedicated to the great-grandson of the poet, the Revd C.W. Wordsworth, essays on the poet of nature, solitude, humanism and joy are grouped with lectures by Bertrand Russell ('The Value of Human Individuality'), Herbert Morrison (the cautionary 'Life of [a] Russian University Student'), together with pieces entitled 'Who Is God?', 'This Cricket', and a 'Mock Session of the U.N.O. on the Declaration of Human Rights' – all in English, and followed by articles in Hindi and Tamil. The journal represents an extraordinary effort at assimilation, reconciliation, and cultural translation still in dialogue with a poetic language that was perceived to have a special power of endorsing an elective western discourse of human dignity and spiritual aspiration.

Hopkins's claims were made in answer to Canon Dixon's expression of disappointment with the 'Great Ode', as with the caginess, or 'sense of baulk' and a resilient 'kind of unhappiness', in his lyrics generally (*Correspondence*, p. 144). The canon's problem does not only apply to what Hopkins acknowledged as Wordsworth's automatic 'Parnassian' style, characteristic of *The Excursion* itself, nor to his 'Castalian', when he is most assured of his own individual voice, but even to what Hopkins regarded as 'the language of inspiration', the 'Great Ode' itself.[11] Dixon was by no means alone in finding that Hopkins's reception of what Faraday had by that time theorized as 'the line of electric force' had short-circuited as far as he was concerned. Even Ruskin, who had originally been energized by Wordsworth's poetry, came to judge Wordsworth's endorsement of prestigious discourses as bathetic and hopelessly provincializing, and the Intimations Ode became his prime example of Wordsworth's inadequacy in sustaining the cultural consequence to which it pretended.[12]

The anecdote about Blake that Hopkins cites from Crabb Robinson's *Reminiscences* leads him to explore the metaphor for influence – of an electric shock – that was developing through the passage. '[A] most poetically electric subject' turns out to be 'both active and passive', vacillating between Blake's characteristic aversion to Wordsworth's nature-worship and his acknowledgement that in this poem at least Wordsworth was in contact with 'the visionary gleam'.[13] Coleridge had described Dorothy Wordsworth's 'taste' as 'a perfect electrometer'[14] – preternaturally sensitive to sensory impressions – but unlike her poet-companions she had apparently '[wanted] the accomplishment of verse' (*Excursion*, I. 80) with which to communicate the influence of natural objects. Blake's response, however, is to the effect of poetic language, with which he enjoys a more complicated, interactive engagement. Hopkins suggests that Blake's response to the poem was produced by both positively and negatively charged particles, attraction and repulsion – a *wavering* and *trembling* in which opposite forces generate a flow of energy, (a 'spontaneous overflow of powerful feelings'[15] in associationist terms), and that the activity and passivity *within* the influential charge might bring about conduction from one body to another, first receiving and then relaying it. The sequence through which the electric field is spread becomes 'unstrung' when the reaction is unrestrained (Blake's case), but may continue as one discursive position passes into another (Hopkins's).

There can be no doubt that Wordsworth himself had increasingly come to see his works as deliberately furthering national religious ends, as he spelled out to Benjamin Haydon in 1820: 'I am sending to the press a collection of poems, that conclude the third and *last* Vol: of my miscellaneous pieces. – In more than one passage their publication will evince my wish to uphold the cause of Christianity.'[16] It is equally clear that he based his expectation of eventual fame on the assumption of his representativeness – that his readers would see themselves in a timeless relation to his spiritual discourse – as he stated to another correspondent in 1823:

> The ground upon which I am disposed to meet your anticipation of the spread of my poetry is, that I have endeavoured to dwell with truth upon those points of human nature in which all men resemble each other, rather than on those accidents of manners and character produced by times and circumstances.[17]

But, though he evidently wished to represent his Christian message as one that spoke a universal language with particular power, the question remained as to what extent his works *did* recharge the discourses in which his later poetry became securely inscribed. Coleridge, for example, tried to account to Lady Beaumont for the poetic flatness of these discourses in *The Excursion* that had been made live for Wordsworth in a way that did not carry for readers such as himself:

> As proofs meet me in every part of the Excursion, that the Poet's genius has not flagged, I have sometimes fancied that having by the conjoint operation of his own experiences, feelings, and reason *himself* convinced *himself* of Truths, which the generality of persons have either taken for granted from their Infancy, or at least adopted early in life, he has attached all their own depth and weight to doctrines and words, which come almost as Truisms or Common-place to others.[18]

The conclusion is that for Wordsworth the language of spiritual orthodoxy was endorsed by a private conviction based upon 'his own experiences, feelings, and reason': that it represented a secret, self-originating history that was of peculiar significance in his relation to language itself. What concerns me in this present essay is not so much the ulteriority of such an elective affinity within Wordsworth's own discourses as the way they may or may not resonate with subsequent literary discourses.

Wordsworth's shocks are characteristically less immediately pleasurable – they contain traces of a higher voltage of psychological trauma – than the tremulous excitement that Hopkins derives from the Ode. None the less, Hopkins's reception does replicate the passage from painful jolting to confirmation that characterizes the original Wordsworthian experience rather than simply inheriting its after-effect. He welcomes, for example, a contact with Wordsworth's poetry that he believes may be sufficiently potent to convert his 'trembling' fear about the fate of the empire expressed in the letter to Patmore into a national crusade.

The French Revolution was, of course, the crucial shock, without which Wordsworth's pre-established pattern of making his peace with elective discourses would not have taken on the powerful reconfiguration of the creative imagination. In 1886, when Hopkins's letters were written, the alternative thrill of Wordsworthian imperialism was being called on once more to absorb and deflect what Hopkins saw as the shock of a possible new revolution. When Gladstone dissolved Parliament in July over the first Home Rule for Ireland bill, and a new House was returned, there ended what has been called 'the most dramatic thirteen months in English party history'.[19] As a diehard conservative imperialist Hopkins only reluctantly supported Home Rule in order to relieve England of what he saw as 'the task of attempting to govern a people who own no principle of civil allegiance' (*Further Letters*, pp. 281–2). 'The hand of unwisdom' which held 'the balance', in which the British Empire was being weighed in June, was that of Gladstone, but Hopkins had a greater contempt for Gladstone's 'dissolution of the empire' than for the Tories' policy of anti-Home Rule, though he feared it would produce further civil rebellion.[20] His Irish apprehensions merged with those that had been aroused by the rise of a popular radical movement driven by the distresses of the unemployed, and commandeered by the Social Democratic Federation, headed by Hyndman, John Burns, and Champion. London got a taste of revolution on 7 February when a meeting in Trafalgar Square led to windows being broken in Pall Mall, and a huge gathering in Hyde Park later that month was broken up by the police. In that context, it is the reactive shock that converts threatened destruction into the empowerment of a counter discourse – reaction – that is topically re-experienced by Hopkins from the spreading tremble of Wordsworth's poetry.

In Dublin in 1886, Hopkins found himself in the right place at the right time to feel the shock of Wordsworth's post-revolutionary discourse of Christian imperialism, a discourse that for Hopkins had been translated so as to be represented by the signifier 'Rome'. The Jesuit convert was in a position to see his own desire to spread the word (while avoiding and blamelessly checking rebellion at home and abroad) mirrored in a poetic discourse that had, however, been created not simply in response to Wordsworth's experience of the French Revolution but, most radically, to a private psychological struggle that the Revolution had retraumatized. By calling attention to the change of ruling discourse, the Revolution had only brought Wordsworth face to face with his founding trauma, that had been repeatedly reawakened by all the other shocks – the acquisition of language in infancy. It took a further protracted trauma, Coleridge's demand for the poetic discourse of what was to have been the 'great philsophical poem' of *The Recluse*, finally to make Wordsworth recognize, in the formulation of the Wordsworthian imagination, how he could deflect the recurrence of that trauma. He did so by converting the shock of literalism – the terryifying awareness that he had entered the domain of the father, language itself – into elective discourses that reflected an elision of the originating oedipal contest for the word of the father.

In the case of Hopkins, therefore, Wordsworth's empowering of Christian imperialism did serve to reflect his own historical convictions, whereas many other Victorians 'wavered' and 'trembled' with half-recognitions, only to feel finally cheated by a current gone dead. On a discursive level, what they were reacting to was the survival of Wordsworthian subjectivity, 'Wordsworth', an autobiography that either did or did not continue to be the story of their own spiritual life.

In March of 1804, Wordsworth registered 'the severest shock ... I think, I have ever received'[21] when he feared that Coleridge might die without imparting to him the philosophical base for *The Recluse*, only to discover, as a result of this desertion, the source of his own alternative imaginative strength in completing *The Prelude*. The second part of 'Intimations of Immortality', written in 1804, asserts the scheme of a continuing 'primal sympathy' (l. 182), and makes claims for a loss-surviving 'habitual sway' (l. 192) that Wordsworth was to elaborate some months later in the Yordas Cave simile for the passages on the crossing of the Alps in Book VI of *The Prelude*. These passages, which describe Wordsworth's analysis of the experience of the shock of sudden dejection and its aftermath, derived centrally from his reaction of disappointment to having 'crossed the Alps', were eventually distributed between Books VI and VIII, to the latter of which the simile in question was transferred. They hinge on the reversal of resistance into a conviction of power that is recorded in the encounter with the imagination in

Book VI: 'I was lost as in a cloud, / Halted without a struggle to break through, / And now, recovering, to my soul I say / "I recognise thy glory".'[22]

Wordsworth's complementary description of the adjustment of internal vision within the cave turns on a reduction to literalism:

> The curious traveller, who, from open day,
> Hath passed with torches into some huge cave,
> The grotto of Antiparos, or the Den
> In old time haunted by that Danish Witch,
> Yordas; he looks around and sees the vault
> Widening on all sides; sees, or thinks he sees,
> Erelong, the massy roof above his head,
> That instantly unsettles and recedes, –
> Substance and shadow, light and darkness, all
> Commingled, making up a canopy
> Of shapes and forms and tendencies to shape
> That shift and vanish, change and interchange
> Like spectres, ferment silent and sublime!
> That after short space works less and less,
> Till, every effort, every motion gone,
> The scene before him stands in perfect view
> Exposed, and lifeless as a written book! –
> (*Prelude*, 1850, VIII. 560–76)

There is an explicit opposition between the initial exhilaration of unbaffling indeterminacy and its termination in linguistic representation that is resolved by a description of the creative imagination:

> But let him pause awhile, and look again,
> And a new quickening shall succeed, at first
> Beginning timidly, then creeping fast,
> Till the whole cave, so late a senseless mass,
> Busies the eye with images and forms
> Boldly assembled, – here is shadowed forth
> From the projections, wrinkles, cavities,
> A variegated landscape, – there the shape
> Of some gigantic warrior clad in mail,
> The ghostly semblance of a hooded monk,
> Veiled nun, or pilgrim resting on his staff:
> Strange congregation! yet not slow to meet
> Eyes that perceive through minds that can inspire.
> (*Prelude*, 1850, VIII. 577–89)

The sights that Wordsworth's inspired eye creates within the cave are not arbitrary, but are in fact allusions to figures that had recurrently processed through his own poetry, so that his analysis of the process is recuperating the significance of his own past work as well as seeing it as exemplary of that to come. (The gigantic mailed warrior, the ghostly hooded monk, the veiled nun, and the pilgrim on his staff had all appeared in his juvenile and earlier poetry.) The shock has after all become one of recognition – confirmatory of something that has persisted through the challenge to expectation and that, after all, can be perceived to go marching on. It is, in effect, *the shock of the old* – of a violence confronted, distanced, and controlled, or 'of old, unhappy, far-off things, / And battles long ago'[23] – which had resulted in victorious expression without violent contestation because the discourse being appropriated was already freely available. As the discourse of Gothic medievalism had been already there, in the air, so the master-discourse he is seeking for his great poem can now be seen to take the shape of an endorsement of the long-known epic and biblical discourses registered in the representation of the Simplon Pass that immediately follows: 'Characters of the great apocalypse, / The types and symbols of eternity, / Of first, and last, and midst, and without end' (*Prelude*, VI. 570–2).

This pattern of entry into self-fulfilling discourses was to continue throughout Wordsworth's works, though the challenged inner transformation of a pre-established discourse might or might not be apparent as in the discourse of religious reaction represented by 'Rome'. Hopkins, for example, may be seen to have been calling on Wordsworth's 'Rome' as a protection from the reappearance of revolution. The power-charge that he inherits attenuatedly is that of transforming the initial language-shock into the discourse of reaction so as unexpectedly to find – and this is the lasting thrill to be derived from the process – a pre-established discourse suddenly re-empowered. The Wordsworthian experience of shock is doubled, so that an unpleasant jolt develops into an animating sensation. But the reason so many readers were to feel well-insulated from the after-effect may be explained in terms of another prestigious city, which is the signifier which 'Rome' rises up against in order to occlude, but which was becoming the site of the representatively modern cultural experience – the revolutionary city of Paris.

It was when Wordsworth remained in Paris on his way back to England for over a month in October 1792 after the Revolution had taken a shape that betokened the Terror to come that he first began to recognize his alienation from revolutionary discourse. He tried unsuccessfully to read the scenes of the horrific recent events – the Temple, where the king and royal family were imprisoned, and the Place du Carrousel, where the bodies had been burned after the September Massacres a few weeks before:

> upon these
> And other sights looking as doth a man
> Upon a volume whose contents he knows
> Are memorable but from him locked up,

> Being written in a tongue he cannot read,
> So that he questions the mute leaves with pain,
> And half upbraids their silence.
>
> *(Prelude,* X. 48–50)

He could not as yet interpret the signs of the popular power of modern urban democracy that would become increasingly represented by the crowd.

In his essay 'On Some Motifs in Baudelaire' Walter Benjamin writes of 'the close connection ... between the figure of shock and contact with the metropolitan masses' of Paris, and discusses the 'hidden figure' of the crowd that is 'imprinted on [Baudelaire's] creativity': 'It is the phantom crowd of the words, the fragments, the beginnings of lines from which the poet, in the deserted streets, wrests the poetic booty.'[24] Baudelaire, he argues, derived his creative energy from the new form of social experience: 'Moving through this traffic involves the individual in a series of shocks and collisions. At dangerous intersections, nervous impulses flow through him in rapid succession, like the energy from a battery. Baudelaire speaks of a man who plunges into the crowd as into a reservoir of electric energy' ('Baudelaire', p. 171). 'The shock experience' which Benjamin finds 'at the very centre' of Baudelaire's work is seen as recording a novel separation of poetic language from the matrix of 'experience' when people are 'increasingly unable to assimilate the data of the world around [them]' (pp. 159, 155), which has since become as automatic as the rhythms of industrial production. But Baudelaire was on the cusp of this new relation to language that set in around 'roughly ... the middle of the last century' (p. 153), and his work still conveys the shock of the new, which disrupts any resemblance that Hopkins's metaphor of an electrical current still bore to an image of organic spreading: '*Les Fleurs du Mal* was the last lyric work that had a European repercussion; no later work penetrated beyond a more or less limited linguistic area' (p. 188).

Benjamin describes an aggressiveness about Baudelaire's *traumatophilia* as he 'wrests the poetic booty', but he also sees the self-defensiveness behind Baudelaire's bravado image of the duel which Benjamin recovers as a kind of creative *parrying*: 'it is easy to trace in his works his defensive reaction to [the masses'] attraction and allure' (p. 164). With recourse to Freud's view that traumatic neurosis can be countered by bringing the origins of a shock to consciousness, Benjamin concludes that the experience of shock can only be 'cushioned' by consciousness (p. 158). But that 'would sterilize this incident for poetic experience' and make it subject to 'a plan [that] was at work in ... composition' (p. 158). His argument proceeds that such planning began to characterize lyrical poetry in response to constant retraumatizations, and he quotes from an essay by

Valéry to define Baudelaire's predicament in relation to his discursive environment as a poet, including his agonistic duelling with precursors, from whose naturalized discourse Baudelaire needed to be consciously alienated: 'The problem for Baudelaire was bound to be this: to become a great poet, yet neither Lamartine nor Hugo nor Musset. I do not claim that this ambition was a conscious one in Baudelaire; but it was bound to be present in him, it was his "reason of state"' (p. 159). It is this self-conscious commission that places Baudelaire at a moment of historical change for Benjamin. Baudelaire was required to emulate a pre-established poetic tradition in a way that no longer came unconsciously: 'He envisioned blank spaces which he filled in with his poems' (p. 159).

The parallel with Wordsworth's earlier dilemma over succession in the epic is evident: how to become a great poet, yet not Milton, is the crudest formulation. Wordsworth also had to operate in the context of post-revolutionary trauma that in part called forth a defence of conscious control. Indeed, he had achieved what Benjamin refers to as 'perhaps the special achievement of shock defence ... in its function of assigning to an incident a precise point in time in consciousness at the cost of the integrity of its contents ... a peak achievement of the intellect; it would turn the incident into a moment that has been lived (*Erlebnis*)' (p. 159) when, in the process of composing his account of crossing the Alps in March 1804, he suddenly realizes his own power of conscious control over experience:

> Imagination! – lifting up itself
> Before the eye and progress of my song
> Like an unfathered vapour, here that power,
> In all the might of its endowments, came
> Athwart me. I was lost as in a cloud,
> Halted without a struggle to break through,
> And now, recovering, to my soul I say
> 'I recognise thy glory'.
>
> (*Prelude*, VI. 525–32)

But in the course of writing through the Alps experience when Wordsworth repeated the shock experience in the Yordas cave simile, he refused to face the revolutionary knowledge of discursive alienation in the 'lifeless ... written book'.

Wordsworth's shift, in the cave, to metaphoricity itself demonstrates the imaginative absorption of shock that is formulated in the address to the imagination, and represents a psychological accommodation that is in every sense *avant la lettre*. The cave simile very possibly preceded the address in order of composition, and lays claim to the unplanned Proustian '*mémoire involuntaire*' that Benjamin sees the shock of the new dispelling:

> a new quickening shall succeed, at first
> Beginning timidly, then creeping fast,
> Till the whole cave, so late a senseless mass,
> Busies the eye with images and forms
> Boldly assembled ...
> (*Prelude*, 1850, VIII. 578–82)

Whereas Baudelaire's poetry incorporates a self-defensive consciousness of the shock of the new, Wordsworth's had deflected it by superimposing a shock of the old by rediscovering in pre-established discourses what he took to be after all an adequate medium for expressing and containing his new experience. The way in which political and poetic reaction were mutually reinforcing in the aftermath of the revolutionary trauma in discourse enacts the structure of what for Kant amounted to the 'negative pleasure' in the feeling of the sublime: 'it is produced by the feeling of a momentary checking of the vital powers and a consequent stronger outflow of them, so that it seems to be regarded as emotion – not play, but earnest in the exercise of the Imagination.'[25] An aversion to the revealed inscription in language alternates with the satisfaction at its power to reinstate a structure of feeling within the symbolic order to produce a flow of admiration.

The 'decline of the aura' – or 'the associations which, at home in the *mémoire involuntaire*, tend to cluster around the object of perception' – that Benjamin describes as resulting from the shock of the new derives from a 'prehistory' which has become inaccessible to Baudelaire's splenetic observer in 'Le Gout du neant' ('Baudelaire', pp. 182, 184): 'Je contemple d'en haut le globe en sa rondeur. / Et je n'y cherche plus l'abri d'une cahute.'[26] Wordsworth's eye typically looks rather for traces of human presence:

> Though habitation none appear,
> The greenness tells, man must be there;
> The shelter – that the perspective
> Is of the clime in which we live.
> ('The Pass of Kirkstone', ll. 65–9)

When he encounters that presence, a landscape speaks to him with a delightful shock of recognition:

> For me,
> When it has chanced that I have wandered long
> Among the mountains, I have waked at last
> From dream of motion in some spot like this,
> Shut out from man ...
> If, looking round, I have perchance perceived
> Some vestiges of human hands, some stir
> Of human passion, they to me are sweet
> As lightest sunbreak, or the sudden sound

Of music to a blind man's ear ...
They are as a creation in my heart.[27]

'To perceive the aura of an object we look at', writes Benjamin, 'means to invest it with the ability to look at us in return' ('Baudelaire', p. 184). Wordsworth seeks and finds with gratitude such assurance of imaginary intersubjectivity. The echo in Wordsworth's heart is that of discursive self-recognition. A stone 'Couched on the bald top of an eminence', with 'a flash of mild surprise', begins to speak 'with something of a lofty utterance drest', as 'the voice of inland waters' had come to the boy hooting at owls, 'with a gentle shock of mild surprize'.[28] Instead of the blankness of 'volitional ... memory' ('Baudelaire', p. 183) the Wordsworthian apocalypse turns out to be the reading of a shared language in the physionomy of the outside world, 'like workings of one mind, the features / Of the same face, blossoms upon one tree, / Characters of the great apocalypse' (*Prelude*, VI. 568–71).

The Wordsworthian passage into a restorative discourse can be followed particularly in the disciplining of his shocked perception of the crowd by which 'London' was able to absorb the shock represented in revolutionary Paris. His description in *The Prelude* of Bartholomew Fair, 'that lays, / If any spectacle on earth can do, / The whole creative powers of man asleep' (VII. 653–5), has often been celebrated as a prescient apprehension of the phenomenon that Benjamin describes with the help of an array of European writers from later in the century. Engels's *The Condition of the Working Class in England* broaches some features of the seeming uncontrollability of the metropolis of industrial revolution. His reaction that 'there is something distasteful about the very bustle of the streets, something that is abhorrent to human nature itself' ('Baudelaire', p. 163) is a paler echo of Wordsworth's

> What a hell
> For eyes and ears, what anarchy and din
> Barbarian and infernal – 'tis a dream
> Monstrous in colour, motion, shape, sight, sound.
> (*Prelude*, VII. 659–62)

Engels's unending displacement in the modern city, 'where one can roam about for hours without reaching the beginning of an end' ('Baudelaire', pp. 162–3) chimes in with Wordsworth's desolating apprehension of what Poe in his story 'The Man in the Crowd' terms an 'absurd kind of uniformity' ('Baudelaire', p. 172) in the crowd: 'Living amid the same perpetual flow / Of trivial objects, melted and reduced / To one identity by differences / That have no law, no meaning, and no end' (*Prelude*, VII. 702–5). The relating of the pedestrians' 'uniformly constant movements of an automaton' to the processes of mechanical reproduction 'as if they had adapted themselves to the machines and could express themselves only automatically' ('Baudelaire', p. 172) which Benjamin finds in Poe develops an insight also present in Wordsworth:

> Tents and booths
> Meanwhile – as if the whole were one vast mill –
> Are vomiting, receiving, on all sides,
> Men, women, three-years' children, babes in arms.
> *(Prelude,* VII. 692–5)

Radically, the fair images the modern crisis in representation: it is a blank space, with no given signified, from which meaning is drained rather than generated by pell-mell activities:

> O, blank confusion, and a type not false
> Of what the mighty city is itself
> To all, except a straggler here and there –
> To the whole swarm of its inhabitants –
> An undistinguishable world to men.
> *(Prelude,* VII. 696–700)

As an exceptional *straggler* himself, Wordsworth does not, as does the Benjaminesque 'idler', become a 'reflecting mechanism' to 'mirror' his times, 'capable only of a reflex action'; nor, like the 'flaneur', does he move with 'skill and ease' amid the crush ('Baudelaire', pp. 173, 174, 163). Book VII, 'Residence in London', is impelled mimetically by a stream of spectacles, pageants and processions that evoke in bursts an increasingly ambivalent attitude to the great metropolis, from his 'living chearfully abroad' during his student years, when 'life ... was new' (*Prelude,* VII. 440), to living hell in Bartholomew Fair by the book's end. At first the riot is animating, but it is punctuated by gasping retreats from 'the thickening hubbub' to 'aery lodges' in inns of court, 'privileged regions and inviolate', or 'Some half-frequented scene, where wider streets / Bring straggling breezes of suburban air' (VII. 227, 202, 207–8). The evocation becomes progressively difficult to comprehend as Wordsworth looks in vain for the returned look of a common discourse:

> How often in the overflowing streets
> Have I gone forwards with the crowd, and said
> Unto myself, 'The face of every one
> That passes by me is a mystery.'
> *(Prelude,* VII. 595–8)

Instead, he naturalizes the experience in the imaginary hold of fantasy as 'A second-sight procession' to choreograph its unpredictable dynamism into a 'moving pageant' (VII. 602, 610). When in this frame of mind Wordsworth is 'abruptly ... smitten with the view' of the blind beggar ('upon his chest / Wearing a written paper, to explain / The story of the man, and who he was'), the language-shock is replayed ('My mind did at this spectacle turn round / As with the might of waters'), but this jostling into self-consciousness ('in this label was a type / Or emblem of the utmost that we know / Both of ourselves and of the universe') runs against the grain of Wordsworth's imaginary control, and the extraordinariness of effect that Wordsworth attributes to the impact of what, for most, would be a bathetic enough signified, is after all safely muted by the man's impersonal facelessness ('this unmoving man, / His fixed face and sightless eyes') and the minimalism of self-declaration ('a written paper ... the utmost that we know') (VII. 611–26). As with the 'written book' of Yordas, there was no answering aura of self-representation.

So when it comes to regulating the experience of Bartholomew Fair Wordsworth has sufficient 'attention ... comprehensiveness and memory' to provide an involuntarily 'habitual' dominion over its chaos and enable the fulfilling return of 'The soul of beauty and enduring life' (VII. 717–18, 722, 737). Natural form and outline help group the crowd into more stable and familiar masses, and its variegations are brought into the slower rhythm of atmospheric effects among the mountains so as to allow the scenes to share in a discourse intelligible to Wordsworth:

> nor less
> The changeful language of their countenances
> Gives movement to the thoughts, and multitude,
> With order and relation.
> (*Prelude*, VII. 727–30)

In this way the revolutionary crowd can be re-created as the socially coordinated British nation. The 'strange congregation' (1850, VIII. 588) that Wordsworth's traveller eventually comes to behold in the cave of Yordas is the Wordsworthian version of the crowd:

> the senseless mass,
> In its projections, wrinkles, cavities,
> Through all its surface, with all colours streaming,
> Like a magician's airy pageant, parts,
> Unites, embodying everywhere some pressure
> Or image, recognised or new, some type
> Or picture of the world – forests and lakes,
> Ships, rivers, towers, the warrior clad in mail,
> The prancing steed, the pilgrim with his staff,
> The mitred bishop and the throned king –
> A spectacle to which there is no end.
> (*Prelude*, VIII. 731–41)

The 'Ships, rivers, towers' echo the panorama of 'Composed Upon Westminster Bridge' which is dstanced into a common hieroglyph for British imperialism: 'Ships, towers, domes, theatres, and temples lie /

Open unto the fields, and to the sky' (ll. 6–7). The allusion develops further the representational restraint of Wordsworth's dawn city-scape, that quite relieves itself from the pressure of the masses which is always immanent in Baudelaire's deserted streets.

Yet Wordsworth was notoriously unable to write his epochal epic, *The Recluse*. His peculiar relation to language may have left him as the privileged apologist for a reactionary poetics – one that negotiated the shock of the new in *The Prelude* by attempting to translate it into the milder shock of recognizing the old. A pre-established discourse – of chivalry, for instance – did mean something new *after* the shock of revolution. It had become part of a new discourse of nationalism and tradition, and Wordsworth could greet it on the other side of the Alps as the upshot of a counter-revolutionary presence that had preceded, co-existed with and survived an enormous historical rift: it had never not been there in some form, and now it had become the prevalent British discourse of power: 'The mind beneath such banners militant / Thinks not of spoils or trophies' (*Prelude*, VI. 543–4). It was also possible for relatively isolated readers, like Hopkins, to find an imaginary intersubjectivity represented in Wordsworth's poetry and to read in it the re-empowerment of a threatened reactionary discourse and an endorsement of 'Rome'. Many of Wordsworth's readers, however, who resisted the democratic elbowing and competitive thrusting of Victorian England, were unable to confront a widespread sense of alienated dejection with an inscription in the discourse of Wordsworth's later poetry which, in effect, had not been powerful enough for his own great work. Wordsworth's own peculiar subjective investment – his 'imagination' – had become isolated and had to struggle too much against the grain of the times.

George Eliot is representative of a wide positioning in Victorian culture – somewhere between Hopkins's imaginary relation to the national tradition and Baudelaire's response to novelty – which attempted to view progress only within pre-established discourses. What she referred to as her fictional 'experiments in life'[29] were effectively extensions of the literary 'experiment' in identifying a communal language that Wordsworth had pursued in *The Prelude* after first instituting it in *Lyrical Ballads*: 'to ascertain, how far, by fitting to metrical arrangement a selection of the real language of men in a state of vivid sensation, that sort of pleasure and that quantity of pleasure may be imparted, which a Poet may rationally endeavour to impart'.[30] Some of the observations she made after the appearance of *Middlemarch* in what was posthumously named her *Leaves from a Note-Book* help pithily to characterize her shrewd balancing of old and new forms of expression. In her note on 'Value in Originality', for example, her opinion that 'The supremacy given in European cultures to the literatures of Greece and Rome has had an effect almost equal to that of a common religion in binding Western nations together' leads her to accept the value of a common tradition: 'It is foolish to be for ever complaining of the consequent uniformity, as if there were an endless power of originality in the human mind.'[31] Originality can only be registered by proceeding from a prior inscription in embedded discourses of cultural power: '[masters of language] use words which are already a familiar medium of understanding and sympathy. Originality of this order changes the wild grasses into world-feeding grain' (*Leaves*, pp. 374–5). 'The Form remains',[32] though the function changes. On the other hand, as her note on 'Historical Imagination' makes clear, the participation of later generations in the aura of historical forms of expression is not automatic. The re-creation of aura depends on differences as well as similarities:

> A false kind of idealisation dulls our perception of the meaning in words when they relate to past events which have had a glorious issue: for lack of comparison no warning image rises to check scorn of the very phrases which in other associations are consecrated.
>
> (*Leaves*, p. 373)

The actualities of Hannibal's and Napoleon's Alpine campaigns, for example, would have to be imagined for a phrase such as 'crossing the Alps' to be admitted to the representation of other and later histories, which might then be seen to have conditions in common with the glorious past. For Eliot, in her revision of Wordsworth's symbolic passage ('Imagination! – lifting up itself / Before the eye and progress of my song / … here that power / In all the might of its endowments, came / Athwart me'), it is the creation of what she calls the 'veracious imagination' (*Leaves*, p. 371) which 'lifts itself up' to challenge both the debunking of literalistic reductivism and the fetishizing of the past to effect the restoration of historical aura.

Middlemarch, the novel about coming to acceptable terms with disillusionment set in the age of Reform, constitutes the most substantial critique of the Wordsworthian imagination, neither unusually receptive like Hopkins nor shocked into disengagement like Benjamin's moderns. In particular, the strain on the imagination in attempting to revise a stultifying literalism into cultural self-enlargement can be seen in its curious refashioning of the Wordsworthian passage to 'Rome' in chapter 20 of Book Two, 'Old and Young', concerning the Roman honeymoon, which David Carroll has written of as the crisis of Dorothea's 'religious disposition'.[33] The overall experience presents the intersection of two related major defeats: the anticlimax of Dorothea's rite of passage into wifehood and of her husband's pretension to be producing a great life-work.

Secretly weeping in the 'boudoir of a handsome appartment in the Via Sistina', after six weeks of marriage and five weeks in Rome, Dorothea is registering a series of let-downs that have been exposed by the confrontation with Rome as *the* symbol of cultural fulfilment: 'after the brief narrow experience of her childhood she was beholding Rome, the city of visible history, where the past of a whole hemisphere seems moving in funeral procession with strange ancestral images and trophies gathered from afar.'[34] The echo of the 'Intimations' ode places Rome immediately next to some pre-cultural plenitude from which it is still 'trailing clouds of glory' ('Ode', l. 64): 'The Soul that rises with us, our life's Star, / Hath had elsewhere its setting, / And cometh from afar' (ll. 59–61). But Rome also stands at the point of origin for the fall into the symbolic order – the *setting*, that makes the triumph funereal. She prefers driving out to the Campagna to get away from the urgency of historical and cultural texts – 'the oppressive masquerade of ages' – to which she has no key, and so in whose discourse she can play no part: 'her own life too seemed to become a masque with enigmatic costumes' (p. 158). Her experience of Rome amounts to a failure of the kind of entry into the social domain of language and culture that is celebrated in Wordsworth's entrance into London, and by extension into 'The human nature unto which [he] felt / That [he] belonged' in Book VIII of *The Prelude* (ll. 761–2):

> A weight of ages did at once descend
> Upon my heart – no thought embodied, no
> Distinct remembrances, but weight and power,
> Power growing with the weight.
> (*Prelude*, VIII. 703–6)

On the other hand, the book judges Ladislaw's 'attitude of receptivity towards all sublime chances' (p. 68) as too light-hearted. His affinity with Rome has not accomplished Dorothea's veracious premonition of Baudelaire's modernity and recalls Wordsworth's youthful apprehension of London in a way that appears inauthentic by that removal of time: 'he confessed that Rome had given him quite a new sense of history as a whole: the fragments stimulated his imagination and made him constructive' (p. 174).

And yet, Dorothea's deferral of her anticipated inscription in 'Rome' has begun to disturb undercurrents of other unconscious signifieds that have not yet defined themselves: 'Dorothea had no distinctly shapen grievance that she could state even to herself' (p. 158). The 'stupendous fragmentariness [that] heightened the dream-like strangeness of [Dorothea's] bridal life' (p. 158) in effect recalls that longed-for state which, in the Fenwick note to the 'Intimations' ode, Wordsworth wrote precedes the fall into society: 'that dream-like vividness and splendour which invest objects of sight in childhood'.[35] She is precisely in the position of the Wordsworthian infant before it discovers the need of imaginative redemption – one of the 'many souls [who] in their young nudity are tumbled out among incongruities and left to "find their feet" among them' (p. 159). The echoes from the ode help reveal her experience of 'Rome' as a replay of language-shock with its challenge to the effort of the imagination to persist in finding adequate self-representation. Her crisis dramatizes the painful evolution of the 'veracious imagination', ghosted by that recorded in the crossing of the Alps in Books VI and VIII of *The Prelude*.

Dorothea's inability to comprehend Rome is complicated by the absence of her husband Casaubon's mentoring on which she had been relying. Despite its awakening an ancient sense of loss, Rome had promised to restore childhood intimations that Dorothea had been in no position to recollect and from which she felt she had been particularly barred. Her chance of fulfilment had been multiply derivative, since it was mediated by all 'Rome' had come to signify: her imagination of Casaubon's cultural consummation and particularly his great work, *The Key to All Mythologies*. Because her fulfilment in 'Rome' is invested in her relation to Casaubon, she feels defeated by his literalism, 'the matter-of-course statement and tone of dismissal with which he treated what to her were the most stirring thoughts' (p. 161). She is repelled by his guidebook idiom, 'as of a clergyman reading according to the rubric', which, in drawing attention to the emptying power of language, excites an impulse to rejection rather than trembling receptivity: 'her husband's way of commenting on the strangely impressive objects around them had begun to affect her with a sort of mental shiver' (pp. 162, 161). Neil Hertz has written of Casaubon as 'the personification of the dead letter',[36] and certainly the exhibition of 'a mind in which years full of knowledge seem to have issued in a blank absence of interest or sympathy' (p. 162) records a similar stultification to that which initially jolted Wordsworth's traveller in the cave of Yordas: 'Till, every effort, every motion gone, / The scene before him stands in perfect view / Exposed, and lifeless as a written book! – ' (*Prelude*, 1850, VIII. 574–6). A content beyond literal definition has been forfeited:

> Substance and shadow, light and darkness, all
> Commingled, making up a canopy
> Of shapes and forms and tendencies to shape

> That shift and vanish, change and interchange
> Like spectres, ferment silent and sublime!
> (*Prelude*, 1850, VIII. 568–72)

Dorothea had deliberately associated Casaubon's limitations with her own visionary recalcitrance from the start: 'She filled up all blanks with unmanifested perfections, interpreting him as she interpreted the works of Providence, and accounting for seeming discords by her own deafness to the higher harmonies' (p. 61). But her experience of Rome retains something of its former excess of Casaubon's prosaic closure, and her passionate release in tears keeps this desire alive: 'However, Dorothea was crying, and if she had been required to state the cause, she could only have done so in ... general words ... to have been driven to be more particular would have been like trying to give a history of the light and shadows' (p. 159).

The enlargement of her own sense of 'Rome' would amount to a radical rejection of what Dorothea now sees her husband standing for. She is faced with the marital piety of having to support her husband's claim to be engaged in heroic intellectual struggle (prickly in its discouraging attitude to a kind of 'presumption ... which sees vaguely a great many fine ends, and has not the least notion what it costs to reach them' (pp. 164–5)), while the awareness that her own conception might perhaps all along have been the more powerful was being 'scattered in fits of agitation, of struggle, of despondency, and ... visions of more complete renunciation, transforming all hard conditions into duty' (p. 163). This is her less affirmative version of Wordsworth's self-definition in the received discourse of duty: 'Yet not the less would I throughout / ... feel past doubt / That my submissiveness was choice.'[37] Her criticism of Casaubon's reading of 'Rome', in short, was undergoing an anxiety of influence, as she feels irksomely obliged to subdue her divergent reading to his narrow-mindedness: 'in the midst of her confused thought and passion, the mental act that was struggling forth into clearness was a self-accusing cry that her feeling of desolation was the fault of her own spiritual poverty' (p. 158). At this point in the novel, Dorothea is undergoing a psychomachia between what 'Rome' has been reduced to in Casaubon's case and what she is uneasily conscious that it has been signifying for herself:

> But now, since they had been in Rome, with all the depths of their emotion roused to tumultuous activity, and with life made a new problem by new elements, she had been becoming more and more aware, with a certain terror, that her mind was continually sliding into inward fits of anger and repulsion, or else into forlorn weariness ... What was fresh to her mind was worn out to his; and such capacity of thought and feeling as had ever been stimulated in him

by the general life of mankind had long shrunk to a sort of dried preparation, a lifeless embalmment of knowledge.

(p. 161)

Since Casaubon was certainly failing to measure up to her anticipations, the question remained whether her disappointment related only to her husband, or whether the possibilities of 'Rome' as a reflection of her own separate aspirations were to be totally undermined, or might still be restored in response to the shock of recognizing her mistake. Following the Wordsworthian paradigm: Could the original aura be translated into some different but equivalent discourse? What was changing, of course, was not Casaubon's 'forms of expression' but the primacy of *his* reading of them over the rival interpretations that Dorothea's own attempt to grasp the aura of 'Rome' were producing: 'But was not Mr Casaubon just as learned as before? Had his forms of expression changed, or his sentiments become less laudable? ... And was not Rome the place in all the world to give free play to such accomplishments?' (p. 160).

Dorothea was anticipating the insight that would come from the shock of the old: the sudden illuminating of interior meaning within pre-established forms of expression, 'when the light of sense / Goes out in flashes that have shown to us / The invisible world' (*Prelude*, VI. 600–2). In Hopkins's day, a more assured faith in the transmission of such momentary glimpses might be supported by the more sustained artifice of Edison's electric light, but Casaubon was blind even to the older kind of illumination. Eliot writes, 'no man was more incapable of flashy make-believe than Mr Casaubon' (p. 155). And yet, though there is an inchoate rejection of the damp squib of Casaubon's literalism, Eliot's brilliant picture of Dorothea's 'electric shock' from the 'alien world' of the city of Rome does not after all issue in the instant switch to an alternatively fulfilling discourse:

> To those who have looked at Rome with the quickening power of a knowledge which breathes a growing soul into all historic shapes, and traces out the suppressed transitions which unite all contrasts, Rome may still be the spiritual centre and interpreter of the world. But let them conceive one more historical contrast: the gigantic broken revelations of that Imperial and Papal city thrust abruptly on the notions of a girl who had been brought up in English and Swiss Puritanism, fed on meagre Protestant histories and on art chiefly of the hand-screen sort ... The weight of unintelligible Rome might lie easily on bright nymphs to whom it formed a background for the brilliant picnic of Anglo-foreign society; but Dorothea had no such defence against deep impressions. Ruins and basilicas, palaces and colossi, set in the midst of a sordid present, where all that was living and warm-blooded seemed sunk in the deep degeneracy of a superstition divorced from reverence; the dimmer but yet eager Titanic life gazing on walls and ceilings; the long vistas of

> white forms whose marble eyes seemed to hold the monotonous light of an alien world: all this vast wreck of ambitious ideals, sensuous and spiritual, mixed confusedly with the breathing forgetfulness and degradation, at first jarred her as with an electric shock, and then urged themselves on her with that ache belonging to a glut of confused ideas which check the flow of emotion ... Our moods are apt to bring with them images which succeed each one like the magic-lantern pictures of a doze; and in certain states of dull forlornness Dorothea all her life continued to see the vastness of St Peter's, the huge bronze canopy, the excited intention in the attitudes and garments of the prophets and evangelists in the mosaics above, and the red drapery which was being hung for Christmas spreading itself everywhere like a disease of the retina.
>
> (pp. 158–9)

Because Dorothea has no redeeming discourse into which to translate her experience, there are, in fact, two shocks: that of Casaubon's desiccating literalism, which challenges the recovery of a lost plenitude, and that of Dorothea's own Baudelairean experience of the manifold of the great city which so disconcertingly impairs any straightforward apprehension of its aura. For Dorothea, the traumatic passage into the city both rehearses and falls short of restoration by the Wordsworthian imagination. The allusion to the imaginary structure of Wordsworthian memory (in 'Lines Written a Few Miles above Tintern Abbey'), 'The weight of unintelligible Rome', recalling

> that blessed mood,
> In which the burden of the mystery,
> In which the heavy and the weary weight
> Of all this unintelligible world
> Is lightened
>
> ('Tintern Abbey', ll. 37–41)

– a restorative scheme Eliot had accepted as satisfactory for her purposes in *Silas Marner*[38] – here offers an ineffective resistance to awakened consciousness and the promise of ultimate blinding as the only 'defence against deep impressions'.

When she had first encountered Wordsworth in her own youth, Eliot had found him adequately self-reflective: 'I never before met with so many of my own feelings, expressed just as I could <wish> like them;[39] but Dorothea's response distinctly lacks any awareness of the poet's 'power / Of harmony, and the deep power of joy' ('Tintern Abbey', ll. 47–8) that had repeatedly consolidated Wordsworth's own subject-formation in its encounters with the Other. The opening sentence of the above passage again deprecates any emulation of Wordsworth's imaginary passage into London, the 'centre and interpreter of [*his*] world', described in Book VIII of *The Prelude*:

> London, to thee I willingly return.
> Erewhile my verse played idly with the flowers
> Enwrought upon thy mantle; satisfied
> With that amusement ...
> A weight of ages did at once descend
> Upon my heart; no thought embodied, no
> Distinct remembrancess, but weight and power, –
> Power growing under weight.
> (1850, VIII. 532–5, 552–5)

Instead, the confusion of her Rome is reminiscent of the 'blank confusion' in 'the picture' of Bartholomew Fair, Wordsworth's image of a disorientating exposure to the 'unmanageable sight' of London, that, like Dorothea's Roman gaze, '[wearies] out the eye' in Book VII of *The Prelude*. With the 'oppression' of its 'perpetual flow', 'Monstrous in colour, motion, shape, sight, sound', writes Wordsworth, it 'lays ... / The whole creative powers of man asleep' (VII. 653–732 passim).

The impression of Wordsworth's Bartholomew Fair is superimposed on the spectacle created by the restored Wordsworthian imagination that is brought to crucial definition in the Cave of Yordas simile. Whereas Wordsworth's fantasy pageant promises that 'a new quickening shall succeed' (as he had elsewhere promised that 'the mind's eye [would be] quickened' by looking at Rome 'as a whole'[40]), Eliot specifically lays no claim to a 'quickening power' for Dorothea, whose perception is of 'images which succeed each other like the magic-lantern pictures of a doze ... the vastness of St Peter's, the huge bronze canopy, the excited intention in the attitudes and garments of the prophets and evangelists in the mosaics above' (pp. 158, 159). Though these bring back the cave interior, with its 'canopy / Of shapes and forms and tendencies to shape / That shift and vanish ... there the shape / Of some gigantic warrior clad in mail, / The ghostly semblance of a hooded monk, / Veiled nun, or pilgrim resting on his staff' (*Prelude*, 1850, VIII. 569ff.), they only succeed in mirroring the 'vast wreck of ambitious ideals, sensuous and spiritual'. In sum, she can discover no available discourse in which to re-create the structure of her expectation, so that the shock of disappointment with Casaubon's literalism is in her case answered only by the continuing reverberation of the shock of a new domain of experience with its uncoordinated contrasts. The city's covert dynamics and shameless exhibitionism, as 'the gigantic broken revelations ... thrust abruptly on [her] notions', and its forms 'took possession of her young sense', offer a rude awakening of consciousness to her linguistic and sexual identity, bringing her to 'strange associations'.

In this climax of Book II, 'Old and Young', Dorothea's inner eye, disappointed in its search for the consolatory Wordsworthian shock of the old, has become irreversibly contaminated by the shock of the new.

Her changing relation to Casaubon is after all the key both to her Wordsworthian expectation of continuing tradition *and* her auraless apprehension of modern Rome, and within terms of its revision the necessary process of neither rebellion nor simple restoration has to take place:

> It was too early yet for her fully to recognise or at least admit the change, still more for her to have readjusted that devotedness which was so necessary a part of her mental life that she was almost sure sooner or later to recover it. Permanent rebellion, the disorder of a life without some loving reverent resolve, was not possible to her; but she was now in an interval when the very force of her nature heightened its confusion.
>
> (p. 160)

The revised reading of 'Rome' which she is negotiating in this scene may be viewed as the working of the 'veracious imagination', playing down the disjuncture between her anticipation of an idealized fulfilment and her own actual destiny: 'Some discouragement, some faintness of heart at the new real future which replaces the imaginary, is not unusual' (p. 159). Dorothea's disappointment becomes a process of graduated transformation – a dispersion of the traumatizing moment, or 'spot of time', even at the risk of 'spots of commonness' (p. 123) – that successfully protects her from traumatic foreclosure:

> for that new real future which was replacing the imaginary drew its material from the endless minutiae by which her view of Mr Casaubon and her wifely relation, now that she was married to him, was gradually changing with the secret motion of a watch-hand from what it had been in her maiden dream.
>
> (pp. 159–60)

Unlike Wordsworth in *The Prelude*, Eliot can make no claim for epic equivalence. In the confrontation between puritanical English provincialism and 'Rome', Dorothea becomes just one 'later-born' St Teresa of Avila, who found 'no epic life wherein there was a constant unfolding of far-resonant action' (p. 3). In reality, no plenitudinous discourse had been available in England around the time of the Great Reform in circles that were 'still discussing Mr Peel's late conduct on the Catholic question, innocent of future gold-fields, and of that gorgeous plutocracy which has so nobly exalted the necessities of genteel life' (p. 8). *Middlemarch* imagines such a critical predicament of transition from old to new, in which the aura of the past and the shock of the new are suspended, with a *veracity* that represents the psycho-social reality rather than feeling it can itself effect an intervention by rediscovering that 'epic life':

> With dim lights and tangled circumstance [these later-born Theresas] tried to shape their thought and deed in noble agreement; but after all, to common eyes their struggles seemed mere inconsistency and formlessness; for [they] were helped by no coherent social faith and order which could perform the function of knowledge for the ardently willing soul.
>
> (p. 3)

In effect, Eliot has made Dorothea's realization of her need to find adequate self-expression, that of the readers of her own text.[41] Idealized identifications, or St Teresas, are not supplied, but more is offered the reader than 'common eyes' with which to see more than images of shared confusion. Eliot provides exemplary adaptations of an ideal self to enhance the veracity of a different contemporary experience.

Robert Kiely has argued that Eliot fell under the influence of Feuerbach's stress on 'the psychological and social power of language' in his 'demysticizing' of 'the Johannine conception of Logos' while at the same time she appreciated that, according to Herbert Spencer, 'certain structures and uses [of language] – especially those having to do with religion – retain elementary links to the past and appear almost exempt from the usual flow'.[42] She had been able to recover from her own sudden traumatic loss of faith by rediscovering its values in another form of imaginative self-extension. Her resulting humanistic religion did allow her in this way to complete *her* 'great work' as a Victorian 'realist' novel balancing contradictory detail with universalist implications, though it had been impossible for both Casaubon and Wordsworth who depended simply on a dead or waning aura. As Eliot implies in *her* 'Prelude' to her great work, a continuing involvement in Dorothea's imagination, 'the incalculably diffusive ... effect of her being', requires a recognition of continuing frustrations and limitations as well as longing: 'Here and there is born a Saint Theresa, foundress of nothing, whose loving heart-beats and sobs after an unattained goodness tremble off and are dispersed among hindrances, instead of centering in some long-recognizable deed' (p. 4).

Dorothea's embarrassment is intimately involved in her dawning appreciation that her husband's great work, *The Key to All Mythologies* – a project of such intellectual hubris that the Eternal City had seemed an appropriate venue in which to consummate their dedication to its composition – is in effect being exposed as a private language of ever-recessive pedanticism. What impedes Casaubon from entering into the sublime excess of meaning in 'Rome' is something he has in common with Wordsworth: 'a mind weighted with unpublished matter' (p. 163). Weighing most heavily on Wordsworth's mind too was, of course, his own impracticable life-work, *The Recluse*. This feeling of oppressiveness, which Dorothea shares, is radically that of 'unintelligibility', gloriously alleviated on those occasions when a self-reflective discourse *is* identified in the Other, so that 'weight' becomes 'power', 'Power growing under weight'. Dorothea's impossible aspiration was to lift the burden of unbelief: 'Besides, had not Dorothea's enthusiasm especially dwelt on the prospect of relieving the weight and perhaps the sadness with which great tasks lie on him who has to achieve them? – And that such weight pressed upon Mr Casaubon was only plainer than before' (p. 160).

Like Casaubon, in whose mind Dorothea had found only 'ante-rooms and winding passages which seemed to lead nowhither' (p. 160), Wordsworth had been capable only of the 'ante-chapel' to his barely commenced 'gothic church'.[43] In 1824, Dorothy Wordsworth wrote to Crabb Robinson of the situation throughout the 1820s: 'My brother has not yet looked at *The Recluse*; he seems to feel the task so weighty that he shrinks from beginning with it.'[44] For some time, Mary Wordsworth, shrinking from the inevitable conclusion about her husband's 'great work', had been urging Wordsworth to make the final effort, and she saw the Italian journey of 1837 as a possible stimulus towards that end. In September 1836 she wrote to Henry Crabb Robinson:

> the poet may leave home with a perfect holiday before him – and, but I dare not say so – return to the *Recluse*; – and let me charge you, not to encourage the muse to *vagrant* subjects – but gently recur, upon such indications should they arise, to Rogers' hint that 'jingling rhyme does not become a certain age' entre nous.[45]

Mary's frustration, though longer seasoned, is in origin not far from Dorothea's unwilling apprehension that the grand ambition is incapable of realization:

> 'And all your notes', said Dorothea, whose heart had already burned within her on this subject, so that now she could not help speaking with her tongue. 'All those rows of volumes – will you now not do what you used to speak of? – will you not make up your mind what part of them you will use, and begin to write the book which will make your vast knowledge useful to the world?'
>
> (p. 164)

But his tour effectively brought the recognition of defeat home to Wordsworth himself. By this stage, the philosophical and religious endeavour of his great poem had begun to appeal to a Catholic cultural tradition that would have entailed nothing less than the full imaginary endorsement of 'Rome' which he, unlike Hopkins, barely glimpsed. The huge recalcitrance of the materials – the weight of the dead letter that had been repeatedly lifted in the past by such answering discourses as pantheism or nationalism – is easily sensed. Inevitably, it would have remained 'lifeless as a written book', unilluminated for Wordsworth with a discourse that had not yet sufficiently renewed its currency in England.

If Wordsworth had gone to Rome with an implicit agenda for '[making] details in the present subservient to more adequate comprehension of the past',[46] he lacked, as he saw, the intellectual energy to translate his contemporary social and political disappointments into an original aura. In the course of the journey, according to Crabb Robinson, '"I have matter for volumes," he said once, "had I but youth to work it up"',[47] and he wrote to his family on leaving Italy:

> I have, however, to regret that this journey was not made some years ago, – to regret it, I mean, as a Poet; for though we have had a great disappointment in not seeing Naples, etc., [due to cholera] and more of the country among the Appenines not far from Rome, Horace's country for instance, and Cicero's Tusculum, my mind has been enriched by innumerable images, which I could have turned to account in verse, and vivified by feelings which earlier in my life would have answered noble purposes, in a way they now are little likely to do.[48]

What had been increasingly wanting during the past 30 years had been not the personal ratification of a reactionary poetics – *that* he had fixed on with conviction – but a discourse in which it could more generally find contemporaneous expression. Only so equipped could he have produced a work powerful enough to subdue the shock of industrialized democracy which had reopened the suture of organic nationalism that he had successfully laid over the trauma of the Revolution. In May 1838, in the course of composing the poems that made up the 'Memorials of a Tour in Italy, 1837', he turned 'very decidedly' to George Ticknor, the Harvard professor whom Mary had also commissioned to urge the poem's completion, and said: 'Why did not Gray finish the long poem he began on a similar subject? because he found he had undertaken something beyond his powers to accomplish. And that is my case.'[49]

Notes

1. 18 October 1866; *The Correspondence of G.M. Hopkins and R.W. Dixon*, ed. Claude Colleer Abbott (Oxford: Oxford University Press, 1935), pp. 147–8 (hereafter, *Correspondence*).

2. Matthew Arnold, 'Address to the Wordsworth Society', *Matthew Arnold: Philistinism in England and America*, ed. R.H. Super (Ann Arbor: University of Michigan Press, 1974), p. 133.
3. Wordsworth, 'Tintern Abbey', l. 96; *The Poetical Works of William Wordsworth*, ed. Ernest de Selincourt and Helen Darbishire, 5 vols (Oxford: Clarendon Press, 1940–49), vol. II, p. 262. Unless otherwise specified, all references to Wordsworth's poetry are to this edition (hereafter, *PW*).
4. Wordsworth's note dictated to Isabella Fenwick, 1843; *PW*, vol. IV, p. 463.
5. Matthew Arnold, 'Memorial Verses', ll. 48–9; *Matthew Arnold*, ed. Miriam Allott and R.H. Super (Oxford: Oxford University Press, 1986), p. 139.
6. *The Prose Works of William Wordsworth*, ed. W.J.B. Owen and Jane Worthington Smyser, 3 vols (Oxford: Oxford University Press, 1974), vol. I, p. 340.
7. 4 June 1886; *Further Letters of Gerard Manley Hopkins*, ed. C.C. Abbott, enlarged edition (Oxford: Oxford University Press, 1956), pp. 366–7, 368 (hereafter, *Further Letters*).
8. George Orwell, 'Poetry and the Microphone', *The Collected Essays, Journalism and Letters of George Orwell*, ed. Sonia Orwell and Ian Angus, 4 vols (London: Secker and Warburg, 1968), vol. II, p. 332.
9. Ibid., p. 368.
10. Volume 28. A copy of this publication is held in the University of Chicago Library.
11. *Further Letters*, pp. 218, 216.
12. See Keith Hanley, 'In Wordsworth's Shadow: Ruskin and Neo-Romantic Ecologies', in *Influence and Resistance in Nineteenth-Century English Poetry*, ed. G. Kim Blank and Margot K. Louis (London: Macmillan, 1993), pp. 220–3.
13. For Blake's contradictory view of the 'Ode', see, for instance, *Diary, Reminiscences, and Correspondence of Henry Crabb Robinson*, ed. Thomas Sadler, 3 vols (London: Macmillan, 1869), vol. II, p. 310: 'I fear Wordsworth loves nature, and nature is the work of the Devil.'
14. *Collected Letters of Samuel Taylor Coleridge*, ed. E.L. Griggs, 6 vols (Oxford: Clarendon Press, 1956–71), vol. I, p. 330.
15. Wordsworth, Preface to *Lyrical Ballads*; *PW*, vol. II, p. 387.
16. *The Letters of William and Dorothy Wordsworth: The Middle Years*, ed. E. de Selincourt, second edition, revised Mary Moorman and Alan G. Hill, 2 vols (Oxford: Clarendon Press, 1969–70), vol. II, pp. 593–4.
17. *The Letters of William and Dorothy Wordsworth: The Later Years*, ed. Alan G. Hill, 4 vols (Oxford: Clarendon Press, 1978–88), vol. I, p. 127 (hereafter, *Later Years*).
18. Coleridge, *Collected Letters*, vol. IV, p. 564.
19. R.C.K. Ensor, *England 1870–1914* (Oxford: Clarendon Press, 1936), p. 99.
20. See Norman White, *Hopkins: A Literary Biography* (Oxford: Clarendon Press, 1992), p. 431.
21. *The Letters of William and Dorothy Wordsworth: The Early Years*, ed. E. de Selincourt, revised Chester L. Shaver (Oxford: Clarendon Press, 1967), p. 464.
22. *The Prelude*, VI. 529–32. Unless otherwise indicated, all references to

The Prelude are to the 1805 version in *The Prelude: 1799, 1805, 1850*, ed. Jonathan Wordsworth, M.H. Abrams and Stephen Gill (New York: W.W. Norton & Co, 1979). '1850' specifies the authorized version published in that year.
23. Wordsworth, 'The Solitary Reaper', ll. 19–20.
24. Walter Benjamin, 'Some Motifs in Baudelaire', in his *Illuminations*, ed. Hannah Arendt, translated by Harry Zohn (London: Fontana, 1992), pp. 161, 162 (hereafter, 'Baudelaire').
25. Immanuel Kant, *Kritik of Judgment*, translated by J.H. Bernard (London: Macmillan, 1892), p. 102.
26. Quoted in 'Baudelaire', p. 182.
27. Wordsworth, 'Michael', MSl; *PW*, vol. II, pp. 479–80.
28. Wordsworth, 'Resolution and Independence', ll. 58, 90, 94; *Prelude*, V. 407.
29. *The George Eliot Letters*, ed. Gordon S. Haight, 9 vols (New Haven: Yale University Press, 1954–78), vol. VI, p. 216.
30. Preface to *Lyrical Ballads*; *PW*, vol. II, p. 384.
31. George Eliot, *Essays and Leaves from a Note-Book* (Edinburgh and London: William Blackwood and Sons, 1884), p. 374 (hereafter, *Leaves*).
32. Wordsworth, *The River Duddon*, 'After-thought', l. 6; *PW*, vol. III, p. 261.
33. See David Carroll, *George Eliot and the Conflict of Interpretations: A Reading of the Novels* (Cambridge: Cambridge University Press, 1992), p. 243. I am indebted to David Carroll for some helpful observations on the original draft of this essay.
34. George Eliot, *Middlemarch*, ed. David Carroll, The World's Classics (Oxford: Oxford University Press, 1988), p. 158. All page references are to this edition and are given in the text hereafter.
35. *PW*, vol. IV, pp. 463–4.
36. Neil Hertz, 'Recognizing Casaubon', *The End of the Line: Essays on Psychoanalysis and the Sublime* (New York: Columbia University Press, 1985), p. 78.
37. Wordsworth, 'Ode to Duty', ll. 41–4.
38. See Peter Simpson, 'Crisis and Recovery: William Wordsworth, George Eliot, and Silas Marner', *University of Toronto Quarterly*, 48 (1979), 95–114.
39. George Eliot, *Letters*, vol. I, p. 34.
40. See Wordsworth's note to his poem 'At Rome', dictated to Isabella Fenwick; *PW*, vol. III, p. 494.
41. See J. Hillis Miller, 'Narrative and History', *English Literary History*, 41 (1974), 455–73.
42. Robert Kiely, 'The Limits of Dialogue in *Middlemarch*', in *The Worlds of Victorian Fiction*, ed. Jerome H. Buckley (Cambridge, Mass. and London: Harvard University Press, 1975), pp. 103, 107.
43. See Preface to *The Excursion*; *PW*, vol. V, p. 2.
44. *Later Years*, vol. I, p. 292.
45. *Correspondence of Henry Crabb Robinson with the Wordsworth Circle*, ed. Edith J. Morley, 2 vols (Oxford: Oxford University Press, 1927), vol. I, p. 318.
46. Quoted from Wordsworth's note to 'At Rome'; *PW*, vol. III, p. 494.

47. Quoted by Chistopher Wordsworth, *Memoirs of William Wordsworth*, 2 vols (London: Edward Moxon, 1851), vol. II, p. 329.
48. 5 July 1837; *Later Years*, vol. VI, p. 423.
49. *Life, Letters, and Journals of George Ticknor*, ed. G.S. Hillard, 2 vols (Boston and New York: Houghton Mifflin, 1909), vol. II, p. 167. Gray's reason for leaving his philosophical poem, 'The Alliance of Education and Government', in a fragmentary state resonates with Wordsworth's family's fears that their poet had become habituated to polishing short lyrical poetry. See R.W. Ketton-Cremer, *Thomas Gray: A Biography* (Cambridge: Cambridge University Press, 1955), p. 91.

CHAPTER FOUR

Autobiography as Self-Indulgence: De Quincey and His Reviewers

Julian North

At the beginning of 'Autobiography as De-Facement' Paul de Man comments that 'compared to tragedy, or epic, or lyric poetry, autobiography always looks slightly disreputable and self-indulgent'.[1] One can understand why this might be the case. In yielding to the pleasures of narcissism, autobiography both indulges the self and indulges in the self. But it may also be self-indulgent in a further sense. George Gusdorf argues that 'the task of autobiography is first of all a task of personal salvation'. Its 'deepest intentions ... are directed toward a kind of apologetics or theodicy of the individual being'.[2] If we accept this, then, in the quest for personal salvation autobiography does not only seem to entail self-indulgence and indulgence in the self but indulgence towards the self. An indulgence, or remission of the temporal punishment still due after sacramental absolution, in the Roman Catholic Church, was granted by ecclesiastical authority to the repentant sinner. The autobiographer may ask for this kind of indulgence from the readers – in the same way that Prospero turns to the audience at the end of *The Tempest* and asks: 'As you from crimes would pardoned be / Let your indulgence set me free.'[3] But one characteristic of autobiography might also be that indulgence is granted by the subject to the subject.

The issue of self-indulgence was an important one for nineteenth-century autobiographers and their critics. Anxious disavowals of self-absorption and egotism appear in several autobiographies of the period. At the beginning of the *Biographia Literaria* (1817), for instance, Coleridge assures us that 'the least of what I have written concerns myself personally'.[4] In 1850 Leigh Hunt begins his autobiography similarly by claiming that its only value lies in what goes beyond the self: 'Should I be led into egotism ... I blush beforehand for the mischance, and beg it to be considered as alien from my habits of reflection.'[5] Newman agonizes over the difficulty of exposing himself in his *Apologia*: 'In exculpating myself, it was plain I should be pursuing no mere personal quarrel' and it 'is not at all pleasant for me to be egotistical: nor to be criticized for being so'.[6]

Many nineteenth-century critics were, as this suggests, alert to signs of self-indulgence in autobiographical writing. Coleridge's *Biographia* was famously attacked by John Wilson for 'inveterate and diseased egotism ... a grinning and idiot self-complacency'.[7] Even an extremely favourable review of Wordsworth's *Prelude* ventured, overcautiously one might think, that the poem was marked by 'a tone of very gentle, tender self-appreciation ... a pervading spirit of satisfaction with self', and worried about the 'propriety of the anatomical study, self-description, ending in self-appreciation, here indulged in'.[8]

But what of the autobiography which took mental and physical self-indulgence as a central theme? De Quincey's *Confessions of an English Opium Eater* (1821) was just such a text and proved particularly provocative to its reviewers for this reason.[9] What I want to do in the following discussion is to focus on the *Confessions* and its self-conscious and witty play with the meanings of self-indulgence. I shall then go on to look at its critical reception, particularly in the 1850s, as pointing to what seem to have been more general anxieties in the period over autobiography as a self-indulgent genre.

The *Confessions* opens with De Quincey defending himself from the charge of indecent self-exposure. His life, he claims, will be 'useful and instructive' to his readers,

> and *that* must be my apology for breaking through that delicate and honourable reserve, which, for the most part, restrains us from the public exposure of our own errors and infirmities. Nothing, indeed, is more revolting to English feelings, than the spectacle of a human being obtruding on our notice his moral ulcers or scars, and tearing away that 'decent drapery', which time, or indulgence to human frailty, may have drawn over them: accordingly, the greater part of *our* confessions ... proceed from demireps, adventurers, or swindlers: and for any such acts of gratuitous self-humiliation from those who can be supposed in sympathy with the decent part of society, we must look to French literature, or to that part of the German, which is tainted with the spurious and defective sensibility of the French.[10]

Moral ulcers, decent drapery torn away, 'gratuitous self-humiliation' – De Quincey here apparently distinguishes his 'English' confessional from foreign, masochistic acts of penance. The English, he says, prefer to indulge human frailty by drawing a veil over such unpleasantness. At the same time he is clearly exploiting the *frisson* of association, and we are left in little doubt that De Quincey is about to humiliate himself gratuitously too. He is talking about self-accusation here, rather than self-indulgence, but the one seems to entail the other. This is especially suggested by his dark hints about the sensibility of the French – hints which unmistakably allude to Rousseau's *Confessions*, an autobiography which had gained a reputation in Britain as the very pinnacle of self-indulgence.

Rousseau's *Confessions* had been denounced by many British critics of the 1780s and 1790s on the grounds of immorality and vanity, and in the 1790s these traits were condemned with renewed force as smacking of revolution. Edward Duffy writes that 'Eighteenth-century moralists readily discerned a family resemblance between the lewdness of young Rousseau and the Jacobin lust for blood. Both were forms of self-indulgence, a gratification of desire beyond the bounds of decency as well as those of social accommodation and compromise.'[11] Foremost among these critics was Burke, who in 1791 numbered Rousseau among a malign class of 'writers indulgent to the peculiarities of their own complexion'. He was, argued Burke, the founder of a 'philosophy of vanity', of which 'the present rebellion was … [a] legitimate offspring'.[12] For Burke, as for so many other commentators of the period, it was Rousseau's solitary sexual pleasures, as recounted in his *Confessions*, that scandalized particularly. Here, indeed, was evidence of self-indulgence of a peculiarly solipsistic kind. Even Hazlitt, who praised Rousseau for his part in instigating the French Revolution and for his *Confessions*, felt that he showed 'a tendency to indulge merely the impulses of passions'.[13]

Though De Quincey, at the opening of his *Confessions*, seems to take a standard Burkian line on Rousseau, the act of homage implied in imitating Rousseau's title goes a great way to undermining his professions of disgust. More than this, however, De Quincey's autobiography imitates and indeed surpasses Rousseau's in foregrounding acts of self-indulgence. Rousseau's sexual fantasies become De Quincey's opium-eating, which is referred to routinely throughout the narrative as his 'indulgence', or 'self-indulgence', and is given the charge of a solitary erotic pleasure – he first tastes the drug alone in his lodgings with orgasmic results.[14] Moreover, where Rousseau's sexual adventures and misadventures are one thread in the narrative, De Quincey's opium indulgence takes centre stage: this is not merely an autobiography which includes examples of self-indulgence, it is an autobiography to which the concept of self-indulgence is integral.

Opium-eating is not simply represented as a self-gratification in De Quincey's *Confessions*. It operates as a self-indulgence in all three of the senses suggested at the beginning of this paper. It is a solitary pleasure, an 'abyss of divine enjoyment' (p. 71), but it is also a means of indulging in the self. Opium is De Quincey's way of retrieving his past: making it present and harmonious, an experience to be luxuriated in.

He recounts the story of his mother who, as a child, fell in a river 'and being on the very verge of death ... saw in a moment her whole life, in its minutest incidents, arrayed before her simultaneously as in a mirror; and she had a faculty developed as suddenly for comprehending the whole and every part' (p. 104). This, he says, is like the mind of the opium-eater. It is also, we might add, the fantasy of the autobiographer. Earlier in the narrative, De Quincey's indulgence in the self has been exemplified when he goes to hear Grassini sing at the opera, under the influence of the drug, and, like his drowning mother, sees displayed before him 'the whole of my past life – not as if recalled by an act of memory, but as if present and incarnated in the music' (p. 79). Where wine, De Quincey argues, 'robs a man of his self-possession: opium greatly invigorates it ' – enables a man to repossess himself.

Opium, then, allows De Quincey both to indulge and to indulge in himself, but in so doing it also allows him to be indulgent towards himself. In his opium reverie at the opera his past life is blameless – 'no longer painful to dwell upon: but the detail of its incidents removed, or blended in some hazy abstraction; and its passions exalted, spiritualized, and sublimed' (p. 79). In the famous centre-piece of the *Confessions*, an apostrophe to the powers of the drug – 'Oh! just, subtle, and mighty opium!' – opium is hailed as 'an assuaging balm', having the power not only to restore the past, but to wipe it clean from sin: 'eloquent opium! that with thy potent rhetoric stealest away the purposes of wrath; and to the guilty man, for one night givest back the hopes of his youth, and hands washed pure from blood' (p. 83).

De Quincey does not only grant his own indulgences, however, he also asks for the indulgence of his readers. They must allow him 'a few indulgences' towards his sense of humour (p. 72) and he begins one section with 'Courteous, and, I hope, indulgent reader (for all *my* readers must be indulgent ones, or else, I fear, I shall shock them too much to count on their courtesy)' (p. 84). In such instances we see a knowing retailoring of a novelistic convention to the language of confessional autobiography. De Quincey restyles the public as his priest 'into whose private ear I am confidentially whispering my confessions', and asks them to grant him remission from punishment (p. 96). He is looking, in his readership, 'for some courteous and considerate sect ... that are "sweet men", as Chaucer says, "to give absolution", and will show some conscience in the penances they inflict, and the efforts of abstinence they exact, from poor sinners like myself' (p. 88).

What is important here is that the indulgence of readers, but, more crucially, self-indulgence as represented in the *Confessions* in the practice of opium-eating, are shown to be necessary to the process of autobiography. De Quincey's opium habit is an indulgence of, in and towards the self, and it is only thus that his past selves may be recovered, consolidated, restored to innocence. This is the effort of all De Quincey's autobiographical writing – the *Confessions* (1821 and 1856), the 'Sketches of Life and Manners; From the Autobiography of an English Opium-Eater' (1834–36), the 'Suspiria de Profundis' (1845) and 'The English Mail Coach' (1849).

However, this only gives one side of the story. As the irony in some of the extracts I have been quoting suggests, the *Confessions* is nothing if not equivocal on the subject of De Quincey's opium indulgence. The drug is represented as a radically unstable experience. After the pleasures of opium come the pains, both physical and mental. Instead of a self-indulgence opium becomes a scourge, afflicting De Quincey with 'unutterable irritation of stomach ... intense perspirations', physical and intellectual torpor (p. 98). The drug in the later stages of addiction still retrieves De Quincey's past selves for him, but they are no longer brought into a harmonious coexistence, and no longer indulged. Now his dreams are marked by anxiety and melancholy. Episodes in his past, for example with Ann the London prostitute, or with the Malay, who visits him in the Lake District, now return but transformed into chaotic visions where time stretches out into infinity, rather than being brought into simultaneous presence, and where the predominant sensations are of powerlessness, guilt and loss. Opium no longer makes the past present and unified, nor does it cleanse the conscience of guilt. The drug is now represented as self-thwarting and, more specifically, as an impediment to the continuous efforts necessary to the writer.

De Quincey tells us that the pains of opium prevented him from reading or writing – he starts to compose a *Prolegomena to all future Systems of Political Economy*, but is unable to finish it (p. 101). As if to mark this change, De Quincey signals his shift to a more disjointed style of narration in the final section of the *Confessions*: 'For several reasons, I have not been able to compose the notes for this part of my narrative into any regular and connected shape' (p. 96). Accordingly we are given observations in note form, and dream narratives, some of them supplied as extracts from a journal. The opium indulgence which has been represented as enabling autobiography thus ends up by disabling it. It can bring pleasure, it can retrieve past selves and make them present, harmonious and restored to innocence; but it can also bring suffering, the realization that the past is lost and unassimilable to the present, and that the guilt remains. Self-indulgence is thus seen as integral to autobiography in the *Confessions*, but it is also shown to be autobiography's undoing.

We should not be too quick to read a moral here, however. Self-indulgence seems to be shown up as fatal by the end of the narrative, but even after detailing the pains of opium, De Quincey, in the closing paragraphs, calls the drug 'the true hero of the tale' (p. 114). The following passage, on the question of whether or not he is strictly guilty of self-indulgence, typifies the equivocations which mark the *Confessions* as a whole:

> If opium-eating be a sensual pleasure, and if I am bound to confess that I have indulged in it to an excess, not yet *recorded* of any other man, it is no less true, that I have struggled against this fascinating enthralment with a religious zeal ... Such a self-conquest may reasonably be set off in counterbalance to any kind or degree of self-indulgence. Not to insist, that in my case, the self-conquest was unquestionable, the self-indulgence open to doubts of casuistry, according as that name shall be extended to acts aiming at the bare relief of pain, or shall be restricted to such as aim at the excitement of positive pleasure.
>
> (p. 30)

This is casuistry indeed. The conditional clauses and double negatives in this passage ensure that admission and denial of self-indulgence coexist. De Quincey is usually characterized as a purple Tory, but, as far as the politics of autobiography in the period are concerned, he remains elusive, neither aligning himself fully with the school of Burke nor with the school of Rousseau.

De Quincey's critics in his own lifetime (he died in 1859) became increasingly concerned with the issue of self-indulgence in the *Confessions* and in his other autobiographical works, though they were, at the same time, almost wholly insensitive to the subtlety with which he dealt with the subject. If we look at De Quincey's critical reception from the 1820s onwards, we can see how deep-rooted the anti-Jacobin line of protest against autobiography, started by Burke and others, was in Victorian criticism, and how it resurfaced particularly in the middle years of the century. Indeed, the case history of De Quincey's critical reception provides an interesting index of the conception and status of autobiography generally at the time.

Most of the early reviews of the *Confessions*, in the 1820s, enthused over De Quincey's sensational self-revelation. As one reviewer put it: 'egotism is the spirit of the age; and the object of every author is to describe his own thoughts, his own feelings, and his own passions'. The *Confessions* was 'the most original, if not the most powerful, piece of self-biography extant'.[15] De Quincey was also compared, without rancour, to Rousseau.[16]

However, De Quincey's autobiography also came in for some adverse criticism. In direct contrast to the general acceptance and praise of the *Confessions*, one reviewer took De Quincey to task for vanity and morbid self-love,[17] and there was a vitriolic attack in the Tory *John Bull*

Magazine from William Maginn. Maginn reviled De Quincey for expecting to be indulged by his readership for his infirmities and, at the same time, for his self-indulgence in painting himself better than he really was – even his name is an affectation, says Maginn: 'His father was an honest shop keeper, who lived and died Quincy [*sic*].' Underneath the personal invective, Maginn was making an objection to the very principle of autobiography. 'There is something excessively disgusting', he says, 'in being obliged to look into any man's private life.'[18]

This kind of sentiment becames a much more marked feature of reviews from the 1850s, when the second burst of critical activity surrounding De Quincey's autobiographical writing took place, following the publication of two editions of his collected works.[19] By this time it is noticeable how the opposing sides in the debate over autobiography and self-indulgence have defined themselves and how both the prosecution and the defence have become more urgent. The distrust of Romantic autobiography as a self-indulgent genre is clear in those critics who attacked De Quincey, but it is also latent in the criticism of those who defended him.

Typical of the attacking school are two articles from the late 1850s. One of these reviewers, in the *London Quarterly Review*, sees egotism and 'self-complacency' as De Quincey's vices. He was 'haunted by the fiend of subjectivity so as never yet was human being'. His imagination was impaired 'by too eager self-scansion'.[20] The second article is an obituary, but nevertheless deplores De Quincey's opium indulgence and what is referred to as the 'diseased introspection' which has made him tolerant of his own moral infirmities.[21] Both these critics imply a connection between the unhealthily self-indulgent life narrated in the *Confessions* and the fact that, as they perceive it, the subjectivity of his autobiographical narrative is, itself, unhealthily self-indulgent. But even the reviewers who championed De Quincey were caught up in the need to defend him from these charges.

Most critics of the 1850s had high praise for De Quincey's autobiographical works for their insight into the darker reaches of the dreaming mind, and for their prose style. However, even the most enthusiastic of these critics were troubled by a feeling that autobiography was a genre in need of justification. They could not pass by the autobiographical writings of De Quincey without excusing him from the charge of self-indulgence – of an egotistical failing in his duty to his readers. So, for instance, though a reviewer in 1854 claims that the charm of De Quincey's work is greatly enhanced by the fact that 'You never lose sight of himself', he adds that 'In a nature so peculiar as his, egotism ceases to be egotism, and assumes a certain catholic air; you feel you cannot spare a single I – since each personal pronoun is an algebraic symbol of great and general truths.' The reviewer groups De Quincey with other Romantic autobiographers – Rousseau, Wordsworth and Byron – but all are men of genius by the token that when they soliloquize they do so like a great mountain, in many voices.[22] The moral infirmities of De Quincey's life may therefore be excused because they function as lessons to his readers – indeed, as such, they make us 'feel he is *entitled* always to use the first person'.[23]

In 1855 Peter Landreth argued that De Quincey's 'very egotism is an impersonal contemplation of the developments and aspects of his own nature'. His 'introverted eye' is thus, paradoxically, 'passionless'. He is, unlike Wordsworth, free from personal pride and thus, 'the entire reverse of a mere artist'.[24] As this last phrase suggests, these critics' distrust of autobiography reflects an increased conviction that literature should serve a didactic function. A dangerous aestheticism would be the result of genuine self-indulgence. Indeed, for the more hostile reviewers this was the point at which De Quincey had already arrived – his 'finest productions teach nothing, are sullied with sadness and melancholy, disposed rather to weaken than to strengthen';[25] his career was 'sad and almost profitless' – his intellect had never been 'of much service to his fellow-men'.[26]

De Quincey's critical reception in the 1850s suggests both a particular alertness at this period to the dangers of self-indulgence in autobiography, and the identification of such autobiographical writing with an immoral or even amoral aestheticism. Autobiography is only justified for these critics if it in some way achieves the paradox of being at once subjective and objective; personal and impersonal. It is interesting that there should have been this concern, in the 1850s, since it suggests that the backlash against what was perceived as the ineffectual solipsism of much Romantic poetry (a backlash seen, for instance, in the Spasmodic controversy of the 1840s and 1850s and in Arnold's 1853 preface to his own poems) also affected Romantic autobiography.[27] But perhaps it is the case that, as in the earlier reaction against Rousseau, a conservative criticism will tend to be suspicious of autobiography on grounds of self-indulgence. In the 1980s Marilyn Butler revived the strong moral line of Burke in reading De Quincey's *Confessions* as narcissistic, unrelentingly egotistical and self-advertising.[28] In characterizing De Quincey's autobiography in this way, she was marking it out as something of an anomaly in an era when, as she argued, other writers were self-consciously satirizing this kind of self-indulgence. What I hope I have demonstrated here is, first, that De Quincey was as knowing as any of the Romantics in his self-conscious play with the issue of self-indulgence in autobiography; and, secondly, that his nineteenth-century critics were too busy charging him with, or defending him from the crime, to realize this.

Notes

1. Paul de Man, 'Autobiography as De-Facement', in his *The Rhetoric of Romanticism* (1979; New York: Columbia University Press, 1984), pp. 67–81 (pp. 67–8).
2. Georges Gusdorf, 'Conditions and Limits of Autobiography', in *Autobiography: Essays Theoretical and Critical*, ed. James Olney (1956; Princeton: Princeton University Press, 1980), p. 39.
3. *The Tempest*, Act V, Epilogue.
4. Samuel Taylor Coleridge, *Biographia Literaria, or Biographical Sketches of My Literary Life and Opinions*, ed. James Engell and W. Jackson Bate, 2 vols (Princeton and London: Princeton University Press and Routledge & Kegan Paul, 1983), vol. I, p. 5.
5. *The Autobiography of Leigh Hunt*, ed. J.E. Morpurgo (London: Cresnet Press, 1948), p. 1.
6. J.H. Newman, *Apologia Pro Vita Sua, Being a History of His Religious Opinions*, ed. Martin J. Svaglic (Oxford: Clarendon Press, 1967), pp. 4, 14. The first phrase is taken from Newman's 1865 preface to the *Apologia*, and the second is from the first edition of 1864, excerpted in his expanded preface of 1869.
7. John Wilson, review of *Biographia Literaria*, *Blackwood's Edinburgh Magazine*, 2 (October 1817), 3–18 (p. 5).
8. *Christian Remembrancer*, 20 (1850), 332–73 (pp. 370–1).
9. Thomas De Quincey, 'Confessions of an English Opium Eater', *London Magazine*, 4, no 21 (September 1821), 293–312 and 4, no. 22 (October 1821), 353–79. All references to this in the text will be to Thomas De Quincey, *Confessions of an English Opium Eater*, ed. Alethea Hayter (Harmondsworth: Penguin Books, 1971) (hereafter, *Confessions*).
10. *Confessions*, p. 29. Cf. Wilson's *Blackwood's* review of *Biographia Literaria*, pp. 3–4, where it is argued that every thinking man must shrink from autobiography as 'the tearing away that shroud which oblivion may have kindly flung over his vices and his follies, or that fine and delicate veil which Christian humility draws over his virtues'. Wilson goes on to deplore Rousseau's *Confessions* as degrading to author and reader alike. De Quincey's preamble seems to refer, perhaps parodically, to Wilson's.
11. Edward Duffy, *Rousseau in England* (Berkeley: University of California Press, 1979), p. 50.
12. *The Writings and Speeches of Edmund Burke*, ed. Paul Langford, volume VIII (Oxford: Clarendon Press, 1989), pp. 312–15.
13. *The Complete Works of William Hazlitt*, ed. P.P. Howe, Centenary Edition, 21 vols (London: J.M. Dent, 1930–34), vol. IV, pp. 88–93; vol. VII, pp. 52–3.
14. *Confessions*, p. 71. Opium was thought by several authorities on the subject to be an aphrodisiac. See, for example, John Jones, *The Mysteries of Opium Revealed* (London: Richard Smith, 1700), p. 20 and passim; and Samuel Crumpe, *An Inquiry into the Nature and Properties of Opium* (London: G.G. and J. Robinson, 1793), p. 44.
15. *London Museum*, 28 (November 1822), 433–5 (p. 433).
16. *Monthly Review*, 100 (March 1823), 288–96 (p. 288).
17. *British Critic*, ns 18 (November 1822), 531–4 (p. 531).

18. [William Maginn], 'The Humbugs of the Age. No. 1 – The Opium Eater', *John Bull Magazine and Literary Recorder*, **1** (July 1824), 21–4 (p. 22).
19. The editions were: *De Quincey's Writings*, ed. T.J. Fields, 22 vols (Boston: Ticknor, Reed and Fields, 1851–59); and *Selections Grave and Gay*, ed. Thomas De Quincey, 14 vols (London: R. Groombridge, 1853–60).
20. *London Quarterly Review*, **8** (April 1857), 198–219 (pp. 212, 219, 204, 218).
21. *Athenaeum*, no. 1677 (December 1859), 814–15.
22. *Eclectic Review*, ns **8** (October 1854), 385–99 (p. 387).
23. Ibid., p. 388 (italics mine).
24. [Peter Landreth], *Scottish Review*, **3** (April 1855), 97–114 (p. 100).
25. *London Quarterly Review* (April 1857), p. 218.
26. *Athenaeum* (December 1859), p. 814.
27. For the anti-Romantic backlash evinced in the reaction of critics, including Arnold, to the Spasmodic poets, see M.A. Weinstein, *William Edmonstoune Ayton and the Spasmodic Controversy* (New Haven: Yale University Press, 1968).
28. Marilyn Butler, 'Satire and the Images of Self in the Romantic Period: The Long Tradition of Hazlitt's *Liber Amoris*', *The Yearbook of English Studies*, **14** (1984), 209–25 (pp. 218–19).

CHAPTER FIVE

The Romance of Sickliness: Leigh Hunt's *Autobiography* and the Example of Keats

Nicholas Roe

> We have been so long reading Leigh Hunt's works, and reading of Leigh Hunt himself, that we are surprised at its never having occurred to us to ask, who in the world is he? – what age is he? – where was he born?[1]

At the back of the first volume of Leigh Hunt's *Autobiography*, in the first edition of 1850, appeared a 16-page 'Catalogue of Books in Various Branches of Literature, Published by Smith, Elder and Co.'. The advertisements drew the reader's attention to literary works: *Jane Eyre: an Autobiography*, *Shirley: a Tale* and *Poems. By Currer, Ellis, and Acton Bell*. Also listed are Hunt's *Autobiography* ('just ready') and some of his other writings: *The Town*; *Men, Women, and Books*; *Imagination and Fancy*; and *Wit and Humour*. On turning the page, the reader found a list of books dealing with 'Practical Information': *The Railways of the United Kingdom, Statistically Considered*; histories of the Iron Trade and of Ancient Commerce; Tables of Consols; *Piddington's Sailor's Horn-Book of Storms*; *Storms in the Indian Ocean ... with Suggestions on the Means of Avoiding Them*.[2]

A broad contrast between literature ('imagination and fancy') and practicality is evident in these pages. The blurb for *Jane Eyre* included quotations from reviews which foreground the discourse of romance: 'Freshness and originality, truth and passion ... the bright field of romantic literature ... raciness and ability ... a thoroughly original and unworn pen ... a feeling heart.' All of these qualities are gendered, and predicated on 'the masculine current of noble thoughts' which discloses 'A very pathetic tale – very singular; and so like the truth'.[3] Smith and Elder's 'Works of Practical Information' presented another kind of truth, also masculine, founded on the nineteenth-century science of statistics. In the books catalogued, statistics inform *The Railways of the United Kingdom* ('a complete encyclopaedia of railway information'), the 'Tables of Consols' and, no doubt, *The Farmer's Friend* which was 'calculated to do good service to agricultural science'. Statistics and the calculation of probability also underwrite Edwin James Farren's *Life Contingency Tables* and Pocock's *Assurances upon Lives; Including the Different Systems of Life Assurance Now in Use*.[4]

In these few pages of advertisements one discourse of Romanticism appears alongside that of Tennyson's 'sordid and mean' age of calculation and system, railways, commerce, investment, mercantilism, law and life assurance. The 'feeling heart' and Hunt's resolute 'cheerfulness' confront a new world 'Coherent in statistical despairs / ... in figures on a page', as Elizabeth Barrett Browning wrote in *Aurora Leigh*.[5] John Kerrigan's essay 'Keats, Hopkins, and the History of Chance' has shown how Gerard Manley Hopkins's poetry seeks to ward off that despair, elaborating numerical structures as a kind of mathematic instress that vindicates God's providential design against the new science of probability in which all contingencies may be tabulated.[6] In Hopkins's poem, the wreck of the 'Deutschland' is celebrated as a 'cipher of suffering Christ' (l. 170), not explained as a consequence of 'the law of storms'.

A comparable defence against 'this iron time' appeared in Matthew Arnold's sentimental image of Wordsworth in 'Memorial Verses':

> He too upon a wintry clime
> Had fallen – on this iron time
> Of doubts, disputes, distractions, fears.
> He found us when the age had bound
> Our souls in its benumbing round;
> He spoke, and loosed our heart in tears.
> He laid us as we lay at birth
> On the cool flowery lap of earth,
> Smiles broke from us and we had ease;
> The hills were round us, and the breeze
> Went o'er the sun-lit fields again ... [7]

Tears betoken Wordsworth's 'healing power', releasing the spirit in joyful response to 'nature', recovering 'youth' and the 'freshness of the early world'. Arnold's idea of Wordsworth contributed to an enduring and distinctive image of 'Romanticism' or, more strictly, the Romantic self: turned away from 'the age' to refresh the spirit as a child laid 'On the cool flowery lap of earth'. This essay explores in Leigh Hunt's *Autobiography* a comparable investment of the Romantic self, although Hunt's 'autocriticism' (as he termed his book)[8] invokes Keats more strongly than Wordsworth. Hunt elaborates an alternative Romantic identity, a 'feminized' self associated (after Burke's *Philosophical Inquiry*) with ill-health, weakness and vulnerability – the susceptibility of the 'heart loosed in tears' rather than the supposedly 'masculine vigour' of Currer Bell.

Hunt's *Autobiography* has a broadly chronological arrangement. It opens with a chapter on 'The Author's Progenitors', and it concludes with the reflections of his old age on 'Political and Religious Opinions'.

It is in this last chapter that Hunt writes, 'I consider myself a royalist of the only right English sort; that is to say, as a republican, with royalty for his safeguard and ornament' (III, p. 277). One should recall that during 1813–15 Hunt had been jailed for a libel on the Prince Regent: the motives for his curious affirmation of royalist republicanism will appear in a moment. In other respects the *Autobiography* is digressive and anecdotal, drawing upon and revising his earlier writings, notably *Lord Byron and Some of his Contemporaries* (1828), by way of correcting facts but also as a means of self-justification at a period when those former 'contemporaries' were long dead.[9] Hunt is from the first a reluctant and sickly autobiographer, a descendant of Tristram Shandy. He regrets that his work is an 'involuntarily egotistical book' on which he had been able to proceed only because of his physician's 'attentions to [his] health' (I, p. x). The *Autobiography* also seeks to present the author's humanity in opposition to the materiality of the age, as appears from Hunt's discussion of Benjamin Franklin.

For Hunt, Franklin was 'one of the *cardinal* great men of his time' (I, p. 198), although he stood for all that Hunt did not wish to associate with himself. In other words, he appears in the *Autobiography* as a kind of foil to Hunt's own self-image, representing 'commercialism' as opposed to 'uncalculating persons like myself': Franklin is figurehead of America, 'a rising commercial state', whereas Hunt belongs to 'an old one', Britain (I, p. 197). Franklin works with 'systems'; Hunt is drawn to 'follies', 'intolerances', and to 'higher speculations' (I, p. 197). Franklin is a man of 'few passions and no imagination'; Hunt counters by observing that Franklin's 'line and rule are not everything' (I, pp. 198–9). Franklin stands for the 'present system of money-making'; Hunt for 'the fancies in our heads, and the hearts beating in our bosoms' (I, pp. 199–200). Hunt would not have ventured on this criticism of Franklin, he says,

> had I not been backed by so many powerful interests of humanity, and had I not suffered in common, and more than in common, with the rest of the world, from a system which, under the guise of economy and social advantage, tends to double the love of wealth and the hostility of competition, to force the best things down to a level with the worst, and to reduce mankind to the simplest and most mechanical law of their nature, divested of its heart and soul, – the law of being in motion.
>
> (vol. I, p. 200)

Hunt's self-justification pitches system, economy, social advantage, wealth, and competition against humanity, heart, soul. We might reformulate this in other ways – as capitalism opposed to social welfare, or as utilitarian 'law' versus the claims of feeling. Alternatively, and bearing in mind the advertisements I have already discussed, we might see Hunt's dwelling upon illness, accident, and misfortune as a defence against a world dominated by statistics and calculation; a deliberate sentimentalizing of his earlier career as a radical when, as he now admits, and with the poet laureateship vacant after Wordsworth's death, he had 'been thought ... to speak too severely of kings and princes'.

Thornton Hunt's introduction to the 1867 edition of the *Autobiography* suggests that his father had 'overrated' his 'delicacy of health'.[10] Certainly, Leigh Hunt suffered from 'fits of nervousness' which he associated with 'hypochondria', or 'a melancholy state of mind, produced by ill health' (I, p. 294):

> And what was it that I suffered? and on what account? On no account. On none whatsoever, except my ridiculous super-abstinence, and my equally ridiculous avoidance of speaking about it. The very fact of having no cause whatsoever, was the thing that most frightened me. I thought that if I had but a cause, the cause might have been removed or palliated; but to be haunted by a ghost that was not even ghostly, which was something I never saw, or could even imagine, this, I thought, was the most terrible thing that could befal me. I could see no end to the persecutions of an enemy, who was neither visible nor even existing!

Hamlet and Satan are half-invoked here, but by way of suggesting that Hunt's torment was unaccountable, without cause – indeed, this was the 'thing that most frightened [him]'. Psychoanalysis might diagnose his malaise as acute anxiety. Timothy Webb believes that Hunt was a manic-depressive, and that his philosophy of deliberate 'cheerfulness' was a way of controlling and coming to terms with his depression; 'cheerful habits enabled me to retain an air of cheerfulness, except when I was alone', as Hunt puts it.[11] If this transforms the 'prince of parlour-window writers'[12] into a more modern and a more heroic figure than we might have expected, it also renders him the more incalculable as a personality: as he writes, 'I felt, long before I knew Mr. Wordsworth's poetry, – "the burthen and the mystery / Of all this unintelligible world".'[13]

As that allusion to 'Tintern Abbey' indicates, Hunt's sickliness and vulnerability were a means of achieving a personal sublime, demonstrating what he called his 'spirit of martyrdom'. Recalling his schooldays, he wrote: 'The truth is, I could suffer better than act; for the utmost activity of martyrdom is supported by a certain sense of passiveness' (I, p. 92). This 'passiveness' recalls the 'wise passiveness' of Wordsworth's lyrical ballad 'Expostulation and Reply', and also Keats's idea of 'negative capability' through which the egotistical self is subdued in hospitality to universal experience.[14] As with Keats's reputation during the nineteenth century, Hunt's cultivation of personal susceptibility and vulnerability is consciously feminized: 'I inherit from my mother a tendency to jaundice', he comments 'which at times has made me melancholy enough' (I, p. 44). 'I was the youngest and least robust of her sons, and during early childhood I used hardly to recover from one illness before I was seized with another. The doctor said I must have gone through an extraordinary amount of suffering'; 'illness, imagination, and an ultra tender and anxious rearing, conspired to render me fearful and patient' (I, pp. 51–2, 59). 'I was too delicately bred ... [although] it gave me an ultra-sympathy with the least show of pain and suffering' (I, p. 65). As well as jaundice, he suffered from 'dropsy in the head' as a child (I, p. 45); he stammered at school (I, p. 124); he endured 'palpitations of the heart' (I, p. 295); his imprisonment coincided with 'unceasing ill-health' (II, p. 155) and, 'partly from ill-health', his release 'brought a good deal of pain with it' (II, pp. 155, 158). I could go on citing the numerous references to sickness throughout the *Autobiography*, although a few words from the second volume might serve as an epigraph for the whole enterprise: 'the reader will bear in mind that I was ill' (II, p. 145).

As I have already pointed out, Edmund Burke's *Philosophical Inquiry into the Origin of Our Ideas of the Sublime and Beautiful* had associated 'weakness and imperfection' with 'the cause of beauty' and, specifically, with 'the female sex': 'Women are very sensible of this; for which reason, they learn to lisp, to totter in their walk, to counterfeit weakness, and even sickness. In all this, they are guided by nature. Beauty in distress is much the most affecting beauty.'[15] In the terms of Burke's influential book, Hunt's *Autobiography* deliberately feminizes his childhood. He inherited sickness from his mother, and he grew up to become prey to 'fits of nervousness' – described by him as 'effeminate ills' that might be prevented by 'violent exercise' (II, p. 158) – or what Currer Bell's reviewer would term 'masculine vigour'. Indeed, the portraits of Hunt from each of the three volumes of his *Autobiography* reflect the 'effeminate' characteristics developed in his narrative. In the first volume is the sensitive youth of 17; in the second volume, the plump and dimpled man of 36.[16] In the third volume appears the elderly Hunt aged 66, pale (in comparison with the other portraits) and now somewhat drawn; the sideboards have disappeared, and his hair is worn long over his collar. It might be the portrait of an invalid; it certainly does not conform to the mid-nineteenth-century image of masculinity.

What I have tried to suggest so far is that Hunt's *Autobiography* uses sickness, and its 'effeminate' associations, as a means to draw attention to his fragile presence in a world dominated by the 'masculine' forces of system, statistics, calculation. Equally, by dwelling upon his 'nervousness' and 'ultra-sympathy' with suffering humanity, he could treat his prominent and libellous career as editor of the *Examiner* newspaper without reawakening former controversies. According to the *Autobiography*, the *Examiner* had apparently 'disclaimed all knowledge of statistics; and the rest of its politics were rather a sentiment ... than founded on any particular political reflection' (II, p. 4). I emphasize this feminizing strategy not just to show how Hunt sought to refashion his life for mid-century readers, but because I think it shows us Hunt remaking himself in the nineteenth-century image of his old friend John Keats.

The sentimental and 'effeminate' image of Keats gained currency from Shelley's 'Preface' to *Adonais*. Here, Shelley lamented Keats's 'delicate', 'fragile' and 'beautiful' genius – a 'young flower blighted in the bud':

> The savage criticism on his *Endymion* ... produced the most violent effect on his susceptible mind; the agitation thus originated ended in the rupture of a blood-vessel in the lungs; a rapid consumption ensued, and the succeeding acknowledgements from more candid critics ... were ineffectual to heal the wound thus wantonly inflicted.[17]

In other words, and as Byron wrote in *Don Juan* (XI. 60), Keats had been 'snuff'd out by an article'. More than a quarter of a century later, Hunt returned to the story of Keats's death in his *Autobiography*: 'When I was in Italy', he wrote,

> Lord Byron shewed me in manuscript the well-known passage in *Don Juan*, in which Keats's death is attributed to the *Quarterly Review*; the couplet about the 'fiery particle', that was 'snuff'd out by an article'. I told him the state of the case, proving to him that the supposition was a mistake, and therefore, if printed, would be a misrepresentation. But a stroke of wit was not to be given up.
> (vol. II, p. 210)

The 'real state of the case', as recounted by Hunt in the *Autobiography*, actually elaborates the myth of Keats's sickliness – but by way of vindicating Hunt himself. In only a dozen pages devoted to Keats, Hunt dwells on the poet's 'bad health', his 'irritable morbidity', his 'trembling excess of sensibility', his 'afflicting delusion', his 'severe illness', his 'ill health' – all of which Hunt suggests Keats inherited from his mother (II, pp. 201–3, 207, 213). Hunt is more or less accurate when he observes that 'Keats had felt that his disease was mortal, two or three years before he died':

> He had a constitutional tendency to consumption; a close attendance on the deathbed of a beloved brother, when he ought to have been nursing himself in bed, gave it a blow which he felt for

months. Despairing love (that is to say, despairing of living to enjoy it, for the love was returned) added its hourly torment; and, meanwhile, the hostile critics came up, and roused an indignation in him, both against them and himself, which on so many accounts he could ill afford to endure.

(vol. II, p. 209)

Accurate in some broad matters, Hunt's account of Keats's torment and despair nevertheless obscures the presence of the vigorous young man who had walked through the Lake District and the Scottish Highlands in summer 1818. Keats the tough and ambitious writer who had swiftly outgrown Hunt's example as a poet has no place in Hunt's reminiscences. What we find instead is a constitutionally weak young man, whose sensitivity betrayed 'ill health as well as imagination' (II, p. 212) and whose sickness had caused him to break with Hunt:

> hopeless of recovering his health, under circumstances that made the feeling extremely bitter, an irritable morbidity appears to have driven his suspicions to excess ... Keats at one period of his intercourse with us suspected Shelley and myself of a wish to see him undervalued! Such are the tricks which constant infelicity can play with the most noble natures. For Shelley, let *Adonais* answer. For myself, let every word answer which I uttered about him, living and dead, and such as I now proceed to repeat. I might as well have been told, that I wished to see the flowers or the stars undervalued, or my own heart that loved him.
> But it was sickness, and passed away.
>
> (vol. II, pp. 202–3)

This passage manages to acquit Hunt and Shelley of any responsibility for Keats's suffering and his literary reputation, although there is I believe more to Hunt's treatment of Keats in the *Autobiography* than self-vindication. In the narrative of the *Autobiography*, the passage seems to fashion Keats in the image of Hunt's sickliness; or perhaps one should say that the *Autobiography* recreates Hunt after the prevailing idea of Keats's susceptible genius. In each case the relationship is defined as mutually reflective, a kind of 'doubling'. Moreover, in creating this mutual image of vulnerability Hunt had been influenced by the myth of 'poor Chatterton', the author of the 'Rowley Poems' who had committed suicide in 1770 at the age of 17.

The link with Chatterton offers one explanation for Hunt's reluctance as an autobiographer. The *Autobiography* recounts at embarrassing length the life of a sickly prodigy who should, by rights, have followed Chatterton and Keats to an early grave. Instead of writing a three-volume memoir in his old age, Hunt (deceased) should have left behind him a collection of papers to be published as *The Remains of Leigh Hunt*, prefaced with a portrait of the poet at 17, and a memoir of his brief, suffering existence. Hunt's problem was the early recognition of his *Juvenilia*, which he published at the age of 16, and, worse, his ability to survive and continue writing. His formidable powers of recovery were such that he endured 'all the diseases ... which the infant [hospitals] know' (I, p. 45), prolonging his childish existence into old age:

> He was a little bright creature, with a rather large head; but a delicate face, and a sweet voice, and there was a perfect charm in him. All he said was so free from effort and spontaneous and was said with such a captivating gaiety, that it was fascinating to hear him talk ... he had more the appearance, in all respects, of a damaged young man, than a well-preserved elderly one. There was an easy negligence in his manner, and even in his dress (his hair carelessly disposed, and his necker-chief loose and flowing, as I have seen artists paint their own portraits), which I could not separate from the idea of a romantic youth who had undergone some unique process of depreciation. It struck me as being not at all like the manner or appearance of a man who had advanced in life, by the usual road of years, cares, and experiences.[18]

Charles Dickens's caricature of Hunt as Harold Skimpole was published in *Bleak House* (1853), some three years after the *Autobiography* appeared. Skimpole embodies a deliberate gaiety of manner, a self-consciously 'easy negligence ... as I have seen artists paint their own portraits'. There is some resemblance between Skimpole and Hunt's portrait in the third volume of the *Autobiography*, but this may be coincidental. More telling, however, is Dickens's suggestion that Skimpole's 'perfect charm', his 'gaiety', was a form of defence but also a self-recommendation that is 'captivating' and 'fascinating'. The unworldliness that had contributed to Keats's destruction becomes, in Skimpole, a strong claim for attention: 'He said to the world, "Go your several ways in peace! Wear red coats, blue coats, lawn sleeves, put pens behind your ears, wear aprons; go after glory, holiness, commerce, trade, any object you prefer; only – let Harold Skimpole live!"' (p. 119). Such an attitude represents a kind of 'unwise passiveness', or, same thing, Keats's 'negative capability' dissociated from 'Achievement ... in Literature' and embodied as an 'easy negligence' which cultivates irresponsibility: 'he had no idea of time ... he had no idea of money ... [H]e never kept an appointment, never could transact any business, and never knew the value of anything! Well! So he had got on in life, and here he was!' (p. 119).

Skimpole exists through celebrating his own incapacity for life. He represents a parodic exaggeration of the romantic cult of vulnerable genius, closely akin to Hunt's self-presentation in the *Autobiography* as an abstract of sickliness, 'a damaged young man ... a romantic youth who had undergone some unique process of depreciation'. In bringing together romantic sentiment and some 'unique' (and therefore incalculable) process of 'depreciation', Harold Skimpole focused exactly the ironic presence of Hunt's *Autobiography* on its first publication. That 'involuntary production' (I, p. 1) comprised the history of one who had failed to die like Chatterton and Keats, Byron and Shelley, and had survived into an 'iron time' to be published alongside those volumes in which life expectancy was 'systematically and scientifically' calculated: Pocock's *Assurances upon Lives* and Farren's *Life Contingency Tables*. A sickly youth who endured against the odds tabulated on those mortal pages, in his *Autobiography* Hunt's literary life acquired the aura of romance which an early death would have denied him.

Notes

1. *Dublin University Magazine*, 36 (1850), 268.
2. 'A Catalogue of Books', pp. 4–7; in *The Autobiography of Leigh Hunt; with Reminiscences of Friends and Contemporaries*, 3 vols, (London: Smith and Elder, 1850) (hereafter, *Autobiography*).
3. 'A Catalogue of Books', p. 4.
4. 'A Catalogue of Books', pp. 6–8.
5. Elizabeth Barrett Browning, *Aurora Leigh*, II. 313, 315; see *Elizabeth Barrett Browning: Her Novel in Verse; Aurora Leigh and Other Poems* (London: Women's Press, 1978), p. 84.
6. John Kerrigan, 'Keats, Hopkins, and the History of Chance', in *Keats and History*, ed. Nicholas Roe (Cambridge: Cambridge University Press, 1995), pp. 280–308.
7. Matthew Arnold, 'Memorial Verses', ll. 42–52; *The Poems of Matthew Arnold*, ed. Kenneth Allott (London: Longmans, 1965), p. 228.
8. *Autobiography*, vol. I, p. vi. Subsequent references will be given in the text.
9. On Hunt's revisions, see in particular Timothy Webb, 'Correcting the Irritability of His Temper: The Evolution of Hunt's *Autobiography*', in *Romantic Revisions*, ed. K. Hanley and R. Brinkley (Cambridge: Cambridge University Press, 1992), pp. 268–90.
10. *The Autobiography of Leigh Hunt. A New Edition Revised by the Author* (London: Smith and Elder, 1867), p. xiv.
11. Vol. I, p. 296. I am grateful to Professor Webb for sharing this insight in a conversation about Leigh Hunt.
12. 'A Catalogue of Books', p. 5, quoting a review in the *Athenaeum*.
13. Vol. I, p. 297. Hunt misquotes 'Tintern Abbey', ll. 39–41.
14. See 'Expostulation and Reply', l. 24; and Keats's letter to George and Tom Keats, 27 (?) December 1817, *The Letters of John Keats, 1814–1821*, ed. Hyder Rollins, 2 vols (Cambridge, Mass.: Harvard University Press, 1958), vol. I, p. 193.
15. Edmund Burke, *A Philosophical Inquiry into the Origin of Our Ideas of the Sublime and Beautiful*, ed. A. Phillips (Oxford: Oxford University Press, 1990), p. 100.

16. A participant at the 'Mortal Pages, Literary Lives' conference at Leicester University, September 1994, pointed out that the portrait of Hunt aged 36 resembles George Richmond's 1850 portrait of Currer Bell.
17. *Shelley's Poetry and Prose*, ed. D. Reiman and S. Powers (New York and London: W.W. Norton & Co., 1977), pp. 390–1.
18. Charles Dickens, *Bleak House*, ed. N. Page (Harmondsworth: Penguin Books, 1971), pp. 118–19. Subsequent references will be given in the text.

CHAPTER SIX

Why Do We Remember Forwards and Not Backwards?

Philip Davis

Serial dullness?

'Nobody', said Leslie Stephen, 'ever wrote a dull autobiography.'[1]

But what about this, from Leslie Stephen's own memoir? Here is Stephen describing the courting of Julia, who eventually became his second wife:

> We returned to London, the whole question still in suspense. I went in as usual to sit with her one evening – I think the fifth of January [1878]. We talked the matter over once more and I rose to go. She was sitting in her arm-chair by the fireplace – I can see her now! – when suddenly she looked up and said, 'I will be your wife and will do my best to be a good wife to you'.
> All doubts vanished like a dream.[2]

Is not this dull? Not exceptionally dull, but decently dull, in a way that characterizes the writing of standard Victorian autobiography? A sense of living *time* has been flattened into the dimensions of continuous *story*. The sentences become like facts, and go on successively *past* what they describe. Everything that turned out after all not to happen is made a non-event, relegated to the status of a dream. It is as if the writer could not put too much inventive energy or new life into what seemed to him no more than a second version of that primary text of the past which was already invisibly marked and factually established elsewhere, in life itself. As Sartre puts it in *La Nausée*, such a narrative is in bad faith: written as though merely straight-forward, it is actually composed backwards from the hindsight of its ending.

Such foreclosed accounts are not so much a writing up of the past as a writing off of it. Their sheer serial flatness results from what John Stuart Mill in 'Thoughts on Poetry and its Varieties' called associations 'chiefly of the successive, not the synchronous kind'.[3] To register impressions successively as events is characteristic of those less naturally poetic minds which, like Mill's own, are distinguished by 'a love of science, of abstract truth, with a deficiency of taste and of fervour'.[4]

Mill is indebted here to Coleridge. In his 'Essay on the Principles of Method', Coleridge remarks that in the prosaic circumstantial accounts of ordinary people the shift from one thought to another is measured only by the temporal connective 'and', marking the next move in the mechanical succession of chronologically bound thought. With 'and then' or 'and there' or 'and so', the space between sentences exists only for the gathering of breath or as a matter of typography. There is no tacit thinking, no implicit poetic potential going on, to take the person from one point to the next. Coleridge says of such a narrator, 'He lives in Time, rather than Time lives in him.'[5]

Thus even when we move up from the ignorant reteller in everyday life to the intelligent prose-autobiographer, it is still the mark of a relatively low order of artistic thinking that successiveness should dominate form and that narrative should more or less follow the order in which the events took place. So, my fear is not that autobiography is not a distinct genre, as Paul de Man has suggested, but that increasingly throughout the nineteenth century it was becoming so. Its key form was an unredeemed chronological successiveness, prosaically denying true memory-thinking.

For Victorian autobiographies too often fail to deploy those real workings of memory on which they presume to base themselves. Time does not live in them. Compare for example with Leslie Stephen's account, Scrooge in Stave Two of Dickens's *A Christmas Carol*, looking at how his lonely young self had to try to comfort himself with visions from books:

> 'Why it's Ali Baba!' Scrooge exclaimed in ecstasy ... To hear Scrooge expending all the earnestness of his nature on such subjects, in a most extraordinary voice between laughing and crying; and to see his heightened and excited face, would have been a surprise to his business friends in the city, indeed ...
> Then with a rapidity of transition very foreign to his usual character, he said, in pity of his former self, 'Poor boy!' and cried again.
> 'I wish,' Scrooge muttered, putting his hand in his pocket, and looking about him, after drying his eyes with his cuff: 'but it's too late now.'
> 'What is the matter?' asked the Spirit.
> 'Nothing,' said Scrooge. 'Nothing.'[6]

A reader can spot here that very moment at which, for the protagonist, autobiography-thinking takes over from real memory-thinking. It is the point at which Scrooge loses his 'I wish' and says 'Nothing' or 'It's too late now' instead. 'Real remembering', says Doris Lessing in her own autobiography, 'is – if even for a flash, even a moment – being back in the experience itself. You remember pain with pain, love with love, one's real best self with one's best self.'[7] Unlike a common autobiography, *A Christmas Carol* is 'real remembering', being not only about the past but for whole moments imaginatively in it.

No writer ever makes the spaces between sentences; a writer makes the sentences. But left in between these sentences and phrases from *A Christmas Carol*, there is time itself: inner thinking and inner recollecting time, in the midst of external formulation, marked in the stutters and pauses Scrooge makes. 'What is the matter?' says the Spirit repeatedly, trying to draw out these implicit microseconds in which a thought cannot quite come to be, because its thinker does not sufficiently believe in himself or in his capacity to make it thinkable in him. 'There was a boy singing a Christmas Carol at my door last night', says Scrooge as though in chance association, and then goes on, his inner feelings forced into a scrupulous register of tenses: 'I should like to have given him something: that's all.'[8] 'That's all' is still spoken foreclosingly as if it was still 'Nothing, nothing'. But even when Scrooge snaps out of the memory of the past, he still thinks with a residual 'rapidity of transition' significantly far greater than has become customary with him in his settled self. There is still potential time in this writing, to make repentance itself present not as a merely vain and belated thing but as a desire to learn from the past and to change it, not in the past itself but in the future. This is not just that apology for memory which in autobiography falsely travels forwards, too late, in sequential sentences which only go back over what has already become the story of a settled past. It is memory reaching backwards before it works forward again to the thought of that boy last night.

In 1805 John Foster offered a 'fantastic idea'. In his essay 'On a Man's Writing Memoirs of Himself' Foster speaks of the idea

> of its being possible for a man to live back again to his infancy, through all the scenes of his life, and to give back from his mind and character, at each time and circumstance, as he repassed it, exactly what he took from it, when he was there before.[9]

Such repassing would be a double movement, going through the scene both with the feelings the person had at the time and with the feelings and consequences it left in him later. *A Christmas Carol* can perform that miracle, redeeming the time, but the *Mausoleum Book* cannot.

In a work of fiction, says Paul Auster in *The Invention of Solitude*, there always seems to be something behind the words on the page, intending meaning: an event is not just there because it happened. But in an account of a real life, in comparison with a novel, 'something is missing: the grandeur, the grasp of the general, the illusion of metaphysical truth'.[10]

In the face of such disappointment, there are, I think, two rival explanations, one generic, the other historical. On the one hand, we may claim that autobiography as a genre is inherently faulty, and that nineteenth-century prose autobiography, in what was increasingly the age of the novel, is all the more exposed as an unavoidable failure. On the other hand, we may argue that it is not prose autobiography as such which is a poor thing, but that, historically, it is unadorned secular human life itself, reflected truly if unwillingly in Victorian autobiography, which is in recurring danger of seeming poor and faulty. In what follows, I will start by largely rejecting the first account and then I will investigate the second.

Is the genre inherently faulty? To say that Victorian autobiography is too often not creative may seem like a tautology to those who think that 'creative' writing has to be fiction or poetry. But all writing is potentially creative and I shall argue, after Coleridge, that the smallest testing-ground for its creativeness is the space for mental movement that takes place in between clauses or sentences.

If the Victorian norm in autobiography consisted in dull factual histories retracing the linear career of a finished and responsible autobiographical self, it was formal successiveness, not autobiography, that was the mistake. In the face of so many straight-forward narratives, one finds oneself turning to the question that forms the title of an essay in the October 1887 issue of *Mind*, written by the Idealist philosopher F.H. Bradley: 'Why do we remember forwards and not backwards?' That is to say in this case: could there not have been more room within the form of nineteenth-century prose autobiography for mental, temporal and grammatical movements of mind *other* than that of sheer narrative progression?

Bradley had asked: by what seeming necessity is it that ordinarily we must remember forwards and not backwards? We remember chronologically, still facing forwards, answered Bradley, because in life we survive by anticipation, the future being the place where danger seems to come from. So likewise in memory, almost automatically, 'our thought fronts the same way and ... goes on forward to meet again past experiences face to face'.[11] We think of time as irreversible; it seems as if we cannot make it run backwards.

Yet Bradley suggests that remembering backwards is not a mental or biological impossibility.[12] Indeed, a sudden turn-round into backwards recall was definitely possible within the on-going movement of nineteenth-century autobiographical writing. I have space for just one major example of movement backwards rather than forwards in the act of recall – taken from the fragment concerning his London street childhood which Dickens later incorporated in adapted form in *David Copperfield*:

> For many years, when I came near to Robert Warrens' in the Strand, I crossed over to the opposite side of the way, to avoid a certain smell of the cement they put upon the blacking-corks, which reminded me of what I was once. It was a very long time before I liked to go up Chandos Street. My old way home by the Borough made me cry, after my eldest child could speak.[13]

By the end of this excerpt, that third sentence has turned round on itself, at the very word 'after': as if to say though my son comes after me, I existed before he did, and I still cry like a baby while my own baby has long since learnt to talk. It is as though Dickens can barely understand how the two – the child he was and the adult he is – can exist in the same sentence, alongside his own oblivious son too.

Dickens's account here is not the Victorian success story of secure, achieved adulthood; on the contrary, as Dickens himself puts it elsewhere in this autobiographical fragment:

> My whole nature was so penetrated with the grief and humiliation of such considerations, that even now, famous and caressed and happy, I often forget in my dreams that I have a dear wife and children; even that I am a man; and wander desolately back to that time of my life.[14]

This account is what Mill would call 'synchronous'. Like 'after' in our first passage, 'even now' marks the point of still vulnerable incredulity at his having a wife and children. It is these link words, so unlike Coleridge's 'and so', that indicate the real work of memory, turning both backwards and forwards, between past and present.

Little connectives in the middle of sentences may thus represent the sudden and momentary thought of a man making sense of things in the very midst of his life; then they pass and the sentence goes on to make its grown-up sense again. But those creative instants in the middle of successive life and thought are momentary glimpses of a missing or elusive centre, from which a person steadily weighs and sums what has happened to him in his whole life.

That centre of life-consciousness is a mental place traditionally related not to the middle of a life but to its deathbed close – as Mrs Oliphant fearfully describes at the death of her feckless son in her *Autobiography*:

> Did he find that he had thrown away his life in that last spasm and anguish when he called upon God – God alone? God, above the beginning and end of all things, only can know. He called upon

> God and they say our Lord Jesus, though I did not know that, –
> Did he know then for the moment suddenly what was coming? I
> cannot bear that he should have had even that little time of mortal
> distress – I would rather he had not known at all – but woken in
> God's arms and known no death –[15]

The young man had thrown away his life and now he was going to die. Mrs Oliphant did not want her son to know that, but to think instead that he was still living and still going to live – however much that made him as heedless as he had been in the ruinous past. Yet when her eldest child Maggie had died more than 25 years earlier, at the age of 11, the mother had been scared that even having got into heaven without knowing it, the child would stop short 'and say "Where is Mamma?"' – 'Did not the separation overwhelm her?'.[16] For better or for worse, that is to say, there is no room in life for the full awareness of a life. And likewise a prosaic sentence passes apparently unredeemingly: there is no permanent resting place in a sentence, no place wherein the meaning of the whole is visibly lodged.[17]

What is marvellous, therefore, is that prose sentences, through their very entrapped successiveness, may even thus represent, far better than does poetry with its own more autonomous sense of duration, the truth of life in time: namely, that knowing takes place without transcendence, only in the very midst of life's still passing. These are the near-silenced secrets of an ordinary successive life momentarily registered in the syntax.

There was thus, I submit, no inherent generic reason as to why Victorian prose autobiography, for all its formal commitment to linear successiveness, could not include within it the profounder movements of mind and memory. But given that Dickens abandoned his autobiography in order to write his autobiographical novel instead, and given that Mrs Oliphant wrote her memoir only intermittently and sadly in the midst of failures with her books and bereavements in her life, I must also conclude that autobiography did not seem even to these exceptional practitioners a primary form for creative writers.

Mill's *Autobiography*

But perhaps the reader will think my account still too dismissive of the claims of most Victorian autobiography. What if, turning round on my own argument for a moment, one took seriously an alternative view – that autobiography offered a representation of secularized human life that the Victorian novel merely fictionalized?

As a test case, I shall take an autobiography which more than any other in the nineteenth century is not just thoughtlessly, but philosophically, committed to that form of linear successiveness which I have criticized. I mean the *Autobiography* of John Stuart Mill. For Mill believed in successiveness – not, as we have seen, in the form of mindless retelling but as rational and logical consecutiveness in the quest for future human progress. The charge characteristically made against Mill's memoir is that it is the epitome of Victorian autobiographical dullness: both the book and the self depicted in it short-changing a full sense of what it is to be human. But I shall examine Mill's *Autobiography* with the help of two quite different Victorian critical witnesses: first, John Morley, writing in the book's defence, and then R.H. Hutton, for the opposition.

John Morley, writing in the *Fortnightly Review* of January 1874, rebuts those Rousseauist literati who judge Mill's life, lived and written, to be merely dull:

> who seem to think that a history of a careful man's opinions on grave and difficult subjects ought to have all the rapid movements and unexpected turns of a romance, and that a book without rapture and effusion and a great many capital letters must be joyless and disappointing. Those of us who dislike literary hysteria as much as we dislike that coarseness that mistakes itself for force, may be glad to follow the mental history of a man who knew how to move and grow without any of these reactions and leaps on the one hand, or any of that overdone realism on the other.[18]

Understand the genre, suggests Morley. For plausibly we are spoilt for reading autobiographies by having read too many novels. Perhaps the removal of ulterior significance, fictionally provided, might offer a more barely essential sense of a life, without succumbing to philistinism. Mill's is not, says Morley, 'a work of imagination or art', but 'the practical record of the formation of an eminent thinker's mental habits and the succession of his mental attitudes' (*NCE*, p. 142). John Stuart Mill modified Benthamite utilitarianism by a later appeal to the poetry and feelings of Wordsworth, but Morley's defence of the *Autobiography* reflects the still underlying history in Mill himself of Bentham's and James Mill's opposition of practical utility to Romantic literary sentimentalism.

To Morley, Mill offers a model of what constitutes mature adulthood in the middle of the nineteenth century. It is the sort of progress to adulthood that Dickens never felt secure of, the want of which perhaps led him to abandon the idea of writing autobiography if it involved a position of superiority in relation to his past. But what Mill overcame in order to become a balanced and mature man, says Morley, was not only his own reaction against the philosophy of his father. He also conquered in his very self, as a microcosmic model, the whole tendency of dogmatic reactiveness between schools of thought, dividing rival truths between them down the ages: 'one tending to give to that truth too large, and the other to give it too small, a place: and the history of opinion is generally an oscillation between these extremes'.[19] 'For our own part', says Mill, writing of Bentham, 'we have a large tolerance for one-eyed men': 'If they saw more, they probably would not see so keenly, nor so eagerly pursue one course of inquiry.' But then he adds a second thought: 'whether these new thoughts drive out others as good, or are peacefully superadded to them, depends on whether these half-thinkers are or are not followed in the same track by complete thinkers' ('On Bentham', p. 94). For all his shrewd tolerance, that is what Mill is offering himself as aiming at being – a complete thinker, able to include what Bentham's merits deserve, while also non-reactively incorporating other considerations that superadd more. Mill's mature project was to find a synthesizing syntax by which he could be more than one person with one half-truth standing in opposition to another person with another fraction of truth.

Assimilation, addition, acquisition and cultivation; combination, incorporation, modification and readjustment: these are Mill's key words. Morley praises in Mill that balanced openness of mind which 'adds and assimilates new elements from new quarters, without disturbing the organic structure of the whole' and thereby makes a whole and stable man (*NCE*, p. 140). Victorian liberalism meant that Mill offered in the practical sphere of thinking what Arnold provided equivalently in the aesthetic: the disinterested incorporation of thoughts which would be inconvenient for one-track minds; an insistence on the exercise of mature critical judgement; the cultivation of a powerful Goethe-like many-sidedness.

The self-creation of this balanced rather than merely reactive man is, Morley argues, the sober and austere point of the *Autobiography* – a point missed by those sensationalist critics who prefer to concentrate instead on Mill's more dramatic youthful breakdown:

> The union of boundless patience with unshaken hope was one of Mr. Mill's most conspicuous distinctions. There are two crises in the history of grave and sensitive natures. One on the threshold of manhood, when the youth defines his purpose, his creed, his aspirations; the other towards the later part of middle life, when circumstance has strained his purpose, and tested his creed, and given to his aspirations a cold and practical measure. The second crisis, though less stirring, less vivid, less coloured to the imagination, is the weightier probation of the two, for it is final and decisive ... It

> is the turn which a man takes about the age of five-and-forty, that parts him off among the sheep on the right hand or the poor goats on the left ...
>
> Mr. Mill did not escape the second crisis, any more than he had escaped the first, though he dismisses it in a far more summary manner.
>
> (NCE, p. 155)

What counts is the potential crisis at 45, not 20. At 45, even a man as adaptable as Mill has more or less to settle for having become what he now is. He is, or should be, no longer fuelled by fancied strengths and vague aspirations. Not yet spent, even while also not complete, the middle-aged man is none the less unable to deceive himself that time and change are, at least for him, limitless. It was at this stage of life, says Morley, that Mill

> saw what all ardent lovers of improvement are condemned to see, that their hopes have outstripped the rate of progress; that fulfilment of social aspiration is tardy and very slow of foot; and that the leaders of human thought are never permitted to enter into the Promised Land whither they are conducting others.
>
> (NCE, p. 156)

A sober reality-test faces Mill when, a believer in human improvement, he finds the limitations to further impending improvement, both in his developed self and in the society of his lifetime, brought home to him. Here indeed is what Morley means by the union of boundless patience with unshaken hope in Mill: a large time-scale beyond the measure of one life of effort, whose perspective is exercised none the less within that one life, with due regard there to what is adult not childish, and politically realistic rather than messianically religious or romantically literary.

For Morley therefore, autobiography is not about beginnings but about this second half of a life. It is about Yeats's 'finished man', at what I shall call the macrolevel of life – where what were originally tiny intimations and opportunities become strengthened into characteristic habits and achieved routines or are lost for ever; where possibilities, if they do not become facts, can be held properly only with such reasonably balanced hope as is emphatically not fantasy.

Any study of Victorian autobiography must take note of Morley's argument as to the value of Mill's account of life, albeit as an essentially unliterary way. There *is* a less refined language of practical meaning which adults have to carry about with them. For by the macrolevel in this context, I refer to that overall meaning into which a person's life has shaken down.

And yet if one had to put one's finger on the point at which the Newmanite literary critic, R.H. Hutton, parts company with Mill, perhaps this passage marks it:

> I found the fabric of my old and taught opinions giving way in many fresh places, and I never allowed it to fall to pieces, but was incessantly occupied in weaving it anew. I never, in the course of my transition, was content to remain, for ever so short a time, confused and unsettled. When I had taken in any new idea, I could not rest till I had adjusted its relation to my old opinions, and ascertained exactly how far its effect ought to extend in modifying or superseding them.[20]

Hutton hated the way that Mill got over his breakdown, making it back over into a mere 'transition'.

When in the autumn of 1826 Mill had asked himself his major life-question – 'Suppose that all your objects in life were realized; that all the changes in institutions and opinions which you are looking forward to, could be completely effected at this instant: would this be a great joy and happiness to you?' (*Autobiography*, p. 139) – and when from somewhere deep within himself he found himself involuntarily obliged to answer 'No', then it seemed even to Mill that this was the secular equivalent of the great religious problem of salvation or damnation: 'the state, I should think, in which converts to Methodism usually are, when smitten by their first "conviction of sin"' (p. 137). But so far as Hutton could see, there was no radical revolution, no equivalent to religious conversion for a secularizer such as John Stuart Mill, even when he recognized the limitations of social and political reform: 'a profound sense of the inadequacy of ordinary human success to the cravings of the human spirit was never followed by a less radical moral change'.[21] The original system was patched up again because the person had to be: 'I never allowed it to fall to pieces ... I could not rest till I had adjusted.' For the sake of mental survival and continuance, the principles Mill inherited from his father and from Bentham had to be modified not rejected. Thereafter Mill went forwards again in the cause of improvement and future progress. For Mill was a man who could not believe he was alive unless he was always seeking – albeit prudently and maturely – to go forward.

Bentham had never asked himself whether 'some more important principle, which he did not perceive, supersedes [his] considerations, and turns the scale' ('On Bentham', p. 93); Bentham had never been aware of the subtler danger 'not so much of embracing falsehood for truth, as of mistaking part of the truth for the whole' ('On Coleridge', p. 122). Mill corrected Bentham's errors in himself, in the mind his own father had created in the image of Bentham's. Yet to Hutton that secular liberal consciousness of possible deficiency was not of itself sufficient to make up for the originally damning deficiency itself. Mill's, says Hutton, was 'quite the largest and most catholic intellect that was ever well kept within the limits of a somewhat narrow system, of which, however, he knew well how to stretch the bounds ... He enlarged Utilitarianism in this sense till it was hardly recognisable as Utilitarianism'.[22]

Thus Mill grafted on to the idea of happiness as the supreme end of human being, the strategic thought 'that this end was only to be attained by not making it the direct end' (*Autobiography*, p. 145). Leslie Stephen called this the making of 'a second self' created so as not to know what the first was really up to.[23] Yet for Hutton, it was evidence that such an alleged end as happiness was not properly primary, was not truly an end for us, if happiness was something that human beings could not directly aim for but could only come at by the way. To Hutton, Mill's was a patched-up situation, a compromised adulthood, a second life given only by the addition of an artificial way round the problem. Mill added Wordsworth on to himself and cultivated what Wordsworth stood for. But, as the Kierkegaard of *The Sickness Unto Death* might have argued, if only Mill had broken down more completely and more long-lastingly: it might take just such a breakdown to bring a halt to the tyranny of temporal succession.

Mill was close to that breakdown in 1826. The great future End to which the whole of his life as a social reformer was dedicated had itself come to an end before ever it had come to be – leaving his life still to carry on:

> During this time I was not incapable of my usual occupations. I went on with them mechanically, by the mere force of habit. I had been so drilled in a certain sort of mental exercise, that I could still carry it on when all the spirit had gone out of it.
> (*Autobiography*, p. 143)

Successiveness no longer meant progress; it only meant carrying on. That final sentence is not really going forward: it is governed by 'so drilled', through 'that still', until and despite 'all gone'. No wonder the end of the sentence is so disturbing, for going on so far beyond the inner feeling that should animate it.

The equivocal word 'end' dominates the crisis: 'All my happiness was to have been found in the continual pursuit of this end. The end had ceased to charm, and how could there ever again be any interest in the means?' (*Autobiography*, p. 139); 'My education, which was wholly [my father's] work had been conducted without any regard to the possibility of its ending in this result' (ibid.). The end had ended. The time is out of joint. The sentences are blocked, self-entangled, stranded disinheritedly in a present never foreseen in the plans of the past. They are still the sentences of a logician but a logician in a situation which brings the very shape of his thinking close to that of Thomas Hardy, whose intelligence likewise only increased his sense of deadlock. The loss of rational and progressivist straightforwardness had such an effect on Mill that it haunts his writing long afterwards, in memory, making parts of that fifth chapter of the *Autobiography* ironically enough Mill's finest work.

But for Mill as a logician, sentences should always be capable, like thoughts, of following each other logically and adding up accordingly:

> We say of a fact or statement, that it is proved, when we believe its truth by reason of some other fact or statement from which it is said to follow. Most of the propositions ... which we believe, are not believed on their own evidence, but on the ground of something previously assented to, from which they are said to be inferred.[24]

All persuasive writing, said Mill, 'does make one point at a time' ('On Bentham', p. 114). He positively liked the succession of separate single sentences. From Bentham himself Mill learnt the method of 'treating wholes by separating them into their parts ... [since] the human mind is not capable of embracing a complex whole, until it has surveyed and catalogued the parts of which that whole is made up' ('On Bentham', pp. 83–4). Sentences as separated parts of a complex whole allow, first, division and then, connection. In most present-day controversies, said Mill, one observer sees one thing, a second sees another, and often both sides are in the right in what they affirm and both sides are wrong in what they deny. In contrast, Mill would put the views of two or more people into two or more sentences, like atoms or elements, each containing one part of the wider truth, each momentarily finding free space in which to defend its own right and truth. Then he would seek to combine the preceding two, like 'mutually checking powers in a political constitution', within a third sentence which virtually created for him, in his own mental chemistry, a new combination of mental person whom he could then become ('On Coleridge', p. 122).

Emphatically therefore, Mill did not want thought-sequences that broke down on him, turned round on themselves or had no positive end. No writer was going to be more sensitive than Mill to a condition in which logical successiveness became mentally impossible, when thoughts and sentences no longer seemed to follow from each other or lead anywhere. Yet I repeat: some of the greatest sentences not only in Mill's own *Autobiography* but in nineteenth-century autobiographical writing as a whole occur only when it seemed as if Mill's life itself simply could not go on. Consider two representative passages: 'I sought no comfort by speaking to others of what I felt. If I had loved any one sufficiently to make confiding my griefs a necessity, I should not have been in the condition I was' (*Autobiography*, p. 139) and

> All those to whom I looked up, were of opinion that the pleasure of sympathy with human beings, and the feelings which made the good of others, and especially of mankind on a large scale, the object of existence, were the greatest and surest sources of happiness. Of the truth of this I was convinced, but to know that a feeling would make me happy if I had it, did not give me the feeling.
>
> (*Autobiography*, p. 143)

The sentences are no longer straightforward; trapped, they turn round upon themselves. The man who considered himself above all a thinker now finds that he cannot get his thoughts out of or above the situation they bear upon: 'I frequently asked myself, if I could, or if I was bound to go on living, when life must be passed in this manner' (p. 145). The big thought is no longer an end but is trapped in the *midst* of the sentence, subsumed and succeeded by the later clausal realization that life still '*must* be passed in this manner'. For how long? He can only answer arbitrarily not philosophically, in order to draw some line, make some end in a world where meaningful ends are gone: 'I generally answered to myself, that I did not think I could possibly bear it beyond a year' (ibid.). The situation still continues in time, even as his life and his thinking go on, unwillingly, locked within it.

What Hutton testifies to is this: that these disturbed sentences are the greatest things in the *Autobiography* because they were the greatest moments in Mill's life. And yet Mill did not value them, he wanted only to get over them. From Hutton's point of view 1826 was a lost moment. It only resulted in the compromised adult moderation that Morley admired. The sentences that follow chapter 5 merely return to the syntax of what Morley calls 'the succession of mental attitudes' (NCE, p. 142).

Thus despite Morley's admirable defence, I take my conclusion from Hutton. Namely: the way that Mill got over his early mental crisis, and the way that this is reflected in the very syntax of his *Autobiography*, is an extreme but still symptomatic marker for Victorian autobiography as a whole. For on the whole Victorian autobiography was determined to make life, one way or another, all too straightforward, practical and (implicitly or explicitly) utilitarian in terms of the story of sheer outcomes. It is as though conventional Victorian autobiography offered a false model of both existence and adulthood, resulting from too exclusive a concentration on what could be made explicit and on those practically realizable qualities of character and adulthood which could make it so. There were no great conversions, no great movements to change the form of the life or its memoir. Indeed, those Victorian autobiographies which best succeed do so, like chapter 5 of Mill's memoir, because of the failure and trouble of the life they describe. For in failure and trouble the narratives lose confidence and do not simply keep going to a sense of a securing end. It is only in its breakdowns and its failures – and here I have room only to cite the flawed and vulnerable memoirs of Mrs Oliphant and of John Ruskin – that Victorian autobiography ironically succeeds.

Newman and Mill: ancient and modern

In Mill's world-view, after the recovery from 1826, a man could work on his very self as it were outside-in. A man's character, says Mill, 'is formed by his circumstances' but adds, in the second place, 'his own desire to mould it in a particular way is one of those circumstances'.[25] Logical theory, re-educating the mind through the steps of logically successive sentences, might show a person *ab extra* what personal practice and experience will only waste time in revealing more slowly if at all.

But one Victorian autobiographer above all resists that view of the workings of being, the man whom R.H. Hutton implicitly places in contrast to J.S. Mill – John Henry Newman. For when Newman was in the very midst of what, viewed with hindsight or from outside, was his predictable conversion to Rome, he found himself beset by something very like the Millite world:

> I had a great dislike of paper logic. For myself it was not logic that carried me on; as well might one say that the quicksilver in the barometer changes the weather. It is the concrete being that reasons; pass a number of years, and I find my mind in a new place; how? the whole man moves; paper logic is but the record of it. All the logic in the world would not have made me move faster towards Rome than I did; as well might you say that I have arrived at the end of my journey, because I see the village church before me, as venture to assert that the miles, over which my soul had to pass before it got to Rome, could be annihilated, even though I had had some far clearer view than I then had, that Rome was my ultimate destination. Great acts take time. At least this is what I felt in my own case; and therefore to come to me with methods of logic had in it the nature of a provocation and, though I do not think I ever showed it, made me somewhat indifferent how I met them, and perhaps led me, as means of relieving my impatience, to be mysterious or irrelevant, or to give in because I could not reply.[26]

What this speaks of, in opposition to paper logic, is emphatically autobiographical thinking: thinking that remains internal to the route that its thinker feels himself blindly or even confusedly following; thinking which, immersed in the midst of a real and particular dilemma, has to take its time only from that person's own sense of where he is in his life. It is to no purpose what people say from outside; it makes no difference how far they think they can predict for you ahead; it matters not if you cannot argue back. Over one who can take 'no external survey of himself, the minute intellect of inferior men has its moment of triumph' – for inferior men it is who excel in a 'mere short-sighted perspicacity'.[27] Autobiographical thinking is that which results when, at bottom involuntarily, a person cannot solve his problems except by being and remaining that person. And that *is* the definition of a person, as 'concrete', albeit a definition quite different from Mill's.

It was Newman who understood even in his own autobiography how the writing of conventional autobiography too often became a travesty of a real life. 'A death-bed', says Newman, thinking of the long story of his defection from Anglicanism, 'has scarcely a history; it is a tedious decline, with seasons of rallying and seasons of falling back.' There is no purpose or interest, he says, in spinning out stories in successive detail when 'the end is foreseen, or what is called a matter of time' (*Apologia*, p. 137). For Newman scorns the sort of dead autobiography in which time and its linear events laboriously spell out life-changes and life-movements only after they are already essentially over. When (what turned out to be) his journey to Rome was most deeply in process, Newman could not say, or later recall, where he really was:

> For who can know himself, and the multitude of subtle influences which act upon him? and who can recollect, at the distance of twenty-five years, all that he once knew about his thoughts and deeds, and that, during a portion of his life, when even at the time his observation, whether of himself or of the external world, was less than before or after, by very reason of the perplexity and dismay which weighed upon him, – when, though it would be most unthankful to seem to imply that he had not all-sufficient light amid his darkness, yet a darkness it emphatically was?
>
> (*Apologia*, p. 90)

For Newman there is in real living something finer than explicit accounts in gross can register. And yet the man with perhaps the age's strongest sense of deep personhood did not write the great personal autobiography of the Victorian period. For even the *Apologia* seems reduced by the age's own restricted sense of what, in its temporal explicitness, autobiography could be. It is rather Newman's *University Sermons*, more even than his *Apologia*, that take as their very subject those 'minute circumstances together, which the mind is quite unable to count up and methodize in argument', 'such impressions [as] manner, voice, accent, words uttered, silence instead of words, and all the many subtle symptoms which are felt by the mind' (*University Sermons*, p. 274). It is in these sermons that Newman most shows a faith in what I call the microreality of what is implicit, latent and anterior in being, in preference to the maturely explicit. The sheer recalling language of the sermons, bare of supporting narrative in time, creates, as the *Apologia* largely does not, an imaginative memory of what is too microscopic in our own internal processes of mind for the eye of ordinary life to see or review it. Thus: 'All men have a reason, but not all men can give a reason'; or: 'It is no proof that persons are not possessed, because they are not conscious of, an idea' (pp. 259, 321). The *Apologia* itself is less the story of that deep unspeakable inner life than a defence of such a life against loud social pressures. It is Newman's *secondary* account of himself.

Newman's primary thinking does not have to do with an external clarity of overview, but with staying loyal to the deep dim view from within and not coming out of internal crisis prematurely before it is really worked through.

In contrast, Mill incorporated in himself what Newman would not allow spectators of his life to adopt for him: the view from outside his own life, the external survey. Mill never wanted to forsake that strong sense of intellectual principle which enabled him to see as from above the primary truths hidden and distorted within people's experience of themselves on the ground. Utilitarianism did not rest upon secondary principles or means, but rationally distinguished the primary overarching need to promote human happiness. To Mill the unthinkingly personal was a blind privileging of what was secondary in place of what was rationally primary.

Even thus, then, Mill's intellectual survey from a height was, in the words of R.H. Hutton: 'for those who were able to look down, not for those who felt themselves looked down upon'.[28]

But Newman was for those who felt themselves looked down upon. For he writes of a self which is very much aware of being a creature, living inside a thing called human life, without being able to see it, like God, from above:

> as well might you say that I have arrived at the end of my journey, because I see the village church before me, as venture to assert that the miles, over which my soul had to pass before it got to Rome, could be annihilated, even though I had had some far clearer view than I then had, that Rome was my ultimate destination.
> (*Apologia*, p. 156)

This is a struggling creature that follows some unclear line it cannot get out of or above, while at the same time knowing there *is* some view from above, a dimension unattainable by him, from which the truth of his position can always be gauged. The line is not logically successive, nor does the journey go evenly on in tick-tock narrative: 'It is the concrete being that reasons; pass a number of years, and I find my mind in a new place; how? the whole man moves; paper logic is but the record of it.' That last sentence is sequential, but look at the sudden jumps made, the spaces left behind in the speed of its passionate sense of experience. This is not a sentence of paper logic, like one of Mill's syllogisms: the man finds his mind in a new place as if it had a life of its own which is also his. Nor does the sentence work from part to part, as Mill suggested, 'treating wholes by separating them into their parts', bring[ing] some things into contact which were separate, or separat[ing] others which were in contact'. With Newman this sentence is full of parts which are themselves whole small sentences grammatically unsubordinated and yet felt as incomplete when separate. You are in one place one year, in a different place another year, and the whole gradual process in between is missing, mysteriously implicit, only surfacing suddenly as an expression of the long-gestating whole: 'the whole man moves', 'Great acts take time'.

At such moments of personal conclusiveness there are no explicit connectives between sentences. For the words and the sentences could not be found by argument, though they will have reason implicit in them. These sentences need not have existed: they are only there because a few minutes of writing found behind them years of living. They come not out of the page, they come from him, this man, and the tacit links emerge out of an underlying acquiescence in the risk of accepting what is given. What lies behind the authoritatively self-sustaining syntax of Newman's 'the whole man moves' in the *Apologia* is that passionate statement of everyman's autobiography in Newman's *Essay in Aid of a Grammar of Assent*:

> I am what I am, or I am nothing. I cannot think, reflect, or judge about my being, without starting from the very point which I aim at concluding. My ideas are all assumptions, and I am for ever moving in a circle.
> I cannot avoid being sufficient for myself, for I cannot make myself anything else, and to change me is to destroy me. If I do not use myself, I have no other self to use.[29]

In contrast to Mill's modern progressivism, this is a very ancient and rooted sense of self. Like the sentences it most passionately utters, one cannot tell where it comes from. But it is not a Rousseauist self, defiant, self-willed, free: 'I cannot make myself ...'. It is limited and involuntary. 'I am what I am, or I am nothing' says the creature, and then goes even further back: 'I cannot avoid being sufficient for myself ...'. This self has something behind it, something given.

In *The Idea of a University*, Newman speaks of a writer's style as a deep 'corresponding language' following him as inevitably as his shadow, 'the faithful expression' of his intense personality and 'all that is proper to him'.[30] But R.H. Hutton says in contrast of Mill's writings:

> What we miss in Mr J.S. Mill are personal characteristics beneath and beyond the permanent characteristics of his rational disquisition. There is a monotony in the calm, evenly flowing, impartial, didactic pertinacity of disquisition, which is almost appalling ... Doubtless this is one of the causes of Mr Mill's great doctrinal success. His books diffuse a fine all-penetrating intellectual atmosphere, more even than a body of individual conviction, and the less closely they are associated with his name and personality, the more do they seem to partake of the impersonal intelligence of the age, and the more readily do they pass into the very essence of what is called the Time-Spirit, and win their way without the necessity for a battle and a conquest ... Hardly anywhere will you stop and say, 'There is the very man'.[31]

Where is Mill's equivalent of the sudden but long-won life-utterance 'the whole man moves', 'Great acts take time'?

Unlike Newman, John Stuart Mill could find in self-limitation no message save, in the absence of progress, the necessity for further effort of the mind in the formation of its own character. For Mill's whole philosophy is a defence of the legitimacy of human revising and self-remaking. Art is our nature, and our nature is not to accept but amend things, the making of a second nature being just as natural to us as any conservative acceptance of our first:

> Art has no independent powers of its own: Art is but the employment of the powers of Nature for an end. Phenomena produced by human agency, no less than those which as far as we are concerned are spontaneous, depend on the properties of elementary forces, or of the elementary substances and their compounds. The united powers of the whole human race could not create a new property of matter in general, or of any one of its species. We can only take advantage for our purposes of the properties which we find. A ship floats by the same laws of specific gravity and equilibrium, as a tree uprooted by the wind and blown into the water. The corn which men raise for food, grows and produces its grain by the same laws of vegetation by which the wild rose and the mountain strawberry bring forth their flowers and fruit ... In these and other artificial operations the office of man is, as has been often remarked, a very limited one; it consists in moving things into certain places. We move objects, and by doing this, bring some things into contact which were separate, or separate others which were in contact: and by this simple change of place, natural forces previously dormant are called into action, and produce the desired effect.[32]

'Unpoetical natures are precisely those which require poetic cultivation' (*Autobiography*, p. 153), and Mill needed to graft on Wordsworth, just as surely as he felt that on the other hand the born poet Tennyson needed 'to cultivate, and with no half devotion, philosophy as well as poetry'.[33] To change places; to combine half-thoughts into whole ones; to convert one's limitations into the thought of what was needed to take one beyond them; to create what might be called artificial second natures, new amalgams or grafts; to 'bring some things into contact which were separate, or separate others which were in contact': all this was the work of culture and cultivation in the mind as surely as in the fields. Mill's mind was committed to moving things, and the thoughts of things, into new places and into new relations. He used a knowledge of the laws of necessity precisely in order to create freedom for manoeuvre: 'We can only take advantage for our purposes of the properties which we find.' If you knew that a human might well do x under y circumstances, then you could either re-create or avoid those circumstances and so by a species of inversion convert the fixed physical laws into flexible social tools. That was the limit to Mill's sense of the discovery of what was new. His idea of personhood was essentially social, political and philosophic, as of a man seeking to hold the world itself in his mind, re-creating and amending there the world's various combinations of possibility down the ages.

Between Mill and Newman what is at stake therefore is not only a basic disagreement between what is or makes a person. Between the two the whole order of things, the sheer direction of thinking, is utterly different:

> In the knowledge of scientific truth, men go on from step to step, at every step advancing to the knowledge of a new Truth; which new Truth includes all that was true in previous knowledge, while it adds to it something more ...
> But in Revealed Truth the case is necessarily different ... There the Revelation contains all the Truth; and to this Truth, succeeding thoughts of men cannot add, though they may develop and methodize it.[34]

That is to say: Are we to remember forwards or backwards?

In Science earlier views, so far as they are true, are summed up in the latest discovery, and in that forward-moving sense Mill is a secular man of science.

In Religion, later views are true precisely in so far as they derive from and bring back to life the original revelation. That last is the essence of Newman's great *Essay*, not on progress as Mill would have it, but on *Development*: where a later developed system of doctrine is no more than the explicit expansion of a few words by the fishermen of Galilee, 'being nothing else than what that very idea meant from the first'.[35] For Newman, every way forward into the world was also simultaneously a way back into the story of its creation.

Conclusion

Emphatically, the very greatest ancient autobiographies offer a much bigger, more widely intervolved sense of a life than do their nineteenth-century equivalents. By the greatest of turn-rounds, Augustine's *Confessions* and Dante's *La Vita Nuova* both use autobiographical accounts precisely to uncover what in them it was that finally transcended the autobiographical self. There is, I submit, nothing like this in the Victorian age.

Indeed, in 1838 Pusey, Newman's fellow-leader of the Oxford Movement, said in the introduction to his translation of Augustine's *Confessions* that a reading of Augustine would be useful to 'people now-a-days' who 'think they understand'. In this scientific age, by the sheer accumulation of facts, argues Pusey, we only hide from ourselves 'our ignorance of principles': 'each accession of knowledge discovering to us not only something new, which we may know, but something also which we cannot know' (p. xxiii).

It was for Augustine the very questions and contradictions which beset a man, in his sense of the unknown, that serve to remind him that he himself is indeed secondary and back to front – that somewhere else, somewhere further back and more primary, lie the answers. For his *Confessions* describe a creature who experiences himself as coming first in the world and yet, even within that sense of his own primary existence, begins to intuit that the order of experience is not the order of ontology. He must turn round and recall that, after all, he comes second to that which created him and his kind in the first place. For Augustine, as for all neo-platonists, thinking is a reaching backwards against the grain, against the ever ongoing movement of time on earth. But Pusey believed that this more ancient work of memory was becoming increasingly lost.

To conclude this present argument then, I can only suggest that the reader should go to the deepest autobiographical account of what it was like for a nineteenth-century man to feel himself torn between the two directions of being I have described, forwards with the moderns or back with the ancients. 'Are God and Nature then at strife?' That is to say, the next step would be to return to the Tennyson of *In Memoriam*:

> We ranging down this lower track,
>   The path we came by, thorn and flower,
>   Is shadow'd by the growing hour,
> Lest life should fail in looking back.
>
> So be it: there no shade can last
>   In that deep dawn behind the tomb,
>   But clear from marge to marge shall bloom
> The eternal landscape of the past.
>
> (XLVI)

Notes

1. Leslie Stephen, *Hours in a Library*, 3 vols (London: Smith, Elder & Co., 1892), vol. III, p. 237.
2. *Sir Leslie Stephen's Mausoleum Book*, ed. Alan Bell (Oxford: Clarendon Press, 1977), p. 57.
3. *The Collected Works of John Stuart Mill*, vol. I, ed. J.M. Robson and J. Stillinger (Toronto: University of Toronto Press and Routledge & Kegan Paul, 1971), p. 357.
4. J.S. Mill, *A System of Logic* (1843), ed. J.M. Robson (Toronto: University of Toronto Press and Routledge & Kegan Paul, 1973); vol. VIII of *Collected Works of John Stuart Mill*, pp. 857–8. *A System of Logic* occupies vol. VII (books I–III) and vol. VIII (books IV–VI) of the *Collected Works*, the two volumes numbered successively, pages 1–638, 639–1251.
5. S.T. Coleridge, *The Friend*, ed. Barbara Rooke, 2 vols (Princeton and London: Princeton University Press and Routledge & Kegan Paul, 1969), vol. I, p. 450; vol. IV of *The Collected Works of Samuel Taylor Coleridge*, Bollingen Series, no. 75.
6. Charles Dickens, *A Christmas Carol*, ed. Michael Slater (Harmondsworth, Penguin Books, 1985), pp. 72–3.
7. Doris Lessing, *Under My Skin* (London: HarperCollins, 1994), p. 218.
8. *A Christmas Carol*, p. 73.
9. John Foster, *Essays in a Series of Letters* (London: Holdsworth and Ball, 1865), pp. 22–3.
10. Paul Auster, *The Invention of Solitude* (London: Faber and Faber, 1988), p. 147.
11. F.H. Bradley, *Collected Essays* (Oxford: Clarendon Press, 1969), pp. 242–3.
12. Contrast what Martin Amis does with memory in his novel *Time's Arrow* (London: Cape, 1991). Although time runs from death to life in this narrative of a concentration camp doctor, it is not *remembering* backwards, for there is in the protagonist no repentant consciousness.
13. John Forster, *Life of Dickens* (1872–74), ed. A.J. Hoppé, 2 vols (London: Dent, 1969), vol. I, p. 33.
14. Ibid., p. 23.
15. *The Autobiography of Margaret Oliphant* (1899), ed. Elisabeth Jay (Oxford: Oxford University Press, 1990), p. 47.
16. Ibid., p. 7.
17. Speaking of transience, Augustine says that with the things of this world, the parts make up the whole only as they succeed each other linearly. So it is even with our sentences: a sentence is not complete as a whole until each word has given way to make room for the next: 'This again is not perfected unless one word pass away when it hath sounded its part, that another may succeed ... In these things is no place of repose; they abide not, they flee' (*Confessions*, trans. E. Pusey (1838; London: Dent, 1907), book IV, pp. 60–1). This thought about writing was taken up in the later nineteenth century by Idealist philosophers such as T.H. Green and F.H. Bradley.
18. John Morley, *Nineteenth Century Essays*, ed. Peter Stansky (Chicago: Chicago University Press, 1970), p. 142 (hereafter, *NCE*).
19. J.S. Mill, *Essays on Ethics, Religion and Society*, ed. J.M. Robson (To-

ronto: University of Toronto Press and Routledge & Kegan Paul, 1969); vol. X of *Collected Works*, p. 124 ('On Coleridge', 1840). Hereafter cited as 'On Bentham' (1838) or 'On Coleridge', as appropriate.
20. J.S. Mill, *Autobiography* (1873), in *Autobiography and Literary Essays*, ed. J.H. Robson and J. Stillinger (Toronto: University of Toronto Press and Routledge & Kegan Paul, 1971); vol. I of *Collected Works*, p. 163. Hereafter cited as *Autobiography*.
21. R.H. Hutton, *Contemporary Thought and Thinkers*, 2 vols (London: Macmillan, 1894), vol. I, p. 179.
22. *A Victorian Spectator: Uncollected Writings of R.H. Hutton*, ed. R.H. Tener and M. Woodfield (Bristol: Bristol Press, 1989), p. 206.
23. *Hours in a Library*, vol. III, p. 464.
24. *A System of Logic*, p. 158; book II, ch. 1, para. 2.
25. *A System of Logic*, p. 840.
26. J.H. Newman, *Apologia Pro Vita Sua, Being a History of His Religious Opinions*, (1864), ed. M.J. Svaglic (Oxford: Clarendon Press, 1967), pp. 155–6 (hereafter, *Apologia*).
27. J.H. Newman, *University Sermons* (1826–43; reprint of 1871 edition, London: SPCK, 1970), pp. 83–4.
28. *Spectator*, 7 December 1895, p. 815.
29. J.H. Newman, *Essay in Aid of a Grammar of Assent* (London: Longman, 1870), p. 347.
30. J.H. Newman, *The Idea of a University* (1852; London: Longman, 1912), p. 276 ('University Subjects', II, 3).
31. *A Victorian Spectator*, p. 204.
32. 'Nature' (1874), *Collected Works of John Stuart Mill*, vol. X, ed. J.M. Robson, p. 375.
33. See *Collected Works*, vol. I, p. 417.
34. William Whewell, *Elements of Morality Including Polity* (London: John W. Parker & Son, 1845), p. 593.
35. J.H. Newman, *Essay on the Development of Christian Doctrine* (London: James Toovey, 1845), pp. 36–7. In Mill, in contrast, 'we can see that the way in which the forward-looking concept of deterrence swallows up the backward-looking concept of guilt foreshadows the way in which the forward-looking concept of utility swallows up the backward-looking concept of justice' (Alan Ryan, *The Philosophy of John Stuart Mill* (London: Macmillan, 1970), p. 130).

CHAPTER SEVEN

Autobiography and the Illative Sense

William Myers

Ludwig Wittgenstein begins *Philosophical Investigations* with the description in Augustine's *Confessions* of a child learning to speak: 'thinking primarily of nouns like "table", "chair", "bread", and of people's names', Wittgenstein tells us, Augustine does indeed 'describe a system of communication', but 'not for the whole of what [he was] claiming to describe', only for one of the many discrete language games learnt in infancy.[1] We cannot get outside these rule-governed games, Wittgenstein argues. It is an illusion of depth, a false pointing, to juxtapose one game with another, and imagine there is something further or deeper to be 'seen'. 'Think how many different kinds of thing are called "description": description of a body's position by means of its co-ordinates; description of a facial expression; description of a sensation of touch; of a mood' (*Philosophical Investigations*, p. 12). The mistake, according to Wittgenstein, is to think there is some kind of problem here, something further about 'description' to be grasped in the light of its varied use. In fact there is nothing to be grasped apart from the senses of the word as it is used, now here now there. *Philosophical Investigations* is thus premised on the aphorism with which Wittgenstein ended *Tractatus Logico-Philosophicus*: 'What we cannot speak about we must pass over in silence.'[2]

John Henry Newman, with whose autobiographical writings this paper is chiefly concerned, would have condemned this conclusion as unreal. Admittedly and in fairness, it must be said that *Philosophical Investigations* focuses on the 'real' in a very Newman-like way, notably in its repeated assertion 'You could imagine ...': Newman too appeals repeatedly to the imagination. It is only on the question of the claims of language that there is serious disagreement between them. But that disagreement is important, and there are seemingly powerful grounds, in the plenitude of *apologias pro vita sua* written before and after Newman's conversion, and culminating in, but not concluded by, *Apologia Pro Vita Sua* itself in 1864, for adopting Wittgenstein's and not Newman's view on the limits language imposes on mind. As we read Newman *in extenso* distinctions between his life and his apologies for it get lost; the 'man' seems to disappear in the innumerable stories in which he constructs and reconstructs himself; we are left with writings and no remainder; and the feeling intensifies that any attempt to 'see' an essential Newman between the texts would be a case of false pointing.

The issue is commonplace. From post-Christian theologians such as Don Cupitt,[3] deconstructionist critics such as J. Hillis Miller,[4] and cognitive philosophers such as Daniel C. Dennett, the same – what shall I call it, assertion, truth, dogma? – is promulgated *ex cathedra*: the self is only a story in constant process of revision. Dennett is particularly important because he carries the notion of the fictional self to its logical conclusion. His initial position is one familiar to a range of modern thinkers:

> we are all virtuoso novelists, who find ourselves engaged in all sorts of behaviour, more or less unified, but sometimes disunified ... We try to make all our material cohere into a single good story. And that story is our autobiography.
> The chief fictional character at the centre of that autobiography is one's self.[5]

Dennett compares this self to an object's centre of gravity, a useful reference point, but not a part of the object, as a handle is part of a hammer or a hard disc part of a computer. In his view, the interactive systems which go to make up a single human being are given a single name, and together are capable of using pronouns, including the first person singular, but there is nothing 'in' these systems corresponding to the 'I' so used, not even their combined operations. Using 'I' would be difficult and confusing in these circumstances if it were not shadowed by a story which makes our material cohere, though as new factors emerge which threaten this fictitious coherence, it has to be revised and developed on a more or less *ad hoc* basis. The telling of this story does not, of course, generate an inner core in the array of systems of which the human being is composed, answering to the description the story constructs. Though the story may be essential to that array in the way that a 'history' is essential to the functioning of a country, there is nothing further to be 'seen' other than the story itself.

Perhaps proponents of this view have in mind Wittgenstein's cryptic remarks on the problems of introspection:

> The feeling of an unbridgeable gulf between consciousness and brain-process: how does it come about that this does not come into the considerations of our ordinary life? This idea of a difference in kind is accompanied by slight giddiness, – which occurs when we are performing a piece of logical sleight-of-hand ... When does this feeling occur in the present case? It is when I, for example, turn my attention in a particular way on to my own consciousness, and, astonished, say to myself: THIS is supposed to be produced by a process in the brain! – as it were clutching my forehead. – But what

can it mean to speak of 'turning my attention on to my own consciousness'? This is surely the queerest thing there could be! ...

Here we have a case of introspection, not unlike that from which William James got the idea that the 'self' consisted mainly of 'peculiar motions in the head and between the head and throat'. And James' introspection shewed, not the meaning of the word 'self' (so far as it means something like 'person', 'human being', 'he himself', 'I myself'), nor any analysis of such a thing, but the state of a philosopher's attention when he says the word 'self' to himself and tries to analyse its meaning.
(*Philosophical Investigations*, pp. 124–5)

Whether Wittgenstein can safely be called in aid of the Dennett model remains to be seen. What can be said is that that model is strikingly reflected in the endlessly repeated and modified tellings of his own story in which Newman, apparently compulsively, indulges. To illustrate this I shall briefly summarize the history of the notorious *Tract 90* (1841) in which Newman argues for a Catholic interpretation of the Thirty-nine Articles, mainly on the strength of passages from the Book of Common Prayer, in particular the Visitation of the Sick, and references in the Book of Homilies to the Apochrypha and the Church Fathers. Even in its original version, *Tract 90* engages in self-quotation and retelling, by quoting, in a discussion of the Eucharist, an earlier work of Newman's, published in 1838. Further self-quotation and retelling followed. The huge controversy the Tract provoked quickly led to Newman writing public letters to Dr Jelf and the Bishop of Oxford, elaborately explaining his position and justifying his actions. In spite of these explanations, however, he did, of course, eventually leave the Church of England for the Church of Rome.

So matters rested for 20 years. Then in 1864, in his pamphlet 'What, Then, Does Dr. Newman Mean?' Charles Kingsley brought up the question of *Tract 90* once again. Kingsley insists that he never attributed 'intentional dishonesty' to the author of the tract.[6] Newman was right, he says, to resist a Calvinist reading of the Articles – their framers having wisely made them ambiguous. But Kingsley does profess to being 'shocked' by Newman's commentaries on four Articles in particular, and he thinks that when Newman tries to show that a fifth Article against '"the sacrifice of masses" does not speak against the mass itself' he is in 'fearful danger' of destroying either his 'sense of honesty' or 'his common sense' (*Apologia*, pp. 32–3). In the first Part of *Apologia* Newman protests at this – Kingsley, he says, is always making him seem virtually bad or mad, if not 'a conscious liar and deceiver' (p. 63). Newman does not, however, there or in subsequent parts of *Apologia*, specifically address the argument about the Mass. He focuses instead on the relation of the Articles to the Homilies and the Prayer Book, and the claim that, the intentions of the framers of the Articles being in general political and in detail unknowable, a true interpretation must fall back on the Catholic tradition.

Thirteen years later, in 1877, as part of an extensive programme of revision and republication of his works, Newman reprinted *Tract 90* in the two-volume *The Via Media of the Anglican Church*. Again we are confronted with the problem of self-quotation and retelling. In a Prefatory Notice Newman asserts that both volumes 'contain various statements, which I ... reproduce at the present time not without pain', and he quotes the Advertisement in his essays about 'the chance of [his work] being ... used after his death ... to benefit the cause it was intended to support at the time when it was given to the world', i.e. Anglo-Catholicism, but which he now opposes.[7] Another Notice, introducing *Tract 90*, states that its polemic has been weakened by deletion of quotations from the Homilies, but that this is 'better than the alternative ... It is penance enough to reprint one's own bad language, without burdening it with the blatterant [anti-Catholic] abuse of the Homilies' (*Via Media*, II, p. 265). This clearly represents a hardening of view: *Apologia* refers to the 'eloquent declamation of the Homilies' (*Apologia*, p. 150).

It would seem then that Newman's texts constantly change status. Initially he will make a claim about a controversial topic, about patristic doctrine or the Book of Common Prayer. Almost at once, however, such claims acquire a second order significance, as part of the Newman autobiographical record. In addition to what he said, the circumstances and good faith of his saying it become matters of controversy. In a later edition of *Via Media* (1885), for example, immediately after his remarks about the language of the Homilies, he denies rather tartly the claim by a former fellow-Tractarian, Palmer, that he never allowed his own Tracts to be revised by others: he often did so, he maintains, but emphatically not by Palmer. In the same edition, another Note, dated 'June 14, 1883', dismisses with contempt his original argument that Article XXXI does not condemn the Mass. 'What the Article abjures as a lie', Newman now announces, 'is just that which Pope and Council declare to be a divine truth' (*Via Media*, vol. II, p. 351). No acknowledgement is made of the fact that this is not far removed from Kingsley's original remarks precisely on this topic.

Traditional scholars would sift through this array of quotation, explanation and silence in order to identify the real Newman – the saint, or the equivocator, or the sensitive, suppressed homosexual, or the entrancing preacher, venerable Prince of the Church, and unreconstructed bigot. They might be inclined to think, for example, that the attack by the Newman of 1883 on the Newman of 1841 for advancing a false argument about the Mass undermines the Newman of 1864 who was silent on this very issue, even though it had been trenchantly raised by Kingsley. Newman's defenders, however, would argue that the treatment of the Mass in *Tract 90* is a side-issue; that the text at the centre of Kingsley's offensive was the sermon of 1844 on 'Wisdom and Innocence'; and that the strong rhetoric of some of the later notes in *Via Media* reflect Newman's age – he was 77 when he used the word 'blatterant' of the Homilies, and 83 when he wrote the note on Article XXXI.

But such approaches ignore the mind-crushing problem of quotation – and the omission which quotation always involves – in every one of the texts we have been considering. 'There is no such thing in nature as a naked text, without note or comment', Newman wrote in 1841;[8] but comment itself is text, and calls implicitly for further comment: context requires to be contextualized, and in this sea of relativism the possibility of definitive explanation vanishes. Thus Newman spent the later years of his life dressing up his Anglican writings in Catholic vestments; but they had never gone naked: as we have seen, the habit of self-quotation and retelling in an apparently unending pursuit of self-definition and self-explanation was with Newman when he wore the surplice. And as the poor Bishop of Oxford could have testified, the task was one which it was impossible to bring to any sort of conclusion.

Newman himself was familiar with the problem and saw only one way of resolving it. He described 'truth' as 'vast and far-stretching ... [Its] advocate, unable to exhibit more than a fragment of the whole, must round off its rugged extremities, and unite its straggling lines, by much the same process by which an historical narrative is converted into a tale'.[9] The numerous versions of Newman's Newman are evidently just such tales, rounded off first one way then another, as honesty, self-interest or senility suggest. But would the Newman-story of a scholar-biographer be any the less 'an economy'? In the end, it would seem, there is no canonical 'Newman', just as there is no canonical *Tract 90*, and no canonical *Apologia*.

Dennett's model rationalizes this conclusion. Newman's writings are continually revised for the purpose of self-definition because, for him as for us, identity is always so constituted. Newman's assertions about theology and church history are made in earnest at one time, and repudiated with repugnance at another, but the issues at stake quickly lose their intrinsic importance, and the shifts of feeling in the mind proposing or re-presenting them become their principal significance. Virtually every note in the later editions of Newman's works operates like this, in effect supplementing and qualifying the already much revised *Apologia*, without significantly helping us to reach a clear conclusion about Newman himself. The references to Palmer in 1885, for example, do not quite fit the Palmer of 1864, and we have no way of judging which better represents either Palmer himself or Newman's 'real' feelings about him. But Dennett permits us to stop worrying about such matters. In his view, inconsistency between one autobiographical draft and the next is not only inevitable but essential, because the autobiographical impulse, in which, as he sees it, human subjectivity is founded, only comes into being because the facts never do add up unless we force them to; and that can only be achieved on a strictly temporary basis, that is, until further redrafting is called for.

The problem with this model is the element of unconsciousness entailed in the process it describes. The procedure would fail if it became self-conscious, if its true structure as fiction were always and immediately obvious – if we were all self-consciously Dickenses making ourselves laugh, making ourselves cry, and making ourselves wait. As Wittgenstein noted, one 'can mistrust one's own senses, but not one's own belief' (*Philosophical Investigations*, p. 190). But there is no point at which this unfocused, unselfreflective element reaches its limit. As Dennett has come to realize, entailed in his 'multiple drafts model' of the fictional self is a much more radical 'multiple drafts model' of consciousness itself:

> In the world of publishing [he notes] there is a traditional ... distinction between pre-publication editing, and postpublication correction of 'errata'. In the academic world today, however, things have been speeded up by electronic communication ... [It] now often happens that several different drafts of an article are simultaneously in circulation, with the author readily making revisions in response to comments received by electronic mail. Fixing a moment of publication, and ... the *canonical* text ... becomes a somewhat arbitrary matter ...
>
> Similarly ... if one wants to settle on some moment of processing in the brain as the moment of consciousness, this has to be arbitrary. One can always 'draw a line' in the stream of processing in the brain, but there are no functional differences that could motivate declaring all prior stages and revisions ... unconscious ... and all subsequent emendations to the content ... post-experiential memory contamination.[10]

Newman's autobiographical writings illustrate in a slowed down version how these complex processes of mind might operate. Thus there are no functional differences between early drafts of Newman's writings and later revisions and omissions which enable us to represent the former as straightforward adjustments and the latter as 'post-experiential memory contamination'. But if the radical instability and inconclusiveness of the Newman narratives do indeed model 'consciousness', and the minute and intimate processes of *current* storytelling are in consequence also always provisional, and in the continual flux of 're-vision', then it is not only Newman and the canonical version of his story that disappear, but the story-making process itself. Our consciousness of what constitutes a good story and not just of its content, our hold, in effect, on the rules of narrative coherence, must also be in process of continual redrafting, as indeed they seem to be in dreams. But this violates some of Wittgenstein's fundamental principles, that an 'intention is embedded in its situation, in human customs and institutions' – it cannot be improvised – and that 'to imagine a language means to imagine a form of life' – a foundation of some sort is a condition of any kind of utterance (*Philosophical Investigations*, pp. 108, 8). 'It is what human beings *say* that is true and false; and they agree in the *language* they use. That is not agreement in opinions but in form of life' (ibid., p. 88).

The rules of autobiographical selving must be based, therefore, on public agreement, their breach a matter of public accountability. The whole concept of a 'fictional' self – as distinct from a self closed to full introspective scrutiny – is thus, from Wittgenstein's point of view, surd. That part of me which is determined, not by what I think and say, but by my capacity to think and say it, cannot be opportunistically invented. In violation of this principle, however, there is an unspecifiable, yet necessary, element of 'private language' in the multiple drafts model of the self, and that of consciousness entailed in it. The model, therefore, collapses solipsistically upon itself. If Dennett is right, 'I' have nothing in common with the Gadarene demoniac of the Gospels, 'clothed and in his right mind'; 'I' am not even '"Legion", because we are so many';[11] – even as I write – I am a herd of maddened swine rushing headlong into the sea. One is reminded of the editor-narrator in Thomas Carlyle's *Sartor Resartus*, determined to generate the very presence of his hero, Teufelsdröckh, from 'fragments of all sorts; scraps of regular Memoir, College-Exercises, Programs, Professional Testimoniums, Milkscores, torn Billets, sometimes to appearance of an amatory cast; all blown together as if by merest chance'[12] – yet terrified that he will produce no more than an optical shadow; or of Carlyle himself, temporarily unable to 'disenchant ... the imprisoned facts and secrets of heroes' languishing in seven folios of state papers.[13] Carlyle blew away his doubts with a single blast of the Everlasting Yea. Newman's method was more drawn out, and in order to examine what might have been his response to the issues I have been raising, we must return to Augustine whom Wittgenstein so grieviously misrepresents. My second section will be based on a rereading of Augustine on language.

What, then, does Saint Augustine mean? Wittgenstein ignores a crucial phrase: 'Thus, as I heard words repeatedly used in their proper places in various sentences, I gradually learnt to understand what objects they signified; and after I had trained my mouth to form these signs, I used them to express my own desires' (*Philosophical Investigations*, p. 2). 'To express my own desires': 'the essence of language' for Saint Augustine is not, as Wittgenstein suggests, that 'individual words in language name objects', but that names are memorized to do the bidding of the will. Always already language presupposes the personal – memory, understanding and will. Wittgenstein, of course, believed this as well – his mistake was in not recognizing that Saint Augustine did so also. Wittgenstein writes:

> 'We name things and then we can talk about them: can refer to them in talk.' – As if what we did next were given with the mere act of naming. As if there were only one thing called 'talking about a thing'. Whereas in fact we do the most various things with our sentences. Think of exclamations alone, with their completely different functions.
>
> >Water!
> >Away!
> >Ow!
> >Help!
> >Fine!
> >No!
>
> Are you inclined still to call these words 'names of objects'?
> (*Philosophical Investigations*, p. 13)

But does not Saint Augustine's account imply just such exclamations attaching to words such as 'Apple!' and 'Mother!'? He does not name objects either, he remembers them and their names, he understands the uses to which those names can be put in expressing his state of mind, and so he utters his desires to those around him, whom he has seen using language for similar ends. He has learned the rules of a game from the forms of life in which he is placed.

But more is involved here for Saint Augustine than for Wittgenstein: memory, understanding and will, contemplating themselves and God, constitute for Saint Augustine an image of the Trinity.[14] His account of language is in fact deeply rooted in his dogmatic theology, for it was in the doctrines of three Persons in One God and two natures in Christ that the Church Fathers also clarified the notion of the human person. The Latin term, as it came to be used, combines the senses of the Greek words *prosopon* (character, aspect, appearance) and *hypostasis* (substance). The resulting doctrine is fundamental to Christianity. It is quite distinct from the doctrine of the soul, which is much more ancient than the doctrine of the person.[15] Plants, animals and the world were deemed to have souls, but the human being is a person; nor is it *prima facie* obvious that the personal condition necessarily entails ensoulment, at any rate in a sense stronger than the term is used by Wittgenstein himself.[16] Be that as it may, for Saint Augustine and for Newman, personhood is not a consequence of how the human being is perceived or perceives itself. It is rather the real foundation of all human life.

This concept was virtually a premiss of medieval theology, Renaissance humanism, the Reformation and the Enlightenment. But with the Enlightenment it lost its Christian dogmatic underpinning, as Carlyle recognized. Forced by Reason to repudiate miracle and Revelation, Carlyle quickly discovered that there was also 'a fundamental *infirmity*, vitiating insufficiency, in all *words*' and therefore in Reason also.[17] So he opted for the will – 'man ... can create as by a *Fiat*. Awake, arise! Speak forth what is in thee': summon into existence, in other words, the 'wondrous agency of *Symbols*', through which a Teufelsdröckh or a Cromwell may be made present to you (*Sartor Resartus*, pp. 262, 276).

In his celebrated attack on Newman for failing to recognize the 'free play of the pure intellect ... [as] the necessary and sufficient guarantee of all improvement of the race',[18] Sir Leslie Stephen chose to ignore this problem of language raised by Carlyle. He was content to rely on what Jacques Derrida calls 'the punctual simplicity of the classical subject',[19] and, in Stephen's own words, on a 'core of permanent knowledge [consisting] partly in those beliefs which can be expressed with mathematical precision ... and partly in ... the concurrent testimony of innumerable observers' (*Agnostics Apology*, pp. 213–14). There is thus no room for the will in Stephen's intellectual world. Understanding reigns alone. Stephen in effect assumes the stance attacked by Marx in 'Theses on Feuerbach'; for him, 'the theoretical is the only genuinely human attitude', and the observer is 'superior to society'.[20]

Newman, of course, with whom 'we are knee-deep in the dust of the ancient fathers' (*Agnostic's Apology*, p. 169), moved smoothly between both points of view, with Carlyle at one moment, with Stephen the next. Admittedly, Newman and Stephen disagreed about the uniformity of nature and the progress of the race; but Stephen could have abandoned both beliefs without sacrificing the claims of Locke and Hume, which are at the core of his thought, just as they are at the core of Newman's account of notional assent and inference, that broad territory of shareable conceptions, from mathematics to ideology, which Stephen so egregiously privileges, and which, as Newman describes it in *An Essay in Aid of A Grammar of Assent*, includes formal and informal inference, profession, credence, opinion, presumption and speculation. It is the terrain of discussion and argument, of demonstrable error and of demonstrable coherence of view, of what can be said. It is also the basis of a university education and the formation of a gentleman. And for Newman it was not enough.

He proposed an alternative terrain, that of real assent, reserve and the illative sense. Real assents are convictions that are held unconditionally. We may have forgotten or repudiated our original grounds for holding them – that Great Britain is an island, that a friend is true, or that the promptings of conscience are crucial to the outcome of our lives – but we hold to them none the less, non-inferentially, and we act on them. We may even be prepared to die for them. They provide the basis for certitude and the formation of saints and secular heroes. They 'are of a personal character ... They depend on personal experience; and the experience of one man is not the experience of another. Real assent ... is proper to the individual, and, as such, thwarts rather than promotes the intercourse of man with man.'[21]

Real assents are thus among the things about which it is impossible to speak, as Carlyle recognized. Trying to explain his doctrine of 'Silence', he identified 'Self-renunciation' as one of its thousand senses. 'But', he warned, 'this too if we *talk* much of it will degenerate into an *ism*.'[22] Perhaps Carlyle's 'Silence' is the terrain of another of Saint Augustine's notions about language, his belief that 'when we utter what we know, a word is necessarily born from the knowledge which we hold in the memory, a word which is absolutely the same kind of thing as the knowledge it is born from ... a word that is neither Greek nor Latin nor any other language' (*Trinity*, p. 409). Or, if this seems too Platonic, 'Silence' may be the terrain of Luce Irigaray's '"other meaning" always in the process of weaving itself, of embracing itself with words, but also of getting rid of words in order not to become fixed, congealed in them'.[23] As Newman expressed it: if 'language becomes the measure of thought ... the multiform and intricate assemblage of considerations, which really lead to judgment and action, must be attenuated or mutilated into a major and minor premiss' (*University Sermons*, p. 230).

The faculty which enables us to engage with this 'intricate assemblage' Newman calls the 'illative sense', 'illative' denoting the inferential and so pointing to syllogism and language in regular ordered use, and 'sense' pointing to instinct and so to language which is figurative and exploratory. Irigaray might find this a significant conflation. Three important points need to be made about it.

The first is that the theoretical for Newman is emphatically not the only genuinely human attitude. On the contrary, even the dogmas of the Catholic Church are no more than 'faithful shadows of those truths, which unlearned piety admits and acts upon, without the medium of clear intellectual representation' (*University Sermons*, p. 65). The genuinely human attitude, in other words, is that of unlearned piety, which theologian and philosopher struggle to gloss. And so, to Stephen's disgust, a peasant, in Newman's judgement,

> may take the same view of human affairs in detail as a philosopher ... such persons ... have clear and distinct opinions; they know what they are saying; ... they do not confuse points of primary with those of secondary importance; they never contradict themselves: on the other hand ... they use arguments which appear to be faulty, as being but types and shadows of those which they really feel.
> (*University Sermons*, pp. 304–5)

Here the gulf between Wittgenstein and Newman is clear: for Wittgenstein knowledge is identical with what can be said:

> What does it mean to know what a game is? What does it mean, to know it and not to be able to say it? Is this knowledge somehow equivalent to an unformulated definition? So that if it were formulated I should be able to recognize it as the expression of my knowledge? Isn't my knowledge, my concept of a game, completely expressed in the explanations I could give?
> (*Philosophical Investigations*, p. 35)

On behalf of his peasant Newman would reply, 'No it is not'. It is perfectly possible for a peasant who plays both football and hockey to know how goals may be scored in both games, and to act on that knowledge, as a player, without being able to state the rules or their rationale with the completeness and accuracy demonstrated by his practice. It is perfectly possible to have mastery of the practice without having mastery of the language games by which the rules governing that practice are expressed; and such mastery is knowledge. The peasant spectator, too, may know a referee is applying the rules badly without being able to specify precisely in what way, though he could judge between the views of more verbally gifted spectators when he heard them argue about the matter. Thus if the notional supplies Newman with the equivalents for what Marxists call ideology and hegemony, the illative sense borders on traditional Marxist conceptions of praxis and class consciousness.

Secondly, it 'is the concrete being that reasons' (*Apologia*, p. 218), not Stephen's 'pure intellect'. 'Logicians are more set upon concluding rightly, than on right conclusions ... After all, man is *not* a reasoning animal; he is a seeing, feeling, contemplating, acting animal ... impressions lead to action, and ... reasonings from it. Knowledge of premises, and inferences upon them, – this is not to *live*' ('Tamworth Reading Room', p. 294). He 'asks me what I mean', Newman writes of Kingsley; 'about that living intelligence, by which I write, and argue, and act'. A recurring image in his work is that of the self-precipitating mind: to read the Fathers, a man must throw 'his mind upon their text, and [draw] from them their own doctrines' (*Essays*, I, p. 94). 'To believe in Objective [i.e. Revealed] Truth is to throw ourselves forward upon that which we have but partially mastered' (ibid., I, p. 34). The story of Newman's changing convictions is accordingly identical with Newman himself – not because we have nothing but text or texts without remainder, but because texts *are* his remainder, faithful shadows of a personal substance, his memory, understanding and will, fully and intricately engaged, and disclosed in his writing to the reader's illative sense. As he himself put it, 'the life and writings of Cicero or Dr Johnson, of St Jerome or St Chysostom, leave upon us certain impressions of the intellectual and moral character of each of them, *sui generis* and unmistakable' (*Grammar of Assent*, p. 96) – even if we cannot put those impressions into words.

My third point in a sense undoes the first two. Newman's system, so strategically superior to those of Carlyle and Stephen, is precisely in its own account of itself, fatally subverted. In 1841, he wrote: 'we may surely take it for granted, from the experience of facts, that the human mind is at best in a very unformed and disordered state' ('Tamworth Reading Room', p. 263). This for Stephen was the ultimate scandal in Newman's thought, the assertion that 'every one of us is born into this world in a state of *death* ... under the bondage of an inborn element of evil, which thwarts and stifles whatever principles of truth and goodness remain in us';[24] that precisely in terms of memory, understanding and will,

> we are groping in the dark, and may meet with a fall any moment. Here and there, perhaps, we see a little; or, in our attempts to influence and move our minds, we are making experiments (as it were) with some delicate and dangerous instrument, which works we do not know how, and may produce unexpected and disastrous effects. The management of our hearts is quite above us.
> (*Parochial and Plain Sermons*, vol. I, p. 173)

And consequently the management of our intellects and our words as well.

But what have we, any more than Stephen, to do with such 'darker, deeper views'? (*Parochial and Plain Sermons*, I, p. 311) – 'darker as deeper', Stephen sardonically notes (*Agnostic's Apology*, p. 173). Simply this – that Newman's vision of intellect corrupted transforms postmodernism into a drama. Postmodernism is a game, if it is confined to the realm of language and the notional. It becomes serious in the arena of the real.

Newman was particularly contemptuous of the heretic, Eusebius of Caesarea, for holding out 'the ambiguous language of the schools' as an excuse for not being specific about doctrine.[25] In teaching that orthodoxy consisted simply in adherence to scriptural terms, without regard to how they were interpreted, Eusebius corrupted 'the simplicity of the Gospel with an Eclectic spirit'. In Eusebius's world, the dispute between Kingsley and Newman about what Newman meant, and about what the Articles may mean, would be unnecessary: there would be no wells to poison, just 'sensible, temperate, sober, well-judging persons' (as Newman put it in another context) 'moving through the channel of No-meaning, between the Scylla and Charybdis of Aye and No' (*Essays*, vol. I, p. 301). However, as he also pointed out:

> It is all very well for educated persons, at their ease ... to argue and speculate about the impalpableness and versatility of the divine message, its chameleon–like changeableness, its adaptation to each fresh mind it meets; but when men are conscious of sin, are sorrowful, are weighed down, are desponding ... [they] want to be assured that what seems to them true, is true; they want something to lean on ... more stable than their own minds.[26]

Eclecticism and the scepticism it engenders are the luxuries of Academics. But if in real life things do not add up and make sense, we – theorists and peasants alike – are on the edge of hell.

And making things add up is an immensely difficult task: 'each of us [Newman asserts] has the prerogative of completing his inchoate and rudimental nature, and of developing his own perfection out of the living elements with which his mind began to be' (*Grammar of Assent*, p. 274). I have pointed out elsewhere[27] how this description of personal formation is similar to Derrida's account of the formation of meaning: 'Meaning must await being said or written in order to inhabit itself, and in order to become, by differing from itself, what it is: meaning.'[28] Both definitions undercut the notion of the classical subject. But in the end Derrida is only talking about what can be said or written – he is a secular Eusebius – whereas Newman is talking about the real. The idea of a sentence always already being the future it has yet to become may amuse, intrigue or exasperate us, but having got the point we go on our way, check the time of this evening's showing of *Three Colours White*, and book the table for dinner. Not so, or at any rate not quite so, if it is we – rudimental, inchoate, our souls a chaos', the management of our hearts quite above us – who await our own thoughts and actions in order to inhabit ourselves, and in order to become by differing from ourselves what we already so perilously are: persons.

I conclude then with this suggestion – it is no more. *Apologia Pro Vita Sua* may be fruitfully read in the light of its own insights and notions, which we may sum up thus: that what we cannot speak about we are none the less incapable of passing over in silence; that the inchoate, the rudimental, the reserved and the personal are brought to texts by writer and reader alike – particularly by writers and readers who throw themselves into what they write and read – and that these things, about which we cannot speak, form part of the real outcomes of literature; that in consequence if a text is real it is also autobiographical; and that the whole process of writing and reading, of inference and logic in the world at large, as well as of real assent and certitude in the heart at home, is crossed and recrossed, diverted and thwarted, by what *Apologia* so eloquently calls 'some terrible aboriginal calamity' (p. 276) but which a less theologically minded age may more simply describe as the meaningless mess we get ourselves into.

Notes

1. '["When they (my elders) named some object, and accordingly moved towards something, I saw this and I grasped that the thing was called by the sound they uttered when they meant to point it out. Their intention was shewn in their bodily movements, as it were the natural language of all peoples: the expression of the face, the play of the eyes, the movement of other parts of the body, and the tone of voice which expresses our state of mind in seeking, having, rejecting, or avoiding something. Thus, as I heard words repeatedly used in their proper places in various sentences, I gradually learnt to understand what objects they signified; and after I had trained my mouth to form these signs, I used them to express my own desires."]

   'These words, it seems to me, give us a particular picture of the essence of human language. It is this: the individual words in language name objects, sentences are combinations of such names. – In this picture of language we find the roots of the following idea: Every word has a meaning. The meaning is correlated with the word. It is the object for which the word stands.

   'Augustine does not speak of there being any difference between kinds of word. If you describe the learning of language in this way you are, I believe, thinking primarily of nouns like "table", "chair", "bread", and of people's names, and only secondarily of the names of certain actions and properties; and of the remaining kinds of world as something that will take care of itself.' (Ludwig Wittgenstein, *Philosophical Investigations* (1953), translated by G.E.M. Anscombe (1953; Oxford: Blackwell, 1986), p. 2.

   'Augustine, we might say, does describe a system of communication; only not everything that we call language is this system. And one has to say this in many cases where the question arises "Is this an appropriate description or not?" The answer is: "Yes, it is appropriate, but only for this narrowly circumscribed region, not for the whole of what you are claiming to describe."

'It is as if someone were to say: "A game consists in moving objects about on a surface according to certain rules ..." – and we replied: "You seem to be thinking of board games, but there are other. You can make your definition correct by expressly restricting it to those games."' (Ibid., p. 3).

2. Ludwig Wittgenstein, *Tractatus Logico-Philosophicus* (1921), translated by D.F. Pears and B.F. McGuinness, with an introduction by Bertrand Russell (1961; London: Routledge, 1992), p. 74.
3. See Don Cuppitt, *What is a Story?* (London: SCM Press, 1991), pp. 53–77.
4. See J. Hillis Miller, *Versions of Pygmalion* (Cambridge, Mass. and London: Harvard University Press, 1990), especially pp. 55–6 ('prosopopoeia is always a fiction') and chapter 4, 'Who Is He? Melville's "Bartleby the Scrivener"', pp. 141–78.
5. Daniel C. Dennett, 'Why Everyone Is a Novelist', *TLS*, 16 September 1988, p. 1029. (Substantial sections of this article had been used before in *The Mind's I: Fantasies and Reflections on Self and Soul*, composed and arranged by Douglas Hofstadter and Daniel C. Dennett (Brighton: Harvester Press, 1981), pp. 350–2. Such textual recycling models what it describes.)
6. Charles Kingsley, 'What, Then, Does Dr. Newman Mean?', in John Henry Newman, *Apologia Pro Vita Sua* (1864), ed. William Oddie, Everyman Library (London: Dent, 1993), p. 32 (hereafter, *Apologia*).
7. John Henry Cardinal Newman, *The Via Media of the Anglican Church. Illustrated in Lectures, Letters, and Tracts Written Between 1830 and 1841. In Two Volumes, with a Preface and Notes* (London: Longmans, Green, and Co., 1885), vol. I, pp. v–vi (hereafter, *Via Media*).
8. John Henry Newman, *Essays Critical and Historical*, 2 vols (London: Basil Montague Pickering, 1871), vol. II, p. 252 (hereafter, *Essays*).
9. *Newman's University Sermons. Fifteen Sermons Preached Before the University of Oxford 1826–43*, with Introductory Essays by D.M. MacKinnon and J.D. Holmes, reprinted from the third edition 1871 (London: SPCK, 1970), p. 90 (hereafter, *University Sermons*).
10. Daniel C. Dennett, *Consciousness Explained* (London: Allen Lane, 1992), pp. 125–6.
11. Mark 5: 9–15.
12. Thomas Carlyle, *Sartor Resartus. The Life and Opinions of Herr Teufelsdröckh* (1833–34), in *A Carlyle Reader: Selections from the Writings of Thomas Carlyle*, ed. G.B. Tennyson (Cambridge: Cambridge University Press, 1984), p. 199.
13. Quoted by K.J. Fielding, 'Carlyle and Cromwell: The Writing of History and "DRYASDUST"', in Fred Kaplan, Michael Goldberg and K.J. Fielding, *Lectures on Carlyle and His Era* (Santa Cruz: The University Library, University of California, 1985), p. 57.
14. Saint Augustine, Bishop of Hippo, *The Trinity*, with introduction, translation, and notes by Edmund Hill, OP (New York: New City Press, 1991), Book X, ch. 4 (pp. 298–9); Book XIV, chs 3 and 4 (pp. 378–87) (hereafter, *Trinity*).
15. The inadequacy of the term 'soul' to encompass what is covered by the word 'person' is illustrated in Newman's cautious attitude to the argument for the existence of God from the 'design' of the universe: 'What the

physical creation presents to us in itself is a piece of machinery, and when men speak of a Divine Intelligence as its Author, ... this god of theirs ... is [merely] the animating principle of a vast and complicated system ... subjected to laws, ... connatural and co-extensive with matter' ('The Tamworth Reading Room' (1841), in John Henry Cardinal Newman, *Discussions and Arguments on Various Subjects* (London: Longmans, Green and Co., 1899), p. 302 (hereafter, 'Tamworth Reading Room')). In other words, we may envisage, as Deists did, an *anima mundi* but without the character of a person.

16. 'The human body is the best picture of the human soul' (*Philosophical Investigations*, p. 178).
17. *The Collected Letters of Thomas and Jane Welsh Carlyle*, ed. C.R. Sanders, J.K. Fielding et al. (Durham, North Carolina: Duke University Press, 1970–), vol. XII (1985), p. 165.
18. Leslie Stephen, 'Newman's Theory of Belief', *An Agnostic's Apology and Other Essays* (London: Smith, Elder, & Co., 1893), p. 170 (hereafter, *Agnostic's Apology*).
19. 'The "subject" of writing does not exist if we mean by that some sovereign solitude of the author. The subject of writing is a *system* of relations between strata: the Mystic Pad, the psyche, society, the world. Within that scene, on that stage, the punctual simplicity of the classical subject is not to be found. In order to describe the structure, it is not enough to recall that one always writes for someone; and the oppositions sender-receiver, code-message, etc., remain extremely coarse instruments. We would search the "public" in vain for the first reader: i.e., the first author of a work. And the "sociology of literature" is blind to the war and the ruses perpetrated by the author who reads and by the first reader who dictates, for at stake here is the origin of the work itself. The *sociality* of writing as *drama* requires an entirely different discipline' (Jacques Derrida, *Writing and Difference* (1967), translated, with an introduction and additional notes, by Alan Bass (1978; London and Henley: Routledge & Kegan Paul, 1981), pp. 226–7).

    (This gnomic utterance is interestingly consistent with Dennett, the Mystic Pad in particular being remarkably close to the multiple drafts model of consciousness. I offer my own model of the drama of writing at the end of this paper.)
20. K. Marx, 'Theses on Feuerbach'; in K. Marx and F. Engels, *On Religion* (London: Lawrence and Wishart, second impression, n.d.), pp. 69–70.
21. John Henry Cardinal Newman, *An Essay in Aid of A Grammar of Assent* (1870), with an introduction by Nicholas Lash (Notre Dame and London: University of Notre Dame Press, 1979), p. 82 (hereafter, *Grammar of Assent*).
22. *Collected Letters*, vol. XII, p. 164.
23. Luce Irigaray, *The Sex Which Is Not One*, translated by Catherine Porter (Ithaca: Cornell University Press, 1985), p. 29.
24. John Henry Newman, BD, *Parochial and Plain Sermons. In Eight Volumes* (London, Oxford and Cambridge: Rivingtons, 1870), vol. VI, pp. 76–7 (hereafter, *Parochial and Plain Sermons*).
25. John Henry Cardinal Newman, *The Arians of the Fourth Century*, fifth edition (London: Pickering and Co., 1883), p. 263.
26. 'Scripture and the Creed', *Discussions and Arguments*, p. 133.

27. William Myers, *Milton and Free Will: An Essay in Criticism and Philosophy* (London: Croom Helm, 1987), p. 3.
28. *Writing and Difference*, p. 11.

CHAPTER EIGHT

Displacing the Autobiographical Impulse: A Bakhtinian Reading of Thomas Carlyle's *Reminiscences*

David Amigoni

Thomas Carlyle's controversial *Reminiscences* are best known for the concert of competing voices which greeted their publication in 1881, following Carlyle's death in 1880.[1] The portraits of James Carlyle, Jane Welsh Carlyle and Edward Irving, Francis Jeffrey, Robert Southey and William Wordsworth were undertaken during two separate periods of intense grieving which followed the deaths of Carlyle's father, James, in 1832, and his wife, Jane Welsh Carlyle, in 1866. These portraits were put into the public domain by Carlyle's literary executor and biographer J.A. Froude. Carlyle's will authorized Froude to publish these texts, but Froude, as editor, left the traces of Carlyle's ambivalent intentions towards these writings untouched:

> I still mean mainly to *burn* this book before my own departure; but feel that I shall always have a kind of grudge to do it, and an indolent excuse, 'not *yet*; wait, any day that can be done!' – and that it *is* possible the thing *may* be left behind me, legible to interested survivors, – *friends* only, I will hope, and with *worthy* curiosity, not *un*worthy!
>
> In the event I solemnly forbid them, each and all, to *publish* this Bit of Writing *as it stands here*; and warn them that *without fit editing* no *part* of it should be printed (nor so far as I can order, *shall* ever be); – and that the 'fit editing' of perhaps nine-tenths of it will, after I am gone, have become *impossible*.[2]

Of course, it was the presence of such injunctions which fuelled the case against Froude, which claimed that he had behaved improperly in publishing the *Reminiscences* of the dead Carlyle, when the living Carlyle had been in at least two minds as to whether to destroy them. This perhaps sheds light on the vague sense that this literary life is not quite legitimate, and the late nineteenth-century reluctance to assign canonical status to the *Reminiscences*.[3]

As Ian Campbell has noted, it is precisely such moments as illustrated by the quotation above that comprise problems of reading for present-day readers of the *Reminiscences*. We may be more distant from the domestic mores of Victorian culture, but an uneasy sense of the violation of the Carlyles' privacy pervades the public circulation of these writings. Yet, as Campbell simultaneously notes, the portraits comprising the *Reminiscences* are astonishing rhetorical performances. Even if, as above, we are urged to avert our gaze and respect privacy, then it remains the case, as Campbell argues, that the actual effects of the writing are compelling, combining dazzling narrative skills with forms of 'public tribute and memorial'.[4] Indeed, Carlyle's vehement demand for privacy imagines itself to be in dialogue and seeks to make contact with an other: it anticipates a response.

To raise the problem of reading and responding to the *Reminiscences* is, then, simultaneously to ask what kind of text we are reading: a private act of automatic writing, the guilt-ridden outpourings of a lonely, bitter old man in decline, or a brilliant act of public reminiscence, built around a series of biographical sketches? In the language of generic categories, are the *Reminiscences* writings of the self (autobiography) or writings of the other (biography)? This was precisely the question which original reviewers asked: were the texts biographies or fragments that taken together constituted Carlyle's autobiography? Herbert Carvell's review in *Blackwood's Edinburgh Magazine* argued that the *Reminiscences* are an incomplete autobiography.[5] But this conclusion could be inflected negatively: according to the reviewer in the *Edinburgh*, the *Reminiscences* were the product of an over-inflated ego; if Carlyle began by writing about others, in the role of biographer, he was possessed by an 'incurable' tendency to refer everything, autobiographically, to himself.[6]

Modern accounts of the *Reminiscences* still pose these questions, but consider them anew in the light of recent theoretical work on the genre of autobiography. In one of the few extended analyses of the text, Gerald Wayne Farrar has attempted to account for the *Reminiscences* as an instance of the 'autobiographical impulse'.[7] For Farrar the *Reminiscences* are highly structured despite the apparent randomness of their composition. The split composition of the *Reminiscences* represents Carlyle at different key moments of his writing career: 1832 (James Carlyle) just prior to *Sartor Resartus*; and 1866 (Jane Welsh Carlyle, Edward Irving, Jeffrey, John Wilson, Southey and Wordsworth) when *Frederick the Great* had been completed, and his writing career was all but over. Not only do the *Reminiscences* attempt to come to terms with the loss of family and life partner, as well as friends and public acquaintances; they also attempt to come to terms with the formation of a sense of vocation through writing, and then its loss. Farrar argues that for Carlyle the *Reminiscences* were attempts to locate an integrated self in the face of competing claims between the demands for love placed on him by his wife and his need to work as an intellectual. The *Reminiscences*, then, are organized by a coherent self which is the true centre to the narratives about others. In producing this reading, Farrar acknowledges the work of influential theorists of autobiography such as George Gusdorf and James Olney. For Gusdorf and Olney, autobiography – defined as the complex metaphoric representation in writing (*graphe*) of a specific life-course (*bios*), which is unique to itself (*autos*) but transcendental in its aspirations – is the impulse behind all writing. For Farrar, Carlyle's writings, especially the *Reminiscences*, 'anticipate' this line of critical thinking in which *autos*, or the 'autobiographical impulse', comes to be central.[8]

In this chapter, I shall argue for the displacement of an 'autobiographical impulse' reading of the *Reminiscences* as an end in itself. I shall argue instead that in the autobiographical and biographical modes comprising the *Reminiscences* we witness both a generic quest through which social values are articulated and a 'laying bare' of the practice of life writing as a contestable and contested cultural activity. I agree with Ian Campbell, that the *Reminiscences* pose problems of reading; but whereas Campbell situates these problems at the level of the individual text's oscillation between private and public modes, I shall argue that the private and public discourses of Carlyle's *Reminiscences* address a wider cultural and intertextual field.

In finding our way to this field we might turn to Carlyle's speculative sense of the relationship between life writing and verbal culture outlined in his essay of 1832 entitled 'Biography', written in the same year as the memoir of James Carlyle:

> Observe, accordingly, to what extent, in the actual course of things, this business of biography is practised and relished. Define to thyself, judicious Reader, the real significance of these phenomena, named Gossip, Egoism, Personal Narrative (miraculous or not), Scandal, Raillery, Slander and suchlike; the sum of which ... constitutes that other grand phenomenon still called 'Conversation.' Do they not mean wholly: *Biography* and *Autobiography*?[9]

According to Carlyle, all utterance can be traced back to autobiography and biography, and this would seem to confirm Farrar's point about Carlyle's anticipation of that line of thinking about the 'autobiographical impulse' which is articulated by Gusdorf and Olney. However, there is another way of reading this speculation: that autobiographical and biographical texts are utterances that are grounded in a variety of primary speech genres.

This alternative way of reading Carlyle's sense of the relationship between genres of speech and more formalized written genres such as biography and autobiography can be read in his elucidations upon the letters of Jane Welsh Carlyle, which record the Carlyles' life in London. In 1868 Carlyle prepared the letters for publication, and Froude edited and published them in three volumes in 1883 (two years after the publication of the *Reminiscences*). Elucidating Jane's first letter home from London, Carlyle acts as lexicographer in respect of forms of dialect which appear: 'To see how they live and waste here, it is a wonder the whole city does not "bankrape, and go out o' sicht." To "*bankrape*" is to *bankrupt* (used as a verb passive).'[10] Carlyle also acts as a commentator, tracing the dialect in the quoted speech to an earlier context, an earlier voice:

> a phrase of my father's in the little sketches of Annandale biography he would sometimes give me. During two wholly wet days, on my last visit to Scotsbrig in 1830, he gave me a whole series of such; clearest brief portraiture and life-history of all the noteworthy, vanished figures whom I had known by look only, and now wished to understand. Such a set of *Schilderungen* (human delienations of human life), so admirably brief, luminous, true and man-like, as I never had before or since. I have heard Wordsworth, somewhat on similar terms (twice over had him in a corner engaged on this topic, which was his *best*); but even Wordsworth was inferior.
>
> (*Letters and Memorials*, vol. I, p. 5)

Carlyle's commentary becomes personal reminiscence, which might seem to confirm Fred Kaplan's point that Carlyle used the commentary around Jane's letters as a means of exercising his own autobiographical impulse by indirection.[11] But Carlyle's reminiscence here is concerned with the telling of and listening to narratives about others. What the commentary focuses on is the place of a dialect phrase in the shape of life-course narratives which relate to specific geographical and cultural spaces (Annandale, Scottish Central Lowlands), and the worthiness of the author who utters them. We could say that here *bios*, or the shape of the life course, and the medium in which it is cast, and so the effects it exerts upon its hearers, is prior to *autos*, or experiencing the uniqueness of the revealed self. To be sure, Carlyle's commentary testifies to his desire to 'understand' the hidden, interior motivations of the subjects of his father's biographies which Carlyle had failed to penetrate – but this could only be guaranteed by the quality and situatedness of the author. In a hierarchy of authors of life-course narratives, the authority of James Carlyle of Annandale is approached only by William Wordsworth. The juxtaposition of these two figures returns us to the *Reminiscences*, where both figure prominently.

The observations above are prompted by the writings of Mikhail Bakhtin and his concerns with the dialogic relations between author and hero, self and other, and the rootedness of these relations in generic practices of speech and writing. Carlyle's text may be read in a way which situates it in a line leading to Gusdorf and Olney and their autobiographical criticism which traces metaphors of the 'autobiographical impulse' and the unitary self in all writing. However, for Bakhtin the self can only articulate and know itself in relation to another, and it is possible to read the discourses of the *Reminiscences* as performances of this knowledge. Indeed, to view the *Reminiscences* as a performance of this knowledge is to move towards a way of explaining the generic-border crossings between the biographical and the autobiographical that the text enacts. For Bakhtin, following from his theory of the dialogic self, there were no essential differences between these genres: what united them was the social practice of authorship and their construction according to particular kinds of chronotope, or narrative representations of selves in time and space.

In what follows I shall first read the *Reminiscences* in the light of Bakhtin's work on the dialogic self and discourse. Second, I shall place this reading in a broader cultural context by reading the *Reminiscences* intertextually. I shall argue that reading Carlyle's memoir of Edward Irving intertextually, and in terms of an evaluative quest for genre and position, makes more sense of the contest of competing cultural voices which greeted the publication of the *Reminiscences* in the 1880s. As a consequence, the controversy which ensued on the publication of the *Reminiscences* should not be seen as an embarrassing rancorous adjunct to a literary life – but rather as the necessary continuation of a chain of cultural dialogue and debate.

Reflecting on what came to be published as 'Edward Irving' in the *Reminiscences*, Carlyle observed himself crossing the border between the genres of biography and autobiography. He recorded in his journal (26 September 1866) that his reminiscence of Irving 'turns out hitherto to be more about myself than him' (*Rem*, p. 307). It is worth reflecting, for a moment, on the fact that Carlyle records his observation in his journal, and not in his narrative about Irving. In other words if we move seamlessly between these texts we can elide the fact that we have two distinctive utterances in which different images of Carlyle are authored by two separate acts. In the journal entry commenting on the Irving narrative, Carlyle is clearly outside the image of himself that is taking shape in that narrative. Given that this is the case, we still have to come to terms with the fact that Carlyle the writer is radically 'outside' the image of the Carlyean self which is authored in the Irving narrative.

What Mikhail Bakhtin conceptualized as 'outsidedness' is the logic which governs the presentation of identity in the Irving narrative.[12] When Carlyle represents the clarity of his recollection of Irving's face, he recalls that it is like looking into a mirror (*Rem*, p. 229). At one level, the mirror is a simile for the powers of the celebrated Carlylean memory and its capacity for recalling Irving's features – but at another level, it echoes a moment from Carlyle's 1830 essay on 'Biography' where the biography of 'each individual is a mirror to us' ('Biography', p. 45). If each individual is a mirror, then the individual as other is a source of construction for the self. As a consequence, understanding of the self is achieved through a multiplicity of points outside of the self, a point that Bakhtin makes in the suggestive aphoristic collection of notes entitled 'The Problem of the Text in the Human Sciences'. Under the heading 'Notes in Philosophical Anthropology' Bakhtin reflects – in a form akin to that of an Imagist poem – on the fact of 'The heterogeneous composition of my image', heterogeneity which Bakhtin concretizes in the line that follows, 'A person at the mirror. Not-I in me'.[13]

The Bakhtinian reading strategies that have been introduced here indicate that to represent a self is a complex gesture of rhetorical activity wherein the rhetoric of selfhood is never identical to, but rather outside of, its originator. Thus, the self is an image which is produced by the dialogic relations and tensions not only between genres of discourse within a single textual utterance, but also intertextually, between texts compiled at different points in time.

One has to acknowledge, though, that this approach comes through a reading of Bakhtin which has to be extrapolated from a variety of sources, and which require some discussion. In the essays comprising the collection published in English as *The Dialogic Imagination* Bakhtin's concern with the pre-history of the the novel involves a discussion of the development of associated genres, including those concerned with the narration of lives. For Bakhtin, in the essay 'Forms of Time and Chronotope in the Novel', early Greek and Roman forms of life-course narration were couched in public forms of rhetoric, comprising external, public details, and as such, the distinction between biography and autobiography was not very meaningful – 'there was no distinction, in principle, between the approaches toward the individual adopted by each'.[14] Bakhtin does, however, go on to suggest that there emerged a species of writing, exemplified in Cicero's letters to Atticus, concerned with more 'private' matters; the subject's domestic space and arrangements, intimate relations: in short, a realm of closed, private experience (*DI*, p. 145). This was linked to the emergence of writing – 'Soliloquia', exemplified by the writings of Marcus Aurelius – exploring 'a new relationship to one's own self, one's own particular "I"', in which there were no 'concessions to the voice of a "third person"' (ibid.). For Bakhtin, this seems to represent a staging post on the way to the emergence of the modern individual, the arrival of which he here places in the Middle Ages. In this history of generic development the modern self, in all its immediacy, self-presence and interiority, will come to find its home in autobiography, as distinct from biography.

The picture is different when we look at Bakhtin's earlier writings from the 1920s. These appear to pull us towards a reading which does not accord autobiography a distinctive status. These writings, such as 'Author and Hero in Aesthetic Activity', are concerned with a neo-Kantian construction of the self/other relation and are overtly philosophical.[15] Even so, Bakhtin is still concerned with the self/other relationship as one whose consequences are best seen at work in narrative. Bakhtin argues in this essay that from an aesthetic point of view, the self which writes does not exist as a given: the self can only be articulated evaluatively as a process, through its inscription in and relation to an other – or to use Bakhtin's terminology, a hero, or the topic of a particular utterance.[16] This dialogic, relational phenomenon is, for Bakhtin, ontologically foundational: it underwrites all genres of discourse, from everyday conversation to sophisticated secondary aesthetic genres such as the novel, biography and autobiography.

It also leads Bakhtin to refuse a distinction which, according to Olney, 'every writer on autobiography would feel it necessary to maintain': the generic dividing line between biography and autobiography.[17] For Bakhtin 'There is no clear-cut, essentially necessary dividing line between biography and autobiography, and this is a matter of fundamental importance' (*Art and Answerability*, p. 150). This is the conclusion that we saw Bakhtin reach, above, in connection with early Greek and Roman forms of life-course narration – except now its scope is 'fundamental' and not simply applicable to early cultures and their historically relative preference for public forms of rhetoric which emphasized the 'exterior' bearings and functions of the person.

In order to get around what seems to be an inconsistency in Bakhtin's thinking, we need to consider his notion of the chronotope, a concept formulated during his neo-Kantian period which continued to be central to his later writings.[18] In the essay 'Forms of Time and Chronotope in the Novel' Bakhtin's point about the move from public to private forms of selfhood has to be seen in the context of shifting constructions of human time, and new adaptations of space, or, to use the term that Bakhtin coined, in the context of the chronotope. Authors fashion self-images according to new conceptions of time and experiences of 'private' space, but however immediate that image of selfhood may appear, it is still an image, an utterance divided from its originator, conditioned by the voices of others in being formulated, shaping other possible images of self in being read. While there is no question of disregarding the cultural and historical construction of generic differences between biographies and autobiographies – a point that will be crucial to my intertextual reading of the *Reminiscences* – it is as utterances representing a relationship between author and hero, and organized by particular chronotopes, that biographies and autobiographies can be considered as narrative forms more alike than dissimilar.

The concept of the chronotope has implications for reading the *Reminiscences*. These return us to the cue we took from Carlyle's commentary on James Carlyle's legitimacy as an author of life-course narratives in *The Letters and Memorials of Jane Welsh Carlyle*. We observed at the time that for Carlyle the power of the narrative was the key to the understanding of a life and the self represented by it. This power was conditioned by the place in which a life-course narrative was fashioned, the place that it was about, and the values embedded in particular forms of language which enabled authorship – and in many respects, these factors are constitutive of Bakhtin's notion of the chronotope. The *Reminiscences* were written in London and France, but were about Lowland Scotland; their composition was split between 1832 and 1866. Thus, in the *Reminiscences* the act of authoring a self comes about through divisions and dichotomies: selfhood is rhetorically fashioned out of images of others, across different times, between the effects of quite radically different places. The *Reminiscences* 'lay bare' the architectonics of life-writing as a set of practices through which contests of ideological evaluation can be glimpsed.[19]

> Everything that pertains to me enters my consciousness, beginning with my name, from the external world from the mouths of others (my mother and so forth), with their intonation, in their emotional and value-assigning tonality. I realise myself initially through others: from them I receive words, forms and tonalities for the formation of my initial idea of myself.
>
> (*Speech Genres*, p. 138)

Carlyle's *Reminiscences* 'lay bare' the practices of life-writing, inscribing images of the others who helped to shape the authorial, evaluative act of writing – which produce an 'I', or an image of the self. In the portrait of James Carlyle, the Annandale stonemason, Carlyle's father's utterances are remembered as being 'full of metaphors' used to 'exaggerated ... humorous effect' which have resulted in the tonalities that characterize the 'I' of the narrative (*Rem*, pp. 3–4). The later reminiscences of figures such as Lord Jeffrey and John Wilson ('Christopher North') seek to capture the tones of their voices; '"with *any* man!" answered Wilson in such a tone of broad recognition as completely pictured the truth of the phenomena' (p. 374). The capacity for rhetorical parody displayed by these figures is also recalled: Francis Jeffrey's 'feeling for the *ludicrous*' is remembered in relation to his parodic imitation of the voices of senior Edinburgh judges (p. 314). And a night in the company of John Wilson is memorable for Wilson's parodies of Coleridge in the style of the 'serio-comic' and De Quincy in the mode of 'farce-tragedy' (pp. 375–6). Thus we have a complex chain in which Jeffrey and Wilson author parodic language images of others in order to produce a sense of their own vitality, and Carlyle in turn authors images of Jeffrey and Wilson.

Carlyle's *Reminiscences* take their cue from Jeffrey and Wilson. The writings were controversial for the way in which they used parody in order to stylize others – principally ideological foes, such as Harriet Martineau, who is rendered 'Mistress of some immense Dress-Shop'. Here the authorial tone reveals its evaluative ideological alignment in the broader political struggles of the 1860s: when Carlyle alludes to Martineau's 'nigger fanaticisms', we need to recall the Governor Eyre controversy in which Carlyle was publicly active (*Rem*, p. 118).[20] It is significant that Carlyle should parody Martineau, a link in a metropolitan-based liberal-radical intellectual formation in a style inherited from James Carlyle. Carlyle's *Reminiscences* remain on the outside of the discourses of the metropolitan literary centre, summed up in Leigh Hunt's talk which is styled in catalogue form as 'Literary-Biographical, Autobiographical, wandering into Criticism, *Reform of Society*. Progress etc. etc., – ' (p. 71). Here again we have autobiography and biography, but this time as images of a certain kind of talk, and linked to a progressive politics, fashioned in radical London. The point is that we need to read the *Reminiscences* in terms of a life-writing chronotope which challenges the discourses and values of the metropolitan liberal intelligentsia. The authorial performances of both 1832 and 1866, and the image of the 'I' that is thereby produced, demonstrate a commitment to the language and place – and values – of 'Annandale biography'. 'Annandale biography' as a distinctive kind of chronotope organizes the *Reminiscences* and the image of the self authored therein.

Of what does this distinctiveness consist? It is distinctiveness that was born of a general cultural discourse in which Carlyle as translator and interpreter of German literature was implicated: 'Annandale biography' needs to be seen in terms of broader European cultural trends. In the essay 'The *Bildungsroman* and Its Significance in the History of Realism', Bakhtin considers Goethe's contribution to the history of the realist novel. For Bakhtin, Goethe figures as the architect of a distinctive chronotope – exemplified in Goethe's *Autobiography* – in which 'all criteria for evaluation, all measures, and the entire living human scale of the locality can be understood only from the standpoint of *man the builder*' (*Speech Genres*, p. 35). Bearing in mind Carlyle's reverence for Goethe, and his reminiscence of his father's head resembling that of Goethe's, we should return now to Carlyle's reminiscence of James Carlyle (*Rem*, p. 13). Writing of his father, Carlyle observes that 'a portion of the Planet bears benificent traces of his strong Hand and strong Head' (p. 2). James Carlyle's occupation as a stonemason means that very tangible evidence of his work inscribes the Annandale locality: of the Auldgarth Bridge, which Carlyle's father helped to build, Carlyle writes that 'A good building will last longer than most Books' (p. 24). The image of the self that is produced by this meditation on work, construction and place is summed up in the following rhetorical question: 'Nay, am not I also the humble James Carlyle's work?' (p. 2). The authorial act that reflects on a self has been built out of the materials and rhythms of the locality.

But the *Reminiscences* were not written in Annandale – they were written in London and France. The distinctiveness of Goethe's specific representation of subjectivity as the product of work, time and space, for Bakhtin, resided in its consciousness of being on the threshold of modernity, and all the possibilities and threats associated with that condition: 'this new sense of space and time' wherein the self 'is no longer within an epoch, but on the border between two epochs, at the transition point from one to the other' (*Speech Genres*, p. 50). The sense of being suspended between two epochs is articulated in the *Reminiscences*, and images of social space in the process of transition are one of the means through which this sense of suspension is represented. In remembering Jane Welsh Carlyle's visit to the Sussex coast, Carlyle's horror at St Leonards in the throes of modernization and rebuilding is seen through 'my dialogues with the dusty sceneries there (Fairlight, Crowhurst, Battle, Rye even, Winchealsea), with their novelties and the antiquities, were very sad for the most part, and very grim, – here and there with a kind of wild interest too' (*Rem*, p. 151).

It is through London that the seductive threats and pressures of modernity are most clearly articulated. Again, these threats find their image in an architectural structure, the Caledonian Chapel of the National Church of Scotland (Regent Square), built in the 1820s to house Edward Irving's great mission in the capital. In the same way that the authorial voice presents an image of itself in dialogue with the 'dusty sceneries' of antiquarian places, here the voice itself is in dialogue with the structure: 'Ah you fatal *tombstone* of my lost friend; and did not a sort so strong and *high* avail only to build you' (*Rem*, p. 258). Addressed to an indifferent and inhuman urban structure, what is striking here is the style of the living voice which mourns for the dead and silenced Irving. It is to a discussion of the stylistic formation of this voice and its representation of its generic place in the modern world that I shall now move.

'The author's quests for his own word are basically quests for genre and style, quests for an authorial position' (*Speech Genres*, p. 149). Bakhtin's words are appropriate to a reading of Carlyle's reminiscence of Edward Irving. This reminiscence can be read as a quest for the Carlylean word conducted through an 'Annandale biography' in the tragic mode, in which Irving, the native son of Annandale, plays the tragic subject destroyed by modern metropolitan duplicity and quackery. But the sense in which Carlyle was questing for genre and style in his reminiscence of Irving involves looking beyond the borders of Carlyle's text.

As we have seen, for Bakhtin there is no essential difference between biography and autobiography as genres: biography and autobiography are common instances of life-writing as a performance constituted around the split between author and hero, self and other. In turn, I have argued that Carlyle's *Reminiscences* 'lay bare' the practices constituting life-writing and their embeddedness in ideology. None the less, generic categories and the values attached to them are real products of cultural and intellectual history, and, as I have argued, the form of narrated relationship between author and hero that we have come to recognize as autobiography emerged in history to become the highly valued generic home of the modern, self-conscious individual. It is in this context that we can see Carlyle's quest for an authorial position as a dialogic act which has to engage with some of these assumptions about the generic values associated with autobiography which were set forth in another text about Irving's life. Here I shall focus on Margaret Oliphant's life of Irving, published in 1862, and a text with which Carlyle was familiar – his own reminiscence of Irving alludes to Margaret Oliphant's *Life of Edward Irving*.[21]

Although generically a biography, Margaret Oliphant's *Life of Edward Irving* claims to find in Irving's writings a spontaneous autobiographical impulse and access to an interiority which guarantees the truth, worth and significance of Irving's public actions. In this particular context Carlyle's quest could almost be said to be a quest *against* the implications which follow from casting Irving's life in such a genre.

Moreover, Carlyle's authorial quest for a style which is expressive of *the* authorial word is in large part produced by means of images suggesting Irving's sundered relationship to language and style. It can thus be argued that the autobiographical impulse is not the ultimate destination of the *Reminiscences*; rather, the prestigious values associated with it are rebutted in the course of the formation of an authorial position.

Margaret Oliphant's life of Edward Irving begins by situating its hero in the place of his birth, and in relation to an oral narrative tradition of local Annandale stories, including tales of religious martyrdom. The narrated life is thus structured around an awareness of storytelling traditions specific to a local time and place, and the way in which these are internalized to become the chronotopic mental landscapes of a culturally situated people. The narrative then shifts focus to Irving's specifically Scottish higher education at Edinburgh University, and the training in eloquence that he received. Margaret Oliphant represents Irving reading and reciting passages of text during walks in the country for the benefit of his companions: 'This is the first indication I can find of his oratorical gifts, and the natural magniloquence of style which belonged equally to his mind and person.'[22] In urging that Irving's eloquence belonged indivisibly to his mind and person, Margaret Oliphant constructs an image of Irving's relationship to language which stresses unity.

Carlyle's reminiscence of Irving begins with a genealogy, situating his hero in the history of the Annandale locale. It then introduces an image of the local schoolteacher, Adam Hope – educator of both Irving and Carlyle – whose demeanour was 'humanely contemptuous of the world' (*Rem*, p. 174). Adam Hope's tone of humane contempt for the world is clearly one which has come to define the authorial position and its sense of value: 'I consider Adam an original, meritorious kind of man; and regret to think that his sphere was so limited' (p. 175). Indeed, Adam Hope's inclusion initiates a commentary on politics and society in the 1860s which explicitly opens up a division between the past and present: 'There is a kind of *citizen* which Britain used to have; very different from the millionaire Hebrews, Rothschild money-changers, Demosthenic Disraelis, inspired young Göschens, and the "unexampled prosperity." Weep, Britain, if the latter are among the honourable you now have' (p. 176). The important point here is the form of address which is used, that is at once contemptuous and public: as though Adam Hope's tone has been internalized, while its sphere of influence has been widened. If tones characterize the authorial position, the authorial position also recalls and represents the tones of Hope's former charge on a triumphal return from Edinburgh to his former school: Irving's pronunciation of 'circle' as '"cir*cul*"' is highlighted, which suggests 'a certain *preciosity*'

(p. 180). Thus Carlyle's reminiscence of Irving follows a similar set of introductory moves to that of Margaret Oliphant: both narratives begin by situating Irving in the space of Annandale; both then tell stories about education. However, whereas Margaret Oliphant concentrates on the education that Irving receives in the Athens of the North, Carlyle concentrates on how that education *sounds* from 'rustic, bare' Annandale (p. 179). There is one further point of contrast. Whereas Margaret Oliphant's narrative represents Irving's relationship to utterance as being indivisible, for Carlyle there is something discordant and derivative in Irving's tone and style of utterance.

Carlyle's reminiscence of Irving explores the derivative nature of style and its consequences for both himself and Irving, the heroes of the narrative:

> He affected the Miltonic or Old-English Puritan style ... At this time and for years afterwards there was something of preconceived intention visible in it, in fact of real 'affectation', as there could well not help being: – to his example also, I suppose, I owe something of my own poor affectations in that matter, which are now more or less visible to me, much repented of or not.
> (*Rem*, p. 195)

The quest for style has been recognized as being important to Carlyle's account of Irving: Tom Lloyd has focused on Carlyle's discussion of his and Irving's appropriations of stylistic models derived from English authorities such as Milton and Hooker, a mediation which, for Lloyd, enabled Carlyle to construct 'his own myth of selfhood'.[23] But while the stylistic quest for self is recognizably a performative dimension of Carlyle's narrative, the extent to which the articulation of this quest was shaped dialogically in relation to Margaret Oliphant's narration of the same topic in her life of Irving has not received attention.

In Margaret Oliphant's *Life of Edward Irving*, the author quotes at length from her hero's response to criticisms levelled at the style of his prophetical texts published in 1823, the *Orations* and the *Arguments for Judgments to Come*. The response is couched in the first person singular:

> I have been accused of affecting the antiquated manner of ages and times now forgotten. The writers of those times are too much forgotten, I lament, and their style of writing has fallen out of use; but the time is fast approaching when this stigma shall be wiped away from our prose, as it is fast departing from our poetry. I fear not to confess that Hooker and Taylor and Baxter in Theology, Bacon, Newton and Locke in Philosophy, have been my companions, as Shakespeare, Spenser and Milton have been in poetry.
> (Oliphant, 1864, p. 90)

The first person address, allied to the fact that Irving 'fear[s] not to *confess* [my emphasis]' his stylistic debts, is preparation for the claim advanced by Margaret Oliphant's authorial commentary, that 'in his dedications and prefaces, he carries on a kind of rapid autobiography, and takes his reader into his heart and confidence, in the singular addresses, in a manner, so far as I am aware, quite unprecedented in literature' (p. 91). It is clear that the commentary is less concerned with Irving's commitment to stylistic conservatism than with the confession and articulation of that commitment in itself, which is held to be autobiographical in mode, and – paradoxically, given its alignment to tradition – unprecedented in expressiveness. The authorial commentary continues in this vein by representing, through letters, Irving's so-called 'apostolical journey', which was undertaken after the death of his child. To these letters, comments Margaret Oliphant, 'we owe a closer and more fruitful picture of Irving's life and heart than anything which a biographer could attempt, than anything, indeed, which, so far as I am aware, any man of modern days has left behind him' (p. 115).

Although Margaret Oliphant's text is generically a biography, in constructing its image of Irving the authorial position eschews biographical limits and claims for the image the generic status of an autobiographical representation. That is to say: Irving's writings are held to give the reader immediate access to Irving's interiority, and as a consequence Irving's style must express the unity of his being which is in turn a reflection of the integrity and validity of his public actions. Furthermore, constructing Irving in the image of an autobiographical subject is powerfully linked to claims about Irving's exemplary 'modern' status. Not only is Irving's 'rapid autobiography' 'unprecedented', but his extant utterances provide the reader with an image of the authentic modern self.

Given this, it should then become apparent that Carlyle's recollection of Irving's precious pronunciation and his meditation on Irving's 'affected' borrowing of Miltonic style take on a dialogic hue coloured by Margaret Oliphant's representation of Irving as one whose self is validated by the autobiographical genre. For Carlyle's reminiscence of Irving refashions Margaret Oliphant's image of Irving as the subject of autobiography, and thereby works to undermine the images of the harmonious links between eloquence and self which Oliphant's narrative generated. Thus for Carlyle, Irving 'talked with an undeniable self-consciousness and something which you could not but admit to be religious mannerism ... his brave old self never *once* looked fairly through' (*Rem*, pp. 286–7). The image of Irving that is fashioned here is determined by the governing chronotope of the *Reminiscences*, Annandale biography, for it is Irving's London fame which fractures any possibility of a harmonious relationship between self and style, so that there appeared in him 'a new height of self-consciousness not yet sure of the manner and carriage that was suitablest for it' (p. 239). Focusing on the latter stages of Irving's London career, the representation of Irving's disintegrating self is pursued through vocal images, so that he diffuses first into 'echoes of himself', and is finally drowned out by the voices of 'Hysterical women', or those followers of Irving who claimed, on the basis of Corinthians 13, to possess the Gift of Tongues (pp. 293, 298).

The image of Irving's disintegrating self amidst the modern Babel that is London provides a counterpoint for reading the most memorable construction of the Carlylean self in the *Reminiscences*: 'With all its manifold petty troubles, this year at Hoddam Hill has a rustic beauty and dignity to me; and lies now like a not ignoble russet-coated Idyll in my memory; one of the quietest on the whole, and perhaps the most triumphantly important of my life' (p. 281). Carlyle at Hoddam Hill stands out as a central image of Carlyle's self in the *Reminiscences*. A key moment in Carlyle's life history, the reminiscence is possessed at the moment of writing through the language of rusticity and the conventions of the pastoral idyll, which very clearly contrasts with the negative images of metropolitan modernity in which the narration of Irving's 'tragical' fate is cast. This image of Carlyle's triumphal self is, however, dialogic in that it takes shape through a contest to narrate the nature of modern selfhood and lay claim to its generic models; Carlyle's narration asserts that his intellectual independence has been achieved by following a 'path trodden' first by Goethe, 'the first of the *moderns*' [my italics] (p. 282). We should recall here that Margaret Oliphant's construction of Irving's writings as autobiographical confessionals, disclosing the subject's interiority, was linked to the assertion of their being 'modern' and 'unprecedented'. In Carlyle's account of Irving, urban life is symptomatic of modern destructiveness, and the true, successful 'modern' is one – like Carlyle – who has followed attentively the path taken by Goethe. It is significant that Carlyle's history of himself attends less to the construction of confessional self-images, and more to the discovery of selfhood in images of travel and pilgrimage. Carlyle's history is not so much the product of an autobiographical impulse. Instead, it finds its shape in a generic, chronotopical story already narrated about selves which blend expression and selfhood in a nourishing sense of place: a sense of place which provides protection from, while it is wedged up against, the shattering pressures of modernity. As such, Carlyle's version of Annandale biography was a form of protest.

I shall conclude by exploring the consequences of the reading for which I have argued in this chapter. While the image of Carlyle at Hoddam Hill stresses the unity and transcendence of Carlyle's self, this is a fictive image of unity, performed by a complex act of authorship fashioned out of dialogues first with images of the other within the narrative, and second in response to other authorial acts formed in different contexts. Bakhtin has explored the consequences of this theory of authorship, as a performative act of evaluation oriented towards a hero, for the conventional uses of biography and autobiography in his essay 'Forms of Time and Chronotope in the Novel'. The consequences are, from the point of view of traditional expectations following from the uses of biography and autobiography in literary historical scholarship, rather disabling. Try as we may to recover the 'real' Carlyle from the pages of the *Reminiscences*, we succeed only in constructing, in yet another verbal performance, just another hero: '[in making] use of autobiographical and biographical material ... [the listener or reader] is merely creating an artistic or historical image of the author' (*DI*, pp. 256–7). Yet that 'merely' is misleading: for it is precisely a radically historical and contextual approach to the study of images of selfhood which is enabled by the Bakhtinian reading which is practised in this chapter.

In what sense is a Bakhtinian approach 'radically' historical? The reading that I have practised has sought radically – in the sense of taking the utterance to be the root to which we have to return – to reinstate the utterance in history. A desire to reinstate the utterance in a historical chain of utterances inscribes Carlyle's practice in first writing the narratives that comprised the *Reminiscences*, and second assembling the letters that stood as memorials to Jane Welsh Carlyle. Essential to this operation was the preparatory act of reading – itself charged with rhetorical intent. We should remember that the reminiscence of Jane Welsh Carlyle begins as a reading of a commemorative narrative portrait of Jane written by her friend Geraldine Jewsbury, on which Carlyle writes comments, finally breaking into the authorship of his own reminiscence (*Rem*, pp. 36–48). The reading of utterances is visibly marked by the writing of responsive utterances, and then to the production of narrative. It is in this sense that the *Reminiscences* 'lay bare' the processes leading to the writing of all life-course narratives by exposing the divisions, spaces and opposed discourses of value in which the practice takes shape as a cultural response in history. My approach has read for the manifest textual divisions that fracture and produce the *Reminiscences*: divisions between author and hero; between self and other; between time and space coordinates, and the time and space coordinates in which representations are shaped – all of which expose divisions between different utterances.

Carlyle's reading of the utterances comprising Jane Welsh Carlyle's letters figures in the *Reminiscences*: the painful, laboured process of reading the 'family circle dialect' in which the letters are cast is clearly a prelude to the act of collation that results in the *Letters and Memorials of Jane Welsh Carlyle*, and the lexicographical touches that gloss 'dialect' forms, which I discussed at the beginning of this chapter (*Rem*, p. 138). These letters have attracted an autobiographical reading. Sharon Hileman has argued that Jane Welsh Carlyle's letters can be read as narratives displaying an 'other-directed', frustrated 'autobiographical impulse'.[24] In this context, it is tempting to pursue a gendered reading of Carlyle's preparation of, and commentary upon, Jane Welsh Carlyle's letters as a suppression of her autobiographical impulse, especially if we follow Fred Kaplan's reading of Carlyle's work on the *Letters and Memorials* as an extension of the indirect autobiographical impulsiveness of his *Reminiscences*.[25]

However, this is to bring a gendered reading into contact with an Olneyesque discourse of autobiographical criticism, and to allow the latter to attain an unwarranted ascendancy. If the *Letters and Memorials* are extensions of the *Reminiscences* then they are so because they too present juxtaposed life-course narrative quests for genre and style. For instance, Carlyle's elucidation of Jane's second letter presents his excursion into the public mass-meeting milieux of radical London in the 1830s: the elucidation leads him to analyse the dynamics of the meeting in terms of a quest for a modern public style of address: 'what new *laws* there were for speaking to such a mass' (*Letters and Memorials*, I, p. 9). One of Jane Welsh Carlyle's letters to John Sterling analyses her domestic situation through the form of a fictional dialogue, in which a caged bird, Chico, discusses its captive predicament with an interlocutor whose voice parodies that of the Carlylean public sage: 'unhappy Chico! Not in thy circumstances but in thyself lies the mean impediment over which thou cans't not gain the mastery' (*Letters and Memorials*, I, p. 78). Reading solely for the autobiographical impulse in itself is not quite adequate to the antagonistic authorial quests for style and mode of address that we can read in the *Reminiscences* and the *Letters and Memorials*.

My reading of Carlyle's *Reminiscences* in this chapter argues that Bakhtin's writings give us new ways of critically conceptualizing the relationships between nineteenth-century biography and autobiography and the forms of cultural value attached to their use. Simultaneously this urges that we modify such a critical concept as the 'autobiographical impulse' by bringing it into contact with a view of life-writing as an act of self-fashioning achieved within particular cultural spaces yielding discursive possibilities and limits. Accordingly, my approach may be said to be New Historical and, in response to a recent critique of this method, I want to finish by uttering a few words in its defence.

In his recent study of *The Language of Autobiography* (1993), John Sturrock questions the ultimate viability of New Historicist accounts of autobiography. Sturrock argues that New Historicism fails to account for the theoretical specifics of the autobiographical act through its need to contextualize and situate autobiography in relation to other writings.[26] Although Sturrock involves himself in an elaborate argument concerning the grounds for a theoretical reading of autobiography, he ends on a prescriptive note: read only autobiographies recognized as such by the existing canon.[27] There are manifest problems with this view when applied to the case of the *Reminiscences*. Canonically restricted readings would lead to a disregard for the chains of intertextuality – wherein, incidentally, biographies transmutate into autobiographies – in which the utterances comprising the *Reminiscences* were situated. Sturrock's prescription would tend still to leave the *Reminiscences* at an embarrassed distance from the public controversy which greeted their publication: the approach that I have sketched in this chapter would restore the *Reminiscences* to their generative position in this controversy – which the form of their utterance fully acknowledges.

Notes

1. The controversy was first surveyed by Waldo H. Dunn, *Froude and Carlyle: A Study of the Froude-Carlyle Controversy* (London: Longmans, Green and Co., 1930). For a more recent review of the controversy and the voices that adopted positions in relation to the issues, see D.J. Trela, 'Froude on the Carlyles: The Victorian Debate Over Biography', in *Victorian Scandals: Representations of Class and Gender*, ed. Kristine Ottesen Garrigan (Athens, Ohio: Ohio University Press, 1992), pp. 180–206.
2. Thomas Carlyle, *Reminiscences* (1881), ed. Ian Campbell, Everyman Library (London: Dent, 1972), p. 169 (hereafter, *Rem*).
3. For instance, H.D. Traill did not include it in his Centenary Edition of the works of Carlyle which appeared between 1896 and 1900. Because the publication history of the *Reminiscences* is complex, a note about editions is necessary here. Froude published the *Reminiscences* in two volumes in 1881; however, the text was generally agreed to have been edited without due attention to detail. In 1887 C.E. Norton published an edition of the text which has since been taken to be more reliable. Even so, neither Froude nor Norton published all of Carlyle's biographical sketches – the sketches of John Wilson ('Christopher North') and Sir William Hamilton were omitted. When Ian Campbell published his Everyman edition of the *Reminiscences* in 1972 he followed Norton's 1887 edition but included the portraits of Wilson and Hamilton, thus expanding the work. For the purposes of this chapter, I have followed Campbell's modified Norton edition, from which all references are taken. A completely

new edition of the *Reminiscences*, edited by Ian Campbell and Kenneth Fielding, and published by Oxford University Press, is expected in the near future: see Ian Campbell, 'Reading Carlyle: the *Reminiscences*', in *Carlyle Society Papers, Session 1990–91* (Edinburgh: Carlyle Society, 1991), p. 8.

4. Campbell, 'Reading Carlyle', p. 8.
5. H. Carvell, 'Carlyle's *Reminiscences*', *Blackwood's Edinburgh Magazine*, **132** (July 1882), 18.
6. [Anon], 'Carlyle's *Reminiscences*', *Edinburgh Review*, **153** (April 1881), 496.
7. G.W. Farrar, 'The *Reminiscences*: A Study of the Autobiographical Impulse in the Work of Thomas Carlyle', unpublished PhD thesis, University of Maryland, 1991.
8. Farrar, p. 36. See also, James Olney, *Metaphors of the Self: The Meaning of Autobiography*, (Princeton: Princeton University Press, 1972), pp. 36–7.
9. Thomas Carlyle, 'Biography' (1832); *The Centenary Edition of the Works of Thomas Carlyle*, ed. H.D. Traill, 30 vols (London: Chapman and Hall, 1896–1900), vol. XXVIII, p. 45 (hereafter, 'Biography').
10. *Letters and Memorials of Jane Welsh Carlyle; Prepared for Publication by Thomas Carlyle*, 3 vols (London: Longman, 1883), vol. I, p. 5 (hereafter, *Letters and Memorials*).
11. F. Kaplan, *Thomas Carlyle: A Biography* (Cambridge: Cambridge University Press, 1983), p. 486.
12. P. Morris, *The Bakhtin Reader: Selected Writings of Bakhtin, Medvedev, Voloshinov* (London: Edward Arnold, 1994), p. 250. For readers new to Bakhtin, Pam Morris's excellent *Bakhtin Reader* contains a very helpful glossary, compiled by Graham Roberts, which includes an account of 'outsidedness' and many additional Bakhtinian neologisms and inflections which feature in this chapter, such as: chronotope, utterance, author, genres (speech, primary, secondary), architectonics.
13. M.M. Bakhtin, *Speech Genres and Other Late Essays* (Austin: University of Texas Press, 1986), p. 147 (hereafter, *Speech Genres*).
14. M.M. Bakhtin, *The Dialogic Imagination: Four Essays* (Austin: University of Texas Press, 1981), p. 142 (hereafter, *DI*).
15. See M. Holquist, *Dialogism: Bakhtin and His World* (London and New York: Routledge, 1990), pp. 3–7.
16. M.M. Bakhtin, *Art and Answerability: Early Philosophical Essays* (Austin: University of Texas Press, 1990), p. 188 (hereafter, *Art and Answerability*).
17. Olney, *Metaphors of the Self*, p. 18.
18. Holquist, *Dialogism*, p. 109.
19. Holquist, p. 170. Holquist uses this term in relation to a reading of F. Scott Fitzgerald's *The Great Gatsby*, which, Holquist argues, is concerned to 'lay bare its own architectonics'. The link here is clearly to the avant-garde poetics of the Russian Formalists. It was Victor Shklovsky, in his essay 'Art as Technique' (1917), who formulated the idea of literary art as that which sought to 'lay bare' the devices from which it was constructed. However, the link has been crucially mediated and modified by the Bakhtin School's argument with Russian Formalism as set out in P.M. Medvedev's *The Formal Method in Literary Scholarship* (1928). According to Bakhtin,

Medvedev and Voloshinov, Formalism was flawed in seeing the poetic device as a constituent of a closed system of poetic language: the 'laying bare' of this device could only occur through its deviation from other 'conventional' terms in the closed system. By contrast, the Bakhtin School's sense of the 'laying bare' of the *word* involved making explicit the word's architectonics – that is, its ideologically contested place within the heteroglot diversity of a social formation (architectonics being a science of dynamic relations between parts).

20. The Governor Eyre case was a major public controversy of the 1860s which was precipitated by the events of 1865 when Edward John Eyre, the English governor of Jamaica, responded to the threat of insurrection with ruthless brutality: 439 native Jamaicans executed; 600 flogged; 1000 dwellings burned. On the British mainland, liberal and conservative opinion polarized around the issue: John Stuart Mill chaired the 'Jamaica Committee' which sought the prosecution of Eyre. Carlyle was a member of the 'Defence Committee' which sought to protect Eyre from prosecution. For details see Kaplan, *Thomas Carlyle*, pp. 487–95.

21. *Rem*, p. 305. That Carlyle should have 'opposed' the prominent novelist and woman of letters Margaret Oliphant may seem surprising: as Fred Kaplan records, Margaret Oliphant became a friend to Jane Welsh Carlyle upon the publication of her *Life of Edward Irving* precisely because both Carlyles approved of the memorial of Irving that she had written (Kaplan, p. 449). Moreover, as D.J. Trela points out, Margaret Oliphant was vociferous in her defence of the Carlyles' right to privacy after the controversial publication of Froude's biography of Carlyle and the *Reminiscences* (Trela, 'Froude on the Carlyles', pp. 197–9). It should be stressed that Carlyle's divergence from Margaret Oliphant occurs at the level of the intertext, and in respect of the cultural values attached to generic forms of writing.

22. Margaret Oliphant, *The Life of Edward Irving: Minister of the National Scotch Church, London: Illustrated by His Journals and Correspondence* (1862), third edition (London: Hurst and Blackett, 1864), p. 19 (hereafter, Oliphant).

23. T. Lloyd, 'Thomas Carlyle and Dynamical Symbolism: The Lesson of Edward Irving', *Victorian Newsletter*, 79 (1991), 9–18 (pp. 12–13).

24. S. Hileman, 'Autobiographical Narrative in the Letters of Jane Carlyle', *A/B: Auto/Biography Studies*, 4 (1988), 107–17 (p. 115).

25. Kaplan, p. 486.

26. J. Sturrock, *The Language of Autobiography: Studies in the First Person Singular* (Cambridge: Cambridge University Press, 1993), p. 10.

27. Sturrock, pp. 12–19.

CHAPTER NINE

Victorian Women as Writers and Readers of (Auto)biography

Joanne Shattock

> It is a dangerous thing to have your life written when you are dead and helpless and can do nothing to protest against the judgement ... But if biography is thus dangerous, there is a still more fatal art, more radical in its operation, and infinitely more murderous, against which nothing can defend the predestined victim. This terrible instrument of self-murder is called autobiography.

The words are Margaret Oliphant's, at the beginning of her review of Harriet Martineau's *Autobiography* in *Blackwood's Magazine* (121, April 1877). The tone is uncharacteristically abrasive and masculine, the review measured but severe. Oliphant objected to Martineau's air of self-importance, the 'self applauses' of the work, her inflated sense of her own influence on her times, her ill-tempered comments on her contemporaries. She noted with disapproval Martineau's ungenerous treatment of her home life, particularly her cruel comments on her mother, her lack of feminine interests, apart from her love of babies and needlework, and finally what she saw as the simple-mindedness of Martineau's religious deconversion and subsequent embracing of Comtism. It was to the Martineau constructed by the autobiography and to her abuse of the form, 'a post-scriptal harangue from the tomb' as she called it (p. 475), that Oliphant objected, rather than to the act of writing an autobiography. As a professional woman writer, the experience of reading the autobiography of a yet more successful woman writer and public figure was not without interest.

George Eliot, too, had read the Martineau autobiography, having looked forward to its appearance since the 1850s when she had heard of its being written. 'She is a trump – the only English woman that possesses thoroughly the art of writing', she had once written of Martineau in their early reviewing days.' She had also read Oliphant's review, with which she was broadly in agreement.[1] She found Martineau's account of her childhood and early youth 'pathetic and interesting', approved, not surprisingly, of her silence on the matter of her estrangement from her brother James, but concluded that 'as in all books of the kind, the charm departs as the life advances, and the writer has to tell of her own triumphs'. Writing to John Blackwood, she confessed that having read Martineau's accounts of her writings and what others said and did concerning them she was cross that she had ever said a word to anyone about either criticism or compliments she had herself received, adding, 'assuredly, I shall not write such things down to be published after my death' (*Letters*, VI, pp. 351–2). Two months later, still on the subject of the *Autobiography*, she told Sara Hennell that 'the more I think of the book and all connected with it, the more it deepens my repugnance – or rather creates a new repugnance in me – to autobiography unless it can be so written as to involve neither self-glorification or impeachment of others' (*Letters*, VI, p. 371).

Feminist critics have written extensively of the constraints imposed on women who attempt to engage formally in self-writing, and of the fundamental divergences of women's autobiography from the recognized masculine model.[2] The ambivalence, if not the disinclination, of nineteenth-century English women writers towards the writing of autobiography has also been noted.[3] Harriet Martineau and Margaret Oliphant were exceptions in a period when few women writers ventured on more than fragmentary memoirs or occasional childhood reminiscences.[4] The few autobiographies which were published joined a select group of biographical texts which assumed particular significance for women readers and, more precisely, women writers as readers, in the nineteenth century.

Nancy K. Miller, considering the complexities of self-representation in the work of French women writers, notes the impact on women writers generally of the autobiographical writings of their predecessors. She instances the influence of George Sand, Daniel Stern and Simone de Beauvoir's autobiographies, suggesting that 'this structure of kinship, through which readers as women perceive bonds relating them to writers as women would seem to be a "natural" feature of the autobiographical text'. She goes on to question the authenticity of self-representation in these autobiographical texts: 'Despite the identity between the "I" of authorship and the "I" of narrative, and the pacts of sincerity, reading these lives is rather like shaking hands with one's gloves on.' Miller proposes 'an intratextual practice of interpretation' which privileges neither the autobiography nor the fiction of women writers, but takes the two writings together 'in their status as text'.[5]

Miller's recommended practice of reading autobiographies in conjunction with fiction in order to gain a full representation of the author nicely describes the reading habits of many nineteenth-century English women writers, untroubled by anxieties about the referentiality of language or the authenticity of the self. Ellen Moers first made the point that these women, denied access to metropolitan literary society, universities and clubs, sought and created the sense of a literary community by reading one another's books: 'The normal literary life was closed to them. Without it, they studied with a special closeness the works written by their own sex, and relied on a sense of easy, almost rude familiarity with the women who wrote them.'[6] Autobiographies and biographies, even more than fictional texts, purported to offer real-life heroines and role models. Elaine Showalter has noted how Elizabeth Gaskell's *Life of Charlotte Brontë* helped to construct the Brontë 'legend', 'the myth of the novelist as tragic heroine', and noted too that after the publication of the *Life* the legend rapidly 'took on the psychic properties of a cult'.[7] References to the Gaskell biography proliferate in the letters and memoirs of nineteenth-century women writers on both sides of the Atlantic.[8] The landmark status which it was accorded at mid-century was to be replicated for a later generation of readers by a unique biography of George Eliot.

The writing of autobiography raised anxieties with most women writers. Self-definition and self-exploration implied self-confidence, a sense of the writing self and the acknowledgement of a public role with which they were uncomfortable. Margaret Oliphant's objection to Harriet Martineau's *Autobiography* was in part that she had taken herself too seriously. George Eliot had similarly found her 'self-glorification' repugnant. Biography, or the prospect of it, posed different problems for women writers. Most, like their male colleagues, shrank from the possibility that their lives should be subjected to posthumous scrutiny, however well-intentioned. Margaret Oliphant extracted a deathbed promise that there should be no account of her life, a somewhat ironic request from the author of five biographies and numerous biographical sketches. Her antipathy to biography probably stemmed from what she regarded as the monstrous injustice done to the Carlyles by Froude, a subject which became for her almost an obsession. Elisabeth Jay has noted how she lost no opportunity of commenting on Froude's biography of Carlyle and his editions of the *Reminiscences* and Jane Carlyle's *Letters and Memorials*. Oliphant wrote two articles in the *Contemporary Review* on the subject, the first of which, 'Mrs. Carlyle', exposed the latter's vulnerability in the light of Froude's decision to publish the *Reminiscences* and the *Letters and Memorials*:

> Is it then permissible to outrage the memory of a wife, and betray her secrets because one has received as a gift her husband's papers? She gave no permission, left no authority for such a proceeding ... Did she authorize Mr. Froude to unveil her most secret thoughts, her darkest hours of weakness, which even her husband passed reverently over? No woman of this generation, or of any other we are acquainted with, has had such desperate occasion to be saved

from her friends: and public feeling and sense of honour must be at a low ebb indeed when no one ventures to stand up and stigmatize as it deserves this betrayal and exposure of the secret of a woman's weakness, a secret which throws no light upon anything, which does not add to our knowledge either of her character or her husband's and with which the public had nothing whatever to do.[9]

Feelings ran high over the Froude publications, and not just with Mrs Oliphant. Two years later, however, her attentions, like those of most of her contemporaries, were directed towards another momentous biographical event, the publication of John Walter Cross's biography of his late wife George Eliot.

This biography was ostensibly a pious three-volume 'Life and Letters', of a type so beloved by the Victorians, compiled in this case by the widower rather than widow. The title is significant: *George Eliot's Life as Related in Her Letters and Journals* 'arranged and edited by her husband, J.W. Cross'. In the preface Cross calls the work an *autobiography* (his italics):

> The life has been allowed to write itself in extracts from her letters and journals. Free from the obtrusion of any mind but her own, this method serves, I think, better than any other open to me, to show the development of her intellect and character ... I do not know that the particular method in which I have treated the letters has ever been adopted before. Each letter has been pruned of everything that seemed to me irrelevant to my purpose – of everything that I thought my wife would have wished to be omitted. Every sentence that remains, adds, in my judgement, something (however small it may be) to the means of forming a conclusion about her character ... Excepting a slight introductory sketch of the girlhood up to the time when letters became available and a few words here and there to elucidate the correspondence, I have confined myself to the work of selection and arrangement ... 'All interpretations depend upon the interpreter,' and I have judged it best to let George Eliot be her own interpreter as far as possible.[10]

This of course we now know to be disingenuous. Cross was constructing a version of George Eliot as carefully as if he had written a narrative, by what he left out, the 'prunings' to which he refers, and by his 'selection and arrangement'. Gordon Haight's preface to the first volume of his edition of the George Eliot letters describes in detail Cross's editorial shortcomings, none of which are surprising to anyone familiar with nineteenth-century editions of letters. More interestingly, he gives precise examples of how Cross stripped the correspondence of wit, spontaneity, gaiety and humour, and left the solemn, ponderous, ultra-serious sibylline Eliot which set the seal on her reputation for the next 30 years.[11]

But in spite of Cross's efforts there is much of Eliot in the text, particularly the Journal entries, of which he included a number. The complete edition of the Journals is still to be published.[12] Haight claimed to have included 91 diary and journal entries. Eliot began her journal in 1849 in Geneva, and continued this notebook up to the end of 1861. She began a second in the same year which extended to 1877. In addition she wrote several separate travel journals: Germany (1858), Italy (1860 and 1864) and France (1865), together with two volumes of diaries for 1879 and 1880. Some of the entries are terse accounts of daily events, others are more like short essays, of which the best known are 'How I Came to Write Fiction' (Cross, vol. I, pp. 414–17), written in 1856, and 'The History of Adam Bede', written in 1858 (II, pp. 65–71). There are also extracts of her 'Recollections' of the Scilly Isles, of Ilfracombe and of Jersey. Some of the daily entries are fairly intimate, recording her changing moods, her depressions and the ailments with which she was constantly beset. There are others, more lengthy, which summarize her feelings at the end of an eventful year, or a significant period in her life.[13] Until the Journals are published in full, we shall not know for certain how much Cross left out, or how in other ways they may have been altered. But their presence in the *Life*, together with the almost total absence of a connecting narrative, makes a case for the *Life* as a form of self-writing in the way that Gaskell's *Life of Charlotte Brontë*, or J.E. Austen Leigh's *Memoir of Jane Austen* (1870), for example, do not.

The impact of the biography when it was published in January 1885 was immediate and far-reaching. To readers of both sexes it established Eliot's intellectual pre-eminence in a way that the novels had individually not done, a point reinforced by reviewer after reviewer. It was reviewed widely – by John Morley, by Henry James, by Frederic Harrison, by Lord Acton, among others. There were two reviews by women, both writers, one by Margaret Oliphant in the *Edinburgh* (April 1885) and another, in the same month, in *Temple Bar*, by Eliza Lynn Linton. Both reviews are revealing of their authors, on both of whom the (auto)biography had a profound impact.

Oliphant proved herself a perceptive critic. Eliot had achieved a status unparalleled in the public mind. One indication was the public's willingness to overlook her domestic circumstances, enough to condemn any woman from the duchess to the dressmaker. Another was the absence of any reference to her sex in any critical writing about her, a point Oliphant had made earlier with respect to Eliot in her review of Martineau.[14] Oliphant regarded the biography as the joint product of Eliot and Cross:

> The biography of George Eliot as here given is a gigantic silhouette ... background and figure are alike dull ... But Mr. Cross, who ought to know better, and she herself, who ought, one sup-

poses, to have known best of all, have here put it down for us in black and white ... Let no one say henceforth out of his own lips a man or a woman can be best judged ... Carlyle has been made out of his own mouth to prove himself a snarling Diogenes ... and George Eliot by the same fine process has been made to prove herself a dull woman. We take leave to say that we do not believe her, any more than we believed him.[15]

Oliphant searches for letters which convey the 'real' George Eliot, one from 1841 when she had moved to Coventry, which describes an autumn day, another from Geneva in 1849, which make her letters to the Bray family 'and the other little intellectualities of Coventry read like so many little essays' (*Edinburgh Review*, p. 532).[16] She sees shrewdly that Eliot is herself constructing a persona which is scarcely reconcilable with the rich humour and the sophistication of the novels. 'Is this the woman who wrote *Adam Bede*?', she asks incredulously (*ER*, p. 519).

She quotes at length from the section of the Journal on 'How I Came to Write Fiction' and questions 'the timidity or rather the docility of the new author' as contrasted with 'the mature and easy force of the style, the command of all her materials and the freedom and power' with which she writes *Amos Barton*. 'That it should be George Eliot, with her voice and touch of power, her large freedom of speech, her emancipation from all bondage of the pretty and proper, who was the heroine of this little conjugal drama, is in the highest degree bewildering' (*ER*, p. 542). She quotes, again from the Journal, the passage in which Eliot describes the germ of *Adam Bede*, her Methodist Aunt Samuel's story of the girl who commited a child murder.

> It is evident in all that follows that, to the author, the central and most important figure in the book is Dinah Morris ... The wonderful study of Hetty, made with such boldness ... obtains from the woman scarcely any notice at all ... It is strange to find her, in her own person, so little conscious of excellence in art, even her own, and so artlessly devoted to moral excellence and the ideal.
> (*ER*, pp. 544–5)

She continues:

> The reader will find but little light thrown upon the authoress in these volumes, but he will make acquaintance with a woman of a remarkable character ... The strongest of all female writers, he will find in her what is almost the conventional type of a woman – a creature all conjugal love and dependence ... who is sure of nothing until her god has vouched for it, not even her own powers.
> (*ER*, p. 551)

Oliphant's conclusion anticipates Virginia Woolf's in the 1919 centennial essay[17] which was to trigger the revival of Eliot's reputation, that the real Eliot was to be found in her heroines, in Maggie, in Dorothea:

'With these and a host of other characters to speak for her, George Eliot needs no other expositor' (*ER*, p. 553).

Cross's *Life* was published in January 1885. In February Margaret Oliphant took up again the fragment of an autobiography she had begun in 1864 after the death of her daughter Maggie, prompted, she acknowledged, by the inevitable comparisons with her own writing life. She is touchingly honest about her mixed feelings concerning her celebrated contemporary: 'I have been tempted to begin writing by George Eliot's Life – with that curious kind of self-compassion which one cannot get clear of. I wonder if I am a little envious of her.' Later, she continues:

> I don't quite know why I should put all this down. I suppose because George Eliot's life has, as I said above, stirred me up to an involuntary confession. How I have been handicapped in life! Should I have done better if I had been kept, like her, in a mental greenhouse and taken care of?... Let me be done with this – I wonder if I will ever have time to put a few autobiographical bits down before I die. I am in very little danger of having my life written, and that is all the better in this point of view – for what could be said of me? George Eliot and George Sand make me half inclined to cry over my poor little unappreciated self – 'Many love me (*i.e.*, in a sort of way), but by none am I enough beloved.' These two bigger women did things which I have never felt the least temptation to do – but how much more enjoyment they seem to have got out of their life, how much more praise and homage and honour ... I do feel very small, very obscure, beside them, rather a failure all round.[18]

It was Oliphant's strength as an autobiographer that she was able to lift herself out of her self-pity and to write an autobiography which was not, as were Eliot's and Martineau's, structured as success stories, the emergence of public women. There is no self-aggrandizement, no immodesty, but rather the reverse. Hers is the story of a private life, not a public one.

Four years before resuming the *Autobiography* she had contributed a series of seven articles on 'Autobiographies' to *Blackwood's* (January 1881–April 1883), one of the numerous journalistic projects in which she was engaged at the time and which she crammed into her crowded writing life. The articles are disappointingly descriptive, and lack both the sense of personal engagement of the review of Martineau's *Autobiography* and the critical shrewdness of her piece on 'Miss Austen and Miss Mitford' (*Blackwood's*, March 1870), a review of Austen Leigh's *Memoir of Jane Austen* and of *The Life of Mary Russell Mitford*.

A general theme, though, does emerge. Autobiography on the one hand can offer consolation in old age to the man who has lived 'an active and important life', a consciousness that he 'can leave behind a record of many things worth knowing, clear up, perhaps, some historical mysteries of his period, and keep the incidents of his own life alive among men'. Equally valid, she acknowledges, is the 'domestic record' of the man who has not been involved in great events, 'over whose head these events have passed without ever disturbing his honest rest; every personal experience adds to our knowledge'.[19] Again in her article on Gibbon (August 1881) she reiterates that 'a glimpse into a man's mind, a real portrait of a human creature great or small, is one of the greatest pleasures we can receive'. Autobiography then, is about self-revelation and insight into human nature. She contrasts Gibbon's autobiographical self-portrait with two paintings in the National Gallery, one by Moroni of a tailor, and another, interestingly, of Andrea del Sarto, 'the great painter but feeble soul, whose sad story of vacillation and moral failure, deepened by a never failing consciousness of the higher truth he could not hold by, is written in his eyes'. Gibbon's autobiography, like the paintings, is 'valuable not for the kind of being it depicts, but because it does depict a real kind of being, bringing us into distinct contact with him, and affording a clear perception of his qualities'.[20] In her *Autobiography*, she was to compare herself to Browning's version of Andrea del Sarto, encumbered by domestic responsibilities and producing as a result second-rate art.[21]

The intensely private nature of her own autobiography is less surprising in the light of these journalistic pieces. Elisabeth Jay's 1990 edition incorporates hitherto missing fragments and her introduction outlines the intermittent composition of the work which took place over more than three decades. Jay also demonstrates the efforts of Oliphant's literary executors, her niece Denny and secretary and friend Annie Coghill to mould sections of the autobiography into a more conventional 'life story' and to construct an image of a domestically orientated, charming, self-deprecating woman which, they thought, would prove attractive to late nineteenth-century readers.[22]

There is no linear structure to Oliphant's autobiography although there is a chronological narrative, but rather four fragments, centring around her family, their births and deaths. Linda Peterson argues that the time scheme is a maternal time scheme, that Oliphant's autobiography is a mother's story first, a writer's second.[23] The two are interwoven, but writing, as Oliphant claimed, 'ran through everything':

> Other matters, events even of our uneventful life, took so much more importance in life than these books – nay it must be a kind of affectation to say that, for the writing ran through everything. But then it was also subordinate to everything, to be pushed aside for any little necessity.
>
> (*Autobiography*, p. 23)

Eliot is the role model she expected to be compared with – single-minded, dedicated to her art, cocooned, protected, a thoroughly professional writer for whom writing took precedence over everything else. Oliphant is in turn shocked and envious. She had a similar response to Trollope's posthumously published *Autobiography* two years earlier, with its concentration on the writing life. She by contrast has 'never had any theory on the subject [of writing]'. 'I have written because it gave me pleasure, because it came natural to me, because it was like talking or breathing, besides the big fact that it was necessary for me to work for my children.' She has sloughed off the embarrassing questions about her 'art': 'They are my work, which I like in the doing, which is my natural way of occupying myself, though they are never so good as I meant them to be. And when I have said that, I have said all that is in me to say' (*Autobiography*, pp. 4–5).

Elisabeth Jay sees the tension between the life and the work as the underlying theme of the *Autobiography*. She notes 'the intimate and complex relationship between the writing and the need that generated it' which ran throughout Oliphant's writing life.[24] It was the image of the dedicated life, the literary 'success story' as projected by Eliot's biography and Trollope's autobiography, which spurred her to write an account of a different writing life in which the demands of art and family generated its own creative tension. And in the writing of that life Oliphant deliberately rejected any version of a 'myth of progress', in Jay's words, creating instead a series of fragments centring on domestic memories, friendships, and griefs, the stuff of women's lives. The *Autobiography* has its own narrative strategy and is, Jay argues, a highly experimental text.

A bizarre coda to the reception of Cross's *Life* was presented by the novelist Eliza Lynn Linton. Her *Temple Bar* review in 1885 was followed in 1897 by a chapter on George Eliot in *Women Novelists of Queen Victoria's Reign*, a collection of essays by late nineteenth-century women novelists on their predecessors, published by Hurst and Blackett. Two years later she published an extensive reminiscence of Eliot in *My Literary Life*, a brief collection of memoirs. In addition, her autobiographical novel, *The Autobiography of Christopher Kirkland*, published in the same year as Cross's *Life*, contained veiled references to the Thornton Hunt-G.H. Lewes circle.[25]

Linton's response to George Eliot's biography was as much a venting of personal animus as a considered review. Reading the *Life* had given rise to an amalgam of strong feelings which she had been nurturing since her early days as an aspiring professional writer. She had conceived an intense antipathy to Lewes on their first meeting at John Chapman's house in London in the 1840s. At subsequent meetings with the young Marian Evans, also at Chapman's, she considered herself as having been snubbed. Despite Eliot's kindly interest in her welfare over the ensuing decade, Linton grew intensely jealous of her literary success and her happy liaison with Lewes, circumstances which were not improved by her own indifferent literary career and subsequent broken marriage. A chapter in *My Literary Life* recalled the first meeting with George Eliot:

> She was essentially under-bred and provincial; and I, in the swaddling-clothes of early education and prepossession as I was, saw more of the provincial than the genius, and was repelled by the unformed manner rather than attracted by the learning. She held her hands and arms kangaroo fashion; was badly dressed; had an unwashed, unbrushed, unkempt look altogether; and she assumed a tone of superiority over me which I was not then aware was warranted by her undoubted leadership. From first to last she put up my mental bristles ...[26]

As a reviewer of Cross's *Life* she was scarcely neutral. The review is an interesting mixture of perception, envy and spleen. Cross is virtually absent from his text, she notes at the outset. He lets Eliot tell her own life, the reader is given only her version of events, and therefore never sees her objectively. The book has been written 'to embalm and preserve the image of the Ideal George Eliot, as success made her appear, and as the world accepted for reality'.[27] Eliot was not an original thinker. Her mind was 'chameleon-like', she had great powers of assimilation and therefore grew to be 'a learned woman of rare solidity and thoroughness', but she was eminently the result of other men's teachings (*TB*, pp. 514–16). Her characters were individually memorable but, unlike those of Dickens, Jane Austen or Thackeray, few had entered the national consciousness as unforgettable types.

The *Life* was too long, and her letters as literature were 'in no way superior to those of any intelligent woman who goes to Germany and Italy for the first time and enjoys what she sees' (*TB*, p. 518). Hers was a 'hot-house' nature that needed constant sympathy and protection. Without the encouragement of Lewes she probably would never have found the genius that had lain dormant so long. Without him, it was predictable that she should marry: 'Old as she was, past sixty, she could not live without a lover, a husband.' When the current wave of adulation has subsided, when men no longer 'quote Kant and the author of "Middlemarch" as equals' (*TB*, pp. 523–4), her life and works will take their proper place in history and literature, a place, Linton hints, which will be far less exalted than they at present are given.

Linton mounted a third personal attack on Eliot in her essay for the Hurst and Blackett volume, in which she made no attempt to disguise her hostility to the sibylline Eliot of the later years. Success and adulation had spoilt her, and destroyed all simplicity, all sincerity of character. 'Her whole life and being were moulded to an artificial pose, and the "made" woman could not possibly be the spontaneous artist.'[28]

Linton's valediction, warped though it was by hurt and envy, proved an accurate barometer of Eliot's reputation in the short term. Cross's biography, like Gaskell's *Life of Charlotte Brontë* before it, constructed the image of the writer which was to prevail for decades to come. This 'lifeless silhouette', as David Carroll commented in his introduction to the Critical Heritage volume on Eliot, 'was to intervene stubbornly between the novels and the reading public for many years' and, it is suggested, contributed to the decline in her posthumous reputation.[29]

And yet, in 1919, when Virginia Woolf began to prepare her article for the *Times Literary Supplement* in celebration of the centenary of Eliot's birth, the article which was to launch the revival of her reputation, she began with Cross's *Life*. 'I am reading through the whole of George Eliot, in order to sum her up once and for all, upon her anniversary', she wrote to a friend. 'So far I have only made way with her life, which is a book of the greatest fascination, and I can see already that no one else has ever known her as I know her.'[30] Nearly 40 years after it was published, the biography, or as Woolf describes it, 'the sad soliloquy in which Mr. Cross condemned her to tell the story of her life' proved as potent a revelation to a modernist woman writer as it had done to Eliot's contemporaries.

Despite Margaret Oliphant's warning of the dangers of biography and autobiography in her review of Harriet Martineau's autobiography, both genres have proved to be key sites for the interpretation and understanding of women writers by one another.

Notes

1. *The George Eliot Letters*, ed. Gordon S. Haight, 9 vols (New Haven and London: Yale University Press, 1954–78), vol. II, p. 32 (hereafter, *Letters*).
2. *The Private Self: Theory and Practice of Women's Autobiographical Writings*, ed. Shari Benstock (London: Routledge, 1988); *The Female Autograph: Theory and Practice of Autobiography from the Tenth to the Twentieth Century*, ed. Domna Stanton (Chicago: Chicago University Press, 1987); *Women's Autobiography: Essays in Criticism*, ed. Estelle C. Jelinek (Bloomington: Indiana University Press, 1980), especially her introduction, 'Women's Autobiography and the Male Tradition', pp. 1–20; Linda Anderson, 'At the Threshold of the Self: Women and Autobiography', in *Women's Writing: A Challenge to Theory*, ed. Moira Monteith (Brighton: Harvester Press, 1986), pp. 54–71; *Diaries and Journals of*

Literary Women from Fanny Burney to Virginia Woolf, ed. Judy Simons (London: Macmillan, 1990); Mary Jean Corbett, *Representing Femininity: Middle-Class Subjectivity in Victorian and Edwardian Women's Autobiographies* (Oxford: Oxford University Press, 1992); Sidonie Smith, *A Poetics of Women's Autobiography: Marginality and the Fictions of Self-Representation* (Bloomington: Indiana University Press, 1987).
3. See Valerie Sanders, *The Private Lives of Victorian Women: Autobiography in Nineteenth-Century England* (London: Harvester Press, 1989).
4. For example: Sara Coleridge, 'Recollections of the Early Life of Sara Coleridge, Written by Herself', in *Memoir and Letters of Sara Coleridge, Edited by Her Daughter* (1873); Mary Russell Mitford, *Recollections of a Literary Life; or Books, Places and People* (1852); Anne Thackeray Ritchie, *Chapters from Some Memoirs* (1894); Mary Somerville, *Personal Recollections, from Early Life to Old Age* (1873); Charlotte Elizabeth Tonna, *Personal Recollections* (1841); Mrs Humphry Ward, *A Writer's Recollections 1856–1900* (1918).
5. Nancy K. Miller, 'Writing Fictions: Women's Autobiography in France', in her *Subject to Change: Reading Feminist Writing* (New York: Columbia University Press, 1988), pp. 58–62.
6. Quoted by Elaine Showalter, *A Literature of Their Own: British Women Novelists from Brontë to Lessing* (London: Virago, 1978), p. 101.
7. Showalter, p. 106.
8. See Showalter, pp. 106–7. For example, George Eliot wrote to a friend (*Letters*, vol. II, p. 330): 'Tell me when you have read the Life of Currer Bell. Some people think its revelations in bad taste – making money out of the dead – wounding the feelings of the living etc. etc. ... We thought it admirable – cried over it – and felt the better for it.' Margaret Oliphant, writing on the Brontës in 1897, commented that 'they are the first victims of that ruthless art of biography which is one of the features of our time', a practice in which she regarded Mrs Gaskell as a well-intentioned forerunner (*Women Novelists of Queen Victoria's Reign*, ed. Adeline Sergeant (London: Hurst and Blackett, 1897), p. 56).
9. *Contemporary Review*, 43 (May 1883), 627–8. The second article, 'The Ethics of Biography', was published in the *Contemporary Review*, 44 (July 1883). I am grateful to Elisabeth Jay for drawing these articles to my attention. See also, Elisabeth Jay, *Mrs Oliphant: 'A Fiction to Herself': A Literary Life* (Oxford: Clarendon Press, 1995), p. 256.
10. J.W. Cross, *George Eliot's Life as Related in Her Letters and Journals*, 3 vols (London: Blackwood, 1885), vol. I, pp. v–viii (hereafter, Cross). Cross recalls (vol. I, pp. 36–7) that he had tried to persuade Eliot to write her own autobiography after they were married: 'She said, half sighing, half smiling, "The only thing I should care much to dwell on would be the absolute despair I suffered from of ever being able to achieve anything. No one could ever have felt greater despair, and a knowledge of this might be a help to some other struggler" – adding with a smile, "but, on the other hand, it might only lead to an increase of bad writing".'
11. *Letters*, vol. I, pp. xii–xvi.
12. A complete edition of the Journals is in preparation, edited by Margaret Harris and Judith Johnston, to be published by Cambridge University Press.
13. See, for example, Cross, vol. II, pp. 478–81 and vol. III, pp. 323–4.

14. 'There is no female writer existing who is not benevolently or contemptuously reminded of her sex, except, indeed, George Eliot, whose supremacy is characteristically acknowledged by the absence of this favourite accusation' (*Blackwood's Magazine*, **121** (April 1877), 474).
15. *Edinburgh Review*, **161** (April 1885), 517.
16. There are echoes of this comment in Oliphant's *Autobiography*: 'She took herself with tremendous seriousness, that is evident, and was always on duty, never relaxing, her letters ponderous beyond description – and those to the Bray party giving one the idea of a mutual improvement society for the exchange of essays' (*Autobiography and Letters of Mrs Margaret Oliphant* (1899), ed. Mrs Harry Coghill, reprinted with an introduction by Q.D. Leavis (Leicester: Leicester University Press, 1974), p. 7).
17. 'George Eliot', reprinted in *Collected Essays*, vol. I (London: Hogarth Press, 1966).
18. *Autobiography and Letters of Mrs Oliphant*, ed. Mrs Harry Coghill, pp. 5–8 (hereafter, *Autobiography*).
19. 'Benvenuto Cellini', *Blackwood's Magazine*, **129** (January 1881), 1–3.
20. *Blackwood's Magazine*, **130** (August 1881), 229–30.
21. 'It is a little hard sometimes not to feel with Browning's Andrea, that the men who have no wives, who have given themselves up to their art, have had an almost unfair advantage over us who have been given perhaps more than one Lucrezia to take care of' (*Autobiography*, pp. 5–6).
22. Introduction, *The Autobiography of Margaret Oliphant: The Complete Text*, ed. Elisabeth Jay (Oxford: Oxford University Press, 1990), pp. vii–xvii.
23. Linda H. Peterson, 'Audience and the Autobiographer's Art: An Approach to the *Autobiography* of Mrs M.O.W. Oliphant', in *Approaches to Victorian Autobiography*, ed. George P. Landow (Athens, Ohio: Ohio University Press, 1979), pp. 158–74.
24. Jay, *Autobiography of Margaret Oliphant*, p. vii.
25. On Linton's championing of Thornton Hunt as against Lewes, see Gordon S. Haight, *George Eliot: A Biography* (London: Penguin, 1985), p. 132, and Ruby V. Redinger, *George Eliot: The Emergent Self* (London: Bodley Head, 1975), pp. 248–50.
26. Eliza Lynn Linton, *My Literary Life* (London: Hodder and Stoughton, 1899), p. 95.
27. Eliza Lynn Linton, *Temple Bar* (April 1885), 512 (hereafter, *TB*).
28. Eliza Lynn Linton, 'George Eliot', in *Women Novelists of Queen Victoria's Reign* (London: Hurst and Blackett, 1897), pp. 63–115 (p. 114). Her discussion of the novels, however, was generous and appreciative.
29. Introduction, *George Eliot: The Critical Heritage*, ed. David Carroll (London: Routledge and Kegan Paul, 1971), p. 40.
30. *The Letters of Virginia Woolf*, ed. Nigel Nicholson and Joanne Trautmann (New York: Harcourt, 1975–80), vol. II, p. 321; quoted by Elaine Showalter, 'The Greening of Sister George', *Nineteenth Century Fiction*, **35** (1980–81), 292.

CHAPTER TEN

'Fathers' Daughters': Three Victorian Anti-Feminist Women Autobiographers

Valerie Sanders

> I am not indeed writing an autobiography, or pretending to give an unreserved description of myself, but only offering some slight confessions in an apologetic light ... (George Eliot).[1]
>
> As for what you say about my Memoirs, I am not, you know, writing them, I am only copying and making extracts from my former journals and my early letters to you ... (Fanny Kemble).[2]
>
> Though for the purpose of describing my craft I quote pages from my MS diary, I have neither the desire nor the intention of writing an autobiography (Beatrice Webb).[3]

For centuries, women have been ashamed of writing about themselves, and yet have longed to recount the experiences that have shaped their lives, and share them with other women. Even in the nineteenth century, the great age of biography and autobiography, women writers frequently pretended they were doing something other than telling the story of their lives: writing, for instance, autobiographical fiction, such as *Jane Eyre*, literary memoirs of other people, or reprinting entertaining selections from their letters. It has taken a correspondingly long time for critics to recognize the existence of Victorian women's autobiography, and still longer to acknowledge its importance in the history of self-writing. Until the late 1970s, critics focused on the familiar male canon: Mill, Newman, Ruskin, Trollope and Carlyle – men who recounted their professional lives and the evolution of their opinions and philosophy. Harriet Martineau and Margaret Oliphant were the women most often admitted into this literary version of the male clubland: Martineau because she consciously shapes an account of her personal, professional and spiritual development into a coherent order, and therefore, in some respects, approximates to the format of male-authored autobiography; Oliphant because although she fails in this regard to conform to the accepted pattern, she questions herself about the purpose of autobiography, and places herself at the centre of her own story. Martineau and Oliphant have therefore been the only Victorian women autobiographers to have their work regularly reissued, as well as critically evaluated.

One reason for the neglect of Victorian women's autobiography must be that it raises fundamental difficulties of interpretation: not because it is at all obscure, but because it omits information about those areas of life that we tend to see as the most important in self-writing. It is silent about marriage, for instance, saying very little about the internal dynamics of any relationship with husbands and children (Mrs Oliphant is again the exception in exploring her grief and guilt at the deaths of her children, who all predeceased her). It glosses over feelings about singleness, except in a few cases, such as Harriet Martineau's;[4] like much male self-writing of the time it is reticent about attitudes to parents; and it says little about professional success, except to make light of it, once the first novel has been published, or any other notable achievement reached. What then, is left? Women's autobiography seems to be autobiography with the self left out, concentrating instead on external matters: reminiscences of other people, bygone values, strange schools, London salons, visits to France and Italy, odd religious practices and campaigns to reform schools or start organizations. None of this seems relevant to the critically austere generic approach to autobiography which has emerged from the last two decades. Too much of Victorian women's autobiography is apparently digressive and trivial, long-winded and leisurely. All the interest goes out of it beyond the childhood stage; it is seemingly unaware of the more professional purposes to which the genre was being put by male contemporaries.

The large numbers of Victorian women who wrote oblique or truncated or long-winded forms of autobiography, whether novels, travel memoirs, descriptions of childhood or social reminiscences, tend to be dismissed as unimportant because they fail to focus on a single coherent subject: a defect that may now seem less serious and more interesting because of the critical doubt surrounding the viability of the unified subject, still more the subject's ability to transpose his or her life into 'art'. The present is a key moment to reopen debate about other sorts of autobiography, and to accept that when authors are writing about their friends or ancestors they may still qualify as autobiographers, even though what they do falls far short of the standards set by critics – almost entirely male philosophers and academics. Whether or not we accept the full deconstructionist interpretation of human subjectivity, the point reached by the current critical debate over forms of autobiography permits – even welcomes – a wider discussion of women's autobiography, as attested by the number of women critics who have recently written on the subject (few men yet do so). In 1987, the journal *Women's Studies International Forum* ran a special issue devoted to women's autobiography, which included a review article of Estelle Jelinek's ambitious *Tradition of Women's Autobiography from Antiquity to the Present* (1986). Other critics, such as Domna Stanton, Bella Brodzki, Treva Broughton and Shari Benstock, have made special studies of women's autobiography and drawn attention to texts that have hitherto been largely overlooked.[5]

Nevertheless, there remains a problem with some kinds of women's autobiography: the unfinished, the unfashionable, the kind that refuses to focus on the self, and pads out a rambling narrative with long extracts from letters and diaries. Should these be ignored by the modern critic, or is it possible to find ways of reading them that are both productive and stimulating? Are they, in any helpful sense, commenting on the restrictions surrounding writing women? I wish to return later in this essay to the question of how one should read countless pages of 'reminiscences' in Victorian women's self-writing and find some connection between their thumbnail sketches and the main story of the writer's life. We could take this investigation one step further, and ask what happens when the autobiographer in question is known to express anti-feminist views, and be opposed to most forms of self-advertisement. The writing of autobiography is likely to give her particularly intransigent problems, and lead to various rhetorical strategies to deflect the sense of inconsistency. In the meantime, it is worth pausing for a moment over two recent critical approaches to the autobiographical canon, and the debate about the quality of self-writing.

Two recent critics, John Sturrock (1993) and Sidonie Smith (1987), offer contrasting approaches, demonstrating the range of options still open to the critic of autobiography, and the resistance to accepting women's self-writing as an authentic contribution to the genre. Sturrock focuses entirely on male practitioners, except for Teresa of Avila, defending his loyalty to the traditional canon with the statement: 'There are excellent reasons why certain works become canonical, having to do with their quality and not with the coercive impulses of the canon makers.'[6] Seeing autobiography as, by its nature, 'an authoritarian mode of writing' (p. 15), Sturrock also believes that it wills the unity of its subject. According to him, 'the autobiographer wishes to stand forth in print in the form of a *whole*' (p. 4). Everything about Sturrock's definition of autobiography savours of traditional masculinity, relegating the tentative or the inchoate to the margins of generic acceptability.

On the face of it, of course, Victorian women who regarded their role as essentially private and domestic were supposed to have no business writing autobiography at all. As Sarah Ellis puts it, in *The Women of England* (1839): 'Never yet, however, was woman great because she had great acquirements.' Usefulness, or what she calls 'instrumentality', was in her view the one thing needful for women to make any worthwhile contribution to the running of their households: 'If, therefore, they are endowed only with such faculties as render them striking and distinguished in themselves, without the faculty of instrumentality, they are only as dead as letters in the volume of human life, filling what would otherwise be a blank space, but doing nothing more.'[7]

However useful her work, a woman was not meant to draw attention to herself or her achievements: hence the whole paradox of women writing autobiography, the most attention-seeking literary genre, though also, for that reason, the most apologetic. It was impossible for a Victorian woman to write without acknowledging that she was doing something unbefitting her sex; something that needed both explanation and excuse. Victorian women writing about themselves, either because they wanted other people to know about them, or because they wanted to investigate the evolution of their own involvement in some aspect of public life, were usurping a masculine role and entering a transgressive field of self-expression. Sidonie Smith has gone so far as to suggest that 'They become women writing a man's story'; the woman autobiographer 'assumes the adventurous posture of man'. In doing this, she represses the mother in her, perpetuating 'the political, social and textual disempowerment of mothers and daughters'. Smith suggests that this may cause two patterns to emerge: one of the male-identified self narrating the main story of adventure and achievement; the other, the suppressed female, 'an alternative and private story that qualifies and sometimes even subverts the authorised and public version of herself'.[8] Because most successful Victorian women were *un*typical representatives of their sex, they find it impossible to recount their lives as authentic *women's* lives. Both the nature of their achievements and the masculine parameters of autobiography separate them from other women, even as their acute consciousness of transgression intensifies their feminine self-awareness.

This is a particularly useful model on which to base a discussion of self-writing by Victorian women who had an anti-feminist public profile, and who also understood the anomalousness of their position. How did they sustain the pressure of an inward desire to tell and an outward injunction to remain silent? Is there evidence of the 'self-bafflement' and 'self-counteraction' De Quincey noted in the embarrassed manner of Dorothy Wordsworth?[9] How, in fact, do anti-feminist Victorian women handle the extremely unlikely situation of making their private lives into public property?

The three writers to be discussed in this context are Charlotte Mary Yonge (1823–1901), whose *Autobiography* (1877) breaks off at the end of her childhood; Eliza Lynn Linton (1822-98), author of the transvestite *Autobiography of Christopher Kirkland* (1885), which inverts the gender roles of her own life-story, and of the separate, more formal and impersonal account of her professional role in *My Literary Life* (1899), published posthumously; and Mary Augusta (Mrs Humphry) Ward, whose *A Writer's Recollections* (1918) focuses largely on great men, both family and friends, who impressed and influenced her.

All three women were well known for taking a more or less antifeminist stance on the development of opportunities for women, though Ward was at least a key mover in the campaign to open an Oxford college (Somerville) for women students. Even Ward, however, believed that most women belonged at home, offering support and guidance to their male relatives, while in turn requiring the emotional discipline that comes from having a clear, if circumscribed, purpose in the household. Yonge declared uncompromisingly in *Womankind* (1876): 'I have no hesitation in declaring my full belief in the inferiority of woman, nor that she brought it upon herself.'[10] For her, work in the church offered a dignified way of recovering status, especially for a single woman who had no very pressing family responsibilities. Whenever her young heroines grow impatient with the restrictions of home life, Yonge ensures they are given a sharp reminder that they have no real choice. Two of her cleverest heroines, Ethel May of *The Daisy Chain* (1856) and Rachel Curtis of *The Clever Woman of the Family* (1865), both would-be intellectuals, are first humbled and then retrained to accept domesticity, especially the care of younger children, for which, initially, they have no particular aptitude. As for Linton, she was the most notorious anti-feminist of the three, angrily ridiculing all possible varieties of the modern, emancipated woman in her *Girl of the Period* series in *The Saturday Review* (1868). She deplored the disappearance of the sweet and pure English girl, who had given way to the cigarette-smoking, make-up-flaunting, noisy hoyden of the modern age: the kind of girl she depicted in her attack on women's higher education in her novel, *The One Too Many* (1894). Much of this novel hinges on the contrast between Effie Chegwin, a Girton and London graduate, who smokes cigars, likes omnibuses, and is in love with a handsome policeman, and the beautiful, but doomed, Moira, whose face 'reminded one of a blush-rose, it was so pure in tint and so sweet in expression'.[11] The fact that Moira eventually dies, following an unsuccessful forced marriage, reinforces the pattern of the autobiographies, where images of pure femininity are usually short-lived.

These are all neglected texts, falling short of the classic definitions of autobiography: definitions such as Philippe Lejeune's, which sees the genre as 'retrospective narrative in prose that somebody makes of his own existence, when he places the main emphasis on his individual life, in particular on the history of his personality'.[12] Notoriously, this is something that Victorian women autobiographers fail to do. The history of the 'personality' has far too leisured and self-indulgent a ring to it: where women do write their lives, it is largely to assist others by recounting tribulations, or to tell their descendants about times gone by. Few women autobiographers profess to be recalling the past solely to please themselves or to satisfy their curiosity about the origins of their own uniqueness.

The anti-feminist women writers were, however, keenly interested in the male worlds from which they were excluded, especially the church, the army, Oxford college life and professional journalism. The three discussed here were also conscious of an alternative male paradigm in the reconstruction of their lives. Men's experiences interested them and aroused their curiosity: Mary Ward, like George Eliot, naming her early novels, *Robert Elsmere* (1888), *The History of David Grieve* (1892), *Sir George Tressady* (1896) and *Helbeck of Bannisdale* (1898), after their leading male characters, whose personal and professional trials of character intrigue her as much as those of the women characters. In real life all three were dominated by strong male role models – sometimes more than one – and recalled them in godlike terms. Yonge's military father was a stern teacher who 'thundered' at her, and Linton's was angry and mysterious, driven by contradictory sympathies that prefigured her own. When she first met her idealized substitute father, Walter Savage Landor, she rushed up to him with both hands held out, 'as if he had been a god suddenly revealed'.[13] Mary Ward recalls, in her autobiography, an image of her arrival in Oxford: 'I see a deserted Oxford Street, and a hansom cab coming up it – myself and my father inside it.'[14] She was only 14 and returning home from school for the holidays, but when she reappeared for good, two years later, she slipped into Oxford college life, 'as a fish into water'. From this point onwards, she dissents from the usual prescribed activities of the unmarried daughter waiting for a husband. Much of her time until she was married was spent in Oxford common rooms or in the Bodleian Library, doing research on Spanish history.

All three women were loyal to their fathers' value systems, and chose a way of life very different from their mothers', either avoiding childbearing altogether (Yonge and Linton) or restricting the size of their family (Ward had only three children). Even while running a household, they managed to live a full-time literary life; yet marked dissent from their mothers' values and experiences seems to have confused their sense of self-worth as women, and caused them to compensate by increased criticism of their own sex. Each, however, retained an idealized standard of femininity, an image of the mild and patient mother-figure, who is prepared to subsume her needs in those of her family, and who is rarely the central heroine of their novels. The death of the mother is, in fact, a recurrent feature of their writing: for example, Charlotte Yonge's Mrs May is killed in a carriage accident by her husband's careless driving at the beginning of *The Daisy Chain* (1856), and Christopher Kirkland's died, like Linton's own, when he was five months old. Those that survive, as so often in Victorian women's writing, are feeble and querulous – Mrs Osborn in Linton's *Sowing the Wind* (1867), or Mrs Boyce in Ward's *Marcella* (1894) – or are in other ways unreliable guides, like the worldly Mrs Winstanley in Linton's *The Rebel of the Family* (1880), a Mrs Bennet figure, eager only to get her daughters married off, no matter how unsuitable the husbands, so long as they have money.

In the autobiographies of these writers, mothers play a decidedly minor part. Yonge's helped to educate her, and kept a diary of her progress, but it was clearly her father's lessons she found pleasantly frightening. Georgina Battiscombe has commented: 'Charlotte's father, William Yonge, was without doubt the greatest formative influence in her life. Not even Keble had so large a share in the shaping of her opinions and character.' Battiscombe adds that Mrs Yonge suffered from an inferiority complex, which was something her daughter inherited, always doubting her abilities and her own attractiveness.[15] Ward's mother died painfully and slowly of breast cancer at the time when Ward herself was writing *Robert Elsmere*, the best-seller that launched her career, but even before this time Julia Arnold appears to have had little influence on her daughter's development, especially when compared with the intellectually formidable Arnold clan, with whom Mary Arnold and her family took refuge on their return from Tasmania in 1856. From this moment, the young Mary came under the spell of her aunts, especially Jane and 'Fan', before she was transferred to Miss Clough's boarding-school. All three autobiographies are disturbed by an undercurrent of guilt about the feminine ideal and their failure to achieve it. They recall the aura of illness and frailty surrounding their mothers, even as they are pulled towards the more appealing male-dominated world of achievement in public life. The result is an attempt to reconstruct the contours of a female life, with an unconscious drift towards the masculine, in terms of values, career development and public approbation.

Elizabeth Kowaleski-Wallace has recently traced 'patterns of complicity' and signs of 'women's attraction to patriarchy' in the work of Hannah More and Maria Edgeworth, who found that writing from within their father's ideological position gave them a degree of public empowerment and guaranteed male approval.[16] This pattern is established when the daughters reject their mother's values and focus on their father's, much as Yonge, Linton and Ward did, both in their lives and in their autobiographies. Each of the Victorian anti-feminists begins by prefacing her own personal story either with a sketch of the age (Linton) or with an elaborate family history that stresses the achievements of male ancestors (Yonge and Ward), while subordinating any role played by the women. Yonge's is a striking case in point, with its emphasis on military victory and male heroism. 'Our tradition', she begins the 'Autobiography', 'is that in the time of James, when knights' fees were heavy and zealously exacted, a gentleman of the Norfolk family of Yonge eluded the expensive honour by fleeing into Devonshire.'[17] This man's son acted as a surgeon in the Cavalier army, while another of her more recent family connections, Sir John Colborne, commanded a regiment in the Battle of Waterloo, which she recounts with relish:

> On they went. Sir John's horse was killed under him, and he mounted in haste one near, too full of excitement to see that it was harnessed to a gun-carriage. He spurred in vain, and was heard calling, 'cut me out, cut me out'.
> On they went – the Guard, Napoleon's last hope, breaking and fleeing before them hopelessly.
>
> ('Autobiography', p. 24)

Still further removed from Yonge's own experience was the image of rough male camaraderie among the soldiers, as with limited supplies they prepared to enter Paris: 'In preparation for entering the city they halted at St Cloud, and there all the officers got into one pond, and passed the single razor in their possession from chin to chin' (p. 25).

Christabel Coleridge, who edited Yonge's 'Autobiography' in 1903, has commented that 'Lord Seaton [Colborne], her mother's step-brother, and her cousin by marriage, continued to be her ideal of the virtuous and honourable soldier' (p. 35). So, too, did her father, who seems a direct product of this vigorously muscular background: 'He was a remarkably handsome man, nearly six feet high, and very strong, with dark keen eyes, with the most wonderful power both for sweetness and for sternness that I ever knew' (p. 50). By contrast, Yonge's mother, as described in the 'Autobiography', is meek and shadowy, 'a perfect companion and helpmeet' to her father, but of decidedly unheroic qualities:

> My mother was – as I always remember her, for she altered little – a small woman, with very small delicate hands and feet, and fine-grained skin ... She never had good health, and was capable of little exertion in the way of walking ... She was always nervous,

timid, and easily frightened, and though she controlled herself, excitement told in after illness.

(p. 54)

Yonge describes herself as an even blend of these two influences: a pretty, feminine child with a shrill scream and enormous energy, devoted to her large family of dolls and cousins, but thrilled by boisterous games. The few epochs of her childhood are marked by arrivals and departures of male relatives and friends who exerted a strong influence over her. She states that the 'greatest event' of her life was the birth of her only brother Julian; her three chapters end at the point where John Keble becomes her tutor. 'No one else, save my own father, had so much to do with my whole cast of mind', she wrote of her 'master'. Concerned that she would become too conceited about her success as a novelist, he told her that where possible she should say that 'the real pith of her work came from another mind'.[18] Tutored by men to think of her work as assembled by dialogue with her elders and betters, it is hardly surprising that Yonge constantly sought male approval of her writing from Keble and her father. 'For at least twelve or fifteen years, I never did any literary work without talking it over with Mr and Mrs Keble', she recalled in her informal memoirs of the man who had been her greatest influence.[19] Constantly critical of George Eliot for her want of religious principle, she blames Lewes's worldly attitudes, and felt 'a good man could have made her do grandly good work'.[20]

In recounting her life, Yonge evokes what was largely a communal childhood, shared with her large family of cousins in Devon. In the time she spends on her own, she is only half alive, learning lessons, and awaiting companionship; worrying about whether or not she is attractive, and being sharply rebuked by her mother. She felt her childhood had come to an end when she paid the last of these grand visits to her cousins, and her father became preoccupied with a campaign to extend the parish church. The last family holiday culminated with wild games on the thirteenth birthday of one boy cousin: 'Thus brilliantly ended childhood's wild delights' ('Autobiography', p. 116). Yonge's life was accordingly self-defined in terms of key relationships with strong, intellectual men, or dominant boy cousins; her women friends, who also offered advice, forming a fainter chorus of invalids, whose fragility Yonge, a healthy woman, seems never to have emulated in her own person and way of life, however frequently she drew on them in her novels. She might be seen as recalling a representative female story with a male subtext: an attraction to a more energetic world than the one for which she was destined. Typically, when Yonge later wrote her *Conversations on the Catechism* (1851), which were closely revised by Keble, he commented on one of the female dialogues about the Creed: '"It occurred to me whether, when the ladies quote Greek, they had better not say, they have heard their fathers and brothers say things".'[21]

Eliza Lynn Linton's chief male mentor was Walter Savage Landor, whom she adopted as a father-figure more appealing than her real father, a Cumberland clergyman who neglected his children's education. Explaining that she could not publish her autobiography 'without some such veil as this of changed sex and personation', she turned herself into the fictitious Christopher Kirkland, 'a screen which takes off the sting of boldness and self-exposure', and which enabled her to make boasts such as the following: 'I was comically proud of being an Englishman. I had no doubt that we were God's modern chosen – His eldest sons and peculiar favourites' (instead of being the Revd Lynn's youngest daughter, and something of a nuisance).[22] Like Charlotte Brontë in *The Professor*, Linton as Christopher overstresses the masculine atmosphere of his youth and the uncouth, barbaric conditions of his home community. The other members of his family and the people he meets, all based on real-life originals, quickly divide into the fragilely feminine and the blustering masculine, but not necessarily according to actual gender. His brother, Edwin, for example, is 'the most beautiful of us all'; their father sees in him 'the reproduction of our dead mother' (*Kirkland*, vol. I, p. 58). Edwin, in turn, calls Christopher 'a maniac' who 'ought to be put in a madhouse', while their sister Ellen calls him 'a perfect monster' (ibid., p. 98): Linton's way of marking the anomalousness of her instincts and position. The novel's underlying irony is that although Christopher equates masculinity with freedom – 'When I am my own master I will be happy, because I will conquer fate and compel fortune' (ibid., p. 109) – his is really a feminine life, and his struggles are essentially those experienced by a woman, especially in gaining education and a livelihood away from the family home. His adventures are Linton's own, in that he goes to London, as she did, to become a novelist/journalist, declaring with naïve fervour: 'Yes, I would be a literary man, pure and simple; and I would leave home' (ibid., p. 221). Mr King, the family solicitor, appropriately describes Christopher as 'too big for the house' (ibid., p. 230), and recommends sending him away: an issue likely to have been less controversial in a real man's life. Moreover, Christopher not only wants to 'compel fortune', as he puts it, but win affection: 'I will then make friends who will love and understand me', he declares (ibid., p. 109).

Linton's disguise enables her to voice two desires not normally permitted to women, certainly not to an anti-feminist propagandist like Linton herself: personal ambition and undirected passion:

> I used to dream of the senior wranglership at Cambridge and the leadership of the House of Commons. I would go to the bar and be

> Lord Chancellor, or remain a free lance and be Prime Minister. I would make a name; I would be great. Whatever I did would succeed.
>
> (*Kirkland*, vol. I, p. 109)

In a woman's voice, these ambitions would be outrageous to the point of absurdity; yet Linton's novel, like Mary Shelley's *Frankenstein*, which also employs male narrators, throbs with a sense of soaring aspiration in its male characters, contrasted with the saintly domesticity of its stay-at-home female characters. This enables both writers to explore the lure of ambition, while acknowledging that it is ultimately better to remain quietly indoors: yet both novels also reveal a serious inconsistency. If it is better to stay at home, why do the women in *Frankenstein* die violent deaths, and why does Christopher, the disguised woman, become frustrated and embittered? The fragility of the feminine ideal is marked in Linton's novel by the ephemeral appearance of several perfect women who are extinguished almost as soon as they are mentioned. These include Christopher's mother, who died, as Linton's did, five months after his birth; a modest girl he sees in the British Museum; and Adeline Dalrymple, a woman with whom he falls in love as a teenager, and whose unreality is emphasized by comparison with the heavens: 'I saw her in the stars and found her in the skies ... She was the spirit that animated Nature' (ibid., p. 217).

Both Linton and Ward idealize certain very feminine women in their autobiographies, and then reject them as role models for themselves. Linton's most extreme example of this kind of woman is the Virgin Mary, whose word she had begun to doubt during her religious deconversion, when a pregnant servant-girl in the house had also been mysteriously evasive about the conception of her child. Her publisher, Bentley, made her miss out the allusion to the servant-girl, but Linton was determined to keep the point of the story, merely comparing it with Greek myth: 'Sweet, beautiful and pure as was her personality – Godlike as was that Christ she bore – was that word of more intrinsic value than that of the Greek girl who told how she had met the god in the reeds by the river side?' (ibid., pp. 139–40). This passage indicated Linton's contempt for all amiable, weak-minded girls who think they are right about something, as her other novels confirm. Repeatedly, in her writing, she castigates pure and gentle women characters whom she sees as too feeble to have any real purpose in the world, besides staying at home, and who, moreover, tend to be deceived by scheming men. Her natural survivors are the vigorous eccentrics, such as Jane Osborn, the woman journalist in *Sowing the Wind*, Perdita Winstanley in *The Rebel of the Family*, or Esther Lambert, Christopher Kirkland's undomesticated, disorganized wife, based on William Linton, Eliza's husband. Although this fictitious portrait shares the real William Linton's untidiness, it also resembles Eliza herself, and thus becomes a means of self-castigation. Esther had 'become unsexed in the way of personal independence and political activities; and very soon the restrictions of home began to irk and gall' (*Kirkland*, vol. II, p. 40). If Yonge sees herself as a wild child playing cat and mouse games rampaging through her cousins' houses, Linton shows her characters simply outgrowing the constraints of home and needing a wider field for their ambitions: hence Christopher's departure for London, and ultimately for France, which parallels Linton's own travels.

Half hidden in this narrative of heroic male adventure is a pattern of muted female quest for a purpose in life. The girl in the British Museum is Linton herself, yet her story is left untold, as an undisguised history, until the posthumous *My Literary Life* (1899), when it is pushed aside to leave room for portraits of George Eliot and her circle. Here Linton makes only the briefest appearance, and then as a timid provincial:

> I was intensely shy, and the sound of my own voice frightened me. Also, I had been brought up on the lines of childish effacement and womanly self-suppression, and taught that I ought to have no opinion of my own, or if being unfortunate enough to have one, I ought to keep it to myself, and neither talk glibly nor argue freely.[23]

Linton thus presents herself either as an aggressive male too big for the house, or as a childish woman afraid to speak. It was only as one or the other extreme that she seemed able to project the image of the writing woman: in Sidonie Smith's terms, one is the suppressed, disempowered female, and the other the male adventurer mediated through a transvestite text. Her false first-person autobiographical voice refuses to tell the stories of all the displaced single women in the novel – for example, Felicia Barry, 'type of the Ideal Woman ... Strong, hopeful and unselfish' (*Kirkland*, vol. III, p. 300), or the 'obedient, gentle, steadfast, unselfish' Claudia, with whom Christopher comforts himself when he is disappointed with his feminist wife, Esther Lambert (ibid., p. 237). These are just two of the shadowy female figures who pass in and out of Christopher's life, undemonstratively adrift, quietly going on with their lives, while Christopher rages against the restrictions (really a woman's) in his. Linton thus avoids presenting a fully integrated picture of herself as an anomalous rebel-conformist: a role that was in itself too self-contradictory for coherent explanation. Her multiple selves are scattered through the text, subordinated to the dominant identity of Christopher Kirkland, a doubly religious masculine name cloaking the experiences of a female agnostic.

My third example is Mary Augusta (Mrs Humphry) Ward, the only one of the three to attempt what purports to be a 'straight' and full autobiography, and the one who lived the fullest public life, benefiting from the broadening of opportunities for women writers at the end of the nineteenth century and the beginning of the twentieth. Ward's life was extraordinary, by any standards: her novels selling thousands of copies within a few weeks of publication (at least at the start of her career), and Gladstone himself calling her in to discuss the implications of her agnostic theories. She was friendly with Henry James, attended political and intellectual dinner parties, and towards the end of her life was invited by President Roosevelt to write a series of articles for American readers on the war efforts of the English troops. Perpetually ill with pains in the side, Ward nevertheless toured munitions factories and French battlefields for the writing of *England's Effort* (1916), which her biographer, John Sutherland, believes can be 'plausibly credited with doing much to bring [America] into the European fight'.[24] Ward is a much more modern figure than either Yonge or Linton, yet she too wanted women to be feminine, vulnerable and home-loving, as her chief heroines learn to be. Although women in her novels clearly enjoy political dinner parties and visits to the House of Commons, she remains convinced that they must leave the real work to their husbands, and concentrate on philanthropic and domestic activity closer to home.

As Alan Bellringer has observed, her memoirs are personally unrevealing:[25] they focus on her famous contemporaries, defending her own reputation by extensive quotation from their letters praising her work. What is most noticeable is Ward's determination to exclude almost all female influences on her development (true to a lesser extent of Yonge and Linton). The frontispiece to *A Writer's Recollections* is a picture of Dr Arnold of Rugby, her paternal grandfather, whose death is twice described in the opening chapter. Other illustrations are of Matthew Arnold, John Henry Newman, Benjamin Jowett and Fox How, the Arnolds' home in Westmorland. Her father's family are clearly more important to her partly because she spent more time with them and knew them better, but when she does describe her mother's ancestors, she, like Yonge, in her genealogical preface, is chiefly interested in the men and their adventures. Ward's younger daughter, Janet, was so struck by this, she felt the need to correct the balance in her own memoirs of her mother: 'From a Sorell by birth and temperament, as I believe she was, she gradually became an Arnold by environment.' In other words, she became an Arnold by acculturation, by choosing her father's way of life and intellectual values, though not his religion, which she rejected in favour of her own brand of agnosticism. Janet Trevelyan adds that in her description of Oxford, the only gap left by her mother is 'the portrait of herself'.[26] Indeed Ward gives a picture of an Oxford college life and theological battles waged by the two church parties, as if she herself were a college Fellow, rather than the wife or guest of one; and when she mentions her wedding (in one sentence), the only detail is that the ceremony was performed by 'my father's friend, my grandfather's pupil and biographer, Dean Stanley'.[27]

Each phase of Ward's life, whether focused on home or work, is seen in terms of dominant male personalities (excluding her husband, whose part in the autobiography is minimal): Balfour, Lord Acton, Chamberlain, John Morley, Newman, Jowett, Henry James, Gladstone, Kipling, Wells, Meredith; the list is continuous. The only women she mentions for more than a few sentences are her aunt, Jane Arnold Forster, whose husband's political life in Ireland is still Ward's chief interest, and the tragic Laura Tennant Lyttleton, one of the 'Souls', who died a few days after the birth of her son. In each of these cases, the female image is idealized into something unreachable and unreal: 'How could any one be so good!', was Ward's response to her aunt. 'She was to me "a thing enskied" and heavenly – for all her quick human interests, and her sweet ways with those she loved' (*Recollections*, vol. I, p. 51). Although she credits her aunt with influencing the terms of Forster's 1870 Education Act, she adds that through her, it was infused with 'the convictions and beliefs of her father' (ibid., p. 47). Although Jane was in the political world, she was never truly of it: 'She moved through it, yet veiled from it, by that pure, unconscious selflessness which is still the saint's gift' (ibid., p. 49). Always deeply responsive to personality, and through the influence of a person's manner and magnetism, his or her ideas, Ward says she 'fell in love' with Laura Tennant at a dinner party:

> Suddenly I became aware of a figure opposite to me, the figure of a young girl who seemed to me one of the most ravishing creatures I had ever seen. She was very small, and exquisitely made. Her beautiful head, with its mass of light-brown hair; the small features and delicate neck; the clear, pale skin, the lovely eyes with rather heavy lids, which gave a slight look of melancholy to the face; the grace and fire of every movement when she talked; the dreamy silence into which she sometimes fell without a trace of awkwardness or shyness.
>
> (*Recollections*, vol. II, p. 23)

The description of Laura is the equivalent of the brief sketches of Mrs Yonge or Mrs Dalrymple in the autobiographies of Yonge and Linton: an ephemeral image of idealized feminine beauty, necessarily unattainable and short-lived, and seen as if by the male gaze.

Although Ward has no need of the transvestism adopted by Linton, she boldly recounts her life as a series of intellectual influences and male coteries, quietly coercing the reader into seeing her career development in terms of the normal male trajectories, beginning, like many of her contemporaries, with the shock of Dr Arnold's death, and ending with the continuing trauma of the First World War. Her life thus becomes a representative man's of the nineteenth century, spanning Oxford and London intellectual, religious and political circles, and becoming increasingly involved with an expanding world. The letters of support quoted within the text further bolster Ward's anomalous position as a woman in public life, so that she has to mention few of her achievements directly. Inevitably, most of these letters come from men, themselves successful in public life. Her being a woman ceases to become an issue. She largely avoids the coy protestations common to women autobiographers, and simply assumes her readers will see her life as a natural evolution of achievement, a common Victorian career pattern, irrespective of gender. She believed in teaching morality through the exemplary lives of men, as she does in her own novel *Robert Elsmere* and in the pen portraits of *A Writer's Recollections*; if her novels, beginning with *Marcella*, shifted their focus from the male example to the female, her autobiography remains committed to the superiority of the masculine, with the feminine suppressed or idealized into a fleeting vision.

All three of these anti-feminist women writers were dependent on male approval of their work. While Yonge remained in a childish relationship with her father and Keble, and halted her autobiography on the brink of adolescence, Linton and Ward adopted overt or oblique male personae, displacing the feminine into the 'other' – images of meek or angelic women whom they profess to admire, but whose example they reject as role models for themselves in real life. One could go further and argue that whereas Yonge depicts an overwhelmingly female world of dolls, indoor games and cousinly friendships, with a male subtext (the appeal of military heroism, with which the autobiography opens), Linton employs a male disguise to retell a female story, and Ward, going further still, transforms herself into a late-Victorian career man, retaining in her narrative a feminine subtext (the opposite of Yonge's military undercurrent) of saintly assistance and bodily fragility. Yonge describes the life of a female child looking up to men, but unable to recount her own womanhood – perhaps because in her experience women had no real history, apart from illness, and Yonge herself was never seriously ill. Her constant activity as a novelist and magazine editor (safely distant from London) has no parallel in the life of anyone she knew as a child, and has therefore been established by no written form. Linton, by contrast, fragments every stage of her life into a distinct miniature – a portrait, a sketch, an episode, featuring men or women who briefly embody her previous selves; while the formal 'autobiography', *My Literary Life*, all but erases her altogether. Ward is the most successful in recasting her life as a man's, and so disempowering the feminine, both within herself and in society at large. As a side-effect, however, she also removes a good deal of what is distinctive about her, as an individual: she disappears behind a screen of anecdotes and reminiscences, and reveals less about herself than either Yonge or Linton.

These autobiographies remain frustrating to readers seeking a frank account of a successful, unusual life and its emotional high points. Few autobiographies, whether by men or women, are as revealing as their readers would like, but those by Victorian women are exceptionally reticent, while offering voluminous documentation of events we now find less significant. Yonge, Linton and Ward are alike in providing numerous short sketches of friends and relatives they encountered in the course of their careers, pages modern readers are now tempted to skip in their search for material that is of greater personal interest. To the critic of Victorian women's autobiography, who would like to make a case for its importance as a disregarded genre, rarely reprinted or discussed, these pages of reminiscences still present a difficult problem. How are we to read them? Are we to read them at all? Are they just so much padding, there to satisfy the curiosity of humbler folk who will never mix in these circles themselves, and therefore serving much the same purpose as modern gossip columns and glossy magazines?

At their simplest, these reminiscences function as background: the 'times' part of a 'life and times', establishing a context for the author's professional success, and validating her achievement. Margaret Oliphant is unusual in stressing how few of the great and famous she knew, while in fact slipping in a quiet succession of names, Jane Carlyle's chief among them. Charlotte Yonge takes her reminiscences from a time predating her birth, to give her family its due importance in national history; Eliza Linton cites real-life authors, such as Walter Savage Landor and the Brownings, in her fictitious autobiography, enhancing Christopher Kirkland's credibility as a real hero; and Mary Ward passes judgement on Henry James and other friends, thereby securing her own place in the literary establishment. In each case, the personal is dwarfed by a broader sweep of history, while at the same time gaining validity from it. The author feels she has a double or additional claim on the reader because she has become a piece of living history: by proxy a survivor of Waterloo, or of London literary salons, familiar with names that have now become legendary.

For women specifically, the chance to hitch their wagon to history has a liberating effect. It lifts them out of a parochial context, while acknowledging their relative smallness in the larger plan of things, and it gives them the opportunity to weigh the significance of public achievement. It is common, in autobiographical reminiscences, to criticize as well as applaud: to wish a person's manners had been less artificial, or that he had continued to write in a popular vein, instead of pursuing an eccentric taste. 'If he is without passion', Ward says of Henry James in *Recollections*, 'as some people are ready to declare, so are Stendhal and Turguenieff, and half the great masters of the novel' (II, pp. 209–10) – a comment which places Ward above James, in a position of judgement. 'She was essentially under-bred and provincial', Linton says of George Eliot in *My Literary Life* (p. 95); whereas Landor earned her approval for preferring traditional feminine qualities in women: 'Women were ladies to him, and aught that touched the very fringe of their delicacy was anathema maranatha' (ibid., p. 54). In their passages of reminiscences these Victorian women autobiographers gain an air of worldly wisdom and good taste; knowing the experiences of their friends and contemporaries makes them less likely to err themselves.

These portraits are perhaps their most interesting in indicating what the autobiographers saw as being desirable male and female qualities. To Linton, both George Eliot and Lewes fail as positive examples of their sex. Eliot is too artificial and Lewes too sensual. For Ward, by contrast, Jane Forster and Laura Tennant are perfect women, but beyond the reach of ordinary mortals. For Yonge, most of the men and women she knew in her childhood conformed absolutely to their gender stereotype: the men being strong and military, the women weak and invalidish. In their personal reminiscences all three set out, by indirection, their standards of masculinity and femininity, against which their own achievements may be measured.

Overall, the thumbnail sketch retains a key place in their rhetorical strategy as anti-feminist women writers and specifically as autobiographers. All three withhold admiration from the unwomanly woman, the high achiever who cuts loose from her family responsibilities and enjoys a liberated lifestyle; while Linton, who was, in reality, this kind of woman, gives herself a male identity, and reinforces the disapproval of unattached, freewheeling behaviour. Passing judgement on others and playing down their own successes, anti-feminist women autobiographers quietly atone for their transgression of the formal boundaries.

What remains intriguing for the modern critic, however, is the noticeable gap between what they profess to admire and what the energy of their writing indicates they really approve. Read as split responses from women caught in a web of prohibitions against self-advertisement, they reveal their own frustrations with the womanly paradigm, and a determination to evade the rules for pattern behaviour they themselves have been instrumental in imposing on others. Male adventures remain the exciting and worthwhile ones; female unadventurousness a model more often recommended than followed. Anna Walters has recently commented that when a woman writes an autobiography 'she turns the male value system on its head'.[28] What seems to happen with the Victorian anti-feminist women autobiographers is that the male value system – which values public achievement and heroism over and above domestic unselfishness – triumphs over the image of the 'relative creature',[29] that feminine 'other' of the patriarchal system. While reinforcing the influence of this system, these three autobiographers expose their preference for the masculine role, rather than the function of the domestic 'angel'. This is not to say that they would rather have been men: only that in their autobiographical writing they fail to make the woman's role seem either attainable or enviable.

Notes

1. George Eliot, *Impressions of Theophrastus Such* (1879), Illustrated Copyright Edition (London: Virtue & Co., 1913), p. 7.
2. Frances Anne Kemble, *Further Records 1848–1883*, 2 vols (London: Richard Bentley and Son, 1890), vol. II, p. 70.
3. Beatrice Webb, *My Apprenticeship* (London: Longmans, Green & Co., 1926), p. 1.
4. Harriet Martineau called herself 'probably the happiest single woman in England' (*Harriet Martineau's Autobiography* (1877), ed. Gaby Weiner, 2 vols (London: Virago, 1983), vol. I, p. 133).
5. Anna Walters, 'Self Image and Style: A Discussion Based on Estelle Jelinek's *The Tradition of Women's Autobiography from Antiquity to the Present*', *Women's Studies International Forum*, 10 (1987), 85–93. Recent studies of women's autobiography include: Domna C. Stanton, *The Female Autograph: Theory and Practice of Autobiography from the Tenth to the Twentieth Century* (Chicago and London: Chicago University Press, 1987); *Life/Lines: Theorising Women's Autobiography*, ed. Bella Brodzki and Celeste Schenck (Ithaca and London: Cornell University Press, 1988); *The Private Self: Theory and Practice of Women's Autobiographical Writings*, ed. Shari Benstock (London: Routledge, 1988); and Treva Broughton, 'Margaret Oliphant: The Unbroken Self', *Women's Studies International Forum*, 10 (1987), 41–52.
6. John Sturrock, *The Language of Autobiography: Studies in the First Person Singular* (Cambridge: Cambridge University Press, 1993), p. 19.
7. Sarah Ellis, *The Women of England, Their Social Duties and Domestic Habits* (London: Fisher, Son & Co., 1839), pp. 64, 155.
8. Sidonie Smith, *A Poetics of Women's Autobiography: Marginality and the Fictions of Self-Representation* (Bloomington: Indiana University Press, 1987), pp. 51, 53, 54.
9. Thomas De Quincey, *Recollections of the Lakes and the Lake Poets* (Edinburgh: Adam and Charles Black, 1862), pp. 134–5.
10. Charlotte Mary Yonge, *Womankind* (London: Mozley and Smith, 1876), p. 1

11. Eliza Lynn Linton, *The One Too Many*, 3 vols (London: Chatto and Windus, 1894), vol. I, p. 2.
12. Quoted by Nancy K. Miller, 'Women's Autobiography in France: For a Dialectics of Identification', in *Women and Language in Literature and Society*, ed. Sally McConnell-Ginet, Ruth Borker and Nelly Furman (New York: Praeger Publishers, 1980), p. 260.
13. Quoted by Nancy Fix Anderson, *Woman against Women in Victorian England: A Life of Eliza Lynn Linton* (Bloomington: Indiana University Press, 1987), p. 43.
14. Mrs Humphry Ward, *A Writer's Recollections*, 2 vols (New York and London: Harper & Brothers, 1918), vol. I, p. 135 (hereafter, *Recollections*).
15. Georgina Battiscombe, *Charlotte Mary Yonge: The Story of an Uneventful Life* (London: Constable & Co., 1943), pp. 22–3.
16. Elizabeth Kowaleski-Wallace, *Their Fathers' Daughters: Hannah More, Maria Edgeworth and Patriarchal Complicity* (New York and Oxford: Oxford University Press, 1991), p. ix.
17. Charlotte Mary Yonge, 'Autobiography', in *Charlotte Mary Yonge: Her Life and Letters*, ed. Christabel Coleridge (London: Macmillan, 1903), p. 1 (hereafter, 'Autobiography').
18. Charlotte Mary Yonge, 'Musings Over the "Christian Year" and "Lyra Innocentium"', in her *Gleanings from Thirty Years' Intercourse with the Late Rev. John Keble* (Oxford and London: James Parker & Co., 1871), pp. iv, xxxiii.
19. Ibid., p. xxiv.
20. Quoted by Ethel Romanes, *Charlotte Mary Yonge: An Appreciation* (London and Oxford: A.R. Mowbray & Co., 1908), p. 179.
21. Yonge, 'Musings', pp. i–xxvii.
22. Nancy Fix Anderson, *Woman against Women*, p. 11; Mrs Lynn Linton, *The Autobiography of Christopher Kirkland* (1885), reprinted 3 vols in 1 (New York and London: Garland Publishing, 1976), vol. I, p. 82 (hereafter, *Kirkland*).
23. *My Literary Life. By Mrs Lynn Linton* (London: Hodder and Stoughton, 1899), p. 36.
24. John Sutherland, *Mrs Humphry Ward: Eminent Victorian, Pre-eminent Edwardian* (Oxford: Clarendon Press, 1990), p. 350.
25. Alan Bellringer, 'Mrs Humphry Ward's Autobiographical Tactics: A Writer's Recollections', *Prose Studies*, 8 (December 1985), 40–50.
26. Janet Penrose Trevelyan, *The Life of Mrs Humphry Ward* (London: Constable & Co., 1923), pp. 6–7, 27.
27. *Recollections*, vol. I, p. 159.
28. Anna Walters, 'Self Image and Style', p. 86.
29. Sarah Ellis, *The Women of England*, p. 155.

CHAPTER ELEVEN

Mark Rutherford's Salvation and the Case of Catharine Furze

Vincent Newey

Near the beginning of *Catharine Furze*, published in 1893, the penultimate novel of William Hale White, the man who called himself Mark Rutherford, the eponymous heroine recalls the time she had rescued Tom Catchpole, her father's apprentice, from a fire in the house where the Furzes lived and Mr Furze conducted his ironmonger's business:

> It is as if something or somebody took hold of me, and, before I know where I am, the thing is done, and yet there is no something or somebody – at least, so far as I can see. It is wonderful, for after all it is I who do it.[1]

Catharine seems also to have in mind her own recent impulsive escape from a bargee who had accosted her in a nearby field. Be this as it may, her conscious affirmation of 'I', or what elsewhere Rutherford calls her 'force' (*CF*, pp. 193, 301), should be of interest both to the student of nineteenth-century autobiography and to the student of the 'woman question'. We shall return to *Catharine Furze* in due course.

Hale White's semi-fictional *Autobiography of Mark Rutherford* appeared in 1881, to be followed in 1885 by its sequel, *Mark Rutherford's Deliverance*. One thing that strikes us about these texts is a deliberate fascination with words, of which an obvious example is the way Hale White plays with character names, somewhat in the allegorical tradition of Bunyan, an author he particularly respected. We have the spineless Snale who works against Rutherford when he is a Dissenting minister; or Miss Arbour, under whose protective counsel Rutherford finds shelter from his conflict over whether or not he should marry the woman he no longer loves; or the saintly Theresa, who is based on George Eliot, and whose soothing of Rutherford's frantic self-doubt comes like a replacement of 'visions of torment with dreams of Paradise'.[2] Most important of all, as we shall see, is the atheistical Edward Gibbon Mardon, who had changed his middle name from 'Gibson' so as to identify with the famous eighteenth-century ironist of religion, and whose surname not only suggests 'spoiling' ('to mar') but is intriguingly an anagram of 'random'.

Such devices are an attractive feature of the *Autobiography* and *Deliverance*, and send serious messages to the reader. At a deeper level, however, there is a concern with the possibilities, and the limitations, of language as an instrument for expressing self and the world. In the ambitions of Rutherford's friend M'Kay in *Deliverance*, for example, Hale White projects the idea of a 'higher truthfulness' consisting of the avoidance of 'borrowed expression' in favour of 'perfect exactitude ... point by point, a correspondence of the words with the fact external or internal'.[3] This concept of speaking from the thing and from the heart, a version of the old Puritan commitment to sincerity, may seem an impossible ideal in the light of modern theories of the precedence and autonomy of linguistic forms themselves, but it undoubtedly has a strong influence on Hale White's thinking in the *Autobiography*. Thus, Rutherford's account of his dissatisfaction with the training he received at his Dissenting theological college – an episode recalling Hale White's actual expulsion from a comparable institution – stresses the lack of any vital connection between doctrine and experience or the real needs of humankind: 'The distinctive essence of our orthodoxy was not this or that dogma, but the acceptance of dogmas as communications from without, and not as born from within' (*AMR*, p. 25). The young student tries enthusiastically to revivify the 'terms' of his inherited creed, by, for instance, discoursing on the relevance of Christ's atonement as 'a sublime summing up as it were of what sublime men have to do for their race', an 'exemplification, rather than a contradiction, of nature herself'; but this humanizing approach meets with the President's irate advice simply to repeat the 'old story' of 'sinfulness' and 'safety', and these 'words' of authority 'fell on me like the hand of a corpse' (*AMR*, pp. 26–7). The same cold, hollow thud is felt later by Rutherford when 'not a soul was kindled' by his own sermons at Water Lane Chapel (*AMR*, p. 54), and when the force of his insights into the personal application of Christ's sacrifice is blunted by his necessary routine use of the conventional vocabulary of the Westminster Confession, 'phrases which, though they might be conciliatory, were misleading' (*AMR*, pp. 49–50). There lies on the one side the dead letter and on the other Rutherford's continual effort to see it redeemed, either by actively reinterpreting the Bible and other religious texts or by having them, as he puts it, 'rewritten' for him, as was most notably the case when he encountered Wordsworth's *Lyrical Ballads*, which replaced 'the God of the Church' with 'the God of the hills', 'substituting a new and living spirit for the old deity, once alive, but gradually hardened into an idol' (*AMR*, pp. 21–3).

Hale White is usually classified as an 'honest doubter' – one of the Victorians who lost their faith.[4] But faith is not really the problem if by that term we understand, in the formulations applied to the influence of Wordsworth on Rutherford, habits of 'inner reference', a yearning for things which 'touch the soul' or embody 'some spiritual law' (*AMR*, p. 22). The difficulty is, rather, to discover a focus for this inwardness – a channel through which it might flow and take direction. On several occasions Hale White laments the loss of frameworks of corporate belief and fellowship where the individual could exist unselfconsciously, finding instinctive and secure release for passion. In *Catharine Furze* this golden age is set in the time of Bunyan, when people were 'knit together in everlasting bonds by the same Christ and the same salvation', and all that was in Catharine herself, 'intellect' and 'heart', would have found 'ample room' for satisfaction (*CF*, p. 189). In the *Autobiography* it is located a hundred years back, when Rutherford would have transferred his 'burning longing' to 'the unseen God' (*AMR*, p. 130). In the nineteenth century, however, 'when each man is left to shift for himself, to work out the answers to his own problems, the result is isolation' (*CF*, p. 190).

The *Autobiography* is in large part an account of such isolation, reaching a strange pitch of resonant low-level intensity – an eerily understated climax – when Rutherford runs for his life from the small school where he had found employment after renouncing his ministry among the Unitarians (whom he joins after leaving his earlier orthodox Christian sect). Confined in a small attic bedroom on his first night, he looks out over the urban landscape:

> There were scattered lights here and there marking roads, but as they crossed one another, and now and then stopped where building had ceased, the effect they produced was that of bewilderment with no clue to it. Further off was the great light of London, like some unnatural dawn, or the illumination from a fire which could not itself be seen. I was overcome with the most dreadful sense of loneliness.
>
> (*AMR*, pp. 133–4)

We see in this the emergent city sprawl, signifying the aimlessness and false – merely geophysical – collectivism of modern life. More important than any sociological implications, however, is the projection of an inner mood. There are evocations of Christian's sight of the Celestial City in *The Pilgrim's Progress*, where the streets are 'paved with gold', and, more specifically perhaps, of Dorothea's awakening, in the 'pearly light' of dawn, from self-centred despair to a sympathetic awareness of the 'palpitating life' around her in *Middlemarch*. Rutherford's blank depression is a palpable inversion of both Bunyan's understanding of spiritual triumph and George Eliot's purposeful secular adaptation of it.[5] And for him the only hell is the 'bottomless pit' of madness, on the edge of which he presently totters. So disabling and utterly personal is his aloneness that in the final analysis it cannot be explained in the old language of religion, or even be put into words at all; it is a 'nameless dread' (*AMR*, p. 134).

The condition of stress most commonly dramatized in the *Autobiography*, however, is that of irresolvable mind-debate – the characteristic Victorian battle of the 'two voices', Arnold's 'dialogue of the mind with itself'.[6] This takes two main forms. One of these is interior reflective dialogue, a good instance of which is Rutherford's train of thought as he cuts loose from the Dissenting cause at Water Lane and casts about for principles by which to navigate the future. This is an interesting section because it concentrates so many of the issues then being widely argued over by secularists and the champions of religion. Rutherford's withdrawn speculative state itself seems representative of that 'intense self-consciousness', 'altogether new' to western civilization, which W.H. Mallock places at the centre of the 'crisis' currently facing humankind in his major and ubiquitously noticed arraignment of Positivism, *Is Life Worth Living?*:

> During the last few generations man has been changing. Much of his old spontaneity of action has gone from him. He has become a creature looking before and after; and his native hue of resolution has been sicklied over by thought. We admit nothing now without question; we have learnt to take to pieces all motives and actions. We not only know more than we have done before, but we are perpetually chewing the cud of our knowledge. Thus positive thought reduces all religions to ideals created by man; and as such, not only admits that they have had vast influence, but teaches us also that we in the future must construct new ideals for ourselves.[7]

Hale White's writings, especially the *Autobiography* and *Catharine Furze*, are much about 'constructing new ideals', and the problem of doing so. Rutherford in this chapter considers becoming an instructor of morality, but recoils before the realization that reformations in morals have always depended upon an enthusiasm for 'some City of God, or some supereminent person', rather than following 'mere directions to be good'. There can be no credit or regulation in human behaviour, no genuine aspiration, indeed no vigour or plenitude in life itself, without some given measure of value: 'there must be *distinction*, *difference*, a higher and a lower; and the lower, relatively to the higher, must always be an evil ... The supremest bliss would not be bliss if it were not *definable* bliss, that is to say, in the sense that it has limits, marking it out from something else not so supreme' (*AMR*, pp. 98–9). This is very close to certain of Mallock's arguments, which, for example, attack scientific and humanist Positivism for replacing the struggle for 'supernatural right' with the pursuit of 'natural happiness' and in so doing enfeebling, perhaps fatally, the 'moral end', since under the new dispensation that end 'is nothing absolute, and not being absolute is incapable of being enforced'; or which, more generally, deplore a situation in which, all striving in the face of the 'infinite' or of 'a something beyond' having been abandoned, existence would shrink to one flat level, 'without light and shadow, and with the colours reduced in number, and robbed of all their vividness'.[8] Rutherford uses the same imagery to dismiss the atheist-reformer's shallow dream of a world of 'shadowless light', 'objectless' and robbed alike of pain and the equal 'mystery' of grandeur and glory (*AMR*, pp. 100–1). With Mallock he shares a sure contempt for the narrowness of utilitarian vision: 'Mankind may be improved ... and yet good and evil must exist' (*AMR*, p. 101).

Between the perspectives of Mallock and Rutherford, however, there is a difference. The former envisages what will happen if orthodox religion, and the instincts it has engendered, should fail; and he indeed has a contingency plan ready in case of need, which is – improbable as it may sound – a mass return to Catholicism (a refuge which presumably would not suffer from being an artificial construct since it declares itself as one, or at least as an organism founded on ritual and commitment rather than calling, and is infinitely flexible in adapting to intellectual and social change). Rutherford's is a more drastic situation, for he labours already under the absence of any consoling belief in immortality – 'Why this ceaseless struggle, if in a few short years I was to be asleep for ever?' (*AMR*, p. 90) – and of a personal God, the divine having been attenuated in his perceptions to an awareness of 'immutable laws' governing the universe (*AMR*, p. 99). He trembles before the prospect of 'complete emptiness'. If that nothingness, that entire dissolution of self, is to be avoided, it cannot be by the recovery of orthodoxy; yet neither can Rutherford, or Hale White, do without spirituality and the Word in some form and some degree: they are bound, for better or worse, to logocentric conceptions of being and being-in-the-world. This is clear from Rutherford's relation to Mardon, which constitutes the other manifest psychodrama in the *Autobiography*.

Mardon is Rutherford's double – the projection of an alternative self which he finds at once attractive and threatening, very much in accord with Freud's account of the *alter ego* as a promise of extended life but also a prophecy of death.[9] The ambivalence is brought out forcibly at the opening of the fifth chapter: 'I rather dreaded him. I could not resist him, and I shrank from what I saw to be inevitably true when I talked to him' (*AMR*, p. 65). There is a further clue to Mardon's status as an embodiment of Rutherford's own deepening scepticism in matters of religion when the latter lets slip that 'I knew very well what he thought ... and what he would tell me to do, or rather, what he would tell me not to do' (*AMR*, p. 102). Inside knowledge, however, does not necessarily mean easy negotiations. The metaphors Rutherford uses to describe Mardon's effect upon him signify various degrees of active assault: for example, the 'sledgehammer' blows of Mardon's early criticism of Rutherford's attempt to hold fast to the 'Christ-idea' whether or not it was actually ever incarnated, which leave Rutherford 'stunned, bewildered' (*AMR*, pp. 60–1); or the subtler onslaught, a sort of wizardry, suggested by Rutherford's reference to the painful 'dissolution of Jesus into mythological vapour' when he talks of a further stage in this querying of the efficacy of an ideal as opposed to an inviolable truth (*AMR*, p. 64). Even more disturbing than being bludgeoned, perhaps, would be the relentless 'process of excavation' – being gradually made hollow from within – which is Rutherford's longer-term condition (*AMR*, p. 65).

Certainly, then, the 'spoiling' and 'randomness' in 'Mardon' are a disfigurement wrought upon Rutherford – an undoing, and potential cancellation, of his principles and very identity. It is important to recognize, however, that the movement is by no means all one way. On one occasion Mardon himself is profoundly humbled. Having expressed contempt for any entry into the 'region of sentiment' when Rutherford pleads the value of human instinct, he immediately collapses into silence, 'deeply stirred', when his daughter sings 'He was despised' from Handel's *Messiah*, a song his deceased wife used to sing (*AMR*, pp. 105–7). Like the episode where the stoic philosopher's intellectual propositions crumble before his inconsolable grief over his daughter's death in Dr Johnson's *Rasselas* (a text Hale White might well have in mind),[10] this event affirms, indeed celebrates, the power of love. The feeling Rutherford has pleaded for is not this, but an untaught responsiveness to nature and an inexplicable intuition that bear witness, though not to a conventional God, at least to an 'intellect' or 'mind' of which the 'laws' that 'govern the universe and man' are an expression:

> I cannot encompass God with a well-marked definition, but for all that, I believe in Him ... I cannot help thinking that the man who looks upon the stars, or the articulation of a leaf, is irresistibly impelled, unless he has been corrupted by philosophy, to say, There is intellect there.
>
> (*AMR*, p. 104)

But what matters is the outrunning of Mardon's position – the pointing of its limits. The truly impressive, and disturbing, thing about Mardon, from Rutherford's point of view, had all along been not so much his atheism *per se* as the pure rationalism with which he applied it and of which it was a natural concomitant. Rutherford says of him, for instance, that 'He was perfectly clear, perfectly secular, and was so definitely shaped and settled' (*AMR*, p. 102); and in the present discussion he concedes the force of his habitual cool reasoning, saying 'I have never gained a logical victory over you' (*AMR*, p. 105). Logical, no, imaginative, yes: Mardon's refusal to follow Rutherford 'into the cloud' cannot stop his head being bowed to the table in grief; the rational outlook breaks down.

This episode casts a symbolic light back upon the strangely mundane detail of Rutherford's description of his first visit to Mardon, where we learn of a 'small brick-built cottage' on the 'outskirts' of town, a 'narrow' strip of land separated from those adjacent by 'iron hurdles': 'Mardon had tried to keep his garden in order, and had succeeded, but his neighbour was disorderly, and had allowed weeds to grow, blacking bottles and old tin cans to accumulate, so that whatever pleasure Mardon's labours might have afforded was somewhat spoiled' (*AMR*, p. 57). In the final analysis, Mardon does become a marginal figure, cut off, representing an orderliness of mind that has local force (as in its influence on Rutherford) but which is challenged and charged with irrelevance by the debris that surrounds it – by the life that is altogether messier than rational theory would allow. And we recall, too, the remark in the laconic opening portrait of Mardon, that his eyes indicated a character which 'if it possessed no particular creative power, would not permit self-deception' (*AMR*, p. 53). Mardon rids Rutherford of some illusions, but not of the claims of creativity, which later on take a sociological as well as spiritual dimension; when human clutter again surfaces, in the *Deliverance*, it is the 'uniformity of squalor' of the London slums (*MRD*, p. 26), which Rutherford and M'Kay try to do something about by giving lessons in hope and self-help. Mardon's death, at the end of the *Autobiography*, culminates a process of reversal whereby Rutherford establishes an authority over him. The *alter ego* dissolves not only because its work of specialized 'excavation' has been done but also because it has been transcended. It is notable that Mardon's last words signal a turn-round. In proclaiming the importance of being 'anxious about the Universal' (*AMR*, p. 159) *he* has become more like *Rutherford*, unorthodox yet speculative and metaphysical still.

Another way of seeing this is to say that through the relationship with Mardon, Rutherford progressively defines his own values and personality, and that the text thus reproduces a familiar pattern of traditional spiritual autobiography. But the question of the relation of the *Autobiography* and *Deliverance* to autobiographical form is actually a subtler one deserving closer attention.

Elizabeth K. Helsinger has argued that the Victorians were decidedly uncomfortable with the Romantic and Christian models of purposeful self-revelation and movement towards maturity. Whereas Wordsworth's *Prelude*, locked firmly in a line stemming from St Augustine's *Confessions*, travels to the wholeness of a 'now achieved identity which is profoundly satisfying to the poet', Ruskin's *Praeterita*, Tennyson's 'The Two Voices', Arnold's 'Empedocles on Etna' and Browning's 'Childe Roland to the Dark Tower Came' portray introspective journeying as 'isolated, self-involved, and finally fruitless: incapable of yielding a confident sense of self, or an exhilarating view of ... life'.[11] This is, needless to say, oversure – if only because Wordsworth's own affirmation of a stable selfhood is queried by persistent evidences of psychic tension linked to repression, while there are Christian documents, notably Bunyan's *Grace Abounding to the Chief of Sinners*, where conversion leads not to unity but a split subjectivity, an irresolvable battle between the promptings of the spirit and of nature.[12] As a working generalization, however, Helsinger's summary is helpful; and in certain respects Rutherford belongs clearly enough with the Victorians as she views them. The self-preoccupation which Arnold, Ruskin, and Tennyson all termed 'morbid' is, as we have seen, expressed with blank intensity in the school episode where the constriction Rutherford flees is not that of his surroundings themselves but of the virtual 'madness' of 'nameless dread'. The age is one in which 'We think too much of ourselves', the supposed editor of Rutherford's papers observes in the preface to the *Autobiography* (*AMR*, p. xxxiii), and, as he adds in an afterword, his friend may well be taken as an example of the modern type of 'mere egoist, selfish and self-absorbed' – 'morbid' (*AMR*, p. 165).[13] Similarly, the undoing of Rutherford's beliefs may be associated with the scepticism about the notion of a sustainable coherent identity aired by Pater at the end of *The Renaissance*, where autobiography becomes a 'continual vanishing away, that strange, perpetual weaving and unweaving of ourselves'.[14] But the most apt comparison perhaps is with the deconversion narrative of Edmund Gosse's *Father and Son*. Both Gosse and Rutherford chronicle a transformation that is precisely the opposite of the conversion of Augustine who leaves behind a love of literature and rhetoric for the authority of absolute Truth, so that all inward duality is stilled and 'this debate within my heart ... of myself against myself ... [and] all the dark shadows of doubt fell away'.[15]

For Gosse, the falling away of the submission to Truth means the discovery of the freedom to put on 'the veil of illusion'[16] – to embrace theatricality, acting, as the true condition of being – to take *style*, as Oscar Wilde more flamboyantly does in 'The Decay of Lying', as the only real thing. This, importantly, is not quite the case with the configuration of individuality to be read in the *Autobiography*. There is, as in all Hale White's writings, an earnestness that precludes any temptation to see life simply as a wearing of masks or a playing of parts. Out of the jaws of the denial first of empty dogma and then of faith itself Rutherford works hard to snatch as much residual affirmation as he can. We have already witnessed his cultivation of the numinous in a response to nature and universal laws reminiscent of the Wordsworthian philosophy of the One Life and Spinoza's directive to accept whatever is as a system coterminous with the will of God. Then, however, there is in this ontology an evident strain of compromise, a lowering of spiritual and emotional sights; and we feel this even more acutely in such segments of the *Autobiography* as that covering the butterfly catcher, another *alter ego* and exemplary character, whose history (based this time, I think, on Johnson's mad astronomer)[17] offers a lesson in the dangers of 'metaphysical speculations' about death and our future state (like Rutherford before, he has gazed 'gloomily into dark emptiness') and the therapeutic properties of mastering a science: 'I was the owner of something which other persons did not own, and in a little while, in my own limited domain I was supreme' (*AMR*, p. 127). As a prescription for living this suggests diversionary tactics for hanging on rather than any route to transcendent satisfaction – though in its references to God-surrogacy and the urge to possess, the quotation opens up interesting ways of interpreting the pleasures of collecting dead insects. The two penultimate chapters of the *Autobiography* are entitled 'Emancipation' and 'Progress in Emancipation', but it is difficult to perceive where the release for Rutherford comes, or where he locates it. We are aware not so much of freedom or mobility as of a programme for dogged survival. And this is true also of the *Deliverance*, which, for example, ends with a day's outing away from the London fog:

> We were beyond the smoke, which rested like a low black cloud over the city in the north-east, reaching a third of the way up the zenith ... By moving a little towards the external edge of our canopy we beheld the plain all spread out before us, bounded by the heights of Sussex and Hampshire. It was veiled with the most tender blue, and above it was spread a sky which was white on the horizon and deepened by degrees into azure over our heads. Marie ... wandered about looking for flowers and ferns, and was content. We were all completely happy. We strained our eyes to see the furthest point before us, and we tried to find it on the map we had brought with us ... Rather did summer dying in such fashion fill our hearts with repose, and even more than repose – with actual joy.
>
> (MRD, p. 133)

This is an extreme, even desperate, domestication of the mythic imagination. Edged round by the distant oppressive smoke of the modern industrial hell and by the seasonal signs of inevitable mortality, Rutherford and his family enjoy the temporary paradise of unselfconsciousness and natural beauty. Where Adam and Eve, expelled from Eden, had found the world 'all before them', their descendants snatch a vestigial prelapsarian pleasure from beholding the plain spread out before them; where Christian in *The Pilgrim's Progress* had peered to see 'yonder shining light' of faith and providential guidance, they, on an altogether smaller spiritual scale, entertain themselves by striving to make out and identify the remotest feature of the landscape.[18] Marie, tinged with the aura of Eve gardening, is Rutherford's daughter, but his wife Ellen (another interesting character name, meaning 'courage') is there too: the *telos* of the *Autobiography* and *Deliverance* turns out to be not personal wholeness at all, but mutuality. As a vision of being-in-the-world this is, characteristically of the work, trying rather than triumphant. It pushes at limits without being in any way absurd. It represents a frugal but genuinely practical existentialism.

Where does William Hale White stand in all of this? Certainly, he cannot simply be conflated with Mark Rutherford, his creation, though Rutherford's experiences often echo those of his progenitor. The relationship has been much analysed; but my own emphasis – to use a term applied to Shelley in a similar context – would be on the 'concentrical' aspect of the text, its embodiment of Hale White's current preoccupations.[19] Spiritual autobiography, as in *Grace Abounding* or *The Prelude*, is traditionally both didactic and autodidactic – a route to stability and self-knowledge via a return to the past but also a repository of wisdom for the encouragement and enlightenment of others.[20] Though, as we have seen, an account of personal struggle and development, an unmaking and reconstitution of the self, is present in the *Autobiography*, the work is objectified and set back from Hale White himself, and the autodidactic element is missing. This is the more palpably evident in the *Deliverance*, where the manner is increasingly discursive, taken up with issues rather than with psychodrama – although, to say nothing of the numerous *exempla* ranging from the responsibly free-thinking Theresa to Mary whose conquest of neuralgia represents a commonplace but real heroism, it should be remembered how readily even introspection can turn to evaluative discourse in the *Autobiography* itself, as when we learn of Rutherford's eventual insight into the drawbacks of continually deferring pleasure – 'As I got older I became aware of the folly of this perpetual reaching after the future ... [which] leaves us at death without the thorough enjoyment of a single hour' (*AMR*, p. 65). The greater homiletic content, however, does not mean that there is nothing at stake for Hale White in the matters he rehearses; the issues are live ones, both for him and his readership, and among the most pressing is always the question of how, and how far, the core of Christianity can be preserved for the present:

> We instinctively follow the antecedent form, and consequently we either pass by, or deny altogether, the life of our own time, because its expression has changed. We never do practically believe that the Messiah is not incarnated twice in the same flesh. He came as Jesus, and we look for him as Jesus now, overlooking the manifestation of today, and dying, perhaps, without recognising it.
> (*MRD*, p. 25)

The 'Drury Lane theology' of Rutherford and M'Kay, grounded in the elevation of Christ's attributes and in the watchword 'Love is God', proves powerless to 'stir the soul' among the slum-dwellers to which they preach it (some hooligans actually break up the meeting); intentionally or not, Hale White makes the socio-political point that there is no remedy for the inner-city 'cesspool', which he describes in close physical detail and in accordance with the contemporary liberal spiritualizing tendency and championing of sweetness and light (*MRD*, pp. 26–8). But these urban missionaries do have some success with individuals. John the waiter, for example, they help to perceive what is 'the sole truth of self', which is a sense of the 'universal and impersonal'; through love for his child 'the father passed out of himself, and connected himself with the future' (*MRD*, pp. 90–3). This is said to be John's 'salvation'.

Among the concepts floating free from the unsettlement of orthodox religion, which Hale White is concerned to redefine, 'salvation' is at once one of the most challenging and most rich in possibility. He returns to it in *Catharine Furze*, together with the related themes of latter-day spirituality and manifestations of the divine. When he does so he comes up with an unexpected area of investigation, one which D.H. Lawrence must have found interesting in Hale White's fiction,[21] a different kind of mutuality from that of familial repose or affection – sex.

This is how Catharine's (unacknowledged) love for Mr Cardew, a married parson, is described:

> It was through him the word was spoken to her, and he was the interpreter of the new world to her. She was in love with him – but what is love? There is no such thing: there are loves, and they are all different. Catharine's was the very life of all that was Catharine, senses, heart, and intellect, a summing-up and projection of her

whole selfhood ... When she was in ordinary Eastthorpe society she felt as a pent up lake might feel if the weight of its waters were used in threading needles, but when Mr Cardew talked to her, and she to him, she rejoiced in the flow of all her force, and that horrible oppression in her chest vanished.

(*CF*, pp. 192–3)

Loves may well be 'different' but the one Hale White brings into focus has a definite spiritual dimension, as the reference to 'the word' in particular indicates. Catharine's first awakening, after she has heard Cardew preach at the church near her boarding-school, is cast in terms of natural process, as it might be 'with some bud long folded in darkness which ... bares itself to the depths of its cup to the blue sky and the light' (*CF*, p. 115); but the intertwining of the physical and the inward, at the levels both of release and desire, is plain, and the impression of some kind of conversion experience, suggested by the imagery of darkness and light, is enforced by the fact that Cardew's sermon has been about how Christ will 'come to you in a shape in which it will not be easy to recognise him' (*CF*, p. 113), and by the subsequent exchange between the two on the Pauline theme of breaking out of death-in-life, 'The body of this death' (*CF*, pp. 118–20). We are encouraged to think, somehow, of Cardew entering Catharine's life as a manifestation of divine influence – or as a close substitute for it. Similarly, in Tom Catchpole's yearning for Catharine there is present a sense of a transcendent realm, 'a universe in which other favoured souls are able to live ... and yet its doors are closed to us, or, if sitting outside we catch a glimpse of what is within, we have no power to utter a single sufficient word to acquaint anybody with what we have seen' (*CF*, p. 215). There are intimate evocations here of the dreamer-narrator's glance into the Celestial City in Part One of *The Pilgrim's Progress*.[22] In modern times the journey's end, completion, is not heaven but love. When Catharine rejects him, Tom laments 'you are the one person in the world able to *save* me' (*CF*, p. 232: my italics).

There are many variations on the theme of salvation in *Catharine Furze*. Near the conclusion there is indeed an orthodox old-style conversion when Orkid Jim is rescued from a flood by Tom Catchpole – the man Jim had framed with theft and got sent into exile – and is so struck with repentance that he at once admits all his transgressions, finds the Lord who ''as saved my body and soul this day', and becomes a mighty preacher of God's Word in America (*CF*, pp. 353–7). Rutherford (or Hale White, for after all it is he who is doing it) attempts to disarm the potentially incredulous 'ordinary cultivated reader' with a reminder of comparable sudden transformations witnessed and recorded in the past, not least by John Bunyan; but the effect of this is actually to expose the made-up – fictional – nature of the present example, and to throw into relief the authenticity of modern ways of understanding being 'saved'. We have, for example, the story of Tom's father, Mike, blinded in an accident and face to face with the 'blank wall' of submissive despair, summoning the courage simply to endure, a slow 'deliverance' that 'did not burst upon him in rainbow colours out of the sky complete' (*CF*, p. 35). In a later episode, when we learn how Cardew suddenly awakens from his romantic dream of Catharine and his 'eyes were opened' to the worth of his wife the biblical and soteriological reference is even more overt: 'it smote him as the light from heaven smote Saul of Tarsus journeying to Damascus' (*CF*, p. 342). But in both cases – Noah or Paul – this language, and the general symbolism of blindness and seeing, operate to display the destabilization of once inviolable truths, their dispersal, and a move to redeploy them in the most basic human contexts. Religious doctrine itself – the Word – has status here not for what it says but for what it is. Hale White seeks to retrieve this evacuation of meaning by resituating the old *logos* in the world of common experience; and, vice versa, by so doing he endows that world with a new aura of value and intensity. That love situations are the most important of these areas of relocation is again underlined by the last scene of the book, the death of Catharine, which presents a critical nettle that can usefully be grasped before we then track back to earlier points in her history.

Catharine on her deathbed asks to see Cardew once more:

> 'Mr Cardew, I want to say something.'
> 'Wait a moment, let me tell you — *you have saved me.*'
> She smiled, her lips moved, and she whispered — '*You* have saved *me.*'
> By their love for each other they were both saved. The disguises are manifold which the Immortal Son assumes in the work of our redemption.
>
> (*CF*, p. 365)

It is not difficult to see how Catharine can be said to have 'saved' Cardew. Her renunciation of their love has led him to embrace the 'unexplored excellence' of his wife; the man who 'fell in love with himself, married himself' has come to learn 'who his wife was' (*CF*, p. 184). The same upvaluing of self-abnegation and responsiveness in marriage had been foregrounded in the story of M'Kay and his wife in the *Deliverance*. How Cardew has 'saved' Catharine, however, is harder to determine. John Lucas (who has written better than anyone on Hale White's fiction) thinks the whole idea frankly 'absurd', since 'the plain fact is that Catharine's love for Cardew destroys her'.[23] Yet there is, I think, an explanation for Catharine's claim, a clue to which is given when she twice insists that she be positioned so that she can look out 'across the meadow towards the bridge' (*CF*, p. 364). This spot is described early in the novel as probably the site of mass baptisms (*CF*, p. 53); but it is a holy place in Catharine's history because it is there that her most intense, and deeply erotic, encounters with Cardew have taken place. He has worked her 'redemption' because, to quote from a passage we have already considered, he has opened up to her a 'new world', unblocked 'the flow of all her force' (*CF*, pp. 192–3). That the flow is in the end fatally dammed up makes no difference to its intrinsic nature as an enhancement of her life. Catharine's triumph lies in keeping faith with her 'love', beyond its physical denial and even unto death. There is certainly a strain in the writing, not least the disproportion between the conventional religious formulations – 'Immortal Son' – and their application to ordinary, unmiraculous circumstance. But incongruity is not simple absurdity.

Gaps, things not quite fitting together, failures to cohere, are among the most interesting features of *Catharine Furze*. Nowhere is this more apparent than in the marked ambivalence in the presentation of Catharine herself. Even when he sympathizes with – even celebrates – the way she 'rejoiced in' her 'force' Hale White talks with diagnostic detachment, and a certain critical edge, of a 'cloudy singularity' in her which would have been helped by a modern education (the novel is set back in the year 1840), where books would have made her see that she was 'a part of humanity' in her 'extravagant and personal emotions' (*CF*, p. 192). This suggestion of a dangerous egotism continues a series of references beginning with comments on Catharine's deficient upbringing, when a mixture of parental opposition and weakness in the face of her wishes had accustomed her to assume an accord between her own 'will' and the 'will of the universe', thus preparing the ground for exactly the problem that occurs when the path of destiny does not coincide with her desire for Cardew: for 'the shock then is serious, especially if the collision be postponed till mature years' (*CF*, p. 44).

There is a troublesome cleavage in the text at this very point, because the context in which Catharine's personality is put under a question mark is also one in which she is self-evidently in the right – that is, she is arguing the case for her father's obligation to help the workman, Mike, who has been blinded in an accident in Furze's foundry. Clearly, Hale White is here not so much interested in issues of social justice as in the process of Catharine's development – or underdevelopment – and emergent vulnerability. The Ponsonbys' finishing school, to which she is sent by her mother, does neither harm nor good, though its dryness and superficiality certainly provide perfect conditions for increasing Catharine's receptiveness to Cardew's emotional intensity. Donald Davie (another critic who has written well on Hale White) admires the eighteenth-century restraint of the Misses Ponsonby, which Hale White contrasts, not unfavourably, with the nineteenth-century habit of walking naked in 'doubts, fears, passions' (*CF*, p. 99);[24] but whatever the virtues of 'not crying for the moon' – of suppressing extravagant urges – they make no difference to the shallowness, and in Catharine's case irrelevance, of a curriculum driven by a commitment to enable young ladies 'to move with ease in the best society' and of a system regulated at bottom, not by any sense of individual worth, but by the financial expediency of displaying 'remarkable tact in reconciling parents with the defects and peculiarities of their children' (*CF*, pp. 99, 101).

The most extended critical commentary on Catharine's personality and frame of mind comes from Turnbull, the doctor who is consulted when she begins to fall unaccountably ill. Turnbull steps in as the voice of wisdom and good advice, offering Catharine 'solemn counsel':

> Strive to consider yourself, not as Catharine Furze, a young woman apart, but as a piece of common humanity and bound by its laws. It is infinitely healthier for you ... If you have any originality it will better come out in an improved performance of what everybody ought to do, than in the indulgence of singularity. For one person, who, being a person of genius, has been injured by what is called conventionality – I do not, of course, mean foolish conformity to what is absurd – thousands have been saved by it, and self-separation means mischief. It has been the beginning even of insanity in many cases which have come under my notice.
>
> (*CF*, p. 334)

Now it is through 'conventionality' that one can be 'saved', and what this means in Catharine's case is made clear when Turnbull proceeds to present Mrs Cardew as an ideal of womanhood, 'unobtrusive, devoted to her husband, almost annihilating herself for him', wonderfully fulfilling her role by 'teaching the sick people patience and nursing them' (*CF*, p. 335). Sure enough, when Catharine refuses this guidance in the art of self-control and conformity – 'Commonplace rubbish' is her verdict – she gets worse. Her earlier loss of 'cheerfulness' and 'fight', 'collapse' into bouts of 'silence', possession by 'terrors vague and misty', all linked to the prospect of her love being incapable of realization (*CF*, pp. 299–300), intensifies into moods when she 'wrestled with her fancies, turned this way and that way', sleeplessly 'on fire' with visions of what she most desires but cannot have: 'the arm was behind her – she actually felt it; his eyes were on hers' (*CF*, p. 340).

Catharine's condition is clearly conceived as a case of erotomania, very much in accord with the configuration of female maladies in contemporary medical discourse. Philip W. Martin's recent investigation of nineteenth-century treatises yields several parallels, including a series in J.E.D. Esquirol's *Mental Maladies: A Treatise on Insanity* of 1838 portraying the life-threatening effects of 'amorous sentiments' where these feelings have no release or are bereft of the object of desire, and where the need 'to conceal the emotions of the heart' can be fatal.[25] In the theories of M. Allen the propensity in young women to illness on the grounds of unrequited passion is connected, as it is (if less explicitly) in *Catharine Furze*, with educational causes, so that the tyranny of 'delusive feelings' is most likely to arise in 'those families where ... a constant April atmosphere exists'.[26] The same point emerges in Erasmus Darwin's account of 'Erotomania (or) Sentimental love', where women are more susceptible to insanity because unlike men they have 'not had leisure to cultivate their taste for visible objects, and have not read the works of poets and romance-writers' – a thought which, as we have seen, has a definite counterpart in comments on advances in female education in Hale White's novel, referring especially to the effect of study 'in suppressing sensibility' (*CF*, p. 191).[27] It is George Man Burrows, however, who supplies perhaps the closest comparison, since he tracks debility and potential derangement to the lack, not of a love-object, but of any object whatsoever, which produces a dangerous susceptibility to excitement:

> The education of females is generally showy, rather than substantial, and as they naturally possess more ardent and susceptible minds, want of active occupation becomes a most dangerous enemy to them. Thus circumstanced, if any object present itself sufficiently striking, they are apt to embrace it without due examination; and if of a nature to excite, it soon exercises an inordinate influence. Nothing is so conducive to this effect as new views of religion.[28]

Catharine, 'with no definite object before her', doomed to 'occupy [her strength] in twisting straws' (*CF*, p. 301), finds her 'inordinate influence' in Cardew, and reaps the fatal consequences.

That is one point of view. Yet *Catharine Furze* as a whole – and this is a distinctive strength – also presses us to read against the grain of psychomedical discourse of which Turnbull is the central exponent, and which presents Catharine as a spectacle of deficiency (whether the fault is hers or not) and a suitable case for treatment. Her insistent refusal of Turnbull's verbal prescription for happiness through fitting in – she twice repeats the cry of 'Commonplace rubbish!' – situates her somewhere between obstinacy and admirable courage. Her resistance is not only to a workable moral economy but to being *man-aged*. Though by no means consistently, Hale White's text does see the problem as lying elsewhere than in the female nature itself; when referring to Catharine's future 'twisting straws' he clearly tracks the fault to the way society is organized, for 'It is really this which is at the root of many a poor girl's suffering. As the world is arranged at present, there is too much power for the mills which have to be turned by it' (*CF*, p. 301). Even the medical tracts are patently divided against themselves. They isolate deviation from the norm in the service of correction and the *status quo*, yet they regularly also accuse the norm (a 'showy education', 'want of active occupation'), and, more importantly perhaps, allow the deviant, or problematical, a space in which to put forth its concealed life, its needs and its pain. Hale White's text is similarly, but more intensively, two-sided. Catharine's story is at once a cautionary tale and a sympathetic, at times inspirational, study of 'a poor girl's suffering'.

But before considering further Hale White's treatment of Catharine, and how he opens up the woman question, making fixed assumptions loosely conversible, it is worth looking briefly at other female characters in the novel. Of these, one, Catharine's warm-hearted middle-aged friend Mrs Bellamy, is entirely conventional. All her energy goes into making Chapel Farm, her home, a utopia of cleanliness and hospitality: she 'polished her verses in beeswax and turpentine, and sought on her floors and tables for that which the poet seeks in Eden or Atlantis'; 'the jug was always full to overflowing with beer, and the dishes were always heaped up with good things' (*CF*, p. 57). This is the kind of sublimation Turnbull has in mind for Catharine no doubt, and it is interesting that Mrs Bellamy actually sounds like him when telling Catharine she 'mustn't rebel' against her mother for moving from the old family home to the grander but discomforting surroundings of the Terrace (*CF*, p. 89). Mrs Bellamy is allowed a slice of autobiography when taking an episode in her own past to illustrate to Catharine the wisdom of accepting one's lot (as a newly-wed she had been rescued from gnawing resentment at her interfering sister-in-law by the realization that nothing was meant personally against *her*). Yet even with the good Mrs Bellamy there is something wrong. She 'brooded much' and was 'low-spirited' and 'unwell' the moment she had nothing to do; and her commitment to house-keeping bordered on obsession, so that precautions to prevent dirt – scrapers, mats, druggets, straw – became themselves objects to be protected (*CF*, pp. 56–7). This is no straightforward picture of orthodoxy: occupation is survival, and the limits of opportunity in Mrs Bellamy's world let out her force in curious, neurotic ways. Standard familial and social values, on one level endorsed by her function as a reassuring figure and guiding voice, are on another unsettled by the message of her strange behavioural traits. Her 'symptoms' signal a need not merely for local correction, as Turnbull might have suggested, but for a radical consideration of causes. And so it is with Catharine.

The hidden message of several of the other stories of women in *Catharine Furze* seems to be that status and power are available to them only if they act surreptitiously. Mrs Butcher, a doctor's wife, is an interesting example – one of those marginal characters in fiction who point a very central truth. She wins the respect of her peers and her betters by keeping aloof, hinting but never quite practising the arts of a *femme fatale*, and weaving a mystery around her origins. Her subtlest manoeuvre is to leave open to furtive perusal a letter with a crest on it in a 'most aristocratic hand' and addressing her by a nickname when she is visited by the class-conscious and influential brewer's wife, Mrs Colston (*CF*, pp. 96–7). The tone of the novel at this point – 'Eastthorpe was slightly mistaken' – suggests that Mrs Butcher may well have composed the document herself; but, whether or not this is so, it is certain that she stations herself in the community by an imaginative use of personal history. Whereas Mrs Bellamy extrapolates from her experience a lesson in how to hang on in the face of psychological pressure, Mrs Butcher more assertively – but still in the cause of survival – secures her own position through a manipulative version of the traditional self-constructive purposes of autobiography. Mrs Colston herself exercises a harsh, humiliating control over Mrs Furze, extracting good money from her for the church restoration fund by dangling before her the promise, never realized, of helping to satisfy her obsessive wish for preferment to the upper circles of Eastthorpe society.

Mrs Furze, a major presence in the novel, is also wed to stratagem. She calls her plan to leave the living quarters at the ironmonger's shop for a house in the Terrace her 'little scheme' (*CF*, p. 26), and Hale White goes to some lengths to bring out her unwholesome and devious nature. Her desire for upwards mobility – social as well as physical, not only from town centre to residential area but from chapel to church and from trade to higher circles – is set over against the healthy instincts of her husband, and of Catharine, who wish to stay put, the former because of a natural wisdom rooted in the guiding force of 'past and forgotten experiences' (*CF*, p. 26). That Mrs Furze believes in the false reasons she gives for wanting to move – for example, the perceived advantages to Catharine – is no extenuation of her character; on the contrary, she is one of those continual 'deceivers' for whom 'the word deception has no particular meaning ... and implies a standard which is altogether inapplicable' (*CF*, pp. 50–1). Habituated to 'imposture', she does not know right from wrong.

Mrs Furze's driven blindness to all but her own interests makes her sometimes ridiculous, as when she cringes before the duplicitous Mrs Colston. Always, however, it is a source of danger, and as such must be taken seriously. The translocation to the Terrace contributes, after all, to the collapse of Furze's business, by alienating good friends and customers. More disconcerting still is the plot she later weaves to get honest Tom sent away as a criminal because, entirely misinterpreting a scene outside her house, she thinks that he and Catharine are lovers, and that her (hopeless) plan to get Catharine married to Mrs Colston's rebarbative son will thus be spoilt. Without ever openly doing so, she makes the envious Orkid Jim the agent of her own designs. When he repents near the end of the novel, Orkid Jim says he was 'tempted by the devil' (*CF*, p. 356); but it is Mrs Furze who really draws him in, as, after insinuating that Tom was 'no favourite' of hers, she seizes upon Jim's vague hint of some unspecified secret knowledge – '"What do you mean, Jim? What is it that you see? … I shall really be glad if you will communicate to me anything you may observe which is amiss. You may depend upon it you shall not suffer"' (*CF*, pp. 251–2). The details of the intrigue, which include the planting of false evidence of theft, hardly matter, though they make for a fairly lengthy and not uninteresting narrative.

What is striking is that Mrs Furze, like Shakespeare's Iago, authors a drama that rivals, and threatens to displace, the official direction and values of the text. At a revealing moment in the novel she is parenthesized within a letter she has herself written to Catharine about Tom: 'Catchpole has appropriated money belonging to your father, and the evidence against him is complete. (Mrs Furze then told the story.) You will now, my dear Catharine, be able, I hope, to do justice to your father and mother …' (*CF*, p. 295). This signifies, I think, her whole position in the work, as one who is bracketed off and not allowed (as Turnbull is) a naturally authoritative voice but who, in contradiction to this, insists on constructing a story of her own. Like Mrs Butcher she creates a history, but more formidably and with a bid for wider control. It takes a lot to stop her – no less indeed than that incredible conversion of Orkid Jim, where all claims to realism are sacrificed to the purposes of overthrowing her conclusion in favour of the narrator's. The effort thus required to cut her off is a mark of respect. What might seem at first a simple study in miscreant behaviour emerges, again, as a configuration of the question of woman's 'force' – its irrepressibility and its distortion, its subordination and refusal to submit. Through the negative conditions of its female characters – Mrs Bellamy devotes herself to housework and counselling à la Turnbull but finds no ease, Mrs Butcher resourcefully adopts a narrow persona, Mrs Furze becomes a crook, Catharine falls unmanageably ill – *Catharine Furze* positively acknowledges that 'force' as well as the constrictions acting upon it.

To stop Catharine in her refusal it takes death itself; and whereas the 'force' of Mrs Furze and the rest is brought into view at a secondary level of the text, as it were at cross purposes with the surface, Catharine's often attracts direct recognition. Just before she dies she is actually pictured in exultant mood. Where on the occasion of a meeting with Cardew in the same place the atmosphere, inner and outer, had been 'intense' and 'charged with thunder and lightning' there is now 'nothing but soft, warm showers':

> Never had a day been to her what that day was. She felt as if she lay open to all the life of spring which was pouring up through the earth, and it swept into her as if she were one of those bursting exultant chestnut buds, the sight of which she loved so in April and May ... The bliss of life passed over into contentment with death, and her delight was so great she could happily have lain down amid the hum of the insects to die on the grass.
> (*CF*, pp. 261-2)

This does not escape ambivalence. Catharine's reward for resisting Turnbull's route to sublimation – and indeed the physical realization of her own passion for Cardew – is a sublime intercourse with nature. Her heroism and her pain are glossed by a Romantic ideal. Furthermore, this passage continues a marked element of voyeurism present in previous events – the scuffle with the bargee, Cardew's light 'encircling touch [that] sent a quiver through every nerve in her and shook her like electricity' (*CF*, p. 331), the earlier 'charged' encounter with Cardew (which we shall look at in a moment). Catharine projects repeatedly the desire of the male, in both senses of that phrase. All the same, however, her sexuality is asserted as an independent motive, the more so in the present episode because of its crude melodramatic naturalization in the imagery of lying open, of life pouring up, and bursting buds. A literal eroticism persists, written indelibly upon the very process of its transfiguration into another order of 'bliss'. The effect is oddly present from the beginning; for is 'that day' which meant so much to Catharine the current one of 'contentment' or the one when she had experienced the 'fire' of her need for Cardew?

The earlier scene is perhaps the most finely drawn in the novel, and deserves extensive quotation as an outstanding example of the blend of exposition, analysis and discreet symbolism in which Hale White excels. Catharine is by the riverside, lost in 'simple, uncontaminated bliss'. Cardew suddenly appears, as if in a dream, conjured up by her longing:

> It was curious, but so it was, that her thoughts suddenly turned from the water and the thunderclouds and the blazing heat to Mr Cardew, and it is still more strange that at that moment she saw him coming along the towing-path. In a minute he was at her side, but before he reached her she had risen.
> 'Good morning, Miss Furze.'
> 'Mr Cardew! What brings you here?'

'I have been here several times; I often go out for the day; it is a favourite walk.'

He was silent, and did not move. He seemed prepossessed and anxious, taking no note of the beauty of the scene around him.

'How is Mrs Cardew?'

'She is well, I believe.'

'You have not left home this morning, then?'

'No! I was not at home last night.'

'I think I must be going.'

'I will walk a little way with you.'

'My way is over the bridge to the farmhouse, where I am staying.'

'I will go as far as you go.'

Catharine turned towards the bridge.

'Is it the house beyond the meadows?'

'Yes.'

It is curious how indifferent conversation often is just at the moment when the two who are talking may be trembling with passion.

'You should have brought Mrs Cardew with you,' said Catharine, tearing to pieces a water lily, and letting the beautiful white petals fall bit by bit into the river.

Mr Cardew looked at her steadfastly, scrutinisingly, but her eyes were on the thunderclouds, and the lily fell faster and faster. The face of this girl had hovered before him for weeks, day and night ... He was literally possessed ... Catharine felt his gaze, although her eyes were not towards him. At last the lily came to an end, and she tossed the naked stalk after the flower. She loved this man; it was a perilous moment: one touch, a hair's breadth of oscillation, and the two would have been one. At such a crisis the least external disturbance is often decisive. The first note of the thunder was heard, and suddenly the image of Mrs Cardew presented itself before Catharine's eyes, appealing to her piteously, tragically. She faced Mr Cardew.

'I am sorry Mrs Cardew is not here. I wish I had seen more of her ... Good-bye,' and she was gone.

She did not go straight to the house, however, but went into the garden and again cursed herself that she had dismissed him. Who had dismissed him? Not she ... She tried to make up an excuse for returning; she tried to go back without one, but it was impossible ... Then she leaned upon the wall and found some relief in a great fit of sobbing. Consolation she had none; not even the poor reward of conscience and duty. She had lost him, and she felt that, if she had been left to herself, she would have kept him. She went out again late in the evening. The clouds had passed away to the south and the east, but the lightning still fired the distant horizon ... The sky was clearing in the west, and suddenly in a rift Arcturus, about to set, broke through and looked at her, and in a moment was again eclipsed. What strange confusion! What inexplicable contrasts! Terror and divinest beauty; the calm of the infinite interstellar space and her own anguish; each an undoubted fact, but each to be taken by itself as it stood; the star was there, the dark blue depth was there, but they were no answer to the storm or her sorrow.

(*CF*, pp. 177–81)

The quality of the writing in this has often been admired, but never really explained. Though the control over syntax and punctuation is, as John Lucas comments, 'delicate and exact',[29] more important is the simultaneity of two levels of discourse, conscious and unconscious, occlusive surface and expressive depth. We register the 'trembling ... passion' behind – that is, concealed by *and* patently determining – the opening clipped awkward exchanges well before the narrator enters to underscore the effect; and beyond this the whole notation of suppressed emotion is sharpened by Catharine's urgently defensive repetition of Mrs Cardew's name as if it were a talisman and by the slippage of meaning in Cardew's 'I will go as far as you go', which contains both the promise and the threat of an immeasurable adventure. The 'indifferent conversation' quivers with the very desire it formally masks.

The truth of Catharine's own being, however, is most forcibly expressed here as a silence, accompanied symptomatically by the act of stripping the lily which is the displaced form of her wish to yield to Cardew – to be 'deflowered'. Hale White said that 'If emotion be profound, symbolism, as a means of expression, is indispensable'.[30] Symbolism is crucial to the impact of the present scene, not simply in the way the thunderclouds mirror Catharine's turbulent feelings, nor the signification of the 'bridge' which situates her at a liminal stage of existence where she may take this way or that, but above all in the recurrent focus on the lily, which falls 'faster and faster' as her excitement mounts, until at last it 'came to an end, and she tossed the naked stalk after the flower'. The denuding and casting away of the stalk does more than create an obvious aura of orgasmic intensity, or point Catharine's 'readiness to abandon herself to Cardew';[31] it brings an uncanny psychosexual dimension to her part in the interview, a glimpse of a subconscious urge in her to possess and have power over the object which, in a dual sense, she most wants. Such moments do much to disclose the lure of Hale White's text for the (male?) reader, whose response, in being hooked by the proffered iconography, is parallel to the fixation assigned to Cardew, who is 'literally possessed' (the adverb interestingly suggesting the compulsion of 'the letter') by the image of Catharine and is reduced to the operation of a 'gaze'.

Catharine's silence connects of course with the whole expression in *Catharine Furze* of the limits of female experience and power. As we have seen, other women characters have some command of language whereby, with differing degrees of success, or failure, they station themselves in the world; and it is worth noting that one thing that makes Catharine's mother so dangerous to the prevalent order, and therefore fated to erasure, is a verbal dexterity and capacity for 'logic' (*CF*, p. 28) that is assumed to be a masculine trait and in its conventional form allows Tom Catchpole, who is an excellent business manager, to rise through his merits. Catharine has no self-positioning discourse at all. Some promise of influence is held out when, as a child, she speaks up to persuade her parents to take on Tom as an apprentice in the firm – '"You *must* ... "' is her simple utterance (*CF*, p. 43). Thereafter, however, she is customarily acted upon by words, has texts woven around her, or is prevented from expressing herself. At school she hazards an unsolicited comment on Johnson's *Rasselas*, only to be upbraided for transgressing 'the forms of good society' (*CF*, p. 125). (The reference itself is aptly proleptic, for it is about 'the dreadful effects' of self-absorption and 'uncontrolled imagination' in the episode of the mad astronomer.) She is good at literature and tries to teach the solid, unimaginative Mrs Cardew to appreciate Milton, but the words she uses – 'Cannot you pick out some passage which particularly struck you?' (*CF*, p. 137) – are ones Cardew had already addressed to her – 'Can you select any one part which struck you?' (*CF*, p. 122). Her voice is the repetition of his. It is Cardew's preaching that fires her to the perception of a new world, and the flames are decisively fanned by the story of Charmides and the slave girl which he sends her to read in secret. This strange 'manuscript', which is printed in full (*CF*, pp. 148–70), is supposed to have been written earlier by Cardew but seems very like a seductive response to recent events in its account of the relationship of the artist-philosopher and the beautiful young woman who leads him to Christ and a martyr's death. Its heady mix of sensuality and spiritual idealism reveals much of Cardew himself, and is also a doubling of Hale White's own plucky but uncertain reappraisal of the concept of salvation (while the dying Demariste looks rapturously heavenwards Charmides gazes fixedly on her, so that the status of his self-sacrifice is left specifically 'doubtful'); but what concerns us here is that Cardew is another, like Turnbull, who writes a plot for Catharine, this time a romance in which man and woman defy all convention and journey to an ecstatic consummation.

Catharine plots nothing, authors nothing. Why, then, does she make so great an impression? One answer is indicated, indeed, by the very fact that she is distinct from a whole succession of heroines – Moll Flanders, Pamela, Lucy Snowe, Meredith's Diana of the Crossways – who find in the exercise of the pen a means of negotiating the rocks of recalcitrant structures of authority and gender definition. Her impotence, finally absolute as her 'determination to retaliate by silence' gives way to the 'disappearance of all desire to fight' (*CF*, p. 298), can be seen as a gain in radical complaint, as well as a loss in ideas of tactical redress, because it represents marginalization and meanness of opportunity *in extremis*. Hale White's radicalism is most apparent, however, in the candid way in which he traces Catharine's hidden life – her submerged autobiography – and brings it to light. The configurations of desire are primary here, and have a raw, disconcerting edge and theoretical force that are absent alike from the subtler and more dispersed eroticism of Hardy's fiction and, at the other end of the quality spectrum, the thin idealization of love outside marriage of Grant Allen's once notorious *The Woman Who Did* (belonging like *Catharine Furze* to 1893 but banned in England for many decades) where the heroine consummates her 'espousal' to the man of her free choice dressed symbolically in 'a simple white gown, as pure and sweet as the soul it covered'.[32] Allen now seems rather conservative and naïve in his view of female personality, not least in his unreflective alignment of moral purity and physical choice. Hale White by contrast is everywhere alert to tension and conflict. One of his earliest interpreters, the theologian Thomas Selby, rejoices that Catharine is saved from 'illicit love', and seizes eagerly upon the note of thunder that keeps her and Cardew apart in the above-quoted episode as an interposition of Providence, 'a divine instrument in the election unto life'.[33] But this of course is to put back in what Hale White has written out. In that wonderfully phrased sentence – 'She loved this man; it was a perilous moment: one touch ...' – the sheer fact of Catharine's 'love', which springs proudly to life, is given as much weight as, if not more than, the 'peril' of transgression; the question of providential design is there in the thunder but as an uncertainty, while the motifs of the 'inner light' and 'moral law within', which greatly interested Hale White in the story of Job,[34] have become elements in a palpably secular drama.

Selby's allegiance, and that of Grant Allen, who is his ideological mirror image, is to the Truth that life illustrates, Hale White's is to the life that embodies truth. Hale White respects the claims of moral responsibility and social convention which make Catharine turn away, but, far from rejoicing in their sway, does all he can to stress her pain in the jaws of dilemma and psychological impasse. If she can be said to win a victory it is a truly Pyrrhic one, since it is at the expense of a side of herself that will not be laid to rest, nor, for all Hale White's Puritan heritage, be simply consigned to the sphere of wrongdoing: 'Consolation she had none; not even the poor reward of conscience and duty. She had lost him, and she felt that, if she had been left to herself, she would have kept him.' Yet the language of achievement is not really appropriate at all: Catharine's predicament is to be caught helplessly and impossibly in a field of uncontrollable currents within herself – an irresolvable deadlock between desire and the equally intractable pressure of the prohibition that comes in the form of the piteous image of Mrs Cardew. Nature – the sky clearing, the lightning firing the horizon – provides a spectacular setting for her agony, but also one of indifference. The star Arcturus is said to have 'looked at her', but any suggestion of a benign universal order, or any order at all, is cancelled in its immediate 'eclipse'. Try as Selby might to convince us otherwise, we have only 'strange confusion' and 'inexplicable contrasts' at the levels both of the individual life and the vast drama beyond, and that of the relation between them. Each thing is 'an undoubted fact ... to be taken by itself'. There can be no comforting thoughts of an overarching harmony or purpose – 'no answer to the storm or her sorrow'.

We began our consideration of *Catharine Furze* with a reference to its reorientation of the idea of 'salvation'. A similar unsettlement and recuperation at the level of metaphysical concern is apparent in this 'renunciation' episode, for while 'infinite interstellar space' suggests a universe that is limitless and empty – unbounded and unfilled by God, as was the existence of the deconverted Mark in the *Autobiography* – the reference to 'terror and divinest beauty' reproduces the numinous as a quality of the natural scene and the human experience to which it is a backdrop, a *locus in quo*. The cosmic frame and poetic rendition endow Catharine's 'anguish' with sublimity. The 'vividness' and 'haze of wonder' that W.H. Mallock feared would pass away from the earth and from our being with the contemporary assault on religious belief continue in art's valorization of life – in the secular scripture.[35] This is an important effect; a hard-won plenitude; a notation that inspires even as it tells of lost verities. What is lost in Hale White's work is not only the Deity but that comforting child of the Enlightenment, the stable 'ego' of humanist tradition, able to spread coherent meaning upon the world and to find a home in it. In Catharine, as I have often stressed, we read the problems of being a woman, at least as these are understood by a sympathetic masculine intelligence, but she also figures that same representative modern condition that emerged in the *Autobiography* – a subjectivity marked by division and vulnerability. When Catharine says 'it is I who do it' (*CF*, p. 67) she is fooling herself, not because she is subject to any destiny or divine plan but because she is caught in – indeed is constituted by – a complex of psychic determinants, including interiorized social conventions; and a slightly different way of describing the symbolic text we have just considered is to say that the 'subject' (named Catharine) emerges in a void where there was once free will (that is, in the humanist version of individuality) but is now a fissure between imaginary wholeness (uniting with the 'other', named Cardew) and the internalized cipher of the law (not hurting Mrs Cardew).

I put it like this, with obvious allusion to Jacques Lacan,[36] because it helps to underscore the challengingly transitional nature – the liminal modernity – of Hale White's text. The sublime rendering of Catharine's drama of impulse and denial bears witness to art's abiding function as mourning: it at once declares and accommodates the passing of a Romantic-religious – holistic and anthropocentric – view of the world and being in it; the new 'intense self-consciousness' that worried Mallock is expressed as both chaos and excitement, pain and wonder. In other respects, however, *Catharine Furze* tells more disconcertingly of fragmentation, attenuation, the bewilderment and sheer effort that change can bring. Not only free will and completeness but the very idea of selfhood and personality come under question. Catharine is less a character than a tissue of signs: a signifier above all, as we know, of desire, balanced undecidedly between the affirmation of a 'force', an indictment of repressive influences, and a mapping of mental aberration; a locus of meaning where, at extreme points, 'she' becomes – or *un*becomes – literally an image, a flower opening or bud bursting, energy 'sucked in by a whirlpool' (*CF*, p. 144) or standing 'upright as a spear' (*CF*, p. 331), and even vanishes altogether, unrealized as the moment of her passionate response to Cardew's touch passes – '"Where is Miss Furze?" ... "I do not know"' (*CF*, p. 145).

This 'depersonalization' of Catharine is only one of the ways in which the text deviates from, and seriously undermines, the form of the realist novel and the assumptions that go with it. *Catharine Furze* does follow certain of the procedures of that form. It gives, for example, an outline of the history of Eastthorpe (or lack of it) and of its present geography, and an account of its inhabitants and social hierarchy; it offers Catharine's own progress through childhood, schooldays and early maturity; it respects the common teleological structures that end in a marriage (that of Cardew and Mrs Cardew restored) and transcendence (Catharine and Cardew both being 'saved'). But, as we have already seen, the traditional mimetic, ontological and moral positions inscribed in these conventions are put under severe stress, or are transgressed. The developmental model of the individual life that we tend to associate with high Victorian *bildungsroman* patterning – exemplified, say, in Pip's coming to appreciate human worth in *Great Expectations* or Dorothea's escape in *Middlemarch* from the 'luxurious shelter [of] selfish complaining' and hard-earned recognition of the 'perfect Right' of her duty towards others[37] – is opposed in *Catharine Furze* not only by the fact that Catharine seemingly learns nothing and travels increasingly inwards to self-absorption and premature death but also by the way narrative itself is overcast by the constant repetition of the configurations of Catharine's force – her desire and its outlet or denial – which we have witnessed variously throughout this essay, in her running from the bargee, her three encounters with Cardew, and her bliss in the lap of nature. Drawing attention to itself as device, such repetition instances that general shift to modernity which J. Hillis Miller finds in late-Victorian fiction's anti-mimetic tendency, its readiness to declare its 'fictionality'.[38]

But we can go a little further in considering this effect. All these episodes foreground the dynamic which we earlier identified in one of them, and which is uncovered also in the text Miller is directly concerned with, Hardy's *The Well-Beloved*: voyeurism, or the link between erotic fascination and artistic creation and reception – a connection curiously enforced in the character of the sculptor-lover Charmides in Cardew's attempt at a short story, and by Cardew's own words to Catharine comparing the sculptor's refinement of 'the image which haunts him' and a man's 'image of a woman whom he seeks unceasingly' (*CF*, p. 330). The manifest 'madness' of *Catharine Furze* refers us, then, to the text's subjective origins. There is clearly something in Catherine R. Harland's contention that this novel is, on one level, disguised autobiography, expressing in Catharine's predicament Hale White's own well-documented sexual frustrations.[39] Needless to say, however, the book cannot be consigned either to the enclave of mere aesthetic play or the narrow realm of its author's private places. Its evident fictionality and its subjectivity alike are one side of a duality defined on the other by Hale White's earnest quest to engage with the human condition and serve moral ends. The *telos* of Cardew's 'saved' marriage and that of Catharine's ultimate 'salvation' are the obvious upshot of these objective purposes. That the one does not convince – for the flowers, pet name ('Doss') and passionate kiss that mark Cardew's return to his wife are the laboured signifiers of a completion that reads as emptiness in comparison with Catharine's uncompleted life – and the other strains uneasily, though interestingly, towards affirmation signals the creative uncertainty that is spread throughout the work.

Always trying, never triumphant, *Catharine Furze* is, in the final analysis, a site where questions are raised on the incipient ruins of an old order. Parallels have sometimes been noted between Catharine and Maggie Tulliver, including 'the renunciation by each heroine, in a river scene, of the key temptation, followed in both cases by death'.[40] Just as striking, however, is the difference. Maggie becomes an *exemplum* of the christological ideal of self-sacrifice: 'Is it not right to resign ourselves entirely, whatever ... may be denied us? I have found great peace in that for the last two or three years – even joy in subduing my own will.'[41] Maggie's death can no doubt be read as ironizing the very attitude she voices, but how much more unsettled, and unsettling, is Hale White's novel in its reticence on this matter of recompense and gain. In the body of the novel Catharine's reactions provocatively shut out the idea of reward for self-denial – 'Consolation she had none'. Her final words, '*You* have saved *me*', do suggest, however, that something of the *telos* of transcendence has been salvaged for her. She is at last consciously resigned and at peace, and draws a positive satisfaction from the ideal of self-transformation. But, as we saw at the beginning of our discussion of *Catharine Furze*, what Hale White really offers us here is, not faith in any dogma, but a desperate effort to reapply and restore it to life. He gives us a verbal conundrum telling of a receding past and a potential future, a desperate binding to the vestigial discourse of a once living system and a glimpse of fresh possibilities for understanding the human spirit. It is not so much that he is working out a problem as that language is working through him to propose it.

Notes

1. Mark Rutherford [William Hale White], *Catharine Furze* (1893), ninth edition (London: T. Fisher Unwin, n.d.), p. 67 (hereafter, *CF*).
2. [William Hale White], *The Autobiography of Mark Rutherford, Dissenting Minister, Edited by His Friend, Reuben Shapcott*, ed. William S. Peterson (Oxford: Oxford University Press, 1990), p. 156 (hereafter, *AMR*). All references are to this reproduction of the Oxford University Press edition of 1936, which is based on the text of the second (slightly corrected) edition (London: Trübner & Co., 1888). The name 'Theresa' recalls George Eliot's reflections on the epic life of Saint Teresa in the Prelude to *Middlemarch*.
3. [William Hale White], *Mark Rutherford's Deliverance, Being the Second Part of His Autobiography, Edited by His Friend, Reuben Shapcott* (Oxford: Oxford University Press, 1936), pp. 9–10 (hereafter, *MRD*). The *Deliverance* was first published by Trübner & Co., London.
4. See especially Basil Willey, 'Mark Rutherford', *More Nineteenth Century Studies: A Group of Honest Doubters* (London: Chatto & Windus, 1956), pp. 186–247.
5. For the relevant passages, see: John Bunyan, *The Pilgrim's Progress*, ed. Roger Sharrock (Harmondsworth: Penguin Books, 1984), pp. 197, 200–4 (hereafter, *PP*); George Eliot, *Middlemarch* (1871–72), ed. W.J. Harvey (Harmondsworth: Penguin Books, 1986), p. 846. Certain similarities of phrasing – as in Eliot's 'Far off ... was the pearly light' and Hale White's 'Further off was the great light' – suggest Hale White's definite recollection of Eliot's text. I have discussed Eliot's humanist secularization of Bunyan's orthodox religious vision of spiritual progress, in this latter-day 'conversion' episode, in 'Dorothea's Awakening: the Recall of Bunyan in *Middlemarch*', *Notes and Queries*, 31 (1984), 497–9. Hale White brings

in turn a profound negation of the ideals of inward regeneration and fulfilment.
6. See Matthew Arnold, '1853 Preface'; *The Poems of Matthew Arnold*, ed. Kenneth Allott (London: Longmans, 1965), p. 591. Arnold is referring to his own poem 'Empedocles on Etna', and to the characteristic modern situation 'in which the suffering finds no vent in action; in which a continuous state of mental stress is prolonged, unrelieved by incident, hope, or resistance; in which there is everything to be endured, nothing to be done' (p. 592). The famous 'two voices' are those of Tennyson's poem of that name, where the first voice puts the same desperate question as does Rutherford's 'nameless dread', but more directly: '"Thou art so full of misery, / Were it not better not to be?"' (*The Poems of Tennyson*, ed. Christopher Ricks (London: Longmans, 1969), p. 523).
7. W.H. Mallock, *Is Life Worth Living?* (London: Chatto & Windus, 1880), pp. 19–20.
8. Mallock, pp. 76–77, 104, 111–12.
9. See Sigmund Freud, 'The Uncanny'; *Freud: Art and Literature*, ed. Albert Dickson, Pelican Freud Library, vol. XIV (Harmondsworth: Penguin Books, 1985), pp. 356–7.
10. Catherine R. Harland, *Mark Rutherford: The Art and Mind of William Hale White* (Columbus: Ohio State University Press, 1988), pp. 85–7, documents Hale White's admiration for Johnson, especially as an exemplar of courage. *Rasselas* is referred to directly in *Catharine Furze*, pp. 122–4 (see also note 17 below). For the story of the philosopher whose 'rational fortitude' fails before the impact of feeling, see Samuel Johnson, *The History of Rasselas, Prince of Abyssinia*, ed. J.P. Hardy (Oxford: Oxford University Press, 1968), pp. 46–8.
11. Elizabeth K. Helsinger, 'Ulysses to Penelope: Victorian Experiments in Autobiography', in *Approaches to Victorian Autobiography*, ed. George P. Landow (Athens, Ohio: Ohio University Press, 1979), pp. 3–25 (pp. 16, 12).
12. I have explored the open-endedness and persistent fractures of *The Prelude* and *Grace Abounding* in, respectively: 'Romantic Subjects: Shaping the Self from 1789 to 1989', in *Reviewing Romanticism*, ed. Philip W. Martin and Robin Jarvis (London: Macmillan, 1992), pp. 134–53 (pp. 141–5); and '"With the eyes of my understanding": Bunyan, Experience and Acts of Interpretation', in *John Bunyan, Conventicle and Parnassus: Tercentenary Essays*, ed. N.H. Keeble (Oxford: Oxford University Press, 1988), pp. 189–216.
13. For pointed examples of the use of the term 'morbid' by Arnold, Ruskin and Tennyson, see Helsinger, pp. 4–5. To this short but impressive list we may now add Hale White.
14. Walter Pater, *The Renaissance* (1873; London: Macmillan, 1910), p. 236.
15. *The Confessions of St. Augustine*, trans. John K. Ryan (Garden City: Image Books, 1960), book X, ch. 3, para. 3. For Gosse's reversal of Augustine's account of spiritual progress, see Howard Helsinger, 'Credence and Credibility: The Concern for Honesty in Victorian Autobiography', in *Approaches to Victorian Autobiography*, ed. Landow, pp. 59–60.
16. The phrase is Gosse's own: see Edmund Gosse, *Father and Son* (1907; Harmondsworth: Penguin Books, 1970), p. 218. The way Gosse 'comes

down in favor of the veil of illusion, in defense of the lie that makes life bearable' is traced by Howard Helsinger, *Approaches*, p. 61.

17. Catharine Furze (*CF*, p. 122) identifies as her favourite bit of *Rasselas* 'The part about the astronomer ... about the dreadful effects of the uncontrolled imagination'. For Johnson's study in the 'dangerous prevalence of imagination ... [and] silent speculation', see *Rasselas*, ed. Hardy, pp. 98–115 (pp. 104–5). The astronomer is actually restored, not by taking up a science, but, on the contrary, by renouncing one in favour of friendship and outgoing contact with the world around him. But the fundamental lesson is the same; and it is interesting to note that the butterfly collector's advice that 'men should not be too curious in analysing and condemning any means which nature devises to save them from themselves, whether it be coins, old books, curiosities, butterflies, or fossils' (*AMR*, p. 127) tallies closely with Johnson's remark to Boswell on treating the ills of a mind preying upon itself, 'Let him take a course of chymistry or a course of rope-dancing, or course of anything to which he is inclined at the time' (Boswell's *Life of Johnson*, quoted by Harland, p. 87).

18. See Milton, *Paradise Lost*, XII. 646; *PP*, p. 41.

19. The term is from Christine Gallant, *Shelley's Ambivalence* (London: Macmillan, 1989), p. 21. Among studies explicating Hale White's writings as the expression of his life and opinions, special mention should be made, alongside Catharine Harland's more recent volume (see note 10 above), of the standard source books, Irvin Stock, *William Hale White (Mark Rutherford)* (London: Allen & Unwin, 1956) and Wilfred H. Stone, *Religion and Art of William Hale White* (Stanford: Stanford University Press, 1954).

20. The twin objectives are put with particular clarity in the Preface to *Grace Abounding*, where Bunyan values the personal gains to be had from 'remembrance' of 'the Grace of God towards me' but at once casts himself in the role of a father teaching his children 'for [their] further edifying and building up in Faith' (John Bunyan, *Grace Abounding to the Chief of Sinners*, ed. Roger Sharrock (Oxford: Oxford University Press, 1966), pp. 5, 3). Though *The Prelude* was not published until after Wordsworth's death, it was always inscribed with traditional didactic assumptions, which are emphasized in the conclusion where the poet talks of himself and Coleridge as 'Prophets of Nature' labouring in a work of 'redemption', speaking to men 'A lasting inspiration, sanctified / By reason and by truth' (*Prelude* 1805, XIII. 428–52; ed. E. de Selincourt and H. Darbishire (Oxford: Oxford University Press, 1959), pp. 504, 506).

21. The evidence most often quoted to show Lawrence's admiration of Hale White is the comment, 'I do think he is jolly good – so thorough, so sound and so beautiful' (*The Letters of D.H. Lawrence*, ed. Aldous Huxley (New York: Viking Press, 1932), p. 83). Lionel Trilling, however, in a foreword to Irvin Stock's *William Hale White* (p. vii), reminds us that Lawrence is quoted by his biographer, Harry T. Moore, as also saying that he finds himself 'fearfully fond of Rutherford' because he is 'so just and plucky and sound'. In what could Hale White have been more 'plucky' for Lawrence than in his conflation of spiritual and erotic experience?

22. 'Now just as the Gates were opened to let in the men, I looked in after them; and behold, the City shone like the sun ... and in [the streets] walked many men with crowns on their heads, palms in their hands ...

        And after that, they shut up the Gates: which when I had seen, I wished myself among them' (*PP*, pp. 203–4).
23. John Lucas, 'William Hale White and the Problems of Deliverance', *The Literature of Change: Studies in the Nineteenth-Century Provincial Novel* (Hassocks: Harvester Press, 1977), pp. 57–118 (p. 105).
24. Donald Davie, *A Gathered Church: The Literature of the English Dissenting Interest, 1700–1930* (London and Henley: Routledge & Kegan Paul, 1978), pp. 87–8.
25. J.E.D. Esquirol, *Des Maladies Mental Considérées sous les Rapports Medical, Hygienique et Médico-Legal* (Paris, 1838), trans. E.K. Hunt (Philadelphia, 1845), pp. 342, 338; quoted in Philip W. Martin, *Mad Women in Romantic Writing* (Brighton: Harvester Press, 1988), pp. 185–91 (pp. 185, 188).
26. M. Allen, MD, *Essay on the Classification of the Insane* (London, 1833), p. 146; quoted in Martin, pp. 172–5 (p. 175).
27. Erasmus Darwin, *Zoonomia; or, the Laws of Organic Life*, 2 vols (London, 1794), vol. II, pp. 363–4; quoted in Martin, p. 37.
28. George Man Burrows, *An Enquiry into Certain Errors Relative to Insanity; and Their Consequences; Physical, Moral and Civil* (London, 1820), pp. 215–16; quoted in Martin, p. 36.
29. Lucas, *Literature of Change*, p. 109. My interest in this scene was first stimulated by Lucas's excellent, though brief, commentary.
30. William Hale White, *More Pages from a Journal* (Oxford: Oxford University Press, 1910), pp. 224–5.
31. Lucas, p. 109.
32. Grant Allen, *The Woman Who Did* (London: The Richards Press, 1927), p. 72.
33. Thomas G. Selby, *The Theology of Modern Fiction, Being the Twenty-Sixth Fernley Lecture, Delivered in Liverpool, July, 1896* (London: Charles H. Kelly, 1896), p. 189.
34. For a discussion of Hale White's 'Notes on the Book of Job' (1885) and of these inner promptings as Job's reference points for conduct and relationship with God, see Harland, pp. 194–6.
35. Mallock, pp. 111, 150.
36. I am thinking of Catharine Furze, however, not only as interpretable in terms of the famous Lacanian split, or discord, that comes with the move from the 'imaginary' order (with its illusion of wholeness) to the 'symbolic' (with painful injunctions under the sign of language and of the father) but also as a prior configuration of the more general post-structuralist understanding of the 'subject' as a great absence in a network of determinants, including – as well as linguistic discourse – structures of kinship, culture, and the internal economy of the unconscious. What is involved here is a refusal of the Cartesian *cogito* which supplies 'the notion of a constituting ego which offers itself as a phenomenological centre from which *free will* radiates into the world' (Jean-Marie Benoist, *The Structural Revolution* (London: Weidenfield and Nicholson, 1978), p. 14).
37. *Middlemarch*, ed. Harvey, p. 846. See also note 5 above.
38. J. Hillis Miller, Introduction to Thomas Hardy, *The Well-Beloved* (London: Macmillan, 1975), pp. 11–21.
39. Harland, pp. 161–2.

40. Roger Ebbatson, *Lawrence and the Nature Tradition: A Theme in English Fiction 1859–1914* (Brighton: Harvester Press, 1980), p. 207.
41. George Eliot, *The Mill on the Floss*, Illustrated Copyright Edition, 2 vols (London: Virtue & Co., n.d.), vol. II, book IV, ch. 3, p. 94.

CHAPTER TWELVE

Seconding the Self: *Mary Chesnut's Civil War*

Rosemarie Morgan

It is April 1861, Charleston, South Carolina – at the eleventh-hour. 'There stands Fort Sumter', writes Mary Boykin Chesnut, 'and thereby hangs peace or war':[1]

> The air is too full of war news. And we are all so restless. News so warlike I quake. My husband speaks of joining the artillery ...
> Governor Manning[2] walked in, bowed gravely, and seated himself by me. Again he bowed low, in mock heroic style and, with a grand wave of his hand, said, 'Madame, your country is invaded.'
> When I had breath to speak, I asked, 'What does he mean?'
> 'He means this. There are six men-of-war outside of the bar. Talbot and Chew have come to say that hostilities are to begin. Governor Pickens and Beauregard are holding a council of war.'[3] I crept silently to my room, where I sat down to a good cry.
> (MCCW, p. 43)

This is Chesnut's diary entry for 7 April 1861, some four months after secession and some four days before Confederate General Beauregard will storm Fort Sumter to oust the 'invading' federal troops. Chesnut has recently left the Alabama convention, in company with her husband (newly resigned from the state senate), where 'the brand-new Confederacy' was 'remodelling its Constitution' (p. 6). Here she had 'stood on the balcony to see our Confederate flag go up. Roars of cannon &c&c' (p. 15), and while attending a reception she had ordered the immediate removal of a Union flag still 'floating in the breeze' (p. 19). At the same time, but on a more personal level in response to her husband's anxiety about his cold, reticent public image, she confesses to her diary that 'Truth required me to say that I knew no more what Mr C. thought or felt on any subject now than I did twenty years ago'. 'However', she reminds herself, 'this journal is intended to be entirely *objective*. My subjective days are over', even though 'I think this journal will be disadvantageous for me, for I spend the time now like a spider, spinning my own entrails instead of reading, as my habit was' (p. 23).

The device is a familiar one. In order to exploit the full literary potential of the genre, the diarist invokes an 'objective' stance to authenticate the factual accuracy of the document while disclaiming all pretensions to artistry, or indeed to any non-spontaneous technique that might undermine the sincerity of the unadorned, self-expressive voice. Or, put another way, the realistic immediacy conveyed by the non-retrospective diary mode, the necessary fluctuation in point of view and perception, and the non-linearity of the continually interrupted narration which returns to a new beginning with each entry, may be effectively augmented by an 'objective' narratorial distance artfully appropriate to the historian's act of placing 'facts' on record.

Chesnut goes even further. While implicating intentionality she strips it of false application – as in assuming an inside knowledge of authorial predetermination, or a fixity and singularity of purpose, or a full self-awareness of motivation. Instead, she applies it to the artefact ('this journal is intended to be entirely *objective*'), and, in equal measure, to the diarist (who stands behind the passive construction), who is not the subjective 'I' of earlier days.

Complex as these layered textualities may be, they work in tandem not only to accentuate the self-reflexivity of the diarist's autobiographical act of reading the self in the moment of writing the self, or of reading a second self through the agency of the diary ('However, my subjective days are over'), but also to render transparent those elements of textual self-concealment that convey mimesis, that enhance the illusion of reality. For, in terms of rendering that transparency, it is true to say that both mimesis and the illusion-of-reality, together with sincerity and authenticity (which are more usefully seen not as inherent but adherent), rely extensively upon the reader's double awareness of artlessness in the narrator and the narrative deception of artlessness. Thus, in *Mary Chesnut's Civil War*, both narrator and text 'intend' *objectivity* to remain an open presentational strategy while the autobiographical 'I' will, simultaneously, body forth her *subjective* interiority 'like a spider, spinning my own entrails'.

The extent to which Chesnut uses strategies of objectivity to authenticate not simply the public but also the private self, the inner as well as the outer reality, the personal as well as the political world, becomes more readily apparent through close comparative analysis of her 'private' and 'public' texts. Take, for example, the following account:

> April 9, 1861. I was sitting quietly talking to Mr. G.[4] when John Manning walked in, seated himself by me & in mock heroic style began, 'Madam your country is invaded.' Then as I questioned him told that six men of war were outside the *bar* – & Talbot & Chew had arrived to announce war. Beauregard & Pickens were holding a council of war. I immediately told Mr. C.[5] who came in after inquiry & confirmed the story ... Mrs. W.[6] & I retired to my room, &c, where she silently wept & we disconsolately discoursed upon

> the horrors of Civil War. Directly the boom of a cannon & then *shouts*. I started up & met with blanched face & streaming eyes poor Mrs. Allen Green.[7]
>
> (*PMC*, pp. 56–7)

This is Chesnut's original journal entry. The 7 April account is not an 1861 entry at all, but a revision made in the 1880s in preparation for publication.

The 1860s were, inevitably, chaotic, frightening, uncertain, exciting years for Chesnut. Constantly on the move between war zones, living out of suitcases in hotels and temporary places of refuge, thrown into exceptionally close proximity to political and military leaders, judges, lawyers and doctors, displaced families and wounded soldiers – in field and boudoir alike – this woman of discerning judgement, keen perception, quick wit, fierce intelligence and a 'glad eye' for beautiful young men, took time to study military history for pleasure, political dialogues for scepticism, and knew Shakespeare and the classical poets virtually by heart – the heart that kept missing a beat, literally speaking, and that stopped her at 63.

Preparing her diary-style autobiography, after the war years, Chesnut more than objectified a journal narrative. She also objectified a life in which the seconded self, the erstwhile Mrs Senator Chesnut, now exercised supreme authority over her own domain, over her autonomous self. And, in gaining this dominion the more vulnerable Mary Chesnut who, in April 1861, on the eve of war, had breakfasted almost daily with the amorous John Manning, now disappears in favour of a more commanding figure to whom the 'Governor' now bows and now formally pays his respects before speaking. It is not only that John Manning has become depersonalized in the reconstructed, 'objectified' version, or that he has been transferred to the public domain (albeit, that he was no longer Governor of South Carolina at this time), or that he has been deprived of the (intimate) right to interrupt the lady in her conversation with 'Mr. G.', or that he has to announce himself as if he were an intruder, but that the writer's voice and persona have also changed. The eager interlocutor of the early account becomes the dignified recipient of shocking news in the reconstructed account, and the rather impetuous narrative voice of the first speaker gives way to more balanced, neutral tones in the second (accented by a crisply organized format).

The objectivity 'intended' here has, in part, to do with Chesnut's personal relationship with Manning. There was, during the 1860s, a thrilling emotional attachment between them. But whereas Manning's wife plays little part in the affair, except offstage and cajolingly, Chesnut's husband takes on the full 'conjugal' role:

29 March 1861: 'Mr. Chesnut made himself eminently absurd by accusing me of flirting with John Manning, &c. I could only laugh – too funny!' (*PMC*, pp. 49–50).

And for 1 April: 'Mr. C. came home so enraged with my staying at home, he said to flirt with John Manning, that I went to bed in disgust' (*PMC*, p. 51).

And for 8 April: 'That husband scold made me melancholy last night. I feel he is my all & I should go mad without him' (*PMC*, p. 56).

Some months later, her best friend, Varina Anne Davis (wife of President Jefferson Davis), confides her anxiety: that Mary Chesnut lets her husband bully her. The 'bully', meanwhile, sits up all night giving his wife such a scolding that she takes to her bed with 'so much opium' that her memory goes with it (*PMC*, p. 105).

These stresses remain in muted form in the revised diary-style autobiography – *Mary Chesnut's Civil War*. While the usually reticent husband still occasionally rages, the 'flirtation' is less in evidence. So, how was it for Mary Chesnut? Did the 'Governor' displace that charming admirer, more latterly that 'Snake in the grass – beautiful as he is' (*PMC*, p. 118), because the charm dispelled of its own accord, or because Mr C. dispelled it for her? Because she was forced to look at herself through the perspective of an 'other' and did not recognize, did not identify with, did not like, the empty-headed flirt he made her out to be? We may never know. What we do know is that 'objectivity' has been achieved, in this instance, by means of a profound authorial subjectivity: gazing into the self-reflecting text, Chesnut displaces the self already narrated by the diarist now narrating. The 'spider spins'.

This aspect of subjectivity bodying forth the web of objectivity is most obviously apparent in the diarist's final touch to the April entry. One of the most intriguing of all self-deceptions is that of internalizing the 'other' to such a degree that it replicates itself as subjective experience. Integrating external events, by means of imagining and reimagining them, the 'other' may then be experienced as inseparable from the self that now performs as the subject/object of the construct. This reconstruction is most often an aspect of memory, and a hazard of retrospective autobiography. So that, when the here-and-now narrator of the daily journal discusses the 'horrors of Civil War' with 'Mrs. W' who 'silently wept', as does 'poor Mrs. Allen Green' who is encountered with 'blanched face & streaming eyes', and when our retrospective diarist recalls, 'I crept to my room, where I sat down to a good cry', we might infer that just such a reconstruction has taken place. For, clearly the subject of the 'blanched face & streaming eyes' remains ambiguous in the original, and therefore readily available (to the desiring imagination) to reinterpretation. Equally, in the reconstructed version, the 'I' who 'crept silently to my room' also remains indeterminate: it implies aloneness, by virtue of its singular form, and it implies the absence of Mrs W. Or perhaps 'invisibility' comes closer to it. Thus, re-experiencing – through the agency of self-writing – the many, many hours of solitary misery, together with the intention to displace and pluralize them from the external 'other', the newly autonomous self reconstructs object as subject and becomes the writer's *objective*.

All in all, whether we read reconstruction of this kind as a 'Jungian' objectification of the contents of the unconscious (past repressed misery now expressed), or whether we take it to be simply 'artistic licence' (although, as with 'Freudian slips', there is little that is psychologically simple about this manifestation), the narrative result compounds the notion of subjectivity bodying forth 'objectivity'. The 'I' set in conjunction to the 'other', in the original, transforms into the *sole subject of the action* in the later version while, at the same time, taking on the qualities of the self-expressive 'other' (weeping woman) and, moreover, taking them on with explicit intention to act them out: 'I sat down to a good cry.'

There are indications, in the diary, of Chesnut's literary sensitivity to this manner of bodying forth an objective autobiographical persona – not least in her observation that 'I think I.W. Hayne writes better when he signs himself Professor Holmes than he does over his own signature. His letter which Pickens published was very flat' (*MCCW*, p. 454).[8] Nevertheless, there is no sense, in general, in which Chesnut's autobiographical mode conforms to the 'tradition' that 'autobiography is both introspective and centrally concerned with the problematics of time and memory'; or that it constructs a 'model or exemplary life,' or 'the evocation of a life as a totality'; nor is it founded on the precept that 'the intentions and character of the person, conceptualised in a more psychological register, are made the condition of autobiographical truth'.[9] On the other hand, *Mary Chesnut's Civil War* assuredly mediates the opposition between the public world and the private self, between subjectivity and objectivity, between referential and fictional discourses, and assuredly elects to sustain the fragmented, unstable indeterminacy of each and every one of those oppositions. The diary form in itself exploits these deconstructive elements by virtue of its periodic structure, its incremental repetitions, and its open destiny – the continuous present juxtaposed with the passage of 'real time'.

The hybridity of the genre remains one of its greatest virtues. Another is that literary boundaries remain uncharted and none so much as in the conventions governing the interplay of illusion and reality. Chesnut takes full advantage of the exchange. At the height of the war, in August 1861, when (as she perceives it) rumours play as large a part in decision-making as conflicting military orders play in mortalities caused by 'friendly' fire, she invents the following dialogue: '"Why do you write in your diary at all, if, as you say, you have to contradict every day what you wrote yesterday?" "Because I tell the tale as it is told to me. I write current rumor. I do not vouch for anything"' (*MCCW*, p. 163). This appears to be an imaginary dialogue between an advocate of standard literary conventions questioning the exigencies of contradictory discourses, and an opponent claiming a literary representation of the real – the everyday irrational, incoherent, contradictory, indeterminate 'real'. For to be sure, even as she writes, the London *Post* bears the news that 'The Southern States of America have achieved their independence' (*MCCW*, p. 165), when the somewhat compromised reality is that Confederate victories are still resounding and have not yet met their 'Gettysburg'. And to be sure, even as she notes that Mr Chesnut has 'gone off to see Jeff Davis: he means to take a colonelcy of cavalry if they will give it to him' (*MCCW*, p. 164), the truth of the matter is that Mr Chesnut remains notoriously incapable of making the decision to accept military command and spends the war years instead as (complaining) presidential aide – much to his wife's frustration: 'Oh, if I could put some of my reckless spirit into these discreet, cautious, lazy men', she cries to her quietly sympathetic journal (*PMC*, p. 63).

In an earlier June entry she had once again contemplated the contradictoriness of historical events in the making: 'The war topic is not so much avoided as that everybody has some personal dignity to take care of – and everybody else is indifferent to it ... In this wild confusion everything likely and unlikely is told you – and then everything is as flatly contradicted' (*MCCW*, p. 82). And a year later, in June 1862: 'Now, remember, I write down all that I hear, and the next day, if I hear that it is not so, then I write down the contradiction, too' (*MCCW*, p. 360).

The original journal stresses no such plotted intentions. There are no such overt assertions of preserving the artless, contradictory spontaneity of the diary form. On the contrary, the corresponding entry for August 1861, with its references to news reports and Mr Chesnut's colonelcy, quite simply allows the writing itself to be the plot. Stylistically and artlessly, the uncertainty and incoherency of the self in relation to the world flows through the precariousness of the interrupted syntax, the collapse of linear discourses, and the apt recrudescence of the staggered composition so characteristic of the diary genre:

> August 26, 1861. Richmond. Arlington House. Yesterday went to tea with JC – felt ill – feverish, the old ruinous fever symptoms.

After tea Mr Clayton & Mr Barnwell & a young Stuart from Beaufort. The latter brought the prisoners from the *Thompson*, a merchant vessel.[10] One, a rapid *concessionist*, says he has lost all his property & will prosecute us for life. Yet they turned him loose ... The handsome Anderson talked with us two hours after dinner. Says his wife & child were at Fort Hamilton when Doubleday got there after Fort Sumter.[11] The child not more than 10 months old had been taught to hurra for Davis & Beauregard – which the poor baby called Dadis & Bogar – & Doubleday said such a child must be the product of rebels. Stormed at the little thing & said her father should be arrested ... All the papers favourable to us have been stopped at the north – *Journal of Commerce, Day Book* news[12] – Baltimore also – & a quantity of new arrests made. *Terror* is there no doubt.

That report of Clayton is not true as to our expenses – for the money issued was to pay the troops, therefore cannot be *weekly*.

I saw an immense Brigade go by today. Gonzales made himself very agreeable last night. Mrs. Carter & Miss Barron joined us. Mr. Chesnut went to see Jeff Davis about the colonelcy of *cavalry* – but he was ill in bed. I'm afraid Mr. C. will decide too late as usual. From what I see in the *Journal*, Wm. Shannon, Edward Boykin mean to have superb company. Wilmot D. had been to inspect a cooking stove cut out of earth in the side of a hill– which has succeeded wonderfully. If Mr. C. takes a Colonelcy I will go as *cook* – the men fare so badly.[13]

(*PMC*, p. 140)

Likewise, in corresponding June entries in the original journal, the style and content themselves bespeak the contradictoriness, unsettlement and incoherencies of the world in view:

Richmond. Monday the 24th I left Camden *hot* & dusty, under Mr. Meynardie's care – with Mary Boykin & two Yankee school mistresses. Mr. Meynardie I found very attentive – & a good kind man, slightly *show off* – evidently pleased at the grandees I introduced him to. At Kingsville Tom Waties took charge & at Florence I met Keitt & his family. Mrs. Keitt spanked her *baby well* several times – evidently a bad tempered woman. Keitt[14] had long talks with me, evidently thinks Jeff Davis a failure. Thinks they are playing *Cabinet* to a ridiculous degree. Soldiers all the time. Wrote a note on the cars to Major Jones & himself not to *talk* against the administration for there were Yankees on board ... We dined with the President ... Mr. Chesnut sent by Beauregard for more ammunition & Davis says they have enough there ... The President ridiculed Beauregard's staff – & both Mr. C. & I answered. The president said who ever they did not know how to fit out, they sent to Beauregard's staff. Mr. C. told him they had not enough red tape in his shop to measure Beauregard's staff ... Johnston has not attacked Cadwalader & McClellan[15] because he has not ammunition *enough*! What a *War* department.

(*PMC*, pp. 85–6)

So Johnston's military outfit is ill-equipped – immobilized by lack of ammunition – as, no doubt, Beauregard's will also shortly be if the president refuses further supplies and continues to sabotage his own war effort by furnishing his most prominent general with a motley staff. The anomalies abound. Not least that Mr Chesnut has, himself, accepted a position in Beauregard's ill-equipped staff. So why is he not urging the president for ammunition supplies (as instructed), and why is he playing along with the ridicule, and why is he humouring Davis when he is fully aware that the antagonistic relationship between the president and his most brilliantly successful military commander, Beauregard, is worsening daily and needs urgently to be mediated?

The diarist herself appears to mediate these troubled relations in high places, at this point, in so far as she remains neutral, maintaining the impartiality and inconclusiveness of the account and making every attempt to smooth out the anomalies – anomalies which may well reflect very poorly indeed upon her husband.

Ferocious loyalty flows instinctively from her more composed self, although when discomposed and spontaneously confiding her more intense feelings to her journal, she is divided and conflicted. Notice the entry for 28 June, the day following the presidential dinner:

> The president & I had a long talk – he is despondent, does not see the end of this thing! Gives the north credit for *courage* – says they will fight like devils. Still harping on the *staff* business – says Mr. C. ought to have gotten up a regiment. (So he ought!).
>
> (*PMC*, p. 86)

The parenthetical arrangement here suggests that this (less than loyal) accusation was not communicated to President Jefferson Davis but only to her private journal, and that it is the public self, rather than the private, which usually activates the loyalty. But precisely where the boundaries lie, with regard to the crossover from the one to the other, within the realm of the diary narrative, is not always so syntactically determinable. Clearly, at times, Chesnut takes on a narratorial voice that divulges its self-awareness of an audience. We could call this voice 'public', or at any rate, geared to a listener, as in the segment, 'Now, remember, I write down all that I hear'. Generally speaking, however, the distinction between private and public voices (and which one of them more often articulates the ferocious loyalty) cannot be discerned with any certainty. As with the intersection of objective and subjective selves, so too the public and private voices remain coextensive – the one taking existence from the other.

Take, for example, the November entry below. Five months have passed since the 'despondent' president conversation, and the relationship between Davis and Beauregard (it is hard, now, not to think of them as 'Dadis-and-Bogar') has reached crisis point. For very many weeks now, since July, they have been bitterly at loggerheads over Beauregard's plan of attack on Washington, which Mr Chesnut had presented orally and, it seems, ineffectually, to the president from Beauregard's notes.

> November 2, 1861. Took out a letter [to Camden] from Jeff Davis to JC – asking the particulars of the interview between them on the 13th July! Beauregard it seems has said in his report of the battle that he had offered Jeff Davis a plan of campaign which he would not accept – so JC must remember & write that memorable interview – which I could give pretty well from my journal. He was aide de camp who carried the plan – & John Preston, Gen. Cooper & Gen. Lee were present.
>
> (*PMC*, p. 192)

Needless to say she does give it 'pretty well'. Loyal, in her 'public' role, as ever. The following day she writes up JC's report to Davis – observing privately, in her diary, that 'Lee & Jeff Davis did not agree to [Beauregard's] plan, saying "it was too soon & the enemy too near his cover"' (*PMC*, p. 192). And while adding that she fears this mishap in communications – in Mr Chesnut's oral rendering of General Beauregard's plan – may have ruined them politically, and that 'I dare not look plantation & *Camden* life in the face', she levels no accusations whatsoever at JC himself for once again failing to give Beauregard's proposals due weight.

In this sense, incompletion forms an intrinsic part not only of strategies designed to objectify both text and self, to 'complete' a detached self and to 'finish' a textual emphasis upon external or observable phenomena, but also forms an intrinsic part of the writer's consciousness. The contradictoriness of current rumour, of military information, of human behaviour itself (JC's in particular: he badly wanted a regiment, a military status, but continually defeated his own ends), shape in the writer's consciousness a very profound sense of phenomenal incompletion. 'Incompletion' in the sense that there are half-truths only, or that explanation and rationalization may render these half-truths coherent and whole at the expense of factual or psychological accuracy (therefore the chronicler resists this act of 'completion'), that even personhood itself exists not as an entity but as a process, and therefore, in the interests of mimesis, should neither be explained nor 'finished' in any discursive way – outside the realms of fiction. Accordingly, but not without self-awareness, Chesnut collapses the *completion* of textual order in the very moment of writing the *collapse* of world order, beyond the text. Or, put another way, JC's 'unfinished business' remains 'unfinished business' for the diarist who casts no judgement at all upon his contradictory impulses (to act as aide, yet not to aid) – his failure to complete the task assigned to him.

There are, however, enough crises of passion in Chesnut's consciousness to disable even the most suave of journal discourses. In this respect, there is nothing in the least 'incomplete' and certainly nothing 'complete' about her emotional make-up. The flux is exemplary. Take the following discourse on slavery:

> March 18, 1861: I wonder if it be a sin to think slavery a curse to any land ... God forgive us, but ours is a *monstrous* system and wrong and iniquity. Perhaps the rest of the world is as bad – this *only* I see. Like the patriarchs of old our men live all in one house with their wives and their concubines, and the mulattoes one sees in every family exactly resemble the white children – and every lady tells you who is the father of all the mulatto children in everybody's household, but those in her own she seems to think drop from the clouds ... my disgust sometimes is boiling over ... And all the time they seem to think themselves patterns – models of husbands and fathers.
>
> (MCCW, pp. 30–1)

Or on belief systems:

> June 14–15, 1861. I have been reading the account of Magruder's victory at Bethel's Church. One poor young man found dead with a shot through his heart had a Bible in his pocket in which was written: 'Given to the defender of his country by the Bible Society'. How *dare* men mix up the Bible so with their own *bad* passions.
>
> (PMC, p. 82)

And on the murder of 'dear old cousin Betsey':

> She was smothered – arms & legs bruised & face scratched. William, a man of hers, & several others suspected of her own negroes, people she has pampered & spoiled & done every thing for ... Came here, found Mr. Borman and the children as I left them – & was *ill* ... I had to rush in & was really ill.
>
> (PMC, p. 162)

And although (on a completely different issue) she may not be made physically ill by Milton's *Paradise Lost*, she is made radically oppositional: 'May 17, 1862. See the speech of Adam to Eve in a new light. Women will not stay at home – will go out and be seen, even if it be by the Devil himself' (MCCW, p. 341).[16]

And as the war escalates, and 'The very air darken[s] with generals' (MCCW, p. 552) so the agitated heart of the writer itself sounds notes of warning. It is June 1862. Federal troops have landed on James Island in preparation for an attack on Charleston – 'to erase Charleston from the face of the earth'. Tension mounts daily, casualty figures rise:

Bratton, who married Miss Means, taken prisoner. Beverly Means killed, his mother-in-law a few days ago found *stone dead* in her bed ... A telegram comes to you. And you leave it on your lap. You are pale with fright. You handle it, or dread to touch it, as you would a rattlesnake – worse – worse. A snake would only strike you. How many, many, this scrap of paper may tell you, have gone to their death ... And I am so ill. Mr. Ben Taylor said to Dr. Trezevant: 'Surely she is too ill to be going about. She ought to be in bed. She is very feeble – very nervous, as you say – but, she is living on nervous excitement. If you shut her up she will die at once.' A prostration of the heart, I have. Sometimes it beats so feebly I am sure it has stopped altogether. Then they say I have fainted, but I never lose consciousness.

(MCCW, pp. 370–4)

'Oh God! My poor country', Mary Chesnut cries, again and again, to her waiting war-torn diary – a diary she rips apart and badly mutilates (for security reasons) during a raid upon Richmond in 1863, when the world outside is also being 'kicked to pieces' (*MCCW*, p. 425).

Throughout the 1860s and throughout almost 50 copybooks Chesnut maintained a journal historically coextensive with a world in constant flux, externally and internally. And throughout the years of reconstruction after the war she too settled down to the task of returning every day to a new beginning. Remaking the textual world of what was to become *Mary Chesnut's Civil War*, she created a masterpiece 'more genuinely literary than most Civil War fiction'.[17] She certainly intended the literariness – avid reader, avid writer that she was. Clearly ill-content with the entry-fragments of literary allusion she barely had time to incorporate into her original journal narrative – texts which reflected so much of what she recognized in herself, her philosophical inclinations, her humanitarian interests, her sheer love of writing – she reconstructed the later world of her diary to take account of the many, many internal dialogues she held with those she chose – no needed – to keep company with – from John Julian Chisolm's *Manual of Military Surgery*, Archibald Alison's *Atlas to Alison's History of Europe ... With Vocabulary of Military and Marine Terms*, and Edward Sheperd Creasy's *The Fifteen Decisive Battles of the World*, to George Sand, Balzac, Hugo, Mirabeau, Vigny and Beaumarchais (in French), to Goethe (in German), Milton (in Latin), to practically all the works of Shakespeare and practically all the major Victorian poets and novelists, right down to Thomas Browne's *Sepuchral Urns Lately Found in Norfolk* of 1658. And many, many more.

If, in seconding the self, in the first instance, she adopted the role, form and persona of Mrs Senator Chesnut, it was in the process of narrative reconstruction of her journal that she 'real-ized' a more authentic second self: the literary self, the experimental writer whose subjective consciousness spins forth a web of objectivity – transcending the conventional controls of autobiographical narrative.

Twenty-sixth of June 1865 is the last journal entry on record – self-reflexive in the moment of writing yet prophetically charting what was to become Mary Boykin Chesnut's open destiny: 'Sir Walter Scott says, "Never let me hear that brave blood has been shed in vain. It sends a roaring voice down through all time"' (*PMC*, p. 262).

Notes

1. a) All references to Mary Chesnut's (MC) diary are taken from *Mary Chesnut's Civil War*, ed. C. Vann Woodward (New Haven and London: Yale University Press, 1981) (hereafter, *MCCW*). *MCCW* is based upon the extensive journals kept, irregularly, by Mary Boykin Chesnut during the years of the Confederacy from February 1861 to July 1865. Some of her original journal entries have been lost; some were deliberately destroyed by her when the Confederacy fell. It is not known how much of the original material she had to hand when revising her journals for book publication in the 1880s. She died before completion of this project. It was first published, posthumously, under the title of *A Diary from Dixie, as Written by Mary Boykin Chesnut, Wife of James Chesnut, Jr., United States Senator from South Carolina, 1859–1861, and Afterward Aide to Jefferson Davis and a Brigadier General in the Confederate Army*, ed. Isabella D. Martin and Myrta Lockett Avary (New York, 1905). The marginality this androcentric title enforces upon its author would have drawn contempt from MC who was nothing if not a fierce critic of patriarchy. b) All references to Mary Chesnut's original journal are taken from *The Private Mary Chesnut: The Unpublished Civil War Diaries*, ed. C. Vann Woodward and Elisabeth Muhlenfeld (New York and Oxford: Oxford University Press, 1984) (hereafter, *PMC*).
2. A secessionist serving on the South Carolina (SC) state legislature and a wealthy plantation owner holding 648 slaves, John Laurence Manning took office as Governor of SC from 1852 to 1854.
3. Robert S. Chew, from the State Department, and Theodore Talbot, army officer, had conveyed to Governor Francis Wilkinson Pickens (former congressman; elected governor of SC three days before secession) that Lincoln refused to yield Fort Sumter to the Confederates. Brigadier-General Pierre Gustave Toutant Beauregard of La., ex-US Army, commanded Confederate forces at Charleston, later at Bull Run and Shiloh.
4. Robert Newman Gourdin, lawyer, SC secession convention delegate, formed part of MC's large and privileged circle of friends.
5. MC customarily refers to her husband as Mr C.
6. The excitable Charlotte Maria Wigfall (CMW), wife of Louis Trezevant

Wigfall, US senator 1859–61, secessionist agitator and notorious drunk, found a faithful friend in MC despite her caustic criticisms of the Confederacy to which MC remained stoutly loyal, albeit abolitionist at heart, and despite CMW's conflicts with Varina Anne Davis, wife of President Jefferson Davis whose intimacy MC valued highly and whose difficulties with CMW she mediated patiently and kindly.

7. Mrs Green, nicknamed 'Dame Placid' (by Surgeon-General, Dr Robert W. Gibbes), wife of Allen Jones Green, Jr, physician, planter, state legislator and army captain, drew MC's admiration for remaining constantly calm and gentle with her four small boys despite the terrors and devastation inflicted upon her during the war.
8. Isaac William Hayne was Attorney-General of South Carolina.
9. See Laura Marcus, *Auto/biographical Discourses: Theory, Criticism, Practice* (Manchester and New York: Manchester University Press, 1994), pp. 2–10. Marcus challenges these 'traditions', noting that genres have contestable boundaries, that autobiography also functions as a resource and a site of struggle.
10. This ship had been captured by Confederate forces on 9 July.
11. 'Handsome Anderson' was aide-de-camp to General William Walker; Abner Doubleday (of baseball fame) was a US Army captain stationed at Charleston.
12. These New York papers were suppressed by the US government as being supportive of the Southern cause.
13. Chesnut's war work, aside from that of chronicling events, political hostessing, advising, and writing her husband's letters and reports, also included hospital visiting and handstitching shirts for soldiers.
14. Lawrence Massillon Keitt, ex-US congressman, displayed little discretion or diplomacy in voicing his opinions (sometimes abusive) in public.
15. C. Vann Woodward and Elisabeth Muhlenfeld note that 'Brig. Gen. Joseph Eggleston Johnston of Va. was commander of the Army of the Shenandoah. Maj. Gen. George Brinton McClellan commanded the Union forces which had moved into western Va. from Ohio. George Cadwalader, Maj. Gen. of Penn. Volunteers, was second in command of the Union troops in the lower Shenandoah Valley' (*PMC*, p. 86).
16. C. Vann Woodward notes that MC was probably referring to *Paradise Lost*, Book IX, 'in which Adam blames their troubles on Eve's willfulness and her "strange / Desire of wand'ring ..."' (*MCCW*, p. 341).
17. See Daniel Aaron, *The Unwritten War: American Writers and the Civil War* (New York: Knopf, 1973), pp. 227–9.

CHAPTER THIRTEEN

Autobiography as Prophecy: Walt Whitman's 'Specimen Days'

Nicholas Everett

From the very beginning of his literary career, Walt Whitman constantly strove to present as a unified and coherent structure all the writings he wished to preserve. At first the work consisted (except for prefaces and afterwords) exclusively of poetry and could be contained within a single volume, *Leaves of Grass*, which was revised, rearranged and expanded four times in the two decades following its original appearance in 1855, each edition absorbing and superseding the last. By 1876, however, Whitman had published two books of prose, *Democratic Vistas* (1871), an essay on the future of American democracy, and *Memoranda During the War* (1875), and his conception of the profile of his entire *oeuvre* consequently altered. *Two Rivulets*, the volume he regarded as a necessary complement to what he called the author's edition of *Leaves*, reprinted these books alongside poems, such as 'Passage to India', that had not yet been installed in the main body of his poetry. The complete works took their final and definitive shape just six years later, in 1882, when Whitman published his collected prose in a volume of its own, *Specimen Days & Collect*, together with a reissue of the sixth edition of *Leaves*. 'It is understood', runs one of the sentences he wrote for the use of a potential reviewer, 'that Whitman himself considers "Specimen Days" the exponent and finish of his poetic work "Leaves of Grass", that each of the two volumes is indispensable in his view to the other, and that both together finally begin and illustrate his literary schemes in the New World.'[1] Despite later additions, the forms of both would also remain substantially unchanged.[2]

Specimen Days & Collect, then, was a work of organization rather than of fresh composition. Whitman divided it into two discrete parts, reserving the first, 'Specimen Days', for writings that related to, or stemmed from, some particular moment in his life. These include a sketch of his ancestry and early years originally written to assist Richard Maurice Bucke with his authorized biography, *Walt Whitman* (1883); notes on the Civil War, mainly adapted from *Memoranda During the War* (1875); observations of nature written at Timber Creek, New Jersey, near the home of some friends where he stayed periodically from

1875; records of his visits to the Midwest, Canada and upstate New York in the late 1870s and early 1880s; and memories of contemporary writers such as William Cullen Bryant and, of course, Emerson. Many of the pieces are devoted to essentially public and impersonal themes but qualify for inclusion because of their explicit, even if sometimes rather tenuous, origins in Whitman's experience. The script of his lecture on Thomas Paine, for instance, which exhorts America to value 'the legacy of her good and faithful men' ('Specimen Days', p. 142), has as personal source his memory of becoming acquainted with one Colonel Fellows, Paine's 'most intimate chum' (p. 140); and the sections on Carlyle and Longfellow, though assessments of their literary achievements, were prompted by news of their respective deaths. Whitman then arranged these diverse materials chronologically according to the time of the experience described or, where more appropriate, of their composition or delivery (as with the lecture on Paine which belongs, in the order of his life, with the account of his early manhood, but fitted more easily among the later reflections).

'Collect', meanwhile, as the name suggests (and it had provisionally just been called 'Thoughts'),[3] served as an extended appendix for everything that did not fit into the scheme of 'Specimen Days', 'the odds and ends', as Whitman said, 'of whatever pieces I can now lay hands on' ('Specimen Days', p. 3): *Democratic Vistas*, the prefaces to the various editions of *Leaves of Grass*, an essay on 'Poetry To-Day in America' and a selection, under the title 'Notes Left Over', of miscellaneous shorter pieces on political, cultural and literary topics.

Whitman could thus with some justification call 'Specimen Days' 'an autobiography after its sort' (*Correspondence*, p. 308). But the first question the whole volume prompts, as the official canon of his prose writings, concerns the principle of selection behind it. It contains almost everything he wrote after 1862 but only the preface to the 1855 edition of *Leaves of Grass* written before. Whitman had been a prolific journalist (and diarist) before the Civil War and indeed before 1855. So why was none of the earlier writing included?[4] As editor of *Prose Works 1892*, Floyd Stovall explains:

> Before the period of the Civil War his published prose was written hurriedly, and though clear and often forceful, had the qualities rather of journalism than of literature. After the preface to the 1855 *Leaves of Grass*, *Democratic Vistas* was the first prose publication he had composed with great care. Most of his literary prose was written after his paralysis, between 1875 and 1888, when his poetic genius had spent itself and he had leisure for meditation and deliberate composition.
>
> (vol. I, p. vii)

Though the later prose is definitely of more general and enduring interest (and less narrowly topical) than the earlier, Stovall's explanation should be qualified. His first sentence here applies equally to most of the prose in *Specimen Days & Collect*, which has the generic qualities of journalism (or of the diary) rather than of 'literature'. Much of the volume had already appeared in newspapers or magazines and had been only slightly revised since its first publication. Moreover, while *Democratic Vistas* may have been composed with great care, many other pieces were not and were not meant to seem careful or polished but casual and spontaneous.

I would suggest that Whitman's most important reason for excluding the earlier articles and notes was that, unlike the later prose, they did not conform to the prophetic literary purpose he had discovered and announced back in 1855: to define and celebrate the nature and future of American society (and, by – Whitman's own – extension, all humanity). Radically egalitarian, libertarian and individualistic, democratic America would constitute the fulfilment and culmination of civilization. Its 'genius' would be represented 'not best or most in its executives or legislatures, nor in its ambassadors or authors or colleges or churches or parlors, nor even in its newspapers or inventors ... but always most in the common people' on whose 'measureless' pride in themselves and sympathy for others its political institutions and cultural productions would be founded.[5] Many of its specific features were yet to be elaborated (in *Democratic Vistas* and elsewhere) but its roots in the Jacksonian and predominantly rural America of Whitman's youth are already visible.[6] He imagines a society in which wealth and land are distributed fairly evenly, a country of small farms and city homesteads in which the 'poorest free mechanic or farmer with his hat unmoved from his head' is better respected than a 'bound booby and rogue in office at a high salary' (*Leaves* 1855, p. 16).

For the effective communication of this national vision, Whitman developed an exemplary poetic persona, 'Walt Whitman, an American, ... no stander above men and women or apart from them ... no more modest than immodest' (p. 48, ll. 499, 501), thereby also discovering the foundation of his poetic method. In the very first words of this first edition of *Leaves of Grass* the poet speaks on behalf of his country: 'America does not repel the past or what it has produced under its forms ...' (p. 5). And in the first poem, then untitled, finally called 'Song of Myself' (and in 1856 called 'Poem of Walt Whitman, An American'), he completes his identification with the nation, claiming for his constituency Americans of 'every hue and trade and rank, of every caste and religion' (p. 40, l. 343). Throughout the next two editions (1856 and 1860) defining himself continued to mean defining the nation.

Then, in the Civil War, Whitman found a personal role in which he was able in a sense to embody this persona and so begin the process Mutlu Konuk Blasing has described as 'pattern[ing] his life after the self-image that had been created in 1855'.[7] Drawn to Washington towards the end of 1862 in search of his wounded brother George, he remained there until the end of the war and beyond, visiting the hospitals daily to assist and console the many wounded and dying soldiers. The men were from all over America, had interrupted all sorts of jobs and careers (in this first modern war fought by conscripted civilians) to risk their lives for the Union or the Confederacy, and put Whitman in touch with the scope and character of the country as he had never been before. Visiting them, he became a version of the representative persona he had invented – but with one significant difference. In the Civil War the old young man of the early poems (he was already 37 when they first appeared) became, almost overnight, a young old man, *The Good Gray Poet*, as William O'Connor's book dubbed him (in 1866) when he was still only 46. He could not pretend to be the brother and comrade-in-arms of the wounded young men, so he adopted a paternal role more in keeping with his position. No longer 'one of the roughs', as he was in 'Song of Myself' (*Leaves* 1855, p. 48), he now stood for all of them; no longer the typical American, he now represented America itself, and especially the future for which the soldiers were sacrificing their lives.

For Richard Chase (and several later critics), Whitman's assumption in life of his earlier poetic persona signals the end of his poetic originality; once creatively imagined and invented, Chase argues, the union of self and nation depends for its later achievement on 'extra-poetic means' which result in a merely pedestrian record of its realization in his actual life.[8] Whether or not this is true of the poetry, the Civil War certainly marked the beginning of Whitman's career as a writer of serious prose, as he saw it, as well as providing a vital constituent of the self he wanted to project. From the early 1860s all his writings, whatever their ostensible topics, were devoted to his prophetic purpose; and in his efforts to express it he could, where possible, invoke two significant aspects of his own identity, the poet of *Leaves* and veteran of the war, as heralds and representatives of the glorious democratic future of the United States.

In this limited way, his prose (no less than his poetry) became more predominantly autobiographical which, along with its other peculiarities, appears to have somewhat determined his choice of structure for *Specimen Days & Collect*. To have printed the pieces conventionally in the order in which they had been written or first published would have disrupted the thematic clusters (Civil War memoranda, for example, and the prefaces to *Leaves of Grass*) into which his writings naturally fell. On the other hand, any attempt at a strictly thematic scheme (sections on his own work, on literature in general, on nature, on American society, and so on) would have foundered on a number of problem cases, pieces that would fit into none, or several, of the available categories. A scheme such as this would in any case have established undesirably clear thematic limits to his achievement in prose. Avoiding all these pitfalls, autobiography (plus leftovers) offered the most convenient and expeditious way of arranging such disparate material, much of which was informal and diaristic if not directly autobiographical.

Whitman also had more profound aesthetic and ideological reasons for structuring the volume as he did. Since 1855 he had often asserted that a distinctively American literature should, and would, be factual, personal and artless rather than fictional and decorative. 'The great poets', he declared in the 1855 preface to *Leaves of Grass*, 'are ... to be known by the absence in them of tricks and by the justification of perfect personal candor' (*Leaves* 1855, p. 18); and *Democratic Vistas* argued that the literature of what it called 'Personalism', 'the perfect uncontamination and solitariness of individuality', would provide both the foundation and crowning achievement of American democratic culture ('Collect', p. 398). After the Civil War he became even more intent on fulfilling these injunctions himself, taking pains, when revising earlier poems, to write his life into his work and, in the last decade of his life, insisting that all his work had been an attempt 'to articulate and faithfully express ... [his] physical, emotional, moral, intellectual, and aesthetic Personality' ('Collect', p. 714), 'to put *a Person* ... freely, fully and truly on record' (p. 731). Such assertions are reflected in the organization of 'Specimen Days'. Simply by affixing dates to its sections, ordering them chronologically and (albeit very briefly) accounting for the periods not covered by them, Whitman transformed a largely impersonal collection into a personal expression of himself and product of his life. And when it appeared in London in 1887, as *Specimen Days in America*, he emphasized its autobiographical nature to attract British readers:

> You have had, and have, plenty of public events and facts and general statistics of America; – in the following book is a common individual *private life*, its birth and growth, struggles for a living, its goings and comings and observations (or representative portions of them) amid the United States of America the last thirty or forty years.
>
> ('Collect', p. 598)

He promises a *'private life'* and a 'common', representative American one. Paradoxically, if Whitman's prophetic ambitions determined his choice of genre, they also heavily restricted his movements within it. In a brilliant essay on 'Autobiography in the American Renaissance', Lawrence Buell exposes the 'widely-shared edginess about self-disclosure' in mid-nineteenth-century American autobiographical writings, showing how far they usually are from 'the kind of developed autobiography that one most immediately associates with the term since Rousseau: the detailed, complex secular narrative of the author's unfolding mind and fortunes during a substantial portion if not the entirety of his or her life span'.[9] In 'Specimen Days' he finds

> the period's most conspicuous case of the autobiographer's ambivalence toward his or her genre. Whitman nominally adopts the genre but treats it so cavalierly that his subject becomes not so much the shape of his life as the impossibility of meaningfully shaping it in the terms normally available to the autobiographer.
> ('Specimen Days', p. 62)

A collection of diverse articles and notebook jottings, arranged and advertised as an autobiography yet revealing little (if anything) about the author's personal relationships (even with members of his family) or creative development, 'Specimen Days' is certainly as strikingly ambivalent about its genre as Thoreau's *Walden* (1854) or any of Frederick Douglass's three autobiographical narratives (Buell's main examples).[10] Yet Whitman's refusal to shape his life according to autobiographical convention is also peculiarly his own. Buell points out that in general, nineteenth-century American autobiography is pulled in different directions by conflicting cultural and literary demands. It simultaneously strives to portray the author's life as individual, even unique, and typical or representative. Whitman's life, as his autobiography presents it, isn't typical; but its singularity is representative, as Betsy Erkkila says, of 'national progress'.[11] 'Specimen Days' is not so much about an individual's past as about a nation's future. Or rather it is about an individual's past but presents it only in guises that expound and support his vision of the nation's future. As I hope to show in the following (necessarily selective) examination of its contents, Whitman's prophetic purpose informs its substance and structure alike, dictating which aspects of the man and his life should be highlighted and which falsified, which revealed and which concealed.

The opening account of his personal background and early years is the closest the book comes to conventional autobiography. It alone is written in the past tense and offers a more or less continuous and uninterrupted treatment of his life itself. Like the rest of the book, however, it consists of short sections (often of only one or two paragraphs) which emphasize individual themes and activities ('My Passion for Ferries', 'Plays and Operas Too') at the expense of narrative flow.

Whitman's juggling of titles also suggests that his main priority was simply (and briefly) to cover certain important aspects of his life rather than to tell its story. (The section entitled 'Broadway Omnibusses' in the manuscript presumably became 'Omnibus Jaunts and Drivers', for example, because Broadway had already been featured in the previous section's title, 'Broadway Sights', while his beloved drivers had not yet been featured at all.)[12] Of surprising importance for this most forward-looking and optative of writers are his (Dutch maternal and English paternal) ancestries. In a reversal of the usual dealings between author and biographer, Whitman quotes a couple of long paragraphs from John Burroughs's *Notes on Walt Whitman as Poet and Person* (1867, revised edition 1871), one describing life at the Whitmans' Long Island farmhouse at the turn of the nineteenth century, the other giving thumbnail sketches of various ancestors. The appeal of representing his family by its most recently prosperous times and exemplary members should not be underestimated, perhaps; but the descriptions also serve, in numerous details of person and place, to evoke the essential qualities – including wholesomeness, frugality, resilience and manliness – of Whitman's ideal society much more than to explain the genesis of his personal and creative identity.

> In the house, and in food and furniture, all was rude, but substantial. No carpets or stoves were known, and no coffee, and tea or sugar only for the women. Rousing wood fires gave both warmth and light on winter nights. Pork, poultry, beef, and all the ordinary vegetables and grains were plentiful ... The clothes were mainly homespun. Journeys were made by both men and women on horseback. Both sexes labor'd with their own hands – the men on the farm – the women in the house and around it ...
> The ancestors of Walt Whitman, on both maternal and paternal sides ... were often of mark'd individuality ... His great-grandmother ... for instance, was a large swarthy woman, who lived to a very old age. She smoked tobacco, rode on horseback like a man, managed the most vicious horse, and, becoming a widow in later life, went forth every day over her farm-lands, frequently in the saddle ... The two immediate grandmothers were in the best sense, superior women. The maternal one ... was a Friend, or Quakeress, of sweet, sensible character ... and deeply intuitive and spiritual. The other ... was an equally noble, perhaps stronger character, lived to be very old, had quite a family of sons, was a natural lady, was in early life a school-mistress, and had great solidity of mind. W.W. himself makes much of the women of his ancestry.
> ('Specimen Days', pp. 9–10)

The environments in which Whitman actually grew up played a greater part, no doubt, in shaping his character and along with it his vision of America, but this vision in its turn helped shape his memories of them in 'Specimen Days', where they are selectively and ideally rendered. Fostered alike by country and by town, the young Whitman receives a balanced diet of the influences vital to his later version of healthy democratic life, nature on Long Island ('the horizon boundless, the air too strong for invalids') and ordinary working people in 'teeming Brooklyn and New York' (pp. 12, 23), especially ferry pilots and omnibus drivers to whom he devotes individual sections. The sketch of his ancestry and early years concludes with a summary of the 'leading sources and formative stamps' to his character, the third and last being, incredibly, his 'experiences ... in the secession outbreak' (pp. 22–3). This section is then immediately followed by the 'Opening of the Secession War', as if everything before 1861 had been merely preparatory, his adult life itself on hold until his forty-second year when this national crisis finally let it begin.

Throughout 'Specimen Days' Whitman focuses on aspects of American experience that must (or, very occasionally, must not) be valued or remembered if the nation is to make truly democratic progress. By far the most important of these, the Civil War accounts for almost a third of the book; and its treatment here, as much as in the poetry of *Drum Taps* (1865), fully supports M. Wynn Thomas's observation that its 'primary importance ... lay for Whitman in its significance for the American future'.[13] The war was first of all a successful struggle to secure national unity. In Whitman's account it becomes much more, a reassertion of American democracy and even the ultimate demonstration and justification of democracy itself:

> Down in the abysms of New World humanity there had form'd and harden'd a primal hard-pan of national Union will, determin'd and in the majority, refusing to be tamper'd with or argued against, confronting all emergencies, and capable at any time of bursting all surface bonds, and breaking out like an earthquake. It is indeed my privilege to have been part of it. (Two great spectacles, immortal proofs of democracy, unequall'd in all the history of the past, are furnish'd by the secession war – one at the beginning, the other at its close. Those are, the general, voluntary, arm'd upheaval, and the peaceful and harmonious disbanding of the armies in the summer of 1865.)
>
> ('Specimen Days', pp. 24–5)

The principal representatives of 'New World humanity' are of course the soldiers who emerged in their droves to fight for their vision of America. They represent, for Whitman, not only a noble sacrifice for the United States to come but also an exemplary composite model for its citizens. 'Untold in any official reports or books or journals', their character and contribution nevertheless offer the most 'genuine and precious' lesson of the war ('Specimen Days', p. 62):

> To me the points illustrating the latent personal character and eligibilities of these States, in the two or three millions of American young and middle-aged men, North and South, embodied in those armies – and especially the one-third or one-fourth of their number, stricken by wounds or disease at some time in the course of the contest – were of more significance even than the political interests involved.
>
> ('Specimen Days', p. 116)

In section after section, then, Whitman records and praises the definitively American qualities of the soldiers, individually and collectively, their diverse origins and backgrounds, their ordinariness and unpretentiousness and, above all, their bravery.

He was well qualified for the job. He met thousands of soldiers, witnessed hundreds in extreme trauma and pain, listened to the confidential confessions of many and even attended a few as they died. Although 'Specimen Days' gives due prominence to his role and persona as hospital visitor, it does so carefully and selectively. It presents his role as much as possible as simply a reflection of the lives to which it gives him access. Distracting personal and occupational peculiarities are by and large neglected. Thus, most of 'Our Wounded and Sick Soldiers', first published in the New York *Times* in December 1864, appeared in one place or another in 'Specimen Days', but not its three paragraphs on the 'trade' or 'art' of hospital visiting which, though of considerable documentary and biographical interest, obstruct the reader from the soldiers' heroism with merely administrative details. On the rare occasions when a gap does seem to open up between the public and private man, both turn out to perform an exemplary function. Describing one of the services he provides for the wounded, reading and explaining passages from the Bible, Whitman remarks in parenthesis: 'I think I see my friends smiling at this confession, but I was never more in earnest in my life' ('Specimen Days', pp. 73–4). The individual we briefly glimpse here, with his unorthodox religious views, does not undermine the sincerity of his role as public servant – not least because he is equally public and, far from being anti-Christian, believes in a tolerant and pluralistic society in which a soldier's Christian faith has a perfectly wholesome and respectable place.

Thomas's chapter on 'The Pains and Obligations of Memory' amply demonstrates Whitman's extraordinary and, as he grew older, increasing emotional investment in the war and the ways in which he altered the facts of his life and work to maximize its significance.[14] He attributed to his wartime activities the ill-health he suffered a decade later ('Collect', p. 738); he claimed that the 'whole' of *Leaves of Grass* 'revolves around that Four Years' War',[15] despite the fact that the first three editions, including what would remain his most substantial and original poems, had already appeared before the war began; and he announced that the American 'Union is only now and henceforth (i.e. since the Secession war) to enter on its full Democratic career' ('Collect', p. 748). Many and complex psychological factors probably contributed to this obsession, including, as Thomas suggests, his guilt at having survived 'when so many young men had died in their prime'.[16] Yet it surely resulted, at least in part, from the virtual coincidence of the war with Whitman's discovery of his literary identity. No sooner had he announced his prophetic purpose than the war arrived to test and eventually prove it.[17] What is more, it brought with it a personal role in which the essential attribute of his poetic persona – its identity with the character and fate of the nation as a whole – could be realized in his life. As a result, it was only this role – along with his role as a national poet – by which he would thereafter want to be defined and remembered. Whitman invested nothing less than his creative identity in the war; the success of this identity consequently became firmly attached to the war's significance. Indeed, in Whitman's mind, they became mutually dependent. It is not that surprising, therefore, that he should have continued to see the war as the founding moment both of the nation and of his adult life.

A great deal has been made of the startling thematic and temporal shift in 'Specimen Days' from the Civil War memoranda to the observations on nature composed during Whitman's convalescence from the paralytic stroke he suffered in early 1873. The last section in Washington dates from December 1865, the first in Timber Creek from May 1876. This sudden leap from political crisis to individual recovery a decade later is now commonly regarded as a strategic alignment of personal and national regeneration and thus as the key to understanding 'Specimen Days' as a whole. Linck C. Johnson's account is representative:

> This hiatus undercuts the value of the book for those seeking confession, autobiography, or even factual history, but it is appropriate for what Whitman wishes to convey. Just as Henry Adams would, in *The Education of Henry Adams*, skip twenty of his most productive years in order to shape a story of personal and national failure, so in *Specimen Days* does Whitman reverse the technique by ignoring a decade which would only obscure his story of personal and national success ... [By] resuming his narrative in May of 1876, he can symbolically connect his personal sense of rebirth in the spring with the nation's revival, heralded by the American Centennial celebrations.[18]

Erkkila says very much the same, adding only that Whitman's myth of national revival is effectively undermined by what he omits. The neglected decade, she believes, creates 'an unnatural rupture in the story' at odds with his 'message of natural balance', while 'the historical rupture signified by the Civil War continually breaks the thread of his narrative of restoration'.[19]

Admittedly, Whitman himself founded this tradition of interpretation by offering, in the few sentences added to the first section on nature ('New Themes Entered Upon') especially for 'Specimen Days', some casual links between the personal, national and literary implications of what he called the book's 'abrupt change of field and atmosphere': 'dear, soothing, healthy, restoration-hours – after three confining years of paralysis – after the long strain of the war, and its wounds and death ... After what I have put in the preceding fifty or sixty pages ... I restore my book to the bracing and buoyant equilibrium of concrete outdoor Nature' ('Specimen Days', p. 120). The extent to which the ten-year gap indicates a deliberate accommodation of national to personal (and/or personal to national) history is nevertheless highly questionable. As Joel Myerson's comprehensive bibliography of Whitman's work shows, there were not in fact many published writings that could have filled the gap.[20] His productivity was a victim of his health (these years occupy very few pages in the bibliography compared with the years immediately preceding them). Much of what he did publish concerned the Civil War and appeared earlier in the book; and the rest, including *Democratic Vistas*, did not fulfil the more or less personal requirements of 'Specimen Days' and so ended up in 'Collect'. Moreover, Whitman did very little to reduce or explain the abruptness of the transition, beyond a sentence each about his activities during the late 1860s and his illness of the early 1870s, simply announcing: '[s]everal years now elapse before I resume my diary' ('Specimen Days', p. 118). Even the 'Interregnum Paragraph' between the earlier period and the later, in which he might have taken the opportunity to justify his book's eccentric structure, is largely taken from previously published articles (pp. 118–19). And finally, however selectively he covers his own and American history, he draws no further parallels between personal and national recovery.

Indeed, the sections on nature generally, like those on almost every other subject, concern the nation's future much more than its development in the mid-nineteenth century, culminating as they do in the warning given trenchant expression and pride of place in the concluding section of 'Specimen Days':

> American democracy ... must either be fibred, vitalized, by regular contact with out-door light and air and growths, farm-scenes, animals, fields, trees, birds, sun-warmth and free skies, or it will certainly dwindle and pale. We cannot have grand races of mechanics, work people, and commonalty, (the only specific purpose

of America,) on any less terms. I conceive of no flourishing and heroic elements of Democracy in the United States, or of Democracy maintaining itself at all, without the Nature-element forming a main part – to be its health-element and beauty-element – to really underlie the whole politics, sanity, religion and art of the New World.

(pp. 294–5)

Why should nature have such a crucial role in the survival and prosperity of American democracy? Whitman's answer to this is scattered throughout his earlier and much less formal statements about the secluded creek and his deliciously solitary relationship with it. After the variety of vivid scenes in wartime Washington (which range from the impressive discipline and pageantry of an army on the march to a pile of amputated limbs outside a makeshift hospital), the evocations of nature are disappointingly uniform and secondhand. He looks at a succession of natural features – trees, flowers, birds, sky – but the vocabulary in which he attempts to conjure them is hopelessly archaic and derivative: cedar-apples have 'elfin pates' (p. 126), the clouds are 'silver swirls like locks of toss'd hair' (p. 129). What he is really interested in, though, is what they signify and not, like a natural historian, their specific qualities and their place in the natural order. In his acute diagnosis of Whitman's failings as a nature writer, Chase observes that 'the general motion of his mind is toward transcendental and symbolic formulations'.[21] The sections on nature are primarily didactic and prophetic rather than historical or even descriptive; and in their version nature has a threefold significance.

First it is the source of physical and mental health, 'the only permanent reliance for sanity of book or human life' ('Specimen Days', p. 120). Whitman attributes his 'already much-restored health' after his paralysis to having been 'almost two years, off and on, without drugs and medicines, and daily in the open air' (p. 150). Secondly, nature presents an honest face whose reality is faultlessly and openly reflected in its appearance. 'The Lesson of a Tree', as one section is called, is the lesson of '*being*, as against the human trait of mere *seeming* ... of *what is*, without the least regard to what the looker on (the critic) supposes or says, or whether he likes or dislikes' (p. 130) – a message made especially urgent by the increasing emphasis on wealth and social manners which had followed rapid economic growth and urbanization in the decades since the war. Down at the creek, Whitman imitates this primal integrity, discarding all deceptive human appurtenances, 'no talk, no bonds, no dress, no books, no *manners*' (p. 150). 'Nature was naked', he recalls of his 'Sun-Bath', 'and I was also' (p. 152). And in these sections, as nowhere else in the book, he adopts the manner and rhetoric of casual and honest intimacy, hoping not just that his descriptions will 'prove as glowing to you, reader dear, as the experience itself was to me' (pp. 118–19) but that this intimacy with the reader will reproduce nature's with him.

Thirdly, and most importantly, nature is the tangible manifestation of absolute reality. In whatever shape it appears he finds 'the naked source-life of us all ... the great, silent, savage, all-acceptive Mother' (p. 122) – in the sky, for example, 'the most real reality and formulator of everything' (p. 129), in a tree the 'invisible foundations and hold-together ... the all-basis, the nerve, the great-sympathetic ... giving stamp to everything' (p. 131). Quite often in these sections continuous prose falters into ungrammatical notes; and sometimes it is suspended altogether in favour of bare catalogues. The lists of trees, birds and wild flowers, Whitman explains, express 'A Civility Too Long Neglected' to 'the individualities' which 'have certainly been slighted by folks who make pictures, volumes, poems, out of them' (p. 181). He wants to avoid subordinating them to an abstract, human agenda – which is of course only to say that he is using them for his own agenda in which they function as examples of what is irreducibly itself and real. Imagining nature as an exhibition of the fundamental unity of all creation profoundly alters his relation to it; he no longer simply takes it like a medicine or imitates it but, following the German Romantic theorists, merges with it, feeling 'through his whole being, and pronouncedly the emotional part, that identity between himself subjectively and Nature objectively which Schelling and Fichte are so fond of pressing' (p. 153). The coming generations of Americans will thus, as Whitman sees it, forfeit their honesty, health and sanity and betray their individual, artistic and institutional foundations in reality if they do not preserve and cultivate their 'inner ... rapport' (p. 152) with the natural world.

Which is one reason why he finds the clearest possibilities for an exemplary democratic culture in the prairie states with their 'broad expanses of living green, in every direction', their 'vast Something, stretching out on its own unbounded scale, unconfined ... combining the real and ideal, and beautiful as dreams' ('Specimen Days', p. 208). Whitman's tendency to identify what he sees and likes with what America should and will be is at its most pronounced and explicit on his travels. As Erkkila says, 'he translated his trip West into a prophecy of the American future'.[22] At the same time, the places he visits elicit in quick succession the extreme and conflicting motives behind his nationalism: on the one hand, a final rejection of colonialism and its legacy, a final declaration of cultural independence; and on the other, something that sounds perilously close to incipient imperialism. Out West he finds a life and landscape sufficiently new and remote from Europe to be the potential 'home both of what I would call America's distinctive ideas and distinctive realities' ('Specimen Days', p. 208). Up on the Canadian side of the border, however, he discovers 'hardy, democratic, intelligent, radically sound' individuals who are thus, he reflects appreciatively, 'just as American ... as the average range of best specimens among us' (p. 240); and 'sooner or later', he concludes, 'Canada shall form two or three grand States, equal and independent, with the rest of the American Union' (p. 241). He does not mean this in any sinister or predatory way, of course; still, it does remind us that 'America', as he uses the term, cannot always be conveniently understood as just a metaphor for certain social and political ideals: sometimes it is neither more nor less than the actual nation.

The 'pure breath, primitiveness, boundless prodigality and amplitude' of the West will eventually, Whitman hopes, 'in some sort form a standard' for the nation's 'poetry and art' ('Specimen Days', p. 223). In the mean time, though, he pays tribute in the various literary sections of 'Specimen Days' to the 'poetical beginning and initiation' (p. 267) his celebrated contemporaries on the East coast have provided, identifying the signal contributions of each to American democratic culture. Bryant is praised for loving and singing 'Nature ... so well' (p. 166), Longfellow for his absorption and domestication of European lore and Whittier for his fierce and single-minded 'moral energy' (p. 267). And yet their contributions, as Whitman describes them, are distinctly limited and preparatory, his praises hedged with reservations. Kenneth Price is right to say that 'graciousness ... pervades Whitman's consideration of ... writers in *Specimen Days*', but equally right to add that 'Whitman was enacting ... the role of the poet who synthesizes and subsumes his fellows'.[23] Each writer's achievement is acknowledged but also sharply delimited, while by strong implication his own comes nearest to defining the country's genuine and necessary ideals. Each gets a piece of the pie; only Whitman himself gets the whole of it. He likes Poe, for example, but only as 'that entire contrast and contradiction which is next best to fully exemplifying' the 'perfect and noble life, morally without flaw, happily balanced in activity, physically sound and pure' and so on (pp. 230–1). Similarly, to applaud Longfellow he turns negatives into positives, but the negatives remain to consign this (at the time) much more celebrated and successful poet to an earlier stage of American literary development:

> To the ungracious complaint-charge of his want of racy nativity and special originality, I shall only say that America and the world may well be reverently thankful ... for any such singing-bird vouchsafed out of the centuries, without asking that the notes be different from those other songsters; adding what I have heard Longfellow

himself say, that ere the New World can be worthily original, and announce herself and her own heroes, she must be well saturated with the originality of others, and respectfully consider the heroes that lived before Agamemnon.

(p. 286)

Whitman's keenness to push his American contemporaries into the margins of national tradition, leaving the central position open for occupation by himself, is further suggested by his much more generous and extensive – less threatened – treatment of European writers. A fully-fledged, fairly lengthy essay on Carlyle and Hegel, the section entitled 'Carlyle from American Points of View' (pp. 254–62) rather overwhelms his immediate response to 'The Death of Carlyle' to which it is appended as 'Later Thoughts and Jottings' and would perhaps sit more comfortably among the more formal pieces in 'Collect'.[24] At any rate, it is one of his finest essays and defines his sense of his poetic identity as clearly and coherently as anything he wrote. Hegel's theory of history, in Whitman's estimation, is both right and rightly optimistic even if his style is too abstract and bloodless. Carlyle, meanwhile, is a fiery Jeremiah whose unforgivable hostility to democracy is just another symptom of the 'malady' he so perceptively and 'mercilessly' exposes in Western civilization. Neither can offer a fully rounded expression of American democratic ideals; but both offer vital ingredients of it as none of the Americans do (except possibly Emerson), Hegel the intellect, Carlyle the passion, Hegel the serene optimism, Carlyle the 'rude, rasping, taunting, contradictory tones ... wanted amid the supple, polish'd, money-worshipping, Jesus-and-Judas-equalizing, suffrage-sovereignty echoes of current America'. This neat configuration leaves space for a third, genuinely New World writer – Whitman himself – who combines the positive qualities of each: the 'abysmic inspiration' of a prophet and a passionate belief in the future of democracy (p. 261).

One of Whitman's principal ways of marginalizing, or at least containing, the achievements of other writers is by invoking their lives and personalities. Literature, he believed, is the natural and expressive product of a moral, emotional and even physiological nature as well as of social and biographical circumstance. In Carlyle's work, he says, 'dyspepsia is to be traced in every page, and now and then fills the page. One may include among the lessons of his life ... how behind the tally of genius and morals stands the stomach, and gives a sort of casting vote' ('Specimen Days', p. 249). But while rooting the works of Carlyle and others in their inevitably limiting biographies, in 'Specimen Days' he carefully avoids presenting his own work against the backdrop of his life and thus subordinating the work to the life. We get no specific account of the composition and publication of the first three editions of

Leaves of Grass (nor for that matter of any of the later editions); instead, the story of his adult life effectively begins with the Civil War while the various prefaces to *Leaves* are included not in the autobiography but in 'Collect'.

The substance and structure of 'Specimen Days' also reflect Whitman's more general efforts to evade definition. The final sentence of his brief introduction admits without apology that 'the book is probably without any definite purpose that can be told in a statement' (p. 3); and a later section records that he had at one time 'thought of naming this collection "Cedar-Plums Like"', because like his miscellaneous jottings, those 'acrid plums' are wild, free and useless (pp. 245–6). Having noticed that 'the two major topical centers in *Specimen Days* [the Civil War memoranda and the observations of nature] are not coordinated with each other', Buell goes as far as to claim that Whitman uses an autobiographical arrangement simply 'to supply a nominal principle of coherence that at the same time justifies a strategy of inconclusion'.[25] It seems to me that the strategy of inconclusion is an integral part of the autobiographical project. Whitman wanted to present himself and his life but only in a form that would identify them exclusively with his nation and its prospects. As a result he had to resist other definitions. And this is why, as we have seen, 'Specimen Days' excluded work written before he could present himself as a prophetic poet and wartime hospital visitor, roles in which he represents nothing more specific than the entire nation.

It is easy to see why Whitman should have wanted to portray the nation in his own image: to help bring about his vision of American democratic life and culture. What may remain puzzling is why he should have buried so much of his life to portray himself in the image of the nation. A part of the answer, though, is surely that he was attempting to secure eventual, if not immediate, literary success. Thomas suggests that 'he was as much condemned as committed to optimism' because of his emotional investment in the soldiers who died in the Civil War: he could not bear even to consider the possibility that they had sacrificed their lives in vain.[26] But he was also condemned to optimism because he had invested his literary identity in the nation. Americans might never be interested in him as an individual, but they would always be interested in the state of their country; and he would stand for its glorious future. From the moment he launched his career along these lines, the reward was clearly in his sights. 'The proof of a poet', the preface to the first edition of *Leaves of Grass* concluded, 'is that his country absorbs him as affectionately as he has absorbed it' (*Leaves* 1855, p. 24).

Notes

1. *The Correspondence of Walt Whitman: Volume III; 1876–1885*, ed. Edward Haviland Miller (New York: New York University Press, 1964), p. 309 (hereafter, *Correspondence*); in the New York *Collected Writings of Walt Whitman*, general editors G.W. Allen and S. Bradley.
2. 'Specimen Days' and 'Collect' retained their places in the text, if not the title, of Whitman's final edition of his *Complete Prose Works* (1892) from which Floyd Stovall printed his excellent two-volume edition in *Collected Works: Prose Works 1892: Volume I; 'Specimen Days'* (New York: New York University Press, 1963) and *Prose Works 1892: Volume II; 'Collect'* (New York: New York University Press, 1964). These two volumes will be cited separately as 'Specimen Days' and 'Collect'.
3. See *Correspondence*, p. 269.
4. Admittedly, in the *Complete Prose Works* of a decade later Whitman added a section of 'Pieces in Early Youth'; but Stovall points out that these seem to have been reprinted mainly, as Whitman says in a foreword, 'to avoid the annoyance of their surreptitious issue, (as lately announced, from outsiders)' ('Specimen Days', p. viii). And in fact that final edition of his prose shows him still working with very much the same priorities. Almost all the prose he had written and published since 1882 is included in two additional clusters named after the volumes in which they had previously been collected (along with some poems), *November Boughs* (1988) and *Good-Bye My Fancy* (1891).
5. *Walt Whitman's 'Leaves of Grass': The First (1855) Edition*, ed. Malcolm Cowley (New York: Viking Press, 1959), pp. 5–6, 12 (hereafter, *Leaves 1855*).
6. The extent to which Whitman's political vision remained, even in the later part of his life, rooted in antebellum American society is well documented in both M. Wynn Thomas, *The Lunar Light of Whitman's Poetry* (Cambridge, Mass. and London: Harvard University Press, 1987) and Betsy Erkkila, *Whitman the Political Poet* (New York and Oxford: Oxford University Press, 1989).
7. Mutlu Konuk Blasing, *The Art of Life: Studies in American Autobiographical Literature* (Austin and London: Texas University Press, 1977), p. 47.
8. Richard V. Chase, *Walt Whitman Reconsidered* (London: Victor Gollancz, 1955), p. 46.
9. Lawrence Buell, 'Autobiography in the American Renaissance', in *American Autobiography: Retrospect and Prospect*, ed. Paul John Eakin (Madison: University of Wisconsin Press, 1991), pp. 54, 47.
10. Douglass's three narratives are *Narrative of the Life of Frederick Douglass, An American Slave* (1845), *My Bondage and My Freedom* (1855) and *Life and Times of Frederick Douglass* (1892).
11. Erkkila, p. 301. My understanding of 'Specimen Days' has been greatly assisted by Erkkila's chapter, 'Representing America', which shows how it 'may be as near as Whitman ever came to writing the work of democratic nationality that he proposed in 1871' (p. 294). One point of difference will emerge, however; where Erkkila sees Whitman's self-presentation as a function chiefly of his version of American nineteenth-century history, I see it as a function of his vision of the future.

12. 'Specimen Days', pp. 18, 16.
13. Thomas, p. 222.
14. Thomas, pp. 230–1
15. *Leaves of Grass: Comprehensive Reader's Edition*, ed. H.W. Blodgett and B. Sculley (New York: New York University Press, 1965), p. 750.
16. Thomas, p. 231.
17. The war's immediate outcome proved it but post-war America, as Thomas demonstrates (p. 233), would do its best to disprove it.
18. Linck C. Johnson, 'The Design of Walt Whitman's *Specimen Days*', *Walt Whitman Review*, 21 (1975), 10.
19. Erkkila, pp. 296, 301.
20. Joel Myerson, *Walt Whitman: A Descriptive Bibliography* (Pittsburgh and London: Pittsburgh University Press, 1993), pp. 774–92.
21. Chase, pp. 170–1.
22. Erkkila, p. 299.
23. Kenneth M. Price points out more generally that in 'Specimen Days' Whitman 'seems most interested in maintaining his own consistently genial tone' (*Whitman and Tradition: The Poet in His Century* (New Haven and London: Harvard University Press, 1990), p. 93). Interestingly, several passages seem to have been omitted from this part of the book on the grounds that they were too severely critical of individuals or groups, a furious paragraph about antebellum Southerners being one ('altogether the most impudent persons that have yet appeared in the history of lands …' ('Specimen Days', p. 311)). The fact that passages expressing equally vehement and specifically targeted criticism (such as the list of corrupt types involved in the 'nominating conventions of our Republic') were retained in 'Collect' suggests that Whitman may have wanted to present different identities in the two parts of the book, the autobiographer a sympathetic human being, the cultural historian and analyst (if need be) a sharp and unsparing critic ('Collect', p. 428).
24. Had it been accepted for publication by *The North American Review*, one may conjecture, and thus given some kind of public endorsement, it might have found a place in 'Collect' next to *Democratic Vistas*, which had been previously published (and also provoked in part by Carlyle's ideas). See *Correspondence*, p. 344.
25. Buell, p. 63.
26. Thomas, p. 233.

CHAPTER FOURTEEN

Buried in Laughter:
The *Memories and Adventures* of Sir Arthur Conan Doyle

Diana Barsham

In 1896, three years after he had plunged Sherlock Holmes to his death at the Reichenbach Falls in *The Final Problem*, Arthur Conan Doyle found himself living in Egypt trying to keep his wife, Louise, alive. Louise had developed what was initially diagnosed as a 'galloping consumption' during their recent visit to Switzerland and Doyle was determined to keep pace with this illness which threatened very peremptorily, and pre-emptively, to turn him into a widower.

According to the account given in his autobiography, *Memories and Adventures*, Egypt lived up to its Victorian reputation as an identity-transforming place to visit, for this was a visit that, in the best traditions of Doyle's fiction, 'led up to a most unforeseen climax'.[1] If his wife's consumption ceased to gallop, Doyle himself did not. Egypt was the place where he perfected his riding skills, and he describes vividly a Byronic gallop on one of the 'weird steeds' at the local livery stable, which bolted with him across the desert, threw him off and then literally marked him for life with a star-shaped kick over the eye requiring five stitches (p. 150).

While the notion of the 'unforeseen climax' is introduced at the beginning of the two chapters in *Memories and Adventures* relating Doyle's Egyptian experiences, the climax itself is continually deferred through a series of dream-like adventures of which the encounter with this 'black devil of a horse' is merely the first. On his way to visit a Coptic monastery, Doyle gets lost while crossing the Libyan desert in 'a sort of circus coach' (p. 153), built for Napoleon III, while the teleological outcome of this quest finally reveals itself in the dramatic discovery that war has been declared, and that the British reconquest of the Sudan is under way. In a pattern that is repeated throughout *Memories and Adventures*, personal crisis and cultural dislocation conspire to place the hero of this autobiography on the edge of world events. Doyle comments: 'Thus it was that we learned of the next adventure which was opening up before both us and the British Empire ... Egypt had suddenly become the storm centre of the world, and chance had placed me there at that moment' (p. 157).

As self-elected war correspondent for the *Westminster Gazette*, it was Doyle's intention to report on the British advance on Dongola. In the event, what he saw of the Sudanese War was little more than troop movements and a camel recruitment drive. But Doyle's autobiography is that of a Man of Destiny for whom the interplay of Providential powers and personal ambition is a site of explosive humour which constantly cancels the self-imaging it evokes.

As Doyle struggled towards the centre of world events, his own personal demon, with its 'curious faculty for running into dramatic situations' (p. 76) and coincidental events, was preparing yet another deferral of that narrative climax where selfhood finds itself configured in the historic moment. This time the problematics of destiny presented themselves in the form of a camel, described by Doyle as 'the strangest and most deceptive animal in the world' (p. 163). In an evocative piece of travel writing, Doyle describes his two-day journey across the desert towards Wady Halfa, rising at 2.00 a.m., the noiseless tread of the camels in the sand, the purple velvet sky lit by a half moon and enormous stars, and the beautiful baritone voice of Scudamore, war correspondent for the *Daily News*, rolling out across the desert air. This was as close to action as Doyle was to get in the Sudanese campaign. Suddenly spotting some green stuff on the path, his camel dropped to its knees, catapulting him head foremost down its neck. It was, he said, 'like coming down a hosepipe in some acrobatic performance' (p. 164). Doyle is slipped clown-like out of the frame of the discourse he has been creating through a process of violent symbolization which acts as the main vehicle for the career of the self in its headlong and headstrong search for direction.

Instigators of fall and exponents of vicissitude, the horse and the camel act as quest creatures, articulating the repetitions of an unconscious project and used by Doyle to disguise his knowledge of outcomes. Arriving at Sarras, he is told by Kitchener that nothing will happen by way of military action until thousands of such camels have been collected. Willingly contributing his own beast to the war effort, Doyle prepares to return to Cairo. The curious climax of this Egyptian adventure, so important a turning point in Doyle's life narrative, finally arrives, not in the expected form of military excitements, but in a stasis of self-encounter on an empty cargo boat going back to Assouan. Once aboard, he finds himself without any food except for a few tins of apricots left behind by the British army. On this interminably slow return journey, the tinned apricots gradually merged with the only reading material he chanced to possess – a copy of Rousseau's *Confessions* – into an image of unforgettable repulsion:

> We managed to get some Arab bread from the boatman, and that with the apricots served us all the way. I never wish to see a tinned apricot so long as I live. I associate their cloying sweetness with Rousseau's *Confessions,* a French edition of which came somehow into my hands and was my only reading till I saw Assouan once more. Rousseau also I never wish to read again.
>
> (p. 168)

This rejection of one of the classic texts of Romantic autobiography is more than merely anecdotal. It is a rejection which serves to create and define the project of self-memorialization upon which Doyle is embarked. His distaste for the confessional codes and analytic configurations of Romantic subjectivity is everywhere apparent in *Memories and Adventures* and is a striking feature of his handling of the genre. Pierre Norden, Doyle's biographer, describes him as hesitant 'to draw the reader into purely autobiographical regions' and as 'reluctant to occupy the centre of his own stage'.[2] Richard Lancelyn Green, discussing what he calls Doyle's 'fear of intimacy', comments: 'When he describes his life, he omits the inner man. There are no revelations, no great pangs of remorse, and no sense of personal injustice.'[3]

In this respect *Memories and Adventures* runs counter to that 'shift of attention from *bios* to *autos*' which James Olney sees as largely responsible for opening up 'the subject of autobiography specifically for literary discussion'[4] and may explain in part the lack of attention it has received in discussions of Victorian life-writing. *Memories and Adventures* is a rebellious text, defiantly non-canonical in its concept of identity and in its demarcation of areas considered appropriate for representation. Childhood, that *locus classicus* of nineteenth-century selfhood, receives an epigrammatic dismissal: 'Of my boyhood I need say little, save that it was Spartan at home and more Spartan at ... school' (p. 16). Manhood, its comedies, adventures and responsibilities, forms the burden of this text. One of the few anecdotes of childhood that Doyle does consider worth preserving concerns his passion for street-fighting and the memorable occasion when he was 'knocked pretty well senseless' (p. 17) by the boot of the book-maker's boy. As after so many of Doyle's 'fall-stories', his narrative memory slips immediately into a lateral discontinuity from which he recovers to find himself sitting on the knee of an affable, white-haired gentleman who turns out to be Thackeray.

As the most beaten boy at his Jesuit school, Doyle considered he had learned a valuable lesson in the concealment of the inner man and the non-articulation of feeling. The only occasion in the autobiography when Doyle describes himself giving voice to an agonized selfhood is a significant one, concerning an act of overfamiliarity by an 'exuberant young bounder' who approached Doyle at a railway station during his political campaign for the 1905 elections and squeezed his right hand so hard that his signet ring nearly cut him. As the metonymics of interpretation rush to the aid of this damaged finger, Doyle observes of this incident: 'It opened the sluice and out came a torrent of whaler language which I had hoped that I had long ago forgotten. The blast seemed to blow him bodily across the platform, and formed a strange farewell to my supporters. Thus ended my career in politics ...' (p. 243).

Presenting *Memories and Adventures* as Doyle's 'final tale of chivalry', Lancelyn Green identifies the figurative elements of Doyle's self-portraiture: 'His autobiography does not dwell on the stories that made him famous ... or on the personal and domestic details that were worked into his stories but concentrates instead on his public career, on actions that were at best noble gestures.'[5] This description indicates the structural affinities between *Memories and Adventures* and that type of autobiography identified by William L. Howarth in his useful taxonomy of the genre as 'autobiography as oratory', whereby the 'hero defines his superiority through the power of preaching or public oratory'. According to Howarth, the details of such a life account 'are not literal history but figural narration. They give us selected aspects of a larger allegory': 'Since its purpose is didactic, his story is allegorical, seeking to represent in a single life an idealised pattern of human behaviour. The allegory often has messianic overtones, replete with suffering and martyrdom, as the orator leads his people to their rightful home.'[6]

While I prefer to use the term apothegmic, rather than allegoric, to describe the configurations at work in Doyle's often apparently random memory orderings, the description is useful in helping to identify a peculiarity of literary autobiography that is strongly evident in *Memories and Adventures*, that is, its dependence on writing that has already had its life elsewhere. I mean by this not just a dependence on the already written codes of the autobiographical genre or its frequent ransacking of other forms of discourse and document, such as letters and diaries. What is as striking about *Memories and Adventures* as its subject's avoidance of personal disclosure is its reappropriation of story material that has previously been used by Doyle either in works of fiction or of cultural propaganda. Within the literary academy, Doyle's reputation has never been of the highest; he has been viewed, if at all, as a popularizer and recycler of story codes and structures brought into being by the great mid-Victorian novelists. His autobiography, on the other hand, achieves its highly original and individualistic effect by the conscious ease of its bricolage. The provisionality of much twentieth-century literary autobiography, the sense, exploited by writers such as

Graves and Isherwood, of self-stories shifting in time, is not allowed to disturb the *Memories and Adventures*. The stories that make up this story have been tried and tested as part of the economy of Doyle's professionalism; like the veteran soldiers in Doyle's historical novels, they have done their work elsewhere and returned successful. Provisionality has been present in the discontinuities of a career which has moved from whaling and medicine, through literature and politics, to war and religion. But the stories themselves have the authority of a definitive version and support a work of heroic statuary: though the facets of his career are many, there is only one Sir Arthur. Doyle's self-representation, still intact despite the labours of subsequent biographers, is a triumph of neo-Victorian memorialization.

Despite its insistence on a concept of self that is not an independent agent but is, to use Doyle's own phrase, 'tied to the chariot wheel of history',[7] the rejection of interiority and confession does not lead *Memories and Adventures* away from autobiography and towards the formal Victorian memoir. While sharing that preference for a public discourse of the self, Doyle's individuality is conveyed, not through any attempts at psychological self-realism, but through his continued use of graphic and creative visualization to represent the 'absences' of introspection, offering cartoon images in the places and spaces of private life. Descriptions of his own body, and of the injuries to it, represent one such site for this curious cartoon storage of private experience, often inscribed through the proximity of some animal.

I began this article by referring to the identity-transforming effect of Egypt on Victorian travellers. Doyle's experience there opened up new career adventures for him as well as leading to a romantic involvement with the woman who would eventually become his second wife. The rejection of Rousseau's *Confessions* with which the Egyptian episode concludes, however, is not a rejection of the inner life but is rather an objection to a mode of truth-telling unsettling to the concept of manhood which is Doyle's most obvious project. The notion of transformation, of the story beneath the skin, finds bizarre forms of entrance into the formal narrative, as his experiences on the margins of empire struggle to image their significance back at the centre. In England again, a week after his return from Cairo, Doyle is attending a Royal Academy banquet in London. Suddenly he notices the effects of an unseen process: 'I saw upon my wrists the jagged little ulcers where the poisonous jiggers which had burrowed into my skin while I lay upon the banks of the Nile were hatching out their eggs under the august roof of Burlington House' (p. 144).

As the son, nephew and grandson of well-known artists and cartoonists, Doyle's techniques of indicating aspects of unstoried life assert a continuity of identity with his paternal relatives. Since Doyle's fairy-painting father had been an alcoholic in serious and eventually institutionalized retreat from reality (he died along with Holmes in 1893), this covert identification can be seen as an act of rebellion against his mother, 'the ma'am', who had brought up her family of five children effectively without paternal support and who, in all obvious respects, was the driving force of Doyle's life.

Anyone familiar with Doyle's stories will recognize that the poisonous jiggers burrowing into his skin are activating a metaphor and performing a structural feat which reaches deep into Doyle's imaginative life. A version of the fall, this image of descent through unstable terrain is a recurrent figure in Doyle's fiction, most famously realized in the Great Grimpen mire of *The Hound of the Baskervilles* into which horses, dogs, and the criminal lusts of history all impartially vanish. In *Memories and Adventures* the most unstable terrain is not that of Doyle's personal falls; it is instead the chasm towards which, in 1914, the whole of European culture appeared to be sliding. Doyle writes: 'I can never forget, and our descendants can never imagine, the strange effect upon the mind which was produced by seeing the whole European fabric drifting to the edge of the chasm with absolute uncertainty as to what would happen when it toppled over' (p. 364).

These recurrent images of fall become for Doyle symbolic centres of meaning into which flow the various strands of his narrative; literary and theological allusion, personal mishap and misdemeanour, vocational misdirection and cultural tragedy. They are also the solution to a riddle in which clowning and performing, dying and disappearance become unexpected allies in a deep-seated revolt against cultural, ideological and theological complacency. The importance of falling, of being allowed to fall, is perhaps the apothegm with which Doyle counters that other central imperative of Victorian life-writing: the importance of being earnest. If Doyle, in the early stages of his literary career, has a cultural 'other', it is Oscar Wilde who represents it, the two young authors thrown into conjunction at a literary dinner in 1889 which resulted in the writing of both *The Picture of Dorian Gray* and Doyle's second Sherlock Holmes story, *The Sign of Four*. Doyle describes the meeting as 'a golden evening', but what struck him most about Wilde, apart from the unforgettable brilliance of his conversation, was his self-confessed interest in the primacy of rhetoric and his addiction to the art of lying. He quotes Wilde: 'Between me and life there is a mist of words always. I throw probability out of the window for the sake of a phrase, and the chance of an epigram makes me desert truth' (p. 95).

For Doyle, the 'true' Wilde was a witty and sensitive moralist who left his trace on the characterization and conversation of Sherlock

Holmes; his subsequent career the doctor in Doyle diagnosed as a madness and a monstrous pathological development. But the arts of falling and of lying occupy contiguous space in the genre of autobiography, as too in the comedy of manhood that is the subtext of Doyle's vocational quest. The lively duality of absence involved in Doyle's concept of falling and lying, the absence of life and truth, is amusingly focused in his description of the temporary death of Sherlock Holmes. Visiting the Reichenbach Falls in 1892, Doyle thought them a terrible place but, as he puts it in a phrase which reveals the concealment of Shylock in Sherlock, it was the very place 'that would make a worthy tomb for poor Sherlock, even if I buried my bank account along with him. So there I laid him, fully determined that he should stay there – as indeed for some years he did' (pp. 117–18).

Meaning for Doyle, like the masculinity he constructs, is grounded in the twin concepts of play and attachment. That detachment from 'truth' to which Wilde had confessed was rendered impossible for Doyle by his commitment to essentialist notions of selfhood. What is hidden in his prose, is a concept of inner being as a storehouse for poetry, much of it by Kipling whose works he describes as 'part of my very self' (p. 293). That 'guarantee of honesty'[8] which, according to William L. Howarth, attends the art of nineteenth-century autobiography is here represented, not through the legitimation of approaching death (unsuitable, since Doyle was a Spiritualist), but by the candour with which the text signals its own places of burial.

Like the gaps and holes in his own life story, the version of history with which Doyle wrestles is also discontinuous, a sinking ground for disappearances. Significantly, his sobriquet for the First World War is 'The Great Interruption' (p. 312). As he puts it in *Memories and Adventures*: 'The influence of the lie is one of the strangest problems of life – that which is not continually influences that which is. Within one generation imagination and misrepresentation have destroyed the Boer Republic and Imperial Germany' (p. 343). The lie which Doyle held responsible for the outbreak of war in 1914 was a misrepresentation and a misreading of the British character. One aspect of the strikingly impersonal and apothegmic self-portraiture of *Memories and Adventures* is Doyle's attempt to correct the misrepresentation; to tell the traumatized post-war British public, through the reuse of stories and characters already well known and loved, who they were and what they had meant. In a well-known First World War sonnet, 'When You See Millions of the Mouthless Dead', the poet Charles Sorley had described war as a collective loss of identity:

> Then, scanning all the o'er crowded mass, should you
> Perceive one face that you loved heretofore,

> It is a spook. None wears the face you knew.
> Great death has made all his for evermore.[9]

Memories and Adventures is Doyle's attempt to restore to British cultural identity 'the face you knew' and to illustrate the chivalric codes underlying British behaviour.

The First World War is the culminating point of Doyle's autobiography, the cultural moment at which personal and national destinies unite in a somewhat precarious act of definition:

> And now I turn to the war, the physical climax of my life as it must be of the life of every living man and woman. Each was caught as a separate chip and swept into that fearsome whirlpool, where we all gyrated for four years, some sinking forever, some washed up all twisted and bent, and all of us showing in our souls and bodies some mark of the terrible forces which had controlled us for so long. I will show presently how the war reacted upon me, and also if one may speak without presumption, how in a minute way I in turn reacted upon the war.
>
> (p. 341)

The concept of war is at the centre of the *Memories and Adventures*, just as fighting, rather than writing, is the preferred metaphor for his self-definitions. In describing his ancestry, he explains that he comes on his mother's side from fighting stock and speculates on theories of reincarnation to explain the recurrent return-of-the-soldier motif in his life-story. Part of his justification for the writing of autobiography relies upon the fact that he has 'seen something of three wars, the Soudanese, the South African and the German' (p. 7). During the Boer War he worked first as a doctor through the enteritis epidemic which killed 5000 men, and later as a war correspondent and apologist for the British cause, an activity for which he received his knighthood. While he narrates the encounters of the war with the straight seriousness of a boy's adventure story, even here, however, there is a graphic impulse at work which bespeaks emotions unrepresented in the text, and a sense of the ludicrous which perceives even in appalling suffering a notion of war as masculine cultural play. Enteritis is a terrible illness but in Doyle's account its devastating effects are aided and abetted by grotesquely familiar icons which attempt to contain the self-cancelling incongruities of a war zone. Given a cricket field to serve as their military camp, the main medical ward was established in a cricket pavilion which had at one end a stage with a scene set for a production of *HMS Pinafore*. Doyle observes: 'This was turned into latrines for those who could stagger so far. The rest did the best they could, and we did the best we could in turn' (p. 189).

In his chronicling of war, in his concern for national identity, Doyle wanted to invoke a concept of history which would guarantee to his writing an epic high-seriousness. He had already disposed of the atemporal Holmes in the belief that his overpopular detective was destroying his reputation as a serious historical novelist. In the autobiography, he acknowledges that his failure to gain a reputation as a historian was the most serious disappointment of his life. Yet Doyle's view of history and the concept of war by which it was sustained is irrepressibly one of play, both in the sense of sport and of a dramatic enactment. Equally important, his image of history is an essentialist one, and its essence for Doyle is that of the matriarchal feminine. Quoted as being 'the root of all modern history', Doyle describes his wartime meeting with the aged Empress Eugénie. Glancing into her sitting-room at Farnborough, he sees 'the mind' which had 'played with Empires' 'engaged upon an enormous jigsaw puzzle, a thousand pieces if there were one' (p. 374). Sent to report on the British front line in 1916, Doyle the propagandist uses a more Shakespearean image for the puzzles of history: 'For a moment we had a front seat at the great world-drama, God's own problem play, working surely to its magnificent end' (p. 395).

The play of war and its link with ludic notions of the masculine and with the art of lying is apparent in Doyle's Boer War description of finding a dead Australian soldier. This infantry man with one arm shot off and his stomach gouged out had, even while waiting for death, missed no occasion for play but had amused himself by balancing a red chess pawn on his water bottle. Doyle queries: 'Has he died playing with it? It looks like it. Where are the other chessmen? We find them in his haversack out of reach' (pp. 206–7). By the time Infantryman 410 has been loaded onto a horse, rigor mortis has set in and his one remaining arm with its clenched fist springs upward into a permanent salute. In apparent celebration of this posthumous gesture, Doyle comments blandly: 'Fair fight, open air, and a great cause – I know no better death.' This utter denial of physical pain takes us back to the beatings of Doyle's school-days. None the less, the art of lying is a signalled event in Doyle's writing and something kicks out against the detachment of this account. Ten miles down the track we encounter one of those animal indicators which so frequently attend upon Doyle's emotional burials and his images of essential masculinity. This time it is a black mare that he sees, rolling and kicking on the ground. At first sight he finds it curious 'that she should be so playful'. With a second glance, the picture changes: 'We look again and she lies very quiet.' This cryptic writing concludes on the ambiguity between lying and dying. 'One more', he says, 'has gone to poison the air of the veldt' (p. 207).

If war and fighting provide Doyle with his most cohesive metaphor for selfhood, his quest for vocation is what links together the memories and adventures he recalls. Having worked his way through a variety of careers, all leading to falls of one kind or another, Doyle has a moment of illumination after being heckled by a horse-slaughterer during the parliamentary hustings of 1905. Talking to his soldier brother, Innes, about his gifts as an orator, Doyle finds his normal intelligence taken completely by surprise in a sudden revelation of his real vocation. The illumination, so vital a turning-point in any spiritual autobiography, becomes for Doyle a moment of prophetic hilarity. Innes remarks: '"It would be strange, Arthur, ... if your real career should prove to be political and not literary." "It will be neither. It will be religious," said I. Then we looked at each other in surprise and both burst out laughing' (p. 235). The laughter is relevant to the precariousness and unpredictability of Doyle's autobiographical project as this relentlessly public personality suddenly confesses its other-worldly dimensions and offers its self-writing as a possible history of the hidden and the lost.

Doyle's conversion to Spiritualism, the cause he was to champion until his death in 1930, was announced in the Spiritualist magazine, *Light*, in 1916. Spiritualism, with its central notion of the 'abiding unity' of the self and its 'continuity of personality',[10] countered the gaps and chasms of personal and cultural memory. It also offered a point of intersection whereby Doyle's restless search for vocational direction and the deep psycho-physical identification he had developed for British experience through his historical novels, war journalism and propaganda work could coalesce. As bereavement hit family after family, and as the ghostly stories of returning soldiers continued to proliferate, as grief-stricken women desperately sought channels of comfort for masculine disappearance on a scale beyond Freud's 'fort-da' game, it was Sir Arthur who took up their cause and became their champion. Subsequent to his conversion, Doyle lost five members of his own family in the Great War, including his brother, Innes, and his son, Kingsley. He claimed to have received assurances of survival from all but one of them. In *Memories and Adventures* he describes the certainty of his belief:

> Let me, therefore, confine myself to saying that the studies which have now intermittently occupied my mind for over forty years, culminated at the time of the war, in giving me an absolute conviction that the change of vibration which we call death did not destroy our personalities and that communication was still possible.
>
> (p. 439)

The 1924 version of *Memories and Adventures* had concluded with an image of the Armistice Day celebrations in 1918 and three small 'fall' stories in the last of which – an encounter between the Australian wounded and the War Office flappers – 'the foundations of solid old London got loosened' (p. 437). Beyond this unstable terrain, Doyle asserts his final message of reassurance: 'Britain had not weakened. She was still the Britain of old' (p. 438). This concluding tribute to unfallen nationhood is modified in the 1930 version when, in the year of his death, Doyle added a chapter which returns from the collapse of both the historic moment and the physical body to the still standing edifice of personal achievement:

> When an author is in failing health and has passed his seventieth year he feels, as he surveys the line of his works, like some architect or builder who, having laboured long to complete his edifice, finally stands back to survey it in its entirety ... It is a modest enough structure, no doubt, and yet as I survey it I feel that I could do no better and that any powers which Providence has given me have found their full expression.
>
> (p. 447)

This architectural image of completion and integration concludes the autobiography of a man who felt he had been put on earth for some big purpose and who had, to the best of his abilities, achieved it. It also provides the only version of the self imaged in stasis since his nauseated encounter with Rousseau on the boat back from Dongola. Where that episode had relayed a sickness of the interior, this image presents a structure of achievement and self-representation which the self surveys from without. For the 'inside story' of this edifice we are, rather curiously, referred away from the autobiography and back into the novels and other books which are its building blocks.

As the end of his life approached, Doyle was always asked two questions. One was about the creation of Sherlock Holmes, the other about his involvement with Spiritualism. The two subjects, which he strove to keep apart, mesh into a problematic of identity which is not the subject of *Memories and Adventures*; it is rather a problematic that is kept absent from the text in order to ensure the solidity of its self-memorialization. Doyle's first recorded memory of life is of seeing a white waxen thing on a bed which turns out to be the corpse of his maternal grandmother. The riddle of identity, of what things are, and of what they will turn out to be, and to be part of, is a quest-related question of peculiar importance to the construction of many autobiographical narratives. Certainly, it is a riddle which recurs in stories and anecdotes throughout *Memories and Adventures*, where an endless play of identity around the central subject helps to guarantee both the comic buoyancy of Doyle's adventures and his concept of essential selfhood. His own name is a particular site for these identity-jokes and he relishes occasions when 'Conan' is misread as 'Canon' and he is, for example, asked to say grace at a Chicago dinner party as 'the only ecclesiastic present' (p. 117). The climax of this identity-joke arrives at the time of the Boer War when Doyle forms part of an inspection drill by the ancient Duke of Cambridge, ex-Commander-in-Chief of the British army. Doyle writes:

> I remained quite rigid, looking past him. He continued to stand, so near that I could hear and almost feel his puffy breath ... At last he spoke. 'What is this?' he asked. Then louder, 'What is this?' and finally, in a sort of ecstasy, 'What *is* it?' I never moved an eyelash, but one of a group of journalists upon my right went into hysterical but subdued laughter.
>
> (p. 183)

Memories and Adventures is a book of laughters, the humour serving as one means of protection against the deconstructive demons that surround the concept of unified selfhood. Images of deformed bodies, familiar from the Holmes stories, reappear in the autobiography as twisted identity-jokes which the doctor-turned-writer may be able to straighten out, just as he unfolds from the plethoric activities of his career a purposive linear narrative of discovered vocation. The greatest twist of all in the identity-joke is of course death itself. Doyle describes James Payn, the *Cornhill* editor who once turned down the Holmes stories as 'shilling dreadfuls', so crippled with arthritis (and self-reproach?) that parts of him seemed 'hardly human' but still alive to the humour of this joke against the self. Payn cries out: '"Don't make any mistake, Doyle, death is a horrible thing – horrible! I suffer the agonies of the damned!' Doyle adds, 'five minutes later he would have his audience roaring with laughter, and his own high treble laugh would be the loudest of all"' (p. 306).

It is of course partly through such laughter around the riddle of death that the Spiritualist project unfolds. In the text of another Spiritualist autobiography, that of Frederic Myers – co-founder of the Society for Psychical Research and a man whose work Doyle deeply admired – the new revelation is defined as a 'promise of increased capacity of enjoyment' and the 'strength-giving hope of joy'.[11] The Spiritualist autobiography as a specific subgenre has received little critical attention, perhaps because it is a form of writing predicated on a different set of hypotheses to that of mainstream autobiography. A childhood sensitivity to emotional atmosphere and inner vitalism tends to be a recurrent topos: the young Myers, for instance, had a particularly bad experience with a dead mole. Doyle's conversion to Spiritualism is, however, like the siting of his selfhood generally, configured in external events and empirical 'proofs' of spirit communication. Importantly, it is for him a rationally defensible position not at all incompatible with his knowledge of science and world affairs. His task in *Memories and Adventures* is to present this conversion as a gradual outworking of his destiny rather than as the shocking and radical discontinuity which it appeared to many of his fiction readers. There remains, however, a deep anomaly in Doyle's position which prevented him from describing his convictions convincingly and showing what he calls 'the earnestness' of his 'quest' (p. 277) in its full empirical light.

In Spiritualist autobiographies from Myers to Rosamund Lehmann, the privileged activity is that of trance where the self sinks meaningfully through its own unstable terrains into new domains of interior significance. The description of trance experience was, at the turn of the century, perceived as primarily a gendered discourse, used by women writers such as Anna Kingsford to articulate a sense of difference and of visionary female essence. For Doyle, whose constant falls had announced themselves as talismans against final disappearance, such a descent was, if not unthinkable, at least unwritable; he had excluded himself from such discourse by his relentless encodings of self in concepts of masculine struggle, achievement and physical adventure. Consistent with an overall project that is itself in opposition to the generic expectations of a spiritual autobiography, *Memories and Adventures* deals with this central twist of discourse and identity by ruling it out of court and referring the reader elsewhere in Doyle's writing for information. The autobiography itself deals with its own vocation mainly in terms of number: of miles travelled in the cause (50,000) and of people addressed *en route* (300,000). In the dialectical tensions of Doyle's relationship to his writing personality, this need to evoke and evade his own reflection, and to construct that reflected image as both self and opposition to self, is a defining aspect of his version of masculinity.

In this exclusion of key material, Doyle is reiterating a practice he had employed earlier in the autobiography to ground experiences belonging to the turbulent years of the 1880s. This was the period when Doyle had renounced Catholicism, quarrelled with his family and begun the transformation of his career from medical practitioner to successful author. A crucial figure in this transformation was Dr George Budd with whom Doyle briefly shared a medical practice in 1882. For a full account of his friendship with this man 'born for trouble and adventure' (p. 71) who had 'no doubt a pathological element in his strange explosive character', Doyle refers the reader of *Memories and Adventures* to an avowedly autobiographical novel, *The Stark Munro Letters*, that he had published in 1895, more than ten years after the events it describes. What the novel contains is a hilarious account of a bizarre conflation of identities between two young doctors whose projections and self-mirrorings are gradually transformed into paranoia and rejection. The relationship between the accident-prone, self-reflexive, conscientious and conventional Dr Munro (Doyle) and the 'able, magnetic, unscrupulous, interesting, many-sided'[12] Dr Cullingworth (Budd) whose charisma and exuberance threaten to engulf his less gifted companion is narrated in a clumsily one-sided fashion which easily exposes its own evasions. The struggle for identity, against madness on the one hand, and, on the other, against the creative demon (Cullingworth) whose personality, once subdued, will inform Doyle's writing ever after forms an extraordinary commentary on the smoothly 'definitive' version of the story offered in the autobiography proper. With his art of honest lying, Doyle signals this discrepancy between the accounts by an overt self-contradiction, stating that after the quarrel with Budd he 'put him out of his head forever' and wrote a novel about him at the same time (p. 77).

What this excluded episode reveals is Doyle's guilty conception of identity as a form of theft from some previously more powerful centre of creativity, including of course his own stories. In its constant and explicit concern with narration after the fact, the *Stark Munro Letters* illustrates Doyle's autobiographical determination only to recognize the self once it has gone from the mirror that reflects it. This compulsive need to be several steps ahead of himself and of any act of self-representation had already established itself as part of the fascination of his famous Holmes-Watson investigations.

The writing of autobiography has of course much in common with the detective story; there are many clues and few solutions.[13] In creating Sherlock Holmes, Doyle had released into his own life and that of a whole culture a figure so charismatically addictive that Doyle felt at times he was locked in a life-and-death struggle with this creation he could not control and by whom he did not wish to be defined. According to *Memories and Adventures*, the creation of Holmes had been largely an innovative solution to the demands of magazine serialization, offering a form of narrative unification that, despite the ever-present threat of discontinuity, would catch its readers up into an irresistible double-bind:

> Considering these various journals with their disconnected stories, it had struck me that a single character running through a series, if it only engaged the attention of the reader, would bind that reader to that particular magazine. On the other hand, it had long seemed to me that the ordinary serial might be an impediment rather than a help to a magazine, since, sooner or later, one missed one number and afterwards it had lost all interest. Clearly the ideal compromise was character which carried through, and yet instalments which were complete in themselves, so that the purchaser was always sure that he could relish the whole contents of the magazine.
>
> (p. 113)

Holmes, however, was not just a unifier; he was a monopolizer. Doyle was repeatedly asked whether or not the creation of Holmes was an act of self-representation. In a rare glimpse of autobiographical interiority, Doyle replies to this question by quoting one of his own poems, 'The Inner Room'. This poem, the only one cited in his autobiography, explores the concept of 'multiplex personality' (the term is from F.W.H. Myers, *Human Personality*), and says that among the 'darkling figures' who inhabit 'inner consciousness' there may be 'an astute detective ... but I find that in real life in order to find him I have to inhibit all the others and get into a mood where there is no one in the room but he' (p. 119).

Holmes is an extraordinary personification of some late-Victorian theories of exceptional selfhood and he rises from his cultural sources like a talismanic excalibur. He is Nietzsche's warlike philosopher who 'challenges problems to a dual';[14] half forensic scientist, half spirit medium adept at reading the minor clues of personal history, he is the late-Victorian version of genius defined by Myers in the work already mentioned, a work described by Doyle as 'a great root-book which has marked a date in human thought' (p. 100). According to Myers, 'our psychical unity is federative and unstable ... a limited collaboration of multiple groups'.[15] Manhood establishes itself 'in some example of strongly centralized control over as many elements of the personality as possible',[16] while genius is revealed as a form of calculation, a capacity for utilizing subliminal powers. The man of genius has 'a profounder realization of his environment than is possible for the mass of men'.[17]

Fellow Spiritualist Oliver Lodge said of Doyle that he 'lacked the wisdom of the serpent'.[18] In terms of his autobiographical self-representation, it is possible to say that having Holmes, Doyle had no 'other'. *Memories and Adventures* is something of an attempt to redress the balance of power between a creation who had become more famous than his creator and to return Holmes to his proper sphere in the many-sidedness of Doyle's career. It is Doyle after all, and not Holmes, who solves the great Death Mystery. In the prolonged identity-joke which makes up Doyle's version of autobiography, however, Holmes is the ultimate trickster. As Doyle constructs his apothegmic representation of British manhood, with its unification of self through vocational service, Holmes magnifies a counter notion of identity as a culturally owned multiplicity of representations. In his chapter on Holmes, Doyle stresses the 'many impersonations' which had given 'life' to Holmes via book illustrations, and through stage and film presentations (p. 125). The presence of Holmes, as it reappears throughout the autobiography, curiously challenges the limits of the genre and comes to represent that life of the self that autobiography cannot control: its reception and ownership by other people. This is a version of self analogous not with self-portraiture of the kind discussed by William Howarth[19] but rather with the rapid identity sequences of film, a medium invoked by Doyle both through his images of clowning and in his overt reference to the 'cinema reels of memory' (p. 69).

Doyle frequently returns to his need to separate his own identity from that of Holmes with which it repeatedly threatens to merge. Holmes, he declares, is simply 'a calculating machine' (p. 128), having no inner life and no feeling. If Spiritualist trance represents one sinking hole for Doyle's edifice of selfhood, Holmes's lack of interior meaning offers a mirror to the autobiographer who rejected the model of autobiographical intimacy supplied by Rousseau's *Confessions*. In stressing the calculating aspects of Holmes, Doyle interestingly omits to mention that Holmes's royal road to the solution of crime is via that other absence in Doyle's autobiography, the disappearance into deep trance. It is in this sense that in having Holmes, Doyle has no 'other', for the shadows of his own non-representation are always configured by his famous *alter ego*.

In a recent article, historian Alex Owen has discussed Doyle's involvement in the famous case of the 'Cottingley Fairies', where two young girls, Elsie Wright and Frances Griffiths, effectively hoaxed both Doyle and a large section of his reading public by their claim to have photographed fairies in a Yorkshire dell. The striking point made by Owen is that the girls felt obliged to maintain their hoax despite the damage to their own lives mainly because they could not bear to hurt Doyle's reputation by exposing the truth. These two obscure girls felt sorry for this famous author, who had recently been attacked in the newspapers on account of his belief in Spiritualism. In the words of Elsie Wright, they had seen a cruel cartoon of Doyle 'chained to chair with his head in a cloud, and Sherlock Holmes stood beside him, he had recently lost his son in the war and the poor man was probably trying to comfort himself with unwordly [sic] things. So I said to Frances all right we wont [sic] tell'.[20]

This decision not to tell was made in 1921, shortly before Doyle began work on *Memories and Adventures*. Rather aptly and alarmingly, this incident points to the conspiracies of silence that underpin any autobiographical writing, particularly that which supports a famous, and masculine, name. The silence of the girls is the more disturbing because of the vaunted integrity of Doyle's self-definition. I have tried in the course of this article to indicate some of the protective charms used by Doyle to defend the vulnerabilities of his autobiographical project: the exuberant humour and the comical candour of his identifications with national culture; his strategies for the avoidance of vanity and self-congratulation, the complex guarantees of truthfulness that he constantly maintained. None the less, the testimony of these village girls is interesting in that it asks us to consider how much of an invitation to strangeness and self-opposition the autobiographical act is compelled to supply. Doyle's book on the Cottingley Fairies was published in 1922. In *Memories and Adventures*, he refers to it as possibly 'opening a new vista of knowledge for the human race' (p. 448). Inviting fairies to the christening of a self already buried in laughter is a risky gesture in any genre except the Romance. Revealed here as an act of powerful emptiness, Doyle's autobiography is a memorial to a distinctive neo-Victorian concept of masculinity as a story-centre for the *fabulae* of an entire culture's polymorphic desires. It is a generous and inspiring text, amused by the joke of its own impossibilities. Perhaps that is why, in some rapid movement between two centuries, it is still standing.

Notes

1. Sir Arthur Conan Doyle, *Memories and Adventures* (London: John Murray, 1930), p. 150. All subsequent page references are given in the text and are to this second edition.
2. Quoted by Donald A. Redmond, 'Scholarship Translated into Popular Culture', in *The Quest for Sir Arthur Conan Doyle: Thirteen Biographers in Search of a Life*, ed. Jon L. Lellenberg (Carbondale and Edwardsville: Southern Illinois University Press, 1987), p. 127.
3. Richard Lancelyn Green, 'His Final Tale of Chivalry', in *The Quest for Sir Arthur Conan Doyle*, ed. Lellenberg, p. 43.
4. James Olney, 'Autobiography and the Cultural Moment', in *Autobiography: Essays Theoretical and Critical*, ed. James Olney (Princeton: Princeton University Press, 1980), p. 19.
5. Richard Lancelyn Green, 'His Final Tale of Chivalry', p. 55.
6. William L. Howarth, 'Some Principles of Autobiography', in *Autobiography*, ed. Olney, p. 89.
7. Quoted by Nicholas Utechin, 'A Good-Natured Debunking', in *The Quest for Sir Arthur Conan Doyle*, ed. Lellenberg, p. 100.
8. See Howard Helsinger, 'Credence and Credibility: The Concern for Honesty in Victorian Autobiography', in *Approaches to Victorian Autobiography*, ed. George P. Landow (Athens, Ohio: Ohio University Press, 1979), pp. 39–62.
9. Charles Sorley, 'When You See Millions of the Mouthless Dead'; in *Poetry of the Great War: An Anthology*, ed. D. Hibbert and J. Onions (London: Macmillan, 1986), p. 156.
10. Sir Arthur Conan Doyle, *The History of Spiritualism* (1926; London: The Psychic Press, 1989), vol. II, p. 247.
11. F.W.H. Myers, 'Fragments of Inner Life', *Fragments of Prose and Poetry* (London: Longmans, Green & Co., 1904), p. 43.
12. Sir Arthur Conan Doyle, *The Stark Munro Letters* (London: Longmans, Green & Co., 1895), p. 9.

13. See Dennis Potter, 'An Interview with Alan Yentob', *Seeing the Blossom* (London: Faber & Faber, 1994), pp. 70–1.
14. Friedrich Nietzsche, *Ecce Homo* (1888; Harmondsworth: Penguin Books, 1979), p. 47.
15. F.W.H. Myers, *Human Personality and Its Survival of Bodily Death* (London and Bombay: Longmans, Green & Co., 1904), vol. I, p. 16.
16. Ibid., p. 72.
17. Ibid., p. 20.
18. Quoted by Peter E. Blau and Jon L. Lellenberg, 'A Search for Emotional Peace', in *The Quest for Sir Arthur Conan Doyle*, ed. Lellenberg, p. 156.
19. See William L. Howarth, 'Some Principles of Autobiography', p. 89.
20. Alex Owen, 'Doyle, Albion's Daughters, and the Politics of the Cottingley Fairies', *History Workshop Journal*, 38 (1994), 76–7.

Index

Acton, Sir John, 1st Baron 144, 166
Alderson, Amelia (Mrs Amelia Opie) 26, 27
Alison, Archibald 214
Allen, Grant, *The Woman Who Did* 195
Allen, M., *Essay on the Classification of the Insane* 187
American Civil War 204–16 *passim*, 217, 220–1, 224–7 *passim*
Amigoni, David 4
Amis, Martin, *Time's Arrow* 101
Analytical Review 14
Annandale 123, 128–34 *passim*
Arnold, Julia 159
Arnold, Mary 159
Arnold, Matthew 8, 31, 88, 165, 175, 179; 'Memorial Verses' 32, 72; 'Preface 1853' 68, 200; 'Empedocles on Etna' 179, 200
Arnold, Thomas 165, 167
Athenaeum (quoted) 67, 68
Augustine, St 109, 111, 116; *Confessions* 100, 101, 103, 110, 179; *The Trinity* 110, 112
Aurelius, Marcus 125
Austen, Jane 149
Austen Leigh, J.E., *Memoir of Jane Austen* 144, 146
Auster, Paul 83

Bagot, Richard, Bishop of Oxford 105, 107
Bakhtin, Mikhail 4, 123–30 *passim*, 135
Balfour, Arthur, 1st Earl 166
Balzac, Honoré de 214
Barsham, Diana 11
Barthes, Roland 11
Battiscombe, Georgina 159
Baudelaire, Charles-Pierre 6, 40–3 *passim*, 46, 48; *Les Fleurs du Mal* 40; 'Le Gout du neant' 42
Beaumarchais, Pierre-Augustin Caron de 214
Beaumont, Margaret, Lady 35

Beauregard, Pierre Gustave 204, 210–12 *passim*
Beauvoir, Simone de 141
Bell, Currer, *see* Brontë, Charlotte
Bellringer, Alan 165
Benjamin, Walter 47; 'Some Motifs in Baudelaire' 40–4 *passim*
Benstock, Shari 155
Bentham, Jeremy 87, 88, 90
Bible, Books of: I Corinthians 134; Job 195
Blackwood, John 141
Blackwood's Edinburgh Magazine 121, 140, 146
Blake, William 31, 34, 35
Blasing, Mutlu Konuk 220
Bloom, Harold 4
Boer War 241, 242, 243, 246
Book of Common Prayer, The 105–6
Book of Homilies, The 105–6
Boswell, James, *Tour to the Hebrides* 16
Bradley, F[rancis] H[erbert] 84
Brodzki, Bella 155
Brontë, Charlotte ('Currer Bell') 72, 75, 80, 142; *Jane Eyre* 71, 153; *Poems* 71; *The Professor* 162; *Shirley* 71
Brontë, Emily 8; *Poems* 71
Broughton, Treva 155
Brown, Thomas, 'The Wanderer in Norway' 27
Browne, Sir Thomas, *Sepulchral Urns* 214
Browning, Elizabeth Barrett 168; *Aurora Leigh* 72
Browning, Robert 8, 168; 'Childe Roland' 179
Bryant, William Cullen 218, 230
Bucke, Richard Maurice 217
Budd, George 247
Buell, Lawrence 222
Bunyan, John 10, 183; *Grace Abounding* 179, 181, 201; *The Pilgrim's Progress* 174–5, 181, 183, 199, 201–2

Burke, Edmund 63; *The Sublime and the Beautiful* 10, 72, 75
Burns, John 36
Burns, Robert, 5
Burroughs, John 223
Burrows, George Man, *An Inquiry into Certain Errors Relative to Insanity* 187
Butler, Marilyn 18, 26, 68
Byron, George Gordon, Lord 4, 7, 68; *Don Juan* 28, 76, 79

Campbell, Ian 120-1, 122
Canada 230
Carlyle, James 120-3 *passim*, 127, 128, 129
Carlyle, Jane Welsh 120, 121, 123, 127, 129, 135, 136, 139, 142, 168
Carlyle, Thomas 111, 112, 114, 120-39, 142, 153, 218, 231
  'Biography' 122, 125
  Frederick the Great 121
  Letters and Memorials of Jane Welsh Carlyle 123, 127, 136
  Reminiscences 120-39 *passim*, 142
  Sartor Resartus 109, 111, 121
  letters (quoted) 111, 112
Carroll, David 47-8, 150
Carvell, Herbert 121
Catholic Emancipation 54
Chamberlain, Joseph 166
Champion, H.H. 36
Chapman, John 148
Chaucer, Geoffrey 64
Chase, Richard 220, 228
Chatterton, Thomas 77, 79
Chesnut, James 204-16 *passim*
Chesnut, Mary Boykin 7, **204-16**
  Diary and *Journals* 7, **204-16**
Chisolm, John Julian 214
Christian VII, King of Denmark 25-6
Chysostom, St 114
Cicero, Marcus Tullius 114
Clairmont, Claire (*also* Jane) 26
Clare, John 1-5; 'Autobiographical Fragments' 1-4; 'I Am' 3; 'The Mouse's Nest' 5
Coghill, Annie 147
Colborne, Sir John 160
Coleridge, Christabel 160

Coleridge, Samuel Taylor 19, 26, 84, 85, 128; *Biographia Literaria* 61, 62, 69; 'Essay on Method' 82; 'Religious Musings' 19; *The Ancient Mariner* 24; letters (quoted) 34, 35
Confederate States of America 204-16 *passim*
Contemporary Review 142
Cornhill Magazine 246
Cowper, William 4
Creasy, Edward Sheperd 214
Cross, J[ohn] W[alter], *Life of George Eliot* 9, 143-6, 148-50, 151
Cuppit, Don 104

Darwin, Erasmus, *Zoonomia* 187
Davie, Donald 185-6
Davis, Jefferson 207, 209, 210-12 *passim*
Davis, Philip 5-6
Davis, Varina Anne 207
de Man, Paul 6-7, 61
De Quincey, Thomas 8, 9, 61-70, 128, 156
  Confessions of an English Opium Eater 7, 62-70
  'The English Mail Coach' 65
  'Sketches of Life and Manners' 65
  'Suspiria de Profundis' 65
Dennett, Daniel C. 104, 107-8
Derrida, Jacques 2, 12, 111, 115, 118
Dickens, Charles 85, 86, 87, 149; *Bleak House* 78-9; *A Christmas Carol* 82-3; *David Copperfield* 85; *Great Expectations* 197
Dixon, Richard Watson 31, 34
Douglass, Frederick 222
Doyle, Sir Arthur Conan 235-52
  The Final Problem 235
  The Hound of the Baskervilles 240
  Memories and Adventures 11, 235-52
  The Sign of Four 240
  The Stark Munro Letters 247-8
Dublin University Magazine (quoted) 72
Duffy, Edward 63

Eagleton, Terry 11

INDEX

Eclectic Review (quoted) 67–8
Edgeworth, Maria 159
Edinburgh Review 121, 144–5
Edison, Thomas 51
Egypt 235–6, 239
Eliot, George 6, 9, 10, 46–56, 142, 143–6, 148–50, 153, 158, 161, 169, 172
  Adam Bede 145
  Amos Barton 145
  Leaves from a Note-Book 47
  Letters and Journals 143–5
  Middlemarch 47–56, 149, 174–5, 197, 199
  The Mill on the Floss 198–9
  Silas Marner 52
  letters (quoted) 140–1, 151
Ellis, Sarah 155–6
Emerson, Ralph Waldo 218, 231
Engels, Friedrich, *The Condition of the Working Class in England* 43
Erkkila, Betsy 222, 226, 229, 233
Esquirol, J.E.D., *Mental Maladies* 187
Eugénie, Empress of France 243
Eusebius of Caesarea 114–15
Everett, Nicholas 6
Eyre, John Edward 128, 139

Farrar, Gerald Wayne 121–2
Farren, Edwin James 72, 79
Feuerbach, Ludwig 55, 111
Fichte, Johann Gottlieb 229
Forster, Jane Arnold 166, 169
Forster, John, *Life of Dickens* (quoted) 85
Foster, John 83
Fortnightly Review 87
Foucault, Michel 7
Franklin, Benjamin 73
Frederikstat 21
French Revolution 36–46 *passim*, 57, 63
Freud, Sigmund 40, 176, 244
Froude, J[ames] A[nthony] 120, 123, 142

Gallant, Christine 201
Gaskell, Elizabeth, *Life of Charlotte Brontë* 142–3, 144, 150
Gibbon, Edward 147

Gladstone, William Ewart 36, 165, 166
Godwin, William 19, 26; *Memoirs of Mary Wollstonecraft* 27
Goethe, Johann Wolfgang von 21, 88, 129, 134, 214
Goldsmith, Oliver 4; *The Traveller* 18–19
Gosse, Edmund, *Father and Son* 179
Government College Miscellany, Mangalore 33
Graves, Robert 239
Gray, Thomas 57, 60
Griffiths, Frances 250
Gusdorf, George 61, 122, 124

Haight, Gordon 143
Hamilton, William, *Letters Concerning the Northern Coast of Antrim* 15
Hanley, Keith 6
Hannibal 47
Hardy, Thomas 92; *The Well-Beloved* 198
Harland, Catherine R. 198, 200
Harrison, Frederic 144
Hartman, Geoffrey 29
Haydon, Benjamin 35
Hays, Mary 26, 27
Hazlitt, Sarah, *Journal of My Trip to Scotland* 8–9
Hazlitt, William 26, 63; *Liber Amoris* 8–9
Hegel, G.W.F. 231
Helsinger, Elizabeth K. 179
Hennell, Sara 141
Hertz, Neil 49
Hofkosh, Sonia 8–9, 10
Holmes, Richard 18
Holquist, Michael 138
Home Rule Bill (1886) 36
Hooker, Richard 132
Hope, Adam 131
Hopkins, Gerard Manley 6, 8, 31–7 *passim*, 39, 46, 47, 57, 72; 'The Wreck of the Deutschland' 32, 72
Howarth, William L. 238, 241, 250
Hugo, Victor 41, 214
Hume, David 111
Hunt, Leigh 11, 72–80, 128

Autobiography 10, 72–9
Examiner 76
Juvenilia 78
Lord Byron and Some of his Contemporaries 73
Hunt, Thornton 74, 148
Hutton, R[ichard] H[olt] 87, 90–4 *passim*, 96, 98
Hyndman, Henry M. 36

Imlay, Fanny 17
Imlay, Gilbert 13, 16, 17, 19, 24, 30; *The Emigrants* 29
Irigaray, Luce 112
Irving, Edward 120, 121, 124, 129, 130–4 *passim*; *Arguments for Judgments to Come* 132; *Orations* 132
Isherwood, Christopher 239

James, Henry 144, 165, 166, 168, 169
Jay, Elisabeth 147, 148
Jeffrey, Francis 120, 121, 128
Jelf, Richard William 105
Jelinek, Estelle 155
Jerome, St 114
Jewsbury, Geraldine 135
John Bull Magazine 66–7
Johnson, Joseph 14, 29
Johnson, Linck C. 226
Johnson, Samuel 29, 114; *Journey to the Western Islands* 16; *Rasselas* 177, 180, 194, 200, 201
Jowett, Benjamin 165, 166

Kant, Immanuel 149; *Critique of Judgement* 42
Kaplan, Fred 123, 136, 139
Keats, John 10, 72, 74–5, 76–8 *passim*
Keble, John 159, 161, 167
Kemble, Fanny 153
Kerrigan, John 72
Kiely, Robert 55
Kierkegaard, Søren, *Repetition* 2–3; *The Sickness Unto Death* 91
Kingsford, Anna 247
Kingsley, Charles 105, 107, 113, 115
Kipling, Rudyard 166, 241

Kitchener, Horatio Herbert, 1st Earl 236
Kowaleski-Wallace, Elizabeth 159

Lacan, Jacques 197, 202
Lamartine, Alphonse de 41
Lancelyn Green, Richard 237, 238
Landor, Walter Savage 162, 168, 169
Landreth, Peter 68
Lawrence, D.H. 182, 201
Lehmann, Rosamund 247
Lejeune, Phillipe 157–8
Lessing, Doris 83
Levinson, Majorie 6
Lewes, G[eorge] H[enry] 148, 149, 161, 169
Light 244
Linton, Eliza Lynn 9, 144, 148–50, 156–71 *passim*
  The Autobiography of Christopher Kirkland 148, 157, 159, 162–4, 168
  Girl of the Period 157
  My Literary Life 148, 149, 157, 164, 168, 169
  The One Too Many 157
  The Rebel of the Family 159, 163
  Sowing the Wind 159, 163
Linton, William 163–4
Lloyd, Tom 132
Locke, John 111
Lodge, Oliver 249
Loesberg, Jonathan 12
London Museum (quoted) 66
London Quarterly Review 67
Longfellow, Henry Wadsworth 218, 230
Lucas, John 184, 193, 202

Maginn, William 67
Mallock, W[illiam] H[urrell], *Is Life Worth Living?* 175–6, 196
Manning John 206–7
Marcus, Laura 216
Martin, Philip W. 186
Martineau, Harriet 128, 144, 153–4
  Autobiography 140–2, 146, 150
Marx, Karl 111
Mathias, Thomas James 27
Matilda, Queen of Denmark (Caroline Matilda) 13, 25–6

INDEX

Meredith, George 166, 194
Mill, James 87
Mill, John Stuart 81–2, 85, 86–94, 94–102 passim, 139, 153
   Autobiography 86–94, 98
   'Nature' 98
   'On Bentham' 88, 90, 92
   'On Coleridge' 90, 92
   A System of Logic 81, 92, 94
   'Thoughts on Poetry' 81
Miller, J. Hillis 8, 104, 198
Miller, Nancy K. 141
Milton, John 41, 132, 214; Paradise Lost 213
Mind 84
Mirabeau, H.G.R., Comte de 214
Mitford, Mary Russell 146
Moers, Ellen 141
Monthly Review (quoted) 66
More, Hannah 159
Morgan, Rosemarie 6, 7
Morley, John 87–9, 93, 144, 166
Moroni, Giambattista 147
Morris, Pam 138
Morrison, Herbert 34
Musset, Alfred de 41
Myers, F.W.H. 246; The Human Personality 249
Myers, Mitzi 14, 17
Myers, William 5
Myerson, Joel 227

Napoleon III, Emperor 235
Napoleon Bonaparte 47
Newey, Vincent 10
Newman, John Henry 94–102, 103–18 passim, 153, 165, 166
   Apologia Pro Vita Sua 61, 94–7, 103, 105, 106, 107, 113, 115–16
   Essay in Aid of A Grammar of Assent 97, 111–12, 114, 115
   Essay on Christian Doctrine 99
   Essays Critical and Historical (quoted) 107, 115
   The Idea of a University 97–8
   Parochial and Plain Sermons 114
   'The Tamworth Reading Room' 113, 114, 117–18
   Tract 90 105–7 passim
   University Sermons 95–6, 112–13

The Via Media of the Anglican Church 106–7
Nietzsche, Friedrich 249
Norden, Pierre 237
North, Julian 8
Nyström, Per 29

O'Connor, William 220
Oliphant, Margaret (Mrs Oliphant) 9, 94, 139, 140–50 passim, 153–4, 168
   Autobiography 85–6, 146–8 passim, 152
   Life of Edward Irving 130–4 passim
   journalism 146–7
Olney, James 11, 12, 122, 124, 237
Orwell, George 33
Owen, Alex 250
Oxford Movement, The 100

Paine, Thomas 218
Palmer, William 106, 108
Pater, Walter 10; The Renaissance 179
Patmore, Coventry 33, 36
Paul, St 15, 184
Payn, James 246
Peel, Sir Robert 54
Peterson, Linda 147
Piozzi, Hester Thrale, Observations and Reflections 14
Plato 31
Pocock, Lewis 72, 79
Poe, Edgar Allan 230
Positivism 175
Price, Kenneth M. 230, 233
Prince Regent (George, Prince of Wales) 73
Pusey, Edward 100

Reform Movement, The 47, 54
Richmond, George 80
Robinson, Henry Crabb 34, 56, 57
Roe, Nicholas 10
Rome 46–55 passim
Roosevelt, Franklin D. 165
Rousseau, Jean-Jacques 222; Confessions 2, 7, 11, 24, 63, 66, 68, 236–7, 239, 245, 250
Ruskin, John 34, 94, 153, 179; Praeterita 179

Russell, Bertrand 34
Russian Formalism 138–9
Rutherford, Mark, *see* White,
　　William Hale

St Peter's, Rome 53
Sand, George 141, 146, 214
Sanders, Valerie 9
Sarto, Andrea del 147
Sartre, Jean-Paul, *La Nausée* 81
Saturday Review 157
Schelling, Friedrich von 229
Selby, Thomas 195, 196
Seward, Anna 26
Shakespeare, William 214; *The Tempest* 61
Shattock, Joanne 9
Shelley, Mary 26; *Frankenstein* 163
Shelley, Percy Bysshe 7, 21, 79;
　　Adonais 76; *Alastor* 24, 26, 28;
　　'Julian and Maddalo' 28; *Queen Mab* 26
Showalter, Elaine 142
Siskin, Clifford 6
Smith, Robert 12
Smith, Sidonie 9, 155, 156
Social Democratic Federation 36
Somerville College 157
Sorley, Charles, 'When You See Millions of the Mouthless Dead' 241–2
Southey, Robert 26, 120, 121
Spasmodic School of Poetry 68
Spencer, Herbert 55
Spinoza, Baruch 180
Spiritualism 244–51 *passim*
Stanley, A.P. (Dean Stanley) 166
Stanton, Domna 155
Stendhal 169
Stephen, Sir Leslie 81, 114; *An Agnostic's Apology* 111, 114; *Mausoleum Book* 81, 83
Sterling, John 136
Stern, Daniel 141
Stovall, Floyd 218
Struensee, Johan Frederick 25–6
Sturrock, John 137, 155
Sudan 235, 236, 242
Sutherland, John 165
Swaab, Peter 6, 7

Temple Bar 144, 148
Tennant, Laura 166, 169
Tennyson, Alfred Lord 72, 98–9, 179; *In Memoriam* 100; 'The Two Voices' 179, 200
Teresa of Avila, St 54
Thackeray, William Makepeace 149, 237
Thirty-nine Articles 105–6, 115
Thomas, M. Wynn 224, 232
Thomson, James 4
Thoreau, Henry David, *Walden* 222
Ticknor, George 57
Times Literary Supplement 150
Times, New York 225
Todd, Janet 18, 26
Tomalin, Claire 14, 17
Tønsberg 20, 24, 30
Trela, D.J. 139
Trevelyan, Janet 165
Trollope, Anthony 148, 153
Turgenev, Ivan 169

Utilitarianism 91

Valéry, Paul 41
Vigny, Alfred de 214

Walters, Anna 170
Ward, Mary Augusta (Mrs Humphry Ward) 10, 156–71 *passim*
　　England's Effort 165
　　Helbeck of Bannisdale 158
　　The History of David Grieve 158
　　Marcella 159, 167
　　Robert Elsmere 158, 159, 167
　　Sir George Tressady 158
　　A Writer's Recollections 157, 165–7, 169
Waterloo, Battle of 160, 168
Watson, Nicola J. 28–9
Webb, Beatrice 153
Webb, Timothy 74, 79
Wells, H[erbert] G[eorge] 166
Westminster Gazette 236
White, William Hale ('Mark Rutherford') 10, 11, 172–203
　　The Autobiography of Mark Rutherford 10, 172–82, 196
　　Catharine Furze 10, 172, 174, 175, **182–99**

Mark Rutherford's Deliverance 172, 173, 178, 180–82 *passim*, 184
'Notes on the Book of Job' 195
Whitman, Walt 11, **217–34**
  Leaves of Grass 217–20 *passim*, 225, 232
  'Song of Myself' 219, 220
  Specimen Days & Collect (collected prose) 7, **217–34** *passim*
  letters (quoted) 217, 218
Whittier, John Greenleaf 230
Wilde, Oscar, 'The Decay of Lying' 179, 240; *The Picture of Dorian Gray* 240
Wilson, John 62, 69, 121, 128
Wittgenstein, Ludwig, *Philosophical Investigations* 103, 104–5, 108–11 *passim*, 113, 116–17; *Tractatus* 103
Wollstonecraft, Mary **13–30**
  An Historical and Moral View of the French Revolution 22–3
  Letters in Sweden, Norway and Denmark 7–8, **13–30**
  Mary 13
  Original Stories 13
  Thoughts on the Education of Daughters 14, 21
  Vindication of the Rights of Woman 13, 15, 16, 21
  The Wrongs of Woman 14
  letters (quoted) 13, 18, 29–30
  quoted as reviewer 14–15, 29
Women's Studies International Forum 154–5
Woolf, Virginia 145, 150
Wordsworth, C.W. 34
Wordsworth, Dorothy 9, 34, 56, 156
Wordsworth, Mary 57
Wordsworth, William 3, 4, 6, 7, 10, 20, 26, **31–60**, 68, 72, 87, 91, 98, 120, 121, 123
  'Composed Upon Westminster Bridge' 45–6
  The Convention of Cintra 32
  'Essay Supplementary to 1815 Poems' 20
  The Excursion 28, 33, 34, 35
  'Expostulation and Reply' 74
  'Immortality Ode' 3, 31–2, 34, 36, 37, 48, 49
  'Lines written in Early Spring' 20
  'Memorials of a Tour in Italy' 57
  'The Pass of Kirkstone' 42
  Preface to *Lyrical Ballads* 46
  The Prelude 5, 7, 20, **37–46**, 48–54 *passim*, 62, 179, 181, 201
  The Recluse 37, 56
  'Resolution and Independence' 43
  'The Ruined Cottage' 26, 30
  'Tintern Abbey' 52, 74
  letters (quoted) 35, 37, 57
World War, First 167, 241–5 *passim*, 244–5
World War, Second 33
Wright, Elsie 250

Yeats, W[illiam] B[utler] 89
Yonge, Charlotte Mary 9, **156–71** *passim*
  Autobiography 157, 160–1
  The Clever Woman of the Family 157
  Conversations on the Catechism 161
  The Daisy Chain 157, 159
  Womankind 157
Yonge, William 159